Sport, Ethics and Leadership

Everybody involved in sport, from the bleachers to the boardroom, should develop an understanding of ethics. Sport ethics prompt discussion of the central principles and ideals by which we all live our lives, and effective leadership in sport is invariably ethical leadership. This fascinating new introduction to sport ethics outlines key ethical theories in the context of sport as well as the fundamentals of moral reasoning. It explores all the central ethical issues in contemporary sport: from violence, hazing, and gambling to performance enhancement, doping, and discrimination.

This book not only investigates the ethical, social, and legal underpinnings of the most important issues in sport today, but also introduces the reader to the foundations of ethical leadership in sport and discusses which leadership strategies are most effective. Each chapter includes original real-world case studies, learning exercises, and questions to encourage students to reflect on the ethical problems presented.

Sport, Ethics and Leadership is an essential resource for any course on sport and leisure studies, the ethics and philosophy of sport, or sport and leisure management.

Jack Bowen writes on sports ethics for the Institute of Sports Law and Ethics and Positive Coaching Alliance (PCA), USA. He graduated from Stanford University with Honors in Human Biology and received his Master's from California State University, Long Beach, with an emphasis on the Philosophy of Sport *summa cum laude*. He was a two-time All-American water polo player at Stanford, has been recognized as a national award-winning coach by PCA and USA Water Polo, and has written three books on philosophy.

Ronald S. Katz is a sports attorney at GCA Law Partners LLP, USA. He received his B.A. from New York University *summa cum laude*; his M.A. from Oxford University, where he was a Rhodes Scholar; and his J.D. from Harvard Law School. He co-founded the Institute of Sports Law and Ethics, which is at the University of the Pacific; was its first Chair; and now is Chair Emeritus. He has written extensively on sports ethics, including contributions to Forbes.com in 2015–2016. In 2016 he was a Distinguished Careers Institute Fellow at Stanford University.

Jeffrey R. Mitchell is the Senior Associate Athletic Director for External Operations at Santa Clara University, USA. With a diverse background in intercollegiate athletics administration, Mitchell has experience directing units responsible for revenue generation, media relations, ticketing and marketing, academic support, business operations, and NCAA compliance. Mitchell earned a Bachelor's degree and a Master's in Business Administration from Millsaps College. He also earned a J.D. from the University of Mississippi School of Law.

Donald J. Polden is Dean Emeritus and Professor of Law at Santa Clara University, USA. He received his B.B.A. from George Washington University and his J.D. from Indiana University School of Law, Indianapolis. He teaches courses in sports law and policy, and antitrust law. He is Chair of the Board of Directors of the Institute of Sports Law and Ethics at the University of the Pacific and is the author of several books and articles on competition law, higher education, and employment law. He is a regular contributor to the *Huffington Post* on issues of business and law.

Richard Walden is an attorney in Los Angeles, USA. He obtained his B.A. in Political Science from Texas Christian University and his J.D. from the University of Texas School of Law. He has represented professional athletes for over 20 years. In addition to teaching sports law for the University of San Francisco's Master's Program in Sport Management for over a decade, he has guest lectured on the subject at several colleges and universities.

"*Sport, Ethics and Leadership* is an approachable and readable textbook. The case studies and exercises at the end of each chapter are useful for checking and deepening student learning. This makes it an excellent option for adoption for sport ethics classes."

Shawn E. Klein, Professor of Philosophy, Arizona State University, USA, and blogger at SportsEthicist.com

Sport, Ethics and Leadership

Jack Bowen,
Ronald S. Katz,
Jeffrey R. Mitchell,
Donald J. Polden
and Richard Walden

Routledge
Taylor & Francis Group

LONDON AND NEW YORK

First published 2017
by Routledge
2 Park Square, Milton Park, Abingdon, Oxon OX14 4RN

and by Routledge
711 Third Avenue, New York, NY 10017

Routledge is an imprint of the Taylor & Francis Group, an informa business

© 2017 Jack Bowen, Ronald S. Katz, Jeffrey R. Mitchell, Donald J. Polden and Richard Walden

British Library Cataloguing-in-Publication Data
A catalogue record for this book is available from the British Library

Library of Congress Cataloging in Publication Data
Names: Bowen, Jack, author.
Title: Sport, ethics and leadership / Jack Bowen, Ronald S. Katz, Jeff Mitchell, Donald J. Polden and Richard Walden.
Description: Abingdon, Oxon ; New York, NY : Routledge, an Informa Business, 2017. | Includes bibliographical references and index.
Identifiers: LCCN 2017001826| ISBN 9781138738461 (hbk) | ISBN 9781138738478 (pbk) | ISBN 9781315184739 (ebk)
Subjects: LCSH: Sports—Moral and ethical aspects. | Sports administration—Moral and ethical aspects. | Leadership—Moral and ethical aspects.
Classification: LCC GV706.3 .B68 2017 | DDC 796.01—dc23
LC record available at https://lccn.loc.gov/2017001826

ISBN: 978-1-138-73846-1 (hbk)
ISBN: 978-1-138-73847-8 (pbk)
ISBN: 978-1-315-18473-9 (ebk)

Typeset in Berling and Futura
by Florence Production Ltd, Stoodleigh, Devon, UK

Contents

Preface   *vii*

1   Ethics and moral reasoning   1

2   Ethics in the context of sport   22

3   The importance of leadership and leadership development in sport   35

4   The changing ethical landscape of amateurism   57

5   Fan behavior: ethics, responsibilities, and expectations   74

6   The ethical costs of medical issues   90

7   Social, legal, and ethical issues of performance enhancement in sport   113

8   The ethics of race discrimination in sport   133

9   The ethics of gender discrimination in sport   149

10   Violence and hazing in sport   168

11   Gambling and sport   185

12   Ethical aspects of intellectual property rights in sport   200

13   The ethics of technology in sport   220

14   Value, virtue, and meaning in sport   236

Index   *247*

Preface

A video featured on a youth sports-focused Web page (Bowen, 2015) stimulated an intense discussion, even though the topic may not seem so grave as to incite emotional outbursts and impassioned arguments. That topic was the ethics of pitch framing in baseball, in which catchers subtly shift their glove as they receive a pitch in hopes of garnering a favorable call (a "strike" instead of a "ball"). Although the topic may initially seem quite benign compared with obviously serious issues in sport such as overt violence, athlete drug use, various forms of discrimination, and many others in which real harm results, as it turns out, pitch framing nicely embodies much of the pursuit upon which this book embarks.

The conversation inspired by the pitch-framing video evolved into a conversation about issues much deeper than just framing pitches. In reviewing the arguments given for both sides, respondents often referenced much more profound and foundational issues, including:

- *obligation* of a player to his opponent, referee, fans and the game;
- *strategy* and skill and their relation to cheating;
- what it means to *deserve* and to *earn* something;
- *responsibility* shifting to the umpire for rule enforcement;
- fairness;
- the role *culture* does and should play in ethics;
- *value* and what it means to be a "*good*" player;
- objective versus subjective;
- the role of *rules* and rule-bound enterprises regarding ethics;
- *empathy* for the players involved.

These issues reveal one of the core virtues of a discussion of sport ethics: such discussion serves as an ideal catalyst for framing some of the richest ideals known to humanity. It allows us to explore such complex, abstract topics under the banner of sport without getting into heavier issues often covered in conversations about ethics. In short, a discussion on the ethics of pitch framing boils down to a discussion on the foundation of human morality.

Moreover, sport ethics has pragmatic value. The conclusions reached in such an exploration should be more than just theoretical. Simply discovering the ethical nature of a certain action is only the first step. The next step involves putting what one has discovered into practice. On one hand, this may be on a personal, individual level. If an individual concludes a certain practice is unethical, then that person may put this judgment into practice by avoiding the action. But in the bigger picture, many of these issues run deeper than just one person tweaking an individual moral compass.

This is where the leadership component of this book comes into play. Those of us who hold leadership roles in sports—be it as a coach, athletic director, sports agent, league commissioner, referee, or any other of the myriad leadership positions—are responsible for not just determining ethical action in sport but also implementing it. As the cliché correctly frames such a pursuit, "Doing the right thing isn't always the easy thing." It becomes even more difficult getting entire teams and organizations to do the right thing, especially when it comes at the cost of other goods such as winning.

Along with the benefits of this pursuit—i.e. discovering which actions are ethical; exploring deeper, core values; acting on these conclusions through proper leadership—comes one more, maybe of greatest value to the sport aficionado: a deeper awareness and appreciation of sport and one's role in it. It is important to recognize, for example, that the video referenced above on pitch framing deemed it an ethically allowable strategy in baseball. This is worth noting to demonstrate that the ethical evaluation of an action need not entail a condemnation of that action; such an evaluation can also inspire a deeper understanding. This deeper understanding of an issue and of the institution of sport is an invaluable result of ethical inquiry.

Before getting to the actual issues covered throughout the bulk of the book, the reader will first come to understand just how to develop a cogent logical argument and, from there, will then explore various ethical theories prominent throughout the history of philosophy and the study of ethics. Next, readers will consider how ethical frameworks in sport vary from those in the non-sporting world, and all of the subtlety and nuance entailed in such a venture.

Chapter 3 introduces various foundations of leadership theory, preparing the reader to consider what sort of leadership strategies are effective in various situations. Indeed, many, if not most, ethical problems in sport—for example, unnecessary concussions or the use of performance-enhancing drugs—can be traced to a failure of leadership.

After Chapter 3, the reader is ready to embark on an investigation of the ethical, social, and legal underpinnings of various issues in sport: amateurism, fan behavior, concussions and over use, performance-enhancing drugs, discrimination, violence and hazing, gambling and fantasy sports, intellectual property issues, and technology in sport. In the final chapter, the reader will have a chance to reflect on the profound riches and virtue available to those entrenched in the institution of sport and why sport is worth celebrating.

In delving deeper into various issues in sport, the reader should be open to any and all viewpoints and must understand the true nature of the sport. In so doing, the reader will come to develop an even greater appreciation for sport at the end of the process. Even if the reader doesn't change position on a given topic, he or she will have taken the opportunity to view sport anew, exploring it from various vantage points—legal, psychological, sociological, ethical, and more.

The aim, then, is not to blindly defend one's position nor necessarily to change one's views on all subsequent issues, but to reflect, to be open to opposing positions, and to empathize with all involved. From this place, not only will we reach a heightened appreciation of the richness of sport, but we will connect with the core of our humanity and all those with whom we connect.

BIBLIOGRAPHY

Bowen, Jack, *Framing Pitches in Baseball: Ethical or Not?* Available at: www.facebook.com/Positive CoachingAlliance/posts/10152958399102680 (accessed September 4, 2015).

CHAPTER 1

Ethics and moral reasoning

INTRODUCTION

Before exploring the nuances of sports ethics, it is important to establish a foundation for *ethics* in general. In order to truly pursue *sports ethics*, we need to have a general understanding of how ethics is done on a large scale, to take some time to explore the various moral theories throughout history and currently, and to recognize how to devise moral arguments. From that point, we can engage in a more robust discussion of the ethical aspects of the sporting experience.

As we begin this project we should consider the distinction between morality and ethics. While often used interchangeably, they can and do express slightly different modes of thinking. Ethics typically involves the study of foundational principles, whereas morals tend to focus more on values. Ethics, then, is more of an academic approach to discovering and discussing what is "right" and "good." In a sense, ethical principles serve as a guideline for how one ought to act (or, conversely, how one ought not act), whereas morals express a set of values, such as the importance of generosity, patience, and truth telling. So one might say, for example, that the death penalty is immoral because it infringes on the value of life and that it is unethical because it violates one's right to life.

Discussions of ethics often boil down to some version of people on each side of an argument claiming, "I have a right to my opinion." This sort of comment misses the mark because it assumes discussions of ethics and morality are merely matters of opinion or taste, with no need for logical defense. We will explore the concerns with such a position—more formally known as Moral Subjectivism—but, suffice it to say, employing that sort of rationale makes a discussion of ethics fruitless.

In this chapter we will look at various foundations of moral theory as well as a means for establishing sound, cogent arguments in defense of moral conclusions. In doing so, it will become clear how ethics goes beyond just being a matter of personal taste. In a sense, we'll address the skeptic who says of someone making a moral claim, "Prove it." And it will be clear that, although one may have some sort of "right" to an opinion—essentially, having a right to think things—once those opinions are voiced, they will then need to be defended, especially because they address issues involving the interests of others.

Finally, it is important to keep in mind—in this chapter and throughout this book—the differences between law and ethics. One major such difference is that ethics prescribes what should be done, whereas law prescribes what must be done. Lawmakers are always presumably making laws that reflect the ethics of society, but they do not always succeed—e.g. laws that have legitimized slavery or apartheid.

AN OVERVIEW OF LOGIC AND CONSTRUCTING SOUND MORAL ARGUMENTS

First, we will explore a brief overview of logic. This will help us to both frame our own arguments in a clear, logical manner as well as to clarify the arguments of others—not just *what* they claim but, more importantly, *how* they defend their position.

Moral arguments consist of any number of premises which, together, aim to defend a conclusion. A "good" argument—what we will call a *cogent* argument—is one in which premises logically entail—i.e. they *prove*—the conclusion. For example, in a famous though simple argument from the history of philosophy given by the French philosopher René Descartes, he defends the claim, "I exist," with the premise, "I think" and the assumed premise, "If I think, then I must exist." In this case, the conclusion is *logically entailed* by the premises: if the premises are true, then the conclusion *must be true*. The conclusion here is logically entailed by the premises: for "I" to do anything, it is true that "I" must exist.

In defining a "cogent" argument, we recognize that it must fulfill two conditions:

1. The argument's premises provide grounds for the conclusion in that they logically entail the conclusion. When this condition is met, we consider the argument *valid*. It has only to do with the logic of the argument.
2. The premises are each acceptable.

Thus, all cogent deductive arguments are valid, though not all valid arguments are cogent. In order for a valid argument to be cogent, each of the premises must be acceptable.

To more clearly recognize the logic behind an argument, it often helps to *standardize the argument*. For example, consider an argument often given in defense of an intelligent designer:

> The only way the universe could come to exist is through mere chance *or* the intervention of an intelligent designer. Since the odds are too low for chance to be the cause, then an intelligent designer must exist.

To standardize the argument, we first align all the premises in such a way that they support the conclusion:

1. Either the universe began as a result of mere chance *or* an intelligent designer.
2. It could not have begun as a result of mere chance.
3. *Therefore* an intelligent designer exists.

This argument is *valid*: *if* the premises (one and two) are acceptable then the conclusion (three) must be true. This particular argument is in the form of a logically valid argument structure known as a Disjunctive Syllogism: it exemplifies a logically valid form of reasoning and is disjunctive in that it expresses a choice between two mutually exclusive options. It follows the following structure:

1.   Either A *or* B is true.
2.   A is not true.
3.   *Therefore*, B is true.

In this case, A and B represent statements whose truth can be judged separately. It's important to notice here that this argument is in *valid* argument form: *if* the premises are true, *then* the conclusion *must be true*. An argument in this form is logically valid and will always be so.

With this logical structure in place, we supplement A and B with actual statements as in the above Intelligent Designer argument. Because the argument is in the form of a Disjunctive Syllogism, we know *if* the premises are acceptable, *then* the conclusion must be true. We leave it for the reader to consider the acceptability of the premises of this particular argument. Premise one is nearly universally accepted, while much debate centers around the acceptability of premise two.

There are thirty-two different logical forms such as the Disjunctive Syllogism discussed above. Given that this is not a course on logic, it is not necessary to review all of them. Looking at just two more, however, will allow us to get a better grasp on the concept of deductive *validity* as well as how to best go about constructing cogent arguments.

The following argument structure adheres to the logical form *modus ponens*:

1.   If A is true, then B is true.
2.   A is true.
3.   *Therefore*, B is true.

We can see how the argument is valid: *if* the premises are true, then the conclusion must be true. Look at the following example which aims to defend the practice of baseball's pitch framing, considered in the Preface:

1.   If no rule prohibits an act in baseball, then that act is ethically allowable.
2.   No rule prohibits framing pitches.
3.   *Therefore*, framing pitches is ethically allowable.

Although premise two is a matter of fact regarding the rules of baseball, premise one requires further defense. But in addressing the logical structure of the argument, we recognize that, if both premises are true, then the conclusion must be true, because the argument is valid.

One can more easily recognize the relationship between valid and cogent arguments by looking at the following obviously non-cogent argument, in the form of *modus ponens*:

1.   If the moon is made of green cheese, then we can eat it.
2.   The moon is made of green cheese.
3.   *Therefore*, we can eat the moon.

Here we see, once again, the argument is in *valid* logical form. *If* the premises are true, *then* the conclusion must be true. Clearly, though, the second premise is not true and, thus, the argument, although valid, is not cogent.

Here is a third logically valid argument structure known as *modus tollens*:

1. If A is true, then B is true.
2. B is not true.
3. *Therefore*, A is not true.

Look at the following example of this logical law put to use. Again, look closely as to whether you accept the premises. Remember, for an argument to be valid it says nothing of the truth of the premises, only that if the premises were true, then the conclusion would be true:

1. If framing pitches was wrong, then there would be a rule against it.
2. There is no rule against framing pitches.
3. *Therefore*, framing pitches is not wrong.

Although this argument is in the form of *modus tollens*, some people do not accept the first premise. That being the case, although the argument is valid, it would not be cogent, and thus we would not accept the conclusion as true based on the unacceptability of the first premise. Or, if we accepted the first premise, then we would consider the argument as cogent.

Here it's important to note that deeming an argument as not cogent does not *necessarily* demonstrate that its conclusion is false. Instead, it shows that the conclusion in question cannot be defended with those premises in that way, and must be defended in another manner, through a different, cogent argument.

Before moving on, it is important to mention missing premises because these can often lead one astray if not detected in an argument. A missing premise is one which is missing from an explicitly stated argument and, yet, *must* be there in order for the argument to be valid. It is also referred to as an assumed or implied premise—it is assumed that the listener knows this premise is implied. For example, look at this argument:

> The death penalty deters would-be murderers from killing. Therefore, we ought to implement the death penalty.

Standardizing this argument looks like this:

1. The death penalty deters would-be murderers from killing.
2. *Therefore*, we ought to implement the death penalty.

But, in order for this argument to be valid, it requires the addition of one more premise: "We ought to implement any punishment which deters would-be murderers from killing." So, to properly standardize this argument, we include this missing premise, and we denote it missing from the original argument by underlining the premise number:

1. The death penalty deters would-be murderers from killing.
2. We ought to implement any punishment which deters would-be murderers from killing.
3. *Therefore*, we ought to implement the death penalty.

Once you include the missing premise, you can start to see what is actually being argued.

From here, then, one can use a common and often convincing form of counter-argument known as a *reductio ad absurdum*. This occurs when you use the premise (or, in our case here, an unstated, assumed premise) of an argument to argue a different but absurd conclusion, thus demonstrating that the initially offered premise must not be true.

For example, we could create the following argument using the assumed premise of the previous argument:

1. Sanctioning the brutal torture of convicted murderers would deter would-be murderers from killing.
2. We ought to implement any punishment which deters would-be murderers from killing.
3. Therefore, we should sanction the brutal torture of convicted murderers.

Most consider this conclusion absurd: for various reasons, our government and government workers should not be charged with brutally torturing its citizens. Yet, this absurd conclusion is drawn by way of a previously offered premise (premise two), thus demonstrating that premise two must not be acceptable.

Lastly, as part of an overview of logic, we must briefly examine a different approach to establishing conclusions, which is known as induction. Whereas a deductive, cogent argument results in a conclusion that *must be* true, an inductive argument leads to a conclusion which is true probabilistically and thus could turn out to be false. For example:

1. All swans I have ever seen are white.
2. Therefore, all swans are white.

Although the conclusion could be true—and this person may have seen hundreds of thousands of swans—it could also be false. It is only true with a certain degree of probability, and, in fact, it is false, because there are also black swans. Clearly, the larger the sample size—in this case, the number of swans this person has seen—the greater the degree of acceptability. Science and many forms of information-gathering work inductively. We can imagine a much stronger inductive argument:

1. The sun always sets in the West.
2. Therefore, tomorrow, the sun will set in the West.

In this case, we've formulated an exceptionally strong inductive argument: the conclusion doesn't necessarily follow from the premises but is, instead, a probability and, in this case, a very high probability.

EXPLORING VARIOUS MORAL FRAMEWORKS

With a basic understanding of constructing logical arguments, we can look at just how to go about establishing a moral framework to begin with. In a sense, you can think about this in terms of various defenses of ethical behavior. For example, if a person were confronted with the opportunity to steal a watch knowing they would not be caught, here are some of the possible defenses they might give for not stealing the watch, all in terms of their respective moral foundations. *It would be wrong to steal the watch because*:

a. It seems wrong to me: Moral Subjectivism.
b. Our culture deems it so: Cultural Relativism.
c. I have a moral duty not to: Deontology.
d. God deems it so: Divine Command Theory.
e. Greater good results from not stealing: Utilitarianism.
f. It would not exhibit a sense of caring and relationship: Care Ethics.
g. It would exhibit poor character: Virtue Ethics.

Below, we briefly examine each of these moral theories and, in doing so, highlight the respective strengths and weaknesses of each.

First, we will consider approaches that characterize morality as a matter of personal or cultural taste, and therefore, deem ethical evaluations as a process of subjective judgments rather than objective evaluation.

Moral subjectivism

Moral subjectivists consider an action immoral *only because* they think it is such. With this approach, moral statements are not objectively true but, instead, are merely personal matters of judgment.

However, if determining moral truths was merely a matter of personal judgments, then the pursuit of ethics would be rendered meaningless. It would boil down to an apples-and-oranges sort of discussion. One person could claim, "I think it's unethical to deceptively use one's hands to throw the ball into the goal during a soccer game," and, when asked to defend that position, would respond, "It's just what I think." This exact same defense could be given by someone defending the ethical *acceptability* of the same action.

This situation would be similar to someone saying, "Apples are better than oranges," and someone else responding, "Well, I don't think so. I think oranges are better than apples." All we've done in each case is learn the *feelings* each person has attached to each point of contention.

Here is what the above argument would look like:

1. I think deceptively throwing the ball into the soccer goal is morally allowable.
2. If I think something is morally allowable, then it *is* morally allowable (Moral Subjectivism).
3. *Therefore*, deceptively throwing the ball into the soccer goal is morally allowable.

Accepting Moral Subjectivism removes us from the field of moral theory and places us, instead, in the field of psychology or, really, just interpersonal relations. Then, just as it would be pointless to defend apples as better or worse than oranges, the comment, "Throwing the ball into the soccer goal is unethical," becomes a meaningless statement.

In addition, this approach to ethics could lead to seemingly acceptable conclusions which directly contradict each other: action X is both morally allowable and immoral. One should consider suspicious any theory that results in exactly contradictory conclusions.

Cultural relativism

A similar problem arises in the case of Cultural Relativism, though it is a bit harder to detect as it is both a more commonly given defense and also involves a greater number of people.

Cultural Relativism defends the morality of an action on the basis of the culture's approval or disapproval. For example, a cultural relativist would defend slavery *during the time of slavery* with the following argument:

1. During the time of slavery, the culture participated in and allowed for the practice of slavery.
2. If a culture participates in and allows for an action, then that action is morally allowable (Cultural Relativism).
3. *Therefore*, slavery at the time of slavery was morally allowable.

But this person has confused two different approaches and, in a sense, addressed two different questions. The defender of Cultural Relativism is doing the work of anthropology and sociology, both important in their own right. But they are answering a different question: What *was* the case during a certain time in a certain place? Yet here we are asking a question not of anthropology but of morality: What *should have been* the case at that time and place? It is a question of *ought* and not of *is*.

Cultural Relativism is currently given as a defense of other phenomena, considered by nearly all those outside the respective cultures as immoral. Examples include female genital mutilation, "honor killings" in which women who have been raped are then killed, and various others.

Three pitfalls arise *if we accept Cultural Relativism* as a basis for morality:

1. We could no longer achieve moral progress—for example, the fact that we no longer allow slavery in the United States would be viewed as not morally *better* but, instead, as morally different.
2. We could no longer evaluate the moral status of other cultures—for example, we would be unable to claim, "Culture X is immoral for killing women who are raped," but instead just, "Culture X treats rape victims differently."
3. Determining morality would be as simple as surveying the actions and attitudes in a certain culture. So, for example, if the majority approve of enslaving certain people, then this would be considered moral, regardless of harm done.

Just as Moral Subjectivism resulted in morality being meaningless, Cultural Relativism suffers the same fate. While studying culture and exploring the various cultural practices of different cultures throughout history is an interesting component of our education, it avoids the very question we are addressing here: is a certain act ethical?

Moral nihilism

At this point, it is worth taking a moment to entertain the far-reaching consequences of both Moral Subjectivism and Cultural Relativism, because both result in vacuous claims about morality. Moral Nihilism essentially holds that moral statements are meaningless:

that any values-based statements, such as those about ethics, are vacuous and without any foundation in truth. While not held by many philosophers, Friedrich Nietzsche is the most well-known defender of Nihilism. "Every belief . . . is necessarily false," he wrote, "because there is simply no *true world*" (Nietzsche, 1968 translation).

Suffice it to say, adopting Nihilism as one's framework makes the pursuit of ethics, not to mention sports ethics, somewhat ineffectual. True nihilists, for example, could not defend something as horrendous as the Holocaust as immoral because, for them, there is no immoral action. Typically, this allows us to move beyond Moral Nihilism and explore various approaches of establishing moral statements as objectively true or false.

Deontology

A deontological approach to ethics establishes ethical actions as resulting from doing one's moral duty or, more simply, following a set of moral rules or precepts. It accounts less for the consequences of the action and more for the agent's adherence to moral duty or obligation as the driving force.

Many philosophers have espoused the virtues of a deontological approach to ethics, one of the most well known being 18th-century German philosopher, Immanuel Kant. Kant argued that the *good will* of a person is most important in evaluating them morally. The consequences of an action cannot determine the moral nature of the action because good things may result accidentally from poorly-intentioned people, and bad things may result from otherwise well-intentioned people. In addition, by determining one's moral duty through logic, one can avoid being driven by inclinations which can often cause one to go morally astray.

Kant proposed the Categorical Imperative as a method for determining moral duties. The first "formulation" of the Categorical Imperative instructs one to act only in a way that the maxim underlying the proposed action could be universalized without either of two forms of contradiction resulting: a contradiction in "conception" or a contradiction in "will." That is to say, once we establish a universal law for consideration, it must not result in an inherent contradiction in our ability to even *conceive* of putting it into practice, nor in a prescription for action that no rational person would *will* into existence.

For example, if one were to evaluate the moral status of failing to keep a promise, this practice would be recognized as resulting in a "contradiction in conception": to universalize this action would make promise-making meaningless; if anyone who made a promise could break it whenever it became inconvenient, then the making of promises would carry no weight. Thus, one has a duty to keep promises because failing to do so would violate the Categorical Imperative by a contradiction in conception.

An example of a law failing by a contradiction in will is the following: I will not help others unless I have something to gain. Kant argues this sort of maxim fails because it is not universalizable. The reason for the failure is that then everyone would help others only if there is something to gain. This is not a world we could rationally will into existence: when one is in need of help, one wants another to provide help even if providing help did not benefit the other. Thus, we maintain a moral duty to help others even if we stand to gain nothing ourselves.

Kant's second formulation of the Categorical Imperative demands, essentially, that we ought not use other people. As Kant wrote, we should always treat others, "at the same time as an end, never simply as a means" (Kant, 1959 translation). It is important to note here that Kant instructs us not to treat people *only* as a means to our ends. For example, it is wrong to befriend someone for the sole purpose of attaining a job from the friend's parent, who is the CEO of a company: this is to treat that person solely as a means to one's end of attaining a job. What is morally allowable is if one maintains a true friendship with someone and their parent happens to be the CEO of a company for which that person hopes to work.

Given this brief overview of deontology, we can apply it as a moral argument to defend the immorality of lying:

1.   If I have a duty to do action X, then I ought to do action X.
2.   I have a duty to tell the truth (as demonstrated by the Categorical Imperative in that truth telling passes both the contradiction in conception and the contradiction in will).
3.   *Therefore*, I ought to tell the truth.

Divine command theory

It is important to examine another framework related to Deontology, Divine Command Theory. Divine Command Theory is similar to Kantian theory in that Divine Command Theory sets forth a list of moral rules—duties—to which we are expected to adhere. Kant's laws derive from human logic, whereas those of Divine Command Theory are purported to come from a supernatural, divine being. It is important to see here how Divine Command Theory is strictly duty-based and not reliant on the consequences.

For example, the moral rule given in one form of Divine Command Theory commands us to avoid bearing false witness (i.e. lying). When asked to defend this, it is not the consequences which matter—though positive consequences may often result—but, instead, what counts is following God's will:

1.   A particular God commands us to avoid bearing false witness.
2.   I ought to do what this God commands.
3.   *Therefore*, I ought to avoid bearing false witness.

Given that both approaches to deontology—i.e. Kant's done through logic and Divine Command Theory done through divine inspiration—determine that we have a moral obligation to tell the truth, we can see how this precept would inform a sports-related issue. In a basketball game, for example, the referee often has a difficult time determining who the ball touched immediately prior to going out of bounds. It is common for the players on both teams to put their hands up and claim it didn't touch either of them (though we know, often from instant replay, it touched *one* of them). Look at this in standardized form:

1.   I have a duty to avoid lying.
2.   I know the ball touched me immediately prior to going out of bounds.
3.   Therefore, I have a duty to avoid lying that the ball touched me immediately prior to going out of bounds.

Although Divine Command Theory often provides a great motivation for acting morally in the form of earning the favor of a supernatural being and the hope of a favorable afterlife, certain difficulties arise. It is difficult to know which of the multitudes of purported divine beings one ought to adhere to given that they all make uniquely different demands, many of which contradict each other. Second, it's hard to know exactly what was claimed by such a being as these commands are written by humans. Last, given that most religions pre-date modern-day scientific findings, many of them either make moral claims which are now outdated or do not help us with more recent issues such as affirmative action, cloning, and sports ethics.

Utilitarianism

The deontological approach to ethics has been called into question by the *consequentialist* theory of Utilitarianism. The utilitarian instead considers the *consequences* of an action that determine the moral nature of the action and not the intent nor the issue of adhering to one's moral duty. In short: to act morally is always to act in a way that results in the greatest amount of good or happiness for the greatest number.

For example, when considering the above argument regarding the moral duty of truth-telling, consider the following situation: during the time of the Holocaust, Nazi storm troopers knock on the door of a homeowner housing Jews in his attic to protect them. When the Nazis ask if he is housing Jews, nearly all agree the homeowner *ought not* to tell the truth, despite a so-called duty to do so. Most agree, instead, he *ought* to lie. This intuition defends the underlying precept of Utilitarianism: act always to result in the greatest amount of good or happiness for the greatest number. In this case, while the Nazis are thwarted and thus, for them, some decrease in happiness results, innocent people remain alive versus being killed, which vastly increases overall good.

Thus, the claim of Utilitarianism is that Deontology cannot be the correct moral framework because, when duties conflict, as they often do, this tension can only be adjudicated by way of Utilitarianism. Look at the above situation in standardized argument form:

1. Lying to the Nazi soldiers about hiding Jews results in a greater amount of good for the greatest number of people.
2. One ought to do that which results in a greater amount of good for the greatest number of people (Utilitarianism).
3. *Therefore*, one ought to lie to the Nazi soldiers.

Proponents of Utilitarianism often argue that the entire pursuit of ethics must be to increase happiness—otherwise, why should we be concerned with ethics in the first place? If lying in a certain situation maximizes happiness, this is what one ought to do.

One concern is that Utilitarianism seems to overlook virtues we often hold more dear than just the doing of good: virtues like character, duty—either duty to others, to God, or to oneself—and the value of adhering to moral guidelines in the first place.

Consider the following example: someone spies on a neighbor one morning while the neighbor showers and dresses for the day. This person derives great happiness from the pursuit and the neighbor never discovers the person's spying. In this case, it seems as though the Utilitarian could justify this action: happiness is increased for the one spying and no harm is done to anyone else. Thus, with overall happiness increased, this appears morally justified and, yet, this action certainly seems unethical.

To circumvent this concern, Utilitarianism offers a second version. As opposed to viewing specific actions separately, known as Act Utilitarianism, consider instead examining more general rules from a Utilitarian standpoint, known as Rule Utilitarianism. In the above case, we can imagine testing the moral rule, "One is allowed to spy on others in their own homes." While it might bring some happiness to those doing the spying, it would result in a much greater *decrease* in overall happiness to have this rule in place because people would feel insecure in their homes.

Thus, the Rule Utilitarian posits this moral rule: "It is unethical to spy on others in their own homes for the purpose of the viewer's pleasure." Likewise, in the above situation with Nazi soldiers: "One may tell a lie if the telling of that lie saves the lives of innocent people." Having these rules in place would increase the overall happiness of the greatest number.

Care ethics

Before getting to the crux of Care Ethics, it is worth taking a brief step back to understand the historical context from which it sprang.

Care Ethics is often (though not always) equated with Feminist Ethics, because it was offered by feminist philosophers in reaction to the male-dominated field of philosophy and ethics. Because moral theory through the 1970s was nearly universally proposed by men, the concern became that ethical rules were too aligned with a typically male framework and worldview. Thus, it was argued, greater value was being placed on the male experience, which centered more on contracts and rule-based systems. This emphasis then resulted in women appearing as morally lacking because many of them tend to consider moral issues in terms of interpersonal relationships, community, and caring.

To flesh this out, care ethicists often reference psychologist Lawrence Kohlberg's hierarchy of moral stages. In the 1970s, Kohlberg proposed six stages of moral development regarding motivations for choosing to act ethically, from the least advanced at stage one to the most advanced at stage six:

1. avoid punishment;
2. self-interest;
3. maintain interpersonal relationships;
4. respect authority and social order;
5. act in accord with a social contract;
6. Universal Ethical Principles.

After establishing this framework, Kohlberg interviewed various people about an ethical issue known as the Heinz Dilemma:

> A druggist charges ten times what a rare medicine costs to produce, and a man's wife is dying and needs this particular medicine; after doing all that he can to acquire money through loans, work, etc., yet still not acquiring enough, the man breaks into the druggist's office to steal the drug to give to his wife.

Kohlberg then charted the motivations of respondents: not just whether the husband should or should not have stolen the drug but, *why*. His results showed that women's answers typically averaged at stage three of moral reasoning—based on care for one or more parties and how best to reconcile interpersonal relationships—whereas men tended to respond at levels five and six, using a more distanced, calculated form of reasoning.

This is a good lesson in the potential hegemony of academia: that the "in power" group may set the parameters and then judge everyone by those very parameters. Thus, on this male-dominated scale of moral reasoning, men appeared, naturally, as more advanced and women as more deficient in their respective abilities to reason morally.

It was the contention of feminists—more specifically, of "difference feminists," who argue that women *inherently* view the world differently, versus as a result of their environment—that this approach failed to account for how half of the population views our moral lives and, additionally, that it wrongly devalued the feminine voice simply because academia was dominated by males. In a sense, it was as if the rules of the game were set by one group and then, when those from the other group played differently due to how their brains were wired, they weren't just seen as different but, worse, as deficient.

To combat this mindset, Care Ethics purported to view our moral lives not as cold, distant interactions based on some sort of tacit contract or abstract moral principles. Viewing morality coldly and distantly, they argued, is not how we live our daily lives nor is it, in a deeper sense, what we really want from morality.

Instead, the care ethicist suggests we approach moral issues from a place of caring, which is something universally experienced. Instead of just valuing actions based on duties and rights, we should place greater value on interpersonal relationships and care for others and for community through a lens of empathy and compassion. As the pioneer in Care Ethics, Carol Gilligan, wrote: "The logic underlying an ethic of care is a psychological logic of relationships, which contrasts with the formal logic of fairness that informs the [male-centered] justice approach" (Gilligan, 1982).

As with the Heinz Dilemma above, instead of viewing the ethics of a situation through the deontological framework or utilitarian calculus, care ethicists argue that we ought to consider all interpersonal relationships that are involved, and then act accordingly. It is not just the druggist's *right* to his property nor the woman's *right* to life, nor even achieving the greatest good that we should consider.

Instead, the woman and her husband should reach out to the druggist, connect with the community, and the druggist should do the same, from a place of care and empathy. In this case, the caring thing would be for the druggist to work with the woman to provide a suitable means for her to acquire the drug.

Virtue ethics

Some consider these previous approaches inconsistent with what it means to live a moral life. The primary critique is that they seem too calculated and too sterile while not accounting for a person's moral character and the fact that our moral lives are not so much about encountering various moral dilemmas but, instead, living day-to-day among a community of moral agents. This approach to morality is known as Virtue Ethics, with the most well-known proponent dating back to Aristotle.

Consider which person you value more upon discovering their motivations for behaving ethically in a certain situation, such as not stealing a watch when they could have easily gotten away with it:

a. The person really wanted to steal the watch, struggling with whether to do so, but refrained from doing so because he recognized he had a duty not to.
b. Despite really wanting such a watch, the person never considered stealing it.

The proponent of Virtue Ethics here celebrates the moral character of the second person, because his character was such that he did not even consider acting immorally (this approach to ethics is also known as Character Ethics).

It is worth noting, given the earlier discussion, that the Utilitarian would value them equally: the *consequences* were such that the watch was not stolen and, so, overall happiness was achieved. The virtue ethicist values a person's character and moral disposition, not their ability or willingness to follow moral rules and calculations.

As evident in the above example, virtue ethics approaches morality in a different manner, often framing ethical questions in a completely different way. Those who practice Virtue Ethics consider questions of the form, "Ought I to do X?" to be less significant than questions such as "How should I live my life?" or, "What constitutes a good person?"

Consider the person who consoles a friend following a personal crisis such as a death in the family or a divorce. The virtue ethicist holds that we ought to console this friend because this is what a person of good character would do and not because we maintain some sort of moral duty or because it would result in greater happiness for those involved. This sort of approach, argues the virtue ethicist, makes our moral lives too sterile and, in addition, is not what we value about being a good person and a good friend.

Aristotle helped us frame what it would mean to "live a good life" in accord with virtue and good character. Virtue, he claimed, lies at a point between two extremes or vices. For example, we ought to strive for the mean between the vice of cowardice on the one extreme and of foolhardiness on the other—to do so allows us to achieve courage and to be a courageous person. In like manner, we ought not to lie consistently but also, on the other extreme, we ought to avoid never lying, such as is the case of white lies told in order to protect others' feelings or a lie which may result in some other, greater virtue.

People come to develop virtue and good character over time, through proper education and mentorship, in creating moral habit, much like we develop habits in other areas of our life. Thus, in our earlier example, the virtuous person refrains from stealing the watch simply out of the habit of acting virtuously: no conscious deliberation is required.

It is important to note the distinction in Virtue Ethics between virtue and consequentialism. Although living virtuously certainly may lead to better consequences—i.e. more happiness—better consequences are not the driving force. Instead, living virtuously means living in accord with our highest function and achieving the mean between extremes. Thus, although this approach is certainly likely to bring about greater happiness, that is not the motivation for following it. We act virtuously, not in pursuit of some other end or goal, but as an end in itself: because good is good.

PHILOSOPHICALLY RELEVANT CONCEPTS REGARDING ETHICS

Having framed the predominant moral theories, we can now explore various nuances and philosophically relevant concepts involved in evaluating actions from a moral standpoint.

Intent

Consider the difference between two scenarios: a person is sweeping his third-floor balcony when, unbeknown to him, his broom handle knocks a potted plant off the balcony which hits a pedestrian below, killing him in the process. Contrast that with another person, holding a potted plant on their third-story balcony, awaiting the pedestrian below, and throwing the plant with the intent to kill the person.

In the latter case, we assign moral blame due to the person's intent, whereas we view the moral nature of the former example differently, given no intent to harm. Of course, we might accuse the former person of negligence for keeping his potted plants in a place where they can easily fall and injure someone.

When we turn to the sporting realm, intent becomes increasingly important to consider. Consider the difference between two soccer defenders: one is focused on defending an attacker and then, as a shot is taken from behind him, the ball ricochets off his hand preventing the ball from going into the goal. Compare him with a second defender who, while defending an attacker, sees the ball coming toward the goal and intentionally reaches a hand out to prevent the ball from going into the goal. Our moral evaluation of these two instances differs greatly, all based on intent.

In many cases, intent helps to distinguish between the person who has simply broken a rule (a factual evaluation) and one who has cheated (a moral evaluation). Compare lying to telling a falsehood. If I put a quarter in my pocket but it falls through a hole unbeknown to me, when I tell you I have a quarter in my pocket I have told a falsehood: I have claimed something about the state of affairs which is not true.

But I have not *lied*. To lie requires intent. Lying also usually involves telling the falsehood in order to benefit oneself. However, if you ask me to borrow a quarter and I have one in my pocket but tell you I don't so that I don't feel pressured to give it to you, then I have lied to you: I have *intentionally* told a falsehood.

Intent can often be difficult to decipher, and much of it calls into question metaphysical notions of free will and determinism. In a simple thought experiment aimed to highlight both issues simultaneously, imagine playing a game of tic-tac-toe against a computer. Following two moves by both you and the computer, the computer places two Xs simultaneously, without affording you the opportunity for a move, and flashes the text "You lose" on the screen. Some are inclined to claim that the computer cheated. But, as you likely intuit here, this depends more on one's view of Artificial Intelligence and whether a computer can *intend* anything.

If, as many will argue, a computer merely runs a program, then, although it is true a rule was broken, it would not be true that the computer cheated—certainly not in the way it would be if a human opponent behaved similarly. This analogy helps to frame the relevance of intent as it relates to determining the ethical evaluation of a particular action.

Although a lack of intent lessens the potential for moral blame, it does not necessarily diminish it completely, as in the class of cases involving negligence, carelessness, and neglect. We might assign moral blame, to the person sweeping near a potted plant, which any reasonable person would understand might fall and injure someone—that is, even if they didn't intend to knock the plant over, or if they did knock it over without harming anyone, they could still be held morally accountable to some extent.

This sort of issue arises in sport—for example, regarding the intent to injure a competitor. Consider two football players, both performing the same legal tackle but each with different intent: the first intending to stop the player from progressing the ball and the other intending to injure the player. Regardless of the tackle resulting in an injury, our moral evaluation of the player changes based on his intent.

Moral luck

Most people maintain that being lucky (or unlucky) should not affect a person's moral standing: in a sense, a moral evaluation is something that results completely from intended behaviors and not from circumstances out of one's control. Yet, many evaluate the following two people differently, despite the similarity of their actions:

- "The Unfortunate Driver": A drunk driver kills a child who has run into the street.
- "The Fortunate Driver": A drunk driver arrives home without harming anyone.

Most are quick to find The Unfortunate Driver morally abhorrent and, yet, not assign equally severe moral blame to The Fortunate Driver. Yet this would imply that luck does play a role in our moral evaluation of a person, which seems erroneous: the action itself is what we evaluate from a moral standpoint.

Thus, to alleviate this tension and seeming contradiction, both drivers need to be held equal in moral standing, regardless of the harm they do. The Fortunate Driver behaved immorally and simply got lucky no child ran into the street where he was driving.

Consent

Consent can also play a key role in evaluating actions morally. Especially in the sporting arena, consent is a cornerstone issue, which helps differentiate actions within sport from those outside of sport. To approach a stranger on the sidewalk and punch him in the face would be unethical and illegal, but to do so in a boxing match is permitted, even if the blow is fatal, as has happened on some occasions. The key difference is that the boxer *consented to* being hit in the face while the person on the sidewalk did not.

Consent need not be explicitly given. By voluntarily participating in boxing, for example, one gives tacit consent. Tacit consent also applies to adhering to the rules of a game: by agreeing to play the game, one tacitly agrees to play by the rules. It would not make sense for a soccer player who, after throwing the ball into the goal, responded to objectors, "Well, I never agreed to that."

The analogy to John Locke's Social Contract often works here: simply by choosing to live in a particular country, one tacitly agrees to follow the laws and regulations of that country. Although no one signs a contract agreeing to do so, their participation signals a tacit agreement.

Consent is tricky, though, because it is hard to know exactly what one has consented to. Certainly by playing ice hockey, for example, one consents to being hit and checked. But certain types of hits are explicitly against the rules, yet they do happen somewhat frequently. Therefore, if one were hit illegally from behind, one might claim to have consented to *occasionally* being hit illegally from behind because that is "part of the game."

In addition, consent is not sufficient for deeming a particular act ethically allowable. Professional gladiator-style fights-to-the-death are unethical *even if* both participants consented to the activity and possible outcome. This sort of argument and analogy primes the argument defending the immoral nature of boxing: regardless of the consent of participants, given the potential harm done to boxers (and, many argue, to society at large), we should not consider boxing morally allowable.

Additionally, for consent to hold any weight, it must be freely given and not coerced. This comes into play regarding arguments about boxing (and, obviously, about gladiators): those involved tend to come from lower socioeconomic classes and, because the need for money is greater and the means by which to obtain money more scarce, individuals may consent to something under the duress of simply needing to survive. Consent given under duress or from someone not in a proper state of mind is not true consent. Thus, consent cannot be given by minors, nor by those under the influence of drugs or alcohol, nor from those who suffer severe mental deficiencies, nor by those who have been deliberately misled.

A FINAL REFLECTION ON THE PROCESS OF MORAL REASONING

As you explore ethical issues both in the realm of sport and outside of it, it is worth taking a moment to examine just *how* such moral conclusions are drawn—that is to say, to be conscious of how you arrive at your conclusions. The method assumed by many is that we go through some version of the following: we add up the facts and arguments in order to yield the most suitable conclusion, and this moral conclusion we then adopt. For example, when examining the death penalty, we might look at all the facts and logic behind it—on one hand, all humans have an inalienable right to life, or, on the one hand, by taking a life, a murderer forfeits the right to life—and *then* draw a conclusion—i.e. the death penalty is immoral or is morally required, respectively.

But advances in neuroscience have led some researchers to claim that this is not what we actually do. Instead, findings supporting a model known as social intuitionism suggest that we *first* establish a moral conclusion through our intuition and *then* look for facts and arguments to support this conclusion, in a *post hoc* manner.

For example, one will first intuit the death penalty as morally required and then seek premises to support this intuited conclusion. Thus, even if a person uses data and premises for their argument which are then shown to be incorrect, instead of changing his position, the person will seek to discover another set of premises that suits his initially intuited conclusion.

One might claim, for example, "We should kill murderers because we don't want to spend money imprisoning them when we could spend that money on education." In this case, the argument would be standardized as such:

1. We shouldn't spend money imprisoning murderers when we could spend that money on education.
2. We should punish murderers in the cheapest way possible.
3. We should give murderers the death penalty.

Counter-arguments to the above are that the cheapest available punishment is not necessarily morally favorable and, as a matter of fact, fairly enforcing the death penalty actually costs the state more than life imprisonment. As such, *both* premises would not hold, rendering the argument as not cogent.

But, according to the intuitionist model, instead of abandoning this conclusion in favor of the opposing conclusion as the rational model would predict—the original logic was overturned with facts and data—the person will likely, instead, seek out a different argument with the same conclusion—one that suits his intuition.

Social intuitionism explains why moral disagreements sometimes turn into shouting matches instead of productive discourse: because we do our moral reasoning from an impassioned position and are often more interested in defending our conclusion than finding a logical answer. In addition, it explains why many people experience "moral dumb-founding" in the face of various ethical issues: when the moral evaluation of an action seems obvious, yet no rationale exists to defend it. Such issues include using your country's flag to wash a toilet or eating your family dog after it has been hit by a car. These issues often cause a strong moral response without, some would argue, any obvious harm result-ing from the respective acts.

In framing the neurological nuances of moral reasoning, social intuitionists often refer to a twist on a common thought experiment as further evidence of the intuitionist model. A first thought experiment, known as the Trolley Car Situation, is often given in support of utilitarianism:

> You are the only person on a trolley car speeding downhill with non-functioning brakes. You see five people on the tracks ahead whom you will surely kill if you continue the normal route. You see an out-of-use track just ahead where you could turn the trolley car resulting in just one person's death. *Should* you turn the trolley car? *Would* you turn the trolley car?

Nearly all respondents claim they should turn the car and also would do so if confronted with such a situation.

But now look at the following situation:

> You are on a bridge and see a trolley car speeding downhill out of control with no one on it. You see five people on the tracks ahead whom the car will surely kill if it continues. On the bridge with you, leaning over the edge to see the car, is an extremely large person. You realize if you push this person, their mass will stop the car, but your action will result in that person's death. *Should* you shove the person? *Would* you shove the person?

When presented with this situation, many who previously defended the logic of killing fewer in the previous situation become morally dumbfounded and, even if they continue defending the logic of pushing the one to save the five, many claim they would not do so. As a matter of fact, some scientists say we employ a different part of the brain when considering ethical issues on a more personal level—i.e. actually *touching* someone—versus on a more theoretical and removed level, such as driving a metal car into them. Such discoveries have come to light pragmatically in terms of considering the morality of drone warfare, as well as how automated cars should be programmed when faced with dilemmas which result in unavoidable, collateral harm done to others, including the driver.

Social intuition is important to consider for three reasons. First, many social intuitionists argue on naturalistic lines that we should account for our knowledge of how we do our ethical reasoning: when working through our moral evaluation of a particular action, we *should* consider our intuition on the matter as a factor to help inform us of a proper evaluation of it. As David Hume famously wrote, long before the advent of neuroscience, "The notion of morals implies some sentiment common to all mankind" (Hume, 1975 edition). In a sense, we should consider the pursuit of ethics as *of nature* and, thus, include our natural response to ethical issues as a part of our evaluation of those issues.

In the late 1990s when the possibility of human cloning became a reality, the chair of the President's Council on Bioethics, Leon Kass, used such an argument. He argued that we ought to prohibit the pursuit of human cloning based on, among other things, the "wisdom of repugnance." Repugnance, he wrote, "is the emotional expression of deep wisdom, beyond reason's power fully to articulate it" (Kass, 1997). Thus, Kass argued, moral repugnance, in some cases, may be the only insight into the unethical nature of various acts.

It is worth mentioning, though, that many things people once found distasteful and repugnant are no longer considered as such by many people. Interracial marriage, for example, was once illegal but is now within the law.

Second, and somewhat counter to the initial insight provided by the Social Intuitionist model, it is important to recognize that this is *how* humans often do ethics, but not necessarily how ethics *should be done*. Regarding the above suggestion to "naturalize" ethics, many see ethics as reaching beyond our emotions and instincts, instead relating to such foundations as logic, a utilitarian calculus, or some other benchmark. As Princeton University Ethics Professor, Peter Singer, writes: "Empathy and other emotions often motivate us to do what is right, but they are equally likely to motivate us to do what is wrong. In making ethical decisions, our ability to reason has a crucial role to play" (Singer, 2016).

Lastly, these recent discoveries in neuroscience should encourage us to look inward as we move forward in this inquiry. Be self-aware: are you *first* emoting your moral conclusion only to then find conclusions to fit that intuition, or are you approaching a particular issue with a more open mind, first seeking to understand the facts and arguments on all sides only then to arrive at your conclusion? Although an exploration of ethics and morality should certainly inform us as to the nature of various actions and character traits, it should be a self-exploration as well.

CONCLUSION

Cogent ethical conclusions are grounded in logical arguments: arguments in which acceptable premises entail such a conclusion. In addition, these conclusions reflect a moral foundation that often runs much deeper than just the particular ethical argument at hand. Standardizing these arguments helps us to better recognize not just *what* is being concluded but *how* it is being concluded. This allows us to have a more enriching discussion, to avoid the various logical fallacies, and to know exactly what is being argued.

In addition, various moral frameworks inform our ethical evaluations. Although often alluring, the subjective approaches such as Moral Subjectivism and Cultural Relativism can obstruct our attempt to assert an action as ethical (or not) as they are based more on personal and cultural preference. To avoid the pitfalls of such subjectivism, various moral theories have been posited throughout history which attempt to discern moral conclusions *objectively*. Such attempts include Deontology, Divine Command Theory, Utilitarianism (both Act and Rule Utilitarianism), Virtue Ethics, and Care Ethics. Although each has its virtues, each also comes with concerns.

In developing an understanding of both logic and moral theory, we can more clearly understand what others are arguing and, more importantly, how we develop our own arguments. With this, we will experience a more robust and fruitful discourse, either disagreeing in an informed manner or more confidently accepting a conclusion which, as we will see moving forward, we can implement with proper leadership.

STUDENT LEARNING EXERCISES

Standardize the following moral arguments, listing the premises and then conclusion in standard, logical form. Then, evaluate the argument.

a. The Fosbury Flop was unsportsmanlike. When he did that, high jumpers consented to jumping over the bar on the high jump with their chest closest to the bar. He broke that agreement by jumping with his back closest to the bar.
b. Flopping in soccer is ethically allowable. My coach says so. (Hint: this argument involves an unstated premise. Also: after standardizing, create an argument ad adsurdum arguing against this.)
c. It's unethical to try to lose a match. Sports are about always trying your best. Trying to not win is not trying your best.
d. MMA is not unethical. People chose to do this and anything people chose to do is ethically allowable.
e. It is unethical to take steroids prohibited by the rules of the sport. You can't intentionally do anything rules prohibit.

Address the following situations and sport-specific issues from an ethical position. After formulating one's own position, consider discussing them in small groups looking both for areas of agreement and then also delving deeper into areas of disagreement. Where appropriate, standardize your arguments, listing all premises in defense of the conclusion.

1. A concern stated in the chapter regarding consent, especially of participants in boxing and MMA, is that participation is not as "voluntary" as other sports: that those who participate are predominantly of lower socio-economic status and incur immense, long-lasting harm to their body and brain as a means for earning a living. Some have even made the analogy comparing the athletes to women who "chose" to participate in the sex industry as prostitutes. Evaluate this claim.

2. Various commentators argue that sports such as football, boxing, and MMA are overtly violent and by viewing these sports and/or attending the contests one supports and even endorses the violence and the results (concussions, etc.). How do you address this concern?

3. Evaluate the following statement, given in the text, in defense of a duty-based theory of ethics: "The consequences of an action cannot determine the moral nature of the action because good things may result accidentally from poorly-intentioned people and bad things may result from otherwise well-intentioned people."

4. The text mentions a case in which someone spies on his neighbor showering in the morning and neither the neighbor nor anyone else finds out. It is suggested that, because the spying goes undetected, "no harm is done." Do you agree? Is the spied-upon neighbor harmed?

5. In the section discussing Virtue Ethics, the text suggests that "white lies"—seemingly harmless lies told with the intent to shelter the feelings of another—are morally justifiable. Do you agree? How might one argue white lies are actually *not* morally justifiable? What value might come from constantly telling the truth even about such benign matters as whether a friend's new shirt is attractive?

6. How do you answer the Heinz Dilemma, discussed in the Care Ethics section? What do you argue the husband should do and, more importantly, why should he do that?

7. How do you address the question as to whether a computer could cheat in a game of tic-tac-toe? What does this tell you about the role of intent in regards to cheating in sport?

8. Should we evaluate a football player who intends to injure his opponent when delivering a legal tackle as unethical? Explain.

9. Look at the various examples explicitly involving luck mentioned in the chapter.

    (a) Do you hold the porch sweeper morally blameworthy for sweeping a porch where a potted plant could easily be knocked over and fall three stories to the sidewalk but doesn't? What about the situation in which it does fall but doesn't hit anyone? What if it does fall and kill someone?

    (b) Do you evaluate "The Unfortunate Driver" and "The Fortunate Driver" differently, morally speaking? Why?

10. How do you answer the 4 questions on the Trolley Car Dilemma? What should you do and what would you do in both situations? Why?

11. Explain the relevance of the second Trolley Car Dilemma to:

    (a) Drone warfare
    (b) Programing automated cars.

12. How do you answer this question: "*Why* be moral?" If you could win a game only if you cheated, and no one would find out, would you cheat? Why/why not?

PROBLEMS/QUESTIONS

1. How is it argued that Moral Subjectivism and Cultural Relativism break down into Moral Nihilism? What are the three seemingly unacceptable results of adopting Cultural Relativism as a moral framework?
2. Briefly summarize each of the main moral frameworks explained in the chapter: Deontology, Divine Command Theory, Virtue Ethics, Care Ethics. In doing so, explain the pros and cons of each theory.
3. Explain the difference between Act Utilitarianism and Rule Utilitarianism. What does Rule Utilitarianism hope to achieve which Act Utilitarianism does not? Use the example of the "peeping tom" in your response.
4. What problem with moral theory in general did Care Ethics attempt to overcome?
5. Explain the relevance of the following in evaluating an action, morally:

   (a) Consent
   (b) Intent
   (c) Moral Luck

6. Explain the recent findings in neuroscience and the connection to social intuitionism. What three lessons do we learn in recognizing these findings?

BIBLIOGRAPHY

Aristotle, *Nichomachean Ethics*, translated by W.D. Ross (1925).

Gilligan, Carol, *In a Different Voice: Psychological Theory and Women's Development* (1982).

Hume, David, *Enquiry Concerning the Principles of Morals*, L. A. Selby-Bigge (1975).

Kant, Immanuel, *Foundations of the Metaphysics of Morals*, translated by L.W. Beck (1959).

Kass, Leon, The Wisdom of Repugnance: Why We Should Ban the Cloning of Humans, *The New Republic*, June 2, 1997.

Kohlberg, Lawrence. *The Philosophy of Moral Development: Moral Stages and the Idea of Justice*. San Francisco: Harper & Row, 1981.

Nietzsche, Friedrich, *The Will to Power*, translated by Walter Kaufmann and R.J. Hollingdale (1968).

Singer, Peter, The Empathy Trap, *Project Syndicate*, December 12, 2016.

CHAPTER 2

Ethics in the context of sport

INTRODUCTION

In many ways, determining the ethics of actions in sport is easier than in the non-sporting realm. For one, the rules are clearly stated: for example, soccer's rules explicitly prohibit a non-goalie from intentionally touching the ball with his hands—doing so incurs a stated penalty for the offending player. In addition, we must assume that all players involved have agreed to these rules by virtue of their volunteering to participate.

As with any human construct, however, much gray area exists. Because sport is essentially a cultural, human construct, it comes with various nuances. In much the same way as driving in excess of the posted speed limit on freeways is commonly practiced and allowed, those who participate (and officiate) in sport often hold various interpretations of rules and of the role rules play.

Given the complexities of determining ethical actions in sport, various ethical frameworks have been suggested by philosophers of sport, primarily formalism and an ethos-based account. Along with this, we can better understand such sport-specific issues as what it means to cheat, to display good sportsmanship, and to understand the myriad nuances within the institution of sport.

FORMALISM

Under the framework of formalism, one must first accept the premise that the rules of a game define that very game. For example, if two groups of people on a soccer field are *throwing* a soccer ball to each other and into a goal, it is very unlikely we would call this a *soccer* game. We wouldn't even call it a "poorly played soccer game" as it would fail to adhere to a basic rule of soccer—i.e. players must move the ball using any part of the body except the hands and arms.

Secondly, formalism relies on the notion of tacit consent explored in Chapter 1. John Locke relied on tacit consent in defense of his concept of a Social Contract. In order to avoid the pitfalls of the State of Nature—that is, individuals existing in a community without any form of government in place—people willingly transfer some of their rights to the government. Although they may not maintain total freedom—i.e. they must have a license to drive a car and then pay to maintain that license—they actually achieve greater freedoms as the government then oversees the safe driving of cars through a police force, the maintenance of roads, and so forth, freeing the individuals in a society from those responsibilities.

This compromise may initially seem problematic to someone living in a governed state who may claim "I never agreed to this so-called contract." Locke resolves this dilemma through the notion of tacit consent. Simply by participating in society, one can be said to consent to the contract: by benefiting from the services provided by the government, one consents to forfeiting various freedoms.

The concept of tacit consent is easily applied to a sport contest. Imagine playing tennis with someone and, at one point, she catches your serve, runs up to the net, drops the ball over the net and claims victory. Upon your protest that she did not hit the ball over the net with her racket, she could not, given her tacit consent, validly respond "I never agreed to *that rule*." The proper response, in formalistic terms, would be inevitable: "Yes you did."

Simply by voluntarily walking on the court to play tennis, you implicitly agreed to follow the rules of tennis. Hitting the ball over the net with a racket is just what *playing tennis* entails. Similar to Locke's social contract, by consenting to follow the rules, a tennis player forgoes the ability to perform certain actions. In doing so, the players then receive the various rewards of playing the sport such as fair competition and exercise.

A formalist would argue that to intentionally refuse to follow the rules is to not play the sport at all—what the formalist refers to as the "logical incompatibility thesis." If one intentionally breaks the stated rules of the game in which one voluntarily agreed to participate then, not only can it be said that the person did not win the game, but also that the person fails to play the game in the first place.

The most controversial example formalists use to illustrate the concept of logical incompatibility is the practice typically referred to as basketball's "good foul." It is common in basketball for the team which is losing near the end of the game to foul the offensive team intentionally. The desired outcome of this action is that the referee calls a foul, sending the offensive player to the free throw line, allowing the defense to get the ball sooner and preventing the game clock from winding down. A formalist would interpret this action as unethical, arguing that by intentionally breaking the rules of basketball, an individual ceases to even play basketball—that simultaneous intentional rule breaking and competing are logically incompatible.

ETHOS-BASED APPROACH

In contrast to formalism is the ethos-based perspective of rules in sport. According to this approach, because sport is a social construct and a culture in itself, the participants therefore understand and abide by the ethos—the storied context—of rules and how the game is played. This view takes into account not just the formal rules, but the conventions that develop over time among players as to how they interact with the rules and with each other in the context of a particular sport.

In response to the formalist's argument that the "good foul" in basketball results in the game ceasing to be a game, the ethos proponent would respond, "But fouling in this situation is just how the game is played. All who understand the culture of basketball understand this and accept it."

As a non-sporting analogy, consider the speed limit example mentioned earlier. The clear letter of the rule states, "Do not drive faster than 65 miles per hour on this highway," and yet people consistently drive 5 to 10 miles over the limit, and the practice is generally not considered unethical nor illegal. The understood ethos of the practice is that one may drive slightly over the posted speed limit in accordance with the "flow of traffic."

The ethos-based approach is appealing because it accounts for the fact that human nature is a real aspect of sport and admits that sport is an imprecise human enterprise. In most aspects of life, the letter of the rule can never regulate *all* possible actions available to participants in *any* activity. In almost every situation, humans do not act in *exact* accordance to rules; in a stronger sense, we cannot do so because of the vagueness of language and an inability to behave so precisely in our interactions.

In addition, not every possible circumstance is predictable, and various "solutions" to the myriad problems that arise may be too particular to be so exactly legislated. Aristotle framed this problem with his metaphor of a ruler used by builders on the island of Lesbos which could bend to the various curves of the thing being measured. Known as the Lesbian Rule, Aristotle wrote, "For what is itself indefinite can only be measured by an indefinite standard, like the leaden rule[r] used by Lesbian builders; just as that rule[r] is not rigid but can be bent to the shape of the stone, so a special ordinance is made to fit the circumstances of the case" (Aristotle, 1925 translation). A proponent of the ethos-based account, then, would defend basketball's intentional, "good foul" by referencing basketball's culture and the actions deemed allowable within that culture.

Examining sport violations from the two perspectives

The tension between formalism and an ethos-based account now becomes obvious. On one hand, we want rules to mean something and to serve as proper guides to action. But on the other hand, we recognize that rules cannot perfectly guide every action and so, when participating in a sport, one may instead act based more on the storied-context or, ethos, of the institution. Because this inexactness allows for differences in the way competitors may behave, the temptation is to return to a more formalist approach, demanding strict accordance with the letter of the rules. A return to formalism, of course, simply reintroduces the problems of that approach.

An instance highlighting this problem with the ethos-based account arises when two teams from different cultures, with different approaches to game rules, compete in the same contest. This situation occurred in the 1999 Women's World Cup Soccer Championship match between China and the United States, the outcome of which was determined by penalty kicks.

Immediately prior to China's players kicking the ball, U.S. goalie Briana Scurry took two steps forward (in a quick and subtle manner) in order to block the penalty kicks, a move prohibited by the rules. The goalie of the Chinese team followed the letter of the rule, remaining on the goal line until the ball was struck, forgoing the advantage garnered by Scurry's approach, and failed to block a single shot. Scurry's seemingly illegal save turned out to be the difference, giving the U.S. the victory and the World Cup title.

In an interview following the game, Scurry seemed to justify her actions from an ethos-based perspective, stating, "Everybody does it" (Vecsey, 1998). Another professional soccer goalie shared her view, "People are saying, 'Wow, Briana Scurry cheated.' But they don't understand that part of the game. What Briana did was perfectly normal. . . . I don't call that cheating" (id.). The two players involved in the match, and likely each team, had their own approaches to following game rules, leading to two different actions within the same contest. One approach provided an advantage; the other didn't.

These two ethical frameworks can be used to examine the ethical status of actions in sport. In doing so, they will help frame the concept of cheating and just what, exactly, cheating entails.

Cheating

To cheat is, by definition, to behave unethically. Within the context of sport, much of what people aim to determine is whether a particular player has cheated. In the non-sporting realm, people don't typically use such a term.

If an individual lies to a co-worker to gain an advantage, that person hasn't cheated so much as they have behaved unethically. In the context of sport, people assign the term "cheating" to such ethical violations, so we must define just what cheating entails.

One working definition of cheating in sport is: "Acting with the intent to gain an *advantage* by acting outside the stated rules and context of the sport with the hope of going *undetected*." According to this definition, cheating requires that the following three criteria are met:

1. Rule breaking.
2. Intent to gain an advantage.
3. Attempt to avoid punishment.

Consider simple examples from soccer, in which we examine similar, though slightly varying, actions using the three criteria above:

1. A defender has his back to the ball while tenaciously defending an opposing forward. The ball is struck by another player and, as it heads toward the goal, it ricochets off the defender's hand, causing it to miss the goal.
2. While defending the opposing forward, a defender sees the ball shot toward her goal and subtly puts her hand in the way, preventing undetected by the referee what would have otherwise been a goal.

Here the difference is clear. In the first case, no intent was involved. In the second case, the defender *intended* to break the rules, gained an advantage, and avoided punishment. The action of our second player has met the three criteria for cheating.

Now look at a somewhat trickier example than the previous two:

1. A defender sees the ball shot toward his goal and realizes that neither he nor his goalie will be able to legally prevent it from going into the goal. So he intentionally reaches out with his hand to prevent the ball from entering the goal, knowing the referee will detect it and award the corresponding penalty.

In this example, the criteria of both intent and rule breaking for advantage are met, but avoidance of punishment is not. Therefore, the defender's action is not cheating according to the above definition.

Sportsmanship

Just as in our daily lives, evaluating actions within sport involves more than just meting out judgments of right or wrong. For example, in the non-sporting world, most argue that one is not ethically required to hold the door open for strangers—that is to say, you have not behaved unethically for failing to hold the door open. But, in holding the door for a stranger, you have extended yourself and can be said to have behaved in an ethically praiseworthy manner. By going above and beyond what is required by any ethical precept, one can be said to have behaved in a supererogatory manner.

We can view sportsmanship through a similar lens. In a sense, sportsmanship can be considered the manners of the sporting world. In many senses, exhibiting good sportsmanship goes beyond simple manners; bad sportsmanship can be more than bad manners and lead to negative outcomes.

For example, imagine a baseball player who is rounding third base while the third baseman attempts to catch a high fly ball. Amid the confusion of who will catch the ball, the opposing baserunner shouts, "I got it!" causing the third baseman to step aside to allow the shouter, who the baseman thinks is his teammate, the opportunity to catch the ball. In this case, the actions of the baserunner have caused an error by the other team, resulting in a favorable outcome for the baserunner's team. Yet, he broke no rule.

Poor sportsmanship need not result in an advantage for the participant exhibiting the behavior. Such may be the case at the end of a competition in which the winner taunts or mocks the opposing player. In this situation, no advantage is gained because the competition is over. No rule of the game itself has been violated, yet this behavior is clearly unsportsmanlike. Much of sportsmanship comes down to the question of what the players owe each other and the referee. The answer is not always clear.

Imagine the simple case of a one-on-one basketball game among friends. When the ball goes out of bounds, the person who most recently touched it is usually expected to admit this fact to the other player and relinquish the ball. To fail to do so would not only be unsportsmanlike, but would be a clear case of cheating: intentionally breaking a rule in an attempt to gain an undeserved advantage and go unpunished.

Once there is a referee, however, many sport enthusiasts call this determination into question. Watch almost any basketball game and you will likely see some version of the following: when the ball goes out of bounds, all players from both teams near the ball put their hands up as if to say, "The ball didn't go out off of me." Yet, clearly, we know it did—it must have gone off of someone—and we have video replay to demonstrate this. But the players leave the responsibility to the referee to identify the player.

It seems counter-intuitive to many that a competition becomes *less* fair once a referee is involved in regulating the actions of the players. If anything, we imagine that the competition becomes *more* fair, and not less so. Yet, in this case, we see just the opposite: the ball subtly goes off of Player A and if Player A can convince the referee he was not responsible, then Player A may receive the ball despite not *deserving* it.

Participants and spectators alike treat the inclusion of a referee in a game as the explicit passing off of responsibility for calling rule violations—that is to say, the referee literally becomes "part of the game" in that players are now absolved from determining who violated the rule in this situation.

This view of referee-as-adjudicator has the effect of removing the ethical obligation of players to admit the ball had gone off of them and out of bounds. Though it would still allow for the supererogatory action of a player admitting it had gone off of him even though the referee failed to detect it, it would be an ethically praiseworthy—though not ethically required—action. A question worth addressing here is: shouldn't we strive to be ethically praiseworthy when doing so is relatively feasible?

Flopping and framing

Another action in sport that involves similar controversy is the practice of "flopping." Although nearly all sports have a version of this behavior, it is particularly common in soccer. Flopping occurs when, for example, a soccer player dribbling the ball dives or "flops": falling to the ground, feigning being tripped by the nearby defender and, in some cases, grabbing his ankle or shin and writhing on the ground as if in pain from the feigned strike of the opposing player's cleats. Often the audience can see that the player in question was not touched by the defending player's cleats. Instead, the "flopper" hopes to convince the referee he was fouled, thus being awarded a penalty kick.

Many soccer enthusiasts argue, in a manner consistent with the ethos-based approach, that flopping is just part of the game of soccer. Some go further to say that one's ability to perform this action successfully is a skill of the game: the better players are at flopping, the better they are at getting (could we say *earning* in this case?) penalty kicks and goal-scoring opportunities, making them better players.

Others consider such a practice unethical. For one, the flopper is deceiving the referee. While deception of one's opponent is part of any sport—such as faking to dribble left, yet dribbling right—deceiving the referee in this way would not be considered a soccer skill per se. Second, to get an advantage one doesn't *deserve* seems unethical and may even be considered akin to stealing, as the player acquires something he doesn't deserve. Lastly, this action wrongly punishes a defending player, which many also consider unethical.

To combat flopping, many sports leagues have adopted rules explicitly prohibiting it. For example, the international governing body of soccer, the Federation Internationale de Football Association (FIFA), declares under Law 12 that a player will be cautioned for "unsporting behavior" if that player "attempts to deceive the referee by feigning injury or pretending to be fouled." Given the rules against this behavior and our definition of cheating, this makes flopping another case of cheating. The only real defense of the practice is some form of ethos-based argument, more along the lines of the cultural relativism discussed in the previous chapter.

Within this discussion, the issue of *embellishing* versus outright *flopping* deserves attention. Imagine, instead of a player pretending to be tripped when she was not touched (i.e. flopping), the player actually *was* contacted illegally but, in this instance, she could have continued playing but flops to highlight the transgression. In this case, a foul was committed and, yet, some semblance of flopping also transpired. On one hand, this could be viewed as flopping—acting in a manner solely to receive a call from the referee. On the other hand, it could be seen as aiding the referee to make the proper call.

A similar questionable practice is pitch framing in baseball. When a catcher receives a pitch slightly outside of the strike zone, he will subtly bring his glove into the strike zone in an attempt to "frame" the pitch as a strike. If done well, this action can often be enough to influence an umpire to call a pitch outside of the strike zone a "strike" when it was not. Professional catchers are actually rated on how well they can frame pitches.

In this case, framing shares many—if not all—of the characteristics and corresponding issues of soccer's flopping, except for the rule violation. Additionally, nearly all who are involved in baseball consider it not only ethically allowable, but as a valued skill. Yet, like flopping, the behavior awards pitchers strikes they don't deserve, it wrongly punishes hitters, and it is all done in an attempt to manipulate the umpire.

Many within the culture of baseball, however, argue that pitchers *do* indeed deserve the strike as framing is simply a part of baseball: it's how baseball is played. Likewise, both batters and umpires understand this and, in a sense, consent to framing by playing the game.

Having considered several ethically questionable practices, let's look at examples of morally praiseworthy behavior in sport. For example, in a professional soccer game, an offensive player is awarded a penalty kick when the referee deemed he was tripped inside the penalty box. But the player immediately informs the referee that the defender did not, in fact, trip him: the player instead tripped on the grass. In the same game, a player from the opposing team is awarded a corner kick as the referee deems the ball has most recently touched the defending player and, yet, the offensive player informs the referee it actually touched him most recently. In both cases, the referee uses this information to change the call and award the ball correctly.

As you can see from the previous discussion, awarding ethical praise hinges on the ethical approach used to interpret the situation. On one hand, if an individual views the referee as truly a part of the game and adopts the "how the game is played" approach, then such seemingly praiseworthy acts might be seen as either unnecessary, or as poorly played soccer. In addition, many also consider a player's duty to the team (and to the fans, even) as also relevant here, arguing that a player conceding a penalty kick—even if undeserved—wrongly ignores these other duties. Or, an individual may view these actions as going above and beyond, thus deeming them supererogatory.

If one views these actions as simply playing well—as playing ethically—then, in a sense, these players just did what they *should* or *ought* to have done. In this case, we wouldn't praise these players any more than we would praise a person for handing a $20 bill to someone who has just dropped it while in line at the grocery store.

Examples of clear-cut supererogatory actions abound in sport. Here, we provide just one, as a model case. In a 2008 college softball game, batter Sara Tucholsky hit a home run—the first of her career, in her final game, which decided the conference championship. Upon rounding first base, she tore her ACL, making it impossible for her to round the bases. The rules clearly state that for the home run to count, the hitter must then touch all four bases and cannot receive assistance from any of her teammates in doing so. Two players from the opposing team then carried her around the bases, allowing her home run to stand and allowing Tucholsky's team to win the game, 4–2.

Blowouts

Blowouts occur in a competition when one team is exceptionally dominant over another. It is especially common in youth sports leagues, where teams are not always evenly matched. Numerous instances have occurred in recent history with high school basketball teams winning games by upwards of 100 or more points while maintaining aggressive measures throughout the game such as using a full-court press, shooting three pointers, and keeping the top players in the game.

On one hand, some argue that teams who have clearly asserted themselves as dominant, with the game clearly in control, ought not to run up the score. Out of a sense of sportsmanship and respect for a competitor, these dominant teams should take measures in order to lessen the lopsidedness of the score.

Although devising a respectful method for how to do this can be difficult, the obvious answer, for many, involves substituting the team's second-string or reserve players. But, as is often the case, even these players can dominate players from a much weaker program. Strategies such as slowing down the tempo of the game, having players play with their off-hands (or feet, in the case of soccer) or simply stalling so as to let time expire may alleviate the lopsidedness of the competition. However, these approaches can also exacerbate the dominance of the stronger team, often leading the weaker team to feel even more demeaned.

Even in a more closely contested game, it is widely accepted that when the winning team has the ball during the final seconds and has already secured a victory, it is unsportsmanlike to score even if scoring is easy. For example, if a basketball team is winning by 10 points with 15 seconds remaining and in possession of the ball, there should be no drives to the basket in an attempt to increase the margin to 12. Out of respect, the dominant team should hold the ball until time expires.

On the other hand, some argue that the two teams should play the entire contest to the best of their respective abilities. Although the lesser team may experience a more severe loss, both teams will have played their best. In addition, the lesser team will not feel demeaned by having potentially patronizing strategies adopted on their behalf, and they will have had the experience of playing against and learning from a completely superior team.

It is worth reflecting on whether the considerably weaker team on the losing side of a blowout really should feel demeaned and humiliated any more than is expected when a team loses. When a team enters a contest, the athletes recognize the possibility of losing, and, in losing, an athlete may feel some sense of humiliation. But losing and its attending disappointments are just a part of the sporting experience.

The proponent of playing to the best of one's abilities even when winning by a substantial margin argues that the athletes on the losing team are not demeaned as humans nor as athletes just because another team is considerably stronger. Although the losing athletes may *feel* this way, it is not humiliation in the worst sense (Dixon, 1992). It simply comes with the sporting territory: you win some and you lose some.

The issue boils down to a question of respect for one's competitor and for the game itself. Is it disrespectful to play to your fullest potential throughout an entire contest even if it means running up the score? Or is it disrespectful to intentionally fail to give one's best effort but, in doing so, hopefully diminish the potential humiliation of one's competitor? There are good arguments for and against both positions.

Intentional/strategic losing

Another ethical dilemma unique to sport is that losing a game will sometimes benefit the stronger team. Therefore, the stronger team theoretically has the choice of losing rather than winning the game. This situation typically arises in either tournament play or post-season playoffs, in which a loss provides a team with a weaker opponent in an ensuing round and, thus, a more likely chance to win the tournament or overall competition.

A team may also intentionally lose the first round of a tournament game in order to be placed in the lower bracket, thus greatly increasing the chance they come out of the tournament with a better win-loss record. This situation can also occur near the end of a season, when it has become mathematically impossible for a particular team to qualify for the playoffs. In this situation, losing games—often referred to as "tanking"— becomes beneficial because it can result in various benefits, such as future placement in an easier league or better opportunities to draft players for the next season: the lower-finishing teams are often given higher priority in ensuing drafts to provide some semblance of parity.

One of the more blatant instances of intentional losing occurred in the 2012 Olympic doubles badminton tournament. At one point, both China and South Korea were competing, and each recognized that a loss would put them in a more strategic position to face a weaker opponent in a subsequent round. This awareness resulted in such poor performance that both teams barely placed a serve in bounds and, when they did, the longest rally lasted just four hits in a sport that consistently sees rallies of twenty to thirty hits. As a result, eight players were ejected from the Olympic Games for failing to adhere to the following rules: "Not using best efforts," and, "Conducting oneself in a manner that is clearly abusive or detrimental to the sport" (Saraceno & Johnson, 2012).

In evaluating the ethics of intentionally losing, one must consider the nature of sport: attempting to win within the boundaries of the rules. Clearly, in this case, it was strategically beneficial for the teams to lose that particular competition in order to maximize their chance at winning the overall competition. Yet, as is often the case, just because a particular move in sport is strategic and in the best interests of the athletes and team, it is not sufficient for ethical play. In the case of the badminton tournament, the players actually were charged with breaking the rules.

If this strategy, however, did not break the rules and was considered ethical and sportsmanlike then, in a soccer game, for example, it would be acceptable for both teams to simply stand motionless for the entirety of the 90-minute "competition," allowing the game to end in a tie. If players acted in this way, the event could hardly be considered a "competition" in the first place. To exacerbate the absurdity, one might even imagine the players kicking the ball into their own goal in order to secure the desired outcome—a loss—and, thus, the entire game would break down at its core, becoming the antithesis of competition. Whereas failing to play soccer *well* clearly does not constitute unethical behavior, *intending* to fail might.

Just this sort of absurdity occurred in a 1998 Tiger Cup soccer match. Both Thailand and Indonesia set out to lose the game in order to avoid having to face the home favorite, Vietnam, in a subsequent round. At one point, an Indonesian player kicked the ball into his own goal while Thai players attempted to *prevent* their team being awarded the goal. The player received a lifetime ban from international soccer for "violating the *spirit* of the game."

In a sense, one can argue that within the construct of sport, athletes not only owe each other ethical conduct, but they also owe the referee decorum and respect. Given the public nature of sport, athletes and their teams and leagues also owe the fans and their community something more than just winning a competition at all costs. This idea is best captured by the question of to what extent sport should reflect society's ideals. Can we rightly demand that sport reflect the values we celebrate in society at large? Virtue Ethics, Care Ethics and Utilitarianism point to an affirmative answer to that question.

The problem is made worse—and more evident—when only one team attempts to intentionally lose while the other "uses best efforts." In the 2016 Olympic Qualifying Tournament, the French National Water Polo team was accused of intentionally losing to Canada because the winner of their game would face a considerably weaker team in the next round, in which a win would secure a bid to the 2016 Olympics. France did, in fact, succeed in losing to Canada and then went on to win the next game, qualifying for the Olympics, while Canada lost their next match and, thus, failed to qualify.

The governing body of this competition, FINA, explains in its Rules and Regulations that the rules "seek to preserve what is intrinsically valuable about sport. This intrinsic value is often referred to as 'the spirit of sport.' It is the essence of sport; the pursuit of human excellence . . . it is how we play true" (FINA, 2016). In addition, FINA's rules list values which FINA believes characterize the "spirit of sport":

- Ethics, fair play and honesty.
- Excellence in performance.
- Character and education.
- Respect for self and other participants.
- Community and solidarity.
- Courage.

(id.)

When we know that a team intends to lose, we can recognize how such an approach to a competition clashes with the above values and "spirit of sport." Thus, proper leadership is necessary in such instances from both the team and from the sporting organization in which it competes.

CONCLUSION

Although it may initially seem easy to adjudicate ethical behavior in sport, given its clearly delineated rules and voluntary participation by participants, we quickly recognize many of the subtleties which arise. Two approaches to discerning ethical action in sport are formalism—that rules define the game and, thus, must be strictly adhered to—and an ethos-based approach—that the culture of sport-participants determines how the game ought to be played and how the rules should be interpreted and manipulated. Both approaches have their utility as well as their shortcomings.

These two approaches engender discussion about a more exact definition of cheating in sport, in which someone breaks a rule intending to gain an advantage and attempting to avoid punishment. Additionally, we recognize that ethical behavior extends beyond mere rule following.

Just as we can treat others unethically in life without violating some legal or ethical precept, sport participants can be said to behave in an unsportsmanlike manner. So, too, just as in our daily lives, athletes can behave in a morally praiseworthy manner, going beyond what is expected for the sake of one's competitor.

A closer look at sport-specific issues such as blowouts and intentional losing provides an opportunity to better understand sport's riches, but also to recognize the need for thoughtful, consistent leadership at all levels. The first challenge in this study is determining the ethical actions of participants, and the second challenge is implementing those actions through proper leadership, which we will explore in the next chapter.

ETHICAL LEADERSHIP CASE STUDY

Coach Hackashaq knows that he can increase his basketball team's chances of winning if, toward the end of the game, he instructs his players to foul the worst foul shooter on the opposing team. This practice has resulted in slowing the end of games to a snail's pace, which alienates fans and television networks. Commissioner Sporting wants to end this practice without causing a worse problem. What ethical arguments can he use to convince the team owners that changing this practice will benefit all the stakeholders—fans, players, owners, referees, coaches?

STUDENT LEARNING EXERCISES

Address the ethical nature of the following case studies, situations, and sport-specific issues. After formulating your own position, consider discussing them in small groups looking both for areas of agreement and then also delving deeper into areas of disagreement.

1. Evaluate the following common phrases:

   (a) It's only cheating if you get caught.
   (b) Cheaters never prosper.
   (c) If you're not cheating you're not trying.

2. When playing one-on-one basketball, ought a competitor announce when the ball has gone off his hand and out of bounds? When playing a full-fledged league basketball game with referees, clocks, etc., ought a competitor announce when the ball has gone off his hand and out of bounds when the referee does not detect it? Is there a difference? Should there be? Defend your conclusion.

3. Is it unethical to intentionally lose a game in order to gain something in the future? Consider the following examples:

   (a) Losing a tournament game in order to play a weaker opponent in the next round thus providing a better chance at advancement.
   (b) Losing a game in order to profit monetarily from gambling.
   (c) Losing a game in order to rest the top players for a future game of greater importance.
   (d) Losing a game in order to allow your competitor to make it to the playoffs for the purpose of preventing another team from getting to the playoffs.

(e) Losing the first round of a tournament game in order to make it easier to win the next three games of the tournament, thus improving one's overall record.

(f) When at the end of a season in which it is impossible to make the playoffs, intentionally losing a game in order to secure some advantage the following season (i.e. better draft picks or better league placement).

4. How do you evaluate the following situations? Provide reasons for your answer:

(a) Soccer player faking being tripped—"flopping"—in order to have the referee award him a penalty kick.

(b) Basketball coach spilling water on the court in order to get a timeout without having to use one of his allotted timeouts.

(c) Soccer player deceptively hitting the ball into the goal with his hand for a goal.

(d) Soccer player (non-goalie) intentionally using his hands to prevent a ball from scoring and suffering the consequences (expulsion from the game and a penalty kick for the opposing team).

(e) Baseball team cutting the grass to a height that gives them an advantage.

5. In 2012, two gamblers won over $9 million from a casino playing Baccarat, a luck-based card game. They were later discovered to have spent hundreds of hours memorizing exceptionally subtle patterns on the cards which garnered information about the information on the cards they were not intended to have. A judge ordered them to repay all winnings to the casino for a breach of contract, while their lawyers claimed the gamblers did not break any rules and, instead, relied on keen observation. Is this cheating? How do you evaluate these claims?

6. Are trick plays at the youth sports level ever considered unsportsmanlike? Consider the following:

(a) "Confused quarterback"—The quarterback's coach calls him over before the snap and the quarterback acts like he doesn't understand the play; meanwhile, they hike the ball to a running back and run a play.

(b) "Barking dog"—Before inbounding the ball in basketball, a player gets on his knees and barks like a dog to distract everyone while they inbound the ball for an easy shot.

(c) "Fake inbounds"—A basketball player has the ball out of bounds and hands it to a player inbounds as if telling him to throw the ball in; but instead, because the player is inbounds, he shoots an easy shot.

(d) "Eavesdropping defender"—A football coach yells to his receiver for the sole purpose of the defender hearing him, "Take 'em deep! Sprint all the way to the end zone!" but, instead, they run a short 10-yard play.

(e) "Sneaky kick"—As a soccer player approaches a penalty kick, he walks up to the ball and bends over as if he is going to adjust the ball's placement; immediately prior to touching it with his hands, he cleverly kicks the ball with his toe into the goal, catching the goalie completely off guard.

7. Do you agree or disagree with the statement: "When the winning team has the ball during the final seconds and has already secured a victory, it is unsportsmanlike to score even if easily feasible." Why/why not?

PROBLEMS/QUESTIONS

1. Explain formalism's Logical Incompatibility Thesis as regards the "good foul" in basketball. How does it differ from the ethos-based account of basketball's "good fouls"? Evaluate it in your own terms: do you agree/disagree and why?
2. What role does the ethos of a sport play in rule following? Explain, using the example of baseball's "pitch framing." Explain Aristotle's metaphor of the Lesbian Rule here and the tension between ethos-based sports ethics and formalism.
3. Explain the relevance of implied consent in regards to rule following and violence in a particular game such as football. How does this relate to Locke's notion of tacit consent as it applies to the Social Contract? How does it apply to rule following in general?

BIBLIOGRAPHY

Aristotle, *Nichomachean Ethics*, translated by W.D. Ross (1925).

Dixon, Nicholas, On Sportsmanship and "Running Up the Score", 19, *Journal of the Philosophy of Sport*, 1 (1992).

FINA, *Rules and Regulations* (2016).

Fraleigh, Warren P., Intentional Rules Violations—One More Time, 30 *Journal of the Philosophy of Sport* 166 (2003).

Saraceno, Jon, & Kevin Johnson, London Olympics Badminton Scandal Raises Ethical Issues, *USA Today*, August 1, 2012. Available at: http://usatoday30.usatoday.com/sports/olympics/london/story/2012-07-31/Badminton-players-charged-with-throwing-matches/56630488/1.

Vecsey, George, Backtalk: When is it Gamesmanship, and When is it Cheating?, *The New York Times*, August 8, 1998.

CHAPTER 3

The importance of leadership and leadership development in sport

INTRODUCTION

The purpose of this chapter is to introduce the important role of effective leadership abilities and the development of these abilities in sport-related fields and activities. It will provide students with insights into the importance of leaders in sports leagues, conferences, and activities (as an athlete or coach, for example).

The chapter provides an introduction to leadership theory while also describing the importance of leadership development in sport, including team competition, administration of sport teams and leagues, and preparation of student-athletes for important roles in their communities and organizations. It introduces you to the roles that leaders play in our society, but it also can assist you in understanding the importance of leadership development in their individual lives. Once you understand the critical role of leadership training to our society's future, you can relate that learning to leadership— particularly ethical leadership— in the microcosm of sport.

The chapter also describes examples of exemplary leadership in sport and competitive endeavors by many different participants in the field, from team players to university presidents, from league executives to coaches. Sport provides many opportunities for men and women to demonstrate their leadership abilities as well as to develop and advance those leadership abilities.

The chapter also describes situations where effective, ethical leadership has been lacking and the consequences of failed leadership to fans, sport institutions, players, and coaches. Through an examination of failed as well as exceptional leadership examples, you will gain insights into the central importance of leadership to advancing all aspects of sport management and participation discussed in this book. Students also will recognize that education about leadership in sport is a recurring theme throughout this book; every chapter has examples of good (or poor) leadership in specific areas of sport and competition. Therefore, an overarching goal of this book is to educate and enable students for leadership roles they will play in their careers and to do so in the context of sport.

THE IMPORTANCE OF LEADERSHIP—GENERALLY AND IN SPORT

Leaders and leadership skills in society and our communities

The need for effective leadership is pervasive in our society. Leadership matters in many aspects and sectors of our society and communities, including political and governmental institutions, business organizations, many professions (such as law and medicine) and, significantly, individual personal development. Leaders move our economic institutions, non-profit and philanthropic organizations, and social and community groups, and they undertake the responsibility for articulating the goals and aspirations of the varied groups and entities; they lead the groups' participants—whether participants are coaches or players, shareholders, or clients, advisory boards or employees—to achieve shared goals.

According to Stanford University's Deborah Rhode, leadership training is itself a significant business enterprise which indicates its importance in our social, political, and economic institutions. She notes that "leadership development is now a forty-five-billion dollar industry, and an Amazon search reveals close to 88,000 leadership books in print" (Rhode, 2013). She also writes that leadership education is virtually lacking in some critical areas of our society, but it is abundant in other areas such as business management and operations. More specifically, as noted below, there is considerable interest in research and development of leadership qualities and skills in sport-related fields and organizations.

Leadership education and personal leadership development in the United States occur in several ways. One important avenue is by formal instruction at the college or university level, usually in courses that emphasize the prevalent theories of leadership, the biographies of acknowledged "great" leaders, and information about how leadership is developed in individuals (Northouse, 2015). Another route, which is common in many graduate business school programs, is to use empirical research to develop approaches to the development of sound, effective, or exemplary leadership abilities (Kouzes & Posner, 2014).

Personal and professional leadership development programs often attempt to enhance the leadership abilities of business executives, education administrators, professionals, and others so that those important people can function at higher levels of competence in their positions. There are many providers of these developmental training and personal growth programs; they usually offer the programs for periods of limited duration—for example, three days or one week—to small groups or to individuals. Examples include the Center for Creative Leadership and numerous business schools.

Many professional organizations also offer programs for personal or individual development of key leadership skills and abilities through individual mentoring or coaching. Again, the goal of these intensive educational programs is to enable an employee or executive to improve his or her ability to provide leadership to the organization.

Why do individuals and organizations spend billions of dollars, including the time key employees spend in leadership development programs and skills enhancement seminars, to build stakeholders' abilities to lead? The answer is clear: well-led organizations are more successful—financially and otherwise—than organizations where leadership is lacking or failing. Moreover, many surveys have concluded that citizens have a greater sense of security and optimism if they perceive that their employer, organization, or government is led by capable, ethical leaders (Kouzes & Posner, 2010).

Importantly, countries, such as the United States, that are democratic republics imbue their leaders with roles and responsibilities for maintenance of constitutionally based governance and protection of national institutions and governmental processes. These governmental initiatives and processes require great, effective, and persistent leadership.

Leadership skills in sport

The broad area of sport—from international professional leagues to hundreds of college and university teams to Little League and club sport teams—has an immense economic influence in the United States and the world; it constitutes a multi-billion dollar industry. As one example of revenues in sport, the 2015 National Collegiate Athletic Association (NCAA) basketball tournament generated $71.7 million just from ticket sales with attendance at about 800,000 fans. Another example is the National Football League (NFL) Super Bowl. The 2014 Super Bowl game (played in January 2015) was viewed by 114.4 million viewers and generated advertising revenues alone of $330 million.

Moreover, collegiate sport commentators have argued that sports-related activities on campus enhance the campus community in many respects. They have relied on studies showing that college sport—in conferences as well as intramural on each campus—is a glue that pulls many university campuses together by enhancing a sense of community on the campus both for students and in the community for fans.

> Football, in particular, has been the sport of choice for creating a campus-wide[sense of community] for students and fans. While other benefits such as revenue generation and image enhancement have been sought and attributed to football, fostering [sense of community] is the most pervasive and consistent claim throughout the history of college sport.
>
> (Warner et al., 2011)

Widespread enthusiasm for sport competition, then, sets the stage for great successes in leading these highly visible and important academic institutions that offer venues for competition. Of course, there are also pitfalls because of failure of leadership in sports—for example, in connection with the use of performance-enhancing drugs (see Chapter 7).

Most failures in sport organizations are caused by failures of leadership, so it is important to understand why leadership development is important to the industry. Understanding how sport can be improved and strengthened by effective leadership is, therefore, a key objective of this book.

Instructive examples of failed leadership show their negative effect on public perceptions of the integrity of sport as an integral social activity: one example is the tardy response of the National Football League to the emerging, but clear, evidence that prolonged football competition was a significant contributor to players' concussion-related illness. After a long period of denial of the causal connection between football competition and head concussion-related injuries, the National Football League finally agreed that there was a connection and, more recently, that as many as one in three NFL players could suffer brain trauma as a result of football (Belson, 2014).

The same criticism of the NFL—that the leadership was not proactive or consistent— has also been raised concerning its handling of the rising incidents of domestic violence by NFL players (see Jacobs, 2015). Other examples abound—steroid use in professional baseball, chew-tobacco use by high school players, and corruption in the award of site cities for the Olympic Games and international soccer contests. These examples demonstrate the harmful effects on the positive and personally enhancing attributes of the sport for players and fans.

The many examples of exemplary leadership in sport by coaches, players, league executives, and others, however, serve as a counterbalance to the examples of failed or, occasionally, corrupt leadership. For many sport leadership experts, one coach stands out among leaders: John Wooden, the long-time coach of the University of California, Los Angeles' (UCLA) basketball team. He is an enduring example of positive and ethical leadership in sport. More importantly, he was known for instilling in his players the habits, traits, and skills that helped shape them as admirable citizens and human beings.

Aside from the highly visible examples by sport figures like Coach Wooden, leadership abilities and development in sport are important for other reasons. Leadership training provides opportunities for boys and girls to develop leadership skills and to demonstrate them in sport competition and in life. Sport competition at every level provides participants with examples of good and poor leadership, so sport provides a lens through which we can understand effective and exemplary, or, conversely, inept or negative, leadership in our communities. Sport affects many aspects of our lives, so it is inherently valuable that sport institutions are run ethically and with integrity.

WHAT DO WE MEAN BY LEADERSHIP?

There are many theories of leadership, and many perspectives on how leadership ability emerges. There are also many definitions of what defines an effective and capable leader. Many of these theories and definitions share common aspects. The following sections provide an introduction to definitions of leadership and to prevalent theories of leadership.

At one time, the notion of who is a leader and how he or she leads a group was shaped by human observation and intuition, often influenced by the results or outcomes of the leader's activity. Leadership was defined by what the perceived leaders did or didn't do and how they went about their work for the organization or group. Today, however, a great deal of the knowledge of effective leadership and effective styles of leadership are shaped by empirical analysis and a well-developed body of academic literature. This literature will be introduced through the descriptions of theories and styles of leadership.

Defining leadership

Of the many definitions of leadership, perhaps the simplest, and most inclusive, definition states that it is a process advanced through a personal relationship that influences individuals and groups toward established goals or desired outcomes (Rhode, 2013). Leadership is a process by which an individual or group influences others to achieve positive, ethical change between the leader and his or her followers or constituents. "The functions that leaders perform for human groups are to create meaning and goals, reinforce group identity and cohesion, provide order, and mobilize collective work" (Nye, 2008).

Key concepts underlying the prevalent definitions of leadership (and the corresponding description of what leaders do) are:

- Leadership involves complex behaviors; it is a process of interactions with others.
- Leadership involves change; positive and ethical change; change is an outcome or goal of action by leaders; if an organization does not need change, then it doesn't need leadership.
- Effective leaders have many attributes that enable them to be successful in leading change, but one of the most fundamental is having "vision"—an ability to conceive of a plan of action for how the change to the group or organization will benefit its members and the organization.
- Leaders inspire, motivate, and activate activity by their constituencies (followers, employees, teammates, etc.) toward a goal or goals; trust in the leader's vision for change moves the group toward achievement of the goals (Kouzes & Posner, 2014; Polden, 2012).

Theories of leadership

Human beings have had a long-standing admiration for their heroes and leaders. Bible, Koran and Talmud, for example, all feature stories of great and heroic figures who lead their people to safety, glory or personal and religious growth. Gandhi is an example of someone who rose from obscurity to spark an international movement marked by respect and compassion for the poor and their families.

Early theories of who is a leader were based on great historical leaders and the narrative accounts of their leadership. However, scholars and observers of less exalted, but still important, leaders began to construct more contemporary views of how we understand effectiveness in leadership. These scholars proposed theories why particular leaders came to the forefront in their lives, jobs, or positions to become leaders, and why—and in what contexts—people follow leaders.

The following sections generally describe the most prevalent and historical theories of leadership (Northouse, 2015).

The great man theory

This perspective contends that leaders are born and not made, and that great leaders arise when there is a social or communal need for leadership. This viewpoint is predicated on the idea that leadership ability is innate—you have it or you don't—and, therefore, that it is not an acquired ability. An important, but largely discredited, component of this theory is that leadership cannot be taught or developed in others. Often, great military generals and political figures are identified as examples of this theory as are great movement figures such as Gandhi. The theory has largely been discredited because there is no empirical basis for the underlying notion that leadership ability is inherited or acquired through an inherited position or title.

Trait theory

This perspective is similar to the "great man" theory and assumes that people inherit certain personal qualities that permit them to assume the role of, and be successful in the role of, leader. Again, this view has largely been discarded due to the lack of verifiable evidence that an ability to lead is a trait that one acquires through birth or inherited position.

Behavioral theory

This perspective asserts that leaders can be made and that leadership is a set of behaviors that can be learned. This perspective is the antithesis of the "great man" perspective. It argues that the capacity to lead is not inborn or inherent but rather the product of a deliberative process toward the understanding of, and the development of, the key characteristics and attributes of effective leadership. However, the theory was found to be largely insufficient to explain the various contexts in which leadership occurred and through which it was developed. Advocates of this theory would study the behaviors of acknowledged leaders and then attempt to create a theory of leadership from their documented behaviors. This result-oriented approach is not very predictive and therefore not very helpful.

Contingency theory

This theory is similar to the behavioral perspective. It argues that a person becomes a leader due to the circumstances that he or she *is in* and to which the leader reacts. Some factors (or contingencies) that influence how the leader acts or reacts are the behaviors and needs of followers, the leader's preferred style of leadership, and various other situational factors. While the research on the kinds of situations or contingencies under which a person rose to lead is interesting, the theory was generally not sufficient to explain the full range of leadership activities. The theory assumed that no one leadership style is appropriate or best in all situations and that the "best" approach depended on a number of variables. Therefore, the concern was that the theory was, indeed, no theory at all but a prediction of how people may act under varying circumstances.

Power and influence theory

Another perspective on how leadership is manifested considers the influence process at work between leaders and other individuals in order to gain insights into leadership effectiveness. The power and influence theory considers how the leader can influence, subjugate, or subordinate followers because of the relative positions of power between the leader and the followers. Leaders can acquire power to effect change or enforce their will in a variety of ways. In many situations, leaders possess power because they hold an office or position that carries power or that permits the leader to reward (or punish) followers for their compliance or non-compliance with the wishes of the leader. Similarly, leaders can have and exercise power over or on followers because of their expertise and knowledge or due to their interpersonal skills and charisma. In some contexts—for example, in leadership roles in military conflicts—absolute power wielded by officers is necessary to protect soldiers and to efficiently accomplish the group's mission.

TYPES OF LEADERSHIP

The theories of leadership listed above are not exhaustive. Moreover, the leadership literature often uses "theories" of leadership interchangeably with "styles" or "types" of leadership. However, as is discussed in the following sections, there are important differences between styles of leadership and types of leaders, and those are different than broad theories of the source and nature of leadership.

Related to the literature on theories of leadership are several perspectives on types of or approaches to leadership. The literature attempts to describe how the particular forms of leadership are practiced and conducted by leaders, including the circumstances leaders are in, the situations of their followers and their organizations, and the intended effects of the leadership practices. The following sections describe some of the more commonly known types of leadership practiced today.

Adaptive leadership

This approach to leadership focuses on the activities of a person or persons to mobilize people around them to make progress on important goals, issues, conflicts, and challenges facing them (Heifetz, 2006). They mobilize by motivating, and persuading, organizing, focusing attention on the issues and challenges, and seeking to bring the constituent group together for their common good:

> [a]daptive work consists of the learning required to address conflicts in the values people hold, or to diminish the gap between the values people stand for and the reality they face. Adaptive work requires a change in values, beliefs, or behavior. The exposure and orchestration of conflict—internal contradictions—within the individuals and constituencies provide the leverage for mobility people to learn new ways.
>
> (Hamilton, 2009)

Adaptive leadership requires that leaders utilize a number of skills seeking to mobilize the group but within the context of a conflict or challenge or situation, including the culture of the group or the abilities of group members. Some of the relevant skills applied by an adaptive leader include the ability to help group members understand the situation and manage the contradictions evident in the situation and help address the group's distress (Heifetz & Linsky, 2002).

An important contribution to the literature on leadership made by this perspective is that adaptive leadership does not require a leader with formal directing authority, but rather a member of the group can successfully exercise it for the benefit of the entire group. Thus, leadership in many contexts can be provided by people who do not have formal power or authority over the followers: the leader provides persuasive influence that motivates the group to move in the desired direction.

Transformational leadership

This perspective, which is perhaps the leading theory of leadership used by business and political leaders, contends that people will follow someone who inspires them with a vision for great achievements or improvements. Such leaders inspire followers by articulating a vision for how change (within the organization or in the political environment) can benefit everyone, and then they encourage and inspire followers toward the change. Importantly, the transformation often is reciprocal—leaders change through their leadership conduct and relationship with their constituents, and the constituents or followers are changed by the leadership.

The noted political scientist, James MacGregor Burns, was among the first to describe this form of leadership in the context of political leaders. He explained why people follow leaders who inspire them and who accomplish results by infusing their followers with enthusiasm and excitement about a shared goal or vision for their future (Burns, 1978). According to Burns, transformational leaders bring the vision to life for followers by their example and by effective and inspiring communication.

Transactional leadership

Another type of leadership focuses on transactions or dealings between leaders and their followers or constituents. The proponents of this perspective argue that effective leadership occurs within a framework of transactions in the workplace. Leaders clearly articulate the structures within the workforce and how employees (or followers) are expected to perform. Reciprocally, employees also know their roles and the expectations about their performance.

Transactional leadership focuses on what leaders and their followers gain in exchange for their cooperation and participation. These leaders are a key aspect in the chain of command within the organization, and they articulate what is expected of the workforce. Their job is to see that the work is done, and they often use a reward structure to create incentives for employees to accomplish the goals they set.

Situational leadership

This type of leadership occurs when leaders exhibit no one leadership style or approach, but rather they choose the appropriate course of action based on each situation they encounter. This perspective recognizes that each situation calling for leadership is different and the leader must determine the necessary response in each situation—what forces are pressing on the leader, what forces are pressing on followers, what resources and what competencies are available in the workplace and among the workers. Situational leaders look at the context of the workplace and adapt their approach or style to the developmental level of the employees, including the employees' level of commitment to the organization.

Servant leadership

Servant leaders focus on the growth and well-being of people and their communities, and not, as in other types of leadership, on exercising power at the top of the organization. They share the power of the organization (such as decision-making, planning, managing) with others by putting the others' needs first. These leaders help others to develop professionally, grow personally, and perform as highly as possible (Greenleaf, 2002). Like adaptive leadership, servant leadership can be practiced or implemented by someone who does not have formal authority to lead (Hamilton, 2009).

Servant leaders base their leadership on a moral foundation through self-knowledge and the growth of personal conscience; this foundation permits them to inspire others to ethical, necessary action or activity. The fully formed servant leader demonstrates several key virtues, including stewardship for the benefit of others, empathy, commitment to others' growth, and personal development. Servant leaders also possess key skills and abilities, including listening, reflecting, persuading, providing feedback, and others (Hamilton, 2009).

Participative leadership

This perspective argues that effective leadership is based on democratic decision-making and that effective leaders seek to involve followers in the decision-making process. The wider, participatory process improves understanding of all involved in the situation, builds team loyalty, and generates consensus on how to address organizational problems and challenges.

Ethical leadership

One of the most useful frameworks for understanding leadership in sport is provided by the literature on ethical leadership. Ethics or ethics-based positions, such as those set out in Chapters 1 and 2, can be advanced in any type of leader, but most often in situations involving servant leadership, adaptive leadership, and transformational leadership (Hamilton, 2009). The area of ethical leadership in sport will be discussed further in a later section of this chapter.

LEADERSHIP STYLES

As with the literature on types and theories of leadership, there are many leader styles—i.e. how leaders motivate and encourage followers or constituents to get a job done. The literature on leadership styles attempts to describe how leaders get results through their relationships with their employees, colleagues, or teammates, and how they move or motivate their followers to get results that advance their goals while also making the employees feel important to the mission of the group.

Daniel Goleman, a Harvard University expert on leadership, describes six styles of leadership that are prevalent in workplaces and other settings where there is a relationship between someone in charge and those who follow (Goleman, 1998). Most of these styles are relatively observable in our lives, our work experiences and in public life. Several also are directly observable in sport contexts. Coaches and team leaders often use one or more of the styles in motivating their teams to success.

These leadership styles, according to Goleman, come from aspects of emotional intelligence possessed by effective leaders. Emotional intelligence refers to the capacity for recognizing our own feelings and those of others, for motivating ourselves, and for managing emotions in ourselves and in our relationships (id.).

Four critical and fundamental emotional intelligence-related capabilities of effective leaders are: 1) self-awareness, 2) self-management, 3) social awareness, and 4) social skill (Goleman, 2000). Self-awareness helps us to understand our own emotions and their impact on our relationships and our work, to perform accurate assessments of our strengths and weaknesses, and to develop and exhibit self-confidence.

Self-management is important because it enables self-control, promotes our trust-worthiness, permits us to take the initiative where it is needed, and focuses us on success and achievement of goals. The capacity for social awareness permits us to sense other people's emotions and needs, and to demonstrate empathy for them. It also advances our abilities to organize effectively and to be cognizant of the needs and desires of others, such as customers or sport fans.

Finally, the capacity for "social skill" permits us to provide leadership through conception and articulation of a vision for the group, the ability to build and maintain teams in the workplace, to communicate effectively with our constituents, and to be an honest and capable listener. This capacity also permits us to understand how to help others like our teammates or co-workers to develop their talents and to succeed.

Goleman's sweeping, highly relevant and useful description of these key abilities has greatly advanced thinking and research on how effective leaders can lead groups in both simple and complex organizations. One of the most important findings that came from the research on these capabilities is that leaders with them are more effective in their work than peers who lacked such strengths. Leaders with them were able to create and sustain positive workplace climates that resulted in greater worker satisfaction and success for the organization.

Of course, not every leader has a great abundance of every component of emotional intelligence. Many leaders are continually attempting to develop greater strengths in the components. As they become more proficient in many or all of these capabilities, their abilities to lead increase.

Building on his work on the components of emotional intelligence, Goleman identified six leadership styles that business executives use in the workplace. A description of each style is summarized below. These styles are also observed in highly functioning leaders in other fields, such as non-profit organizations, law firms and hospitals, and, as we shall discuss, in teams and sport organizations.

Coercive style

Leaders using this style simply tell followers (an employee, for example) what they are going to do without soliciting input, feelings, or suggestions. This leader believes in the adage "It's my way or the highway." This leadership style is generally not effective with highly educated or skilled employees. It is often used in situations involving routine work and military combat settings. Also, athletic coaches will often use a coercive, highly directive approach during critical periods of competition or preparation when more participative governance is not possible.

Authoritative style

Authoritative leaders are visionaries and motivate followers by making sure the followers know how their work fits into the bigger vision for the organization. These leaders inspire others by their knowledge, perceptiveness, expertise, and skills. This is one of the more effective methods of leadership with highly educated employees and sport team members. It is also often used when forces facing an organization or group have changed, and a new, responsive vision or change in direction is necessary. Leaders with this style have the ability to inspire followers to view the importance of their work and performances in the broader context of the organization. Of all the leadership styles identified by Goleman, this is the most positive from the perspective of the workplace and the leaders' effects on their constituents or followers.

Affiliative style

These leaders value people highly and, while coercive leaders say "Do what I say," affiliative leaders say "Come with me; people come first, and we go together." Such leaders build cooperative relationships with strong emotional bonds; they build loyalty and trust in the group or organization, especially if the group or organization has experienced challenging times. The affiliative style also has a positive effect on the workplace. Many coaches will use this leadership approach to build cohesion and mutual trust among team members.

Democratic style

Leaders using this style build trust and confidence in followers and spend a lot of time getting "buy-in" from everyone. With this style, all followers have a say in decisions that affect the group's goals. This approach works well when leaders are uncertain about the best outcome and the direction an organization should take. This style also works well in some workplaces where group orientation and shared-commitment to the decision-making process move the organization forward.

However, this style is not useful in some situations, such as when the organization is facing an imminent and complex problem or where the followers lack the ability to make an effective decision in the context of the particular problem or challenge. An example is when a company is approached by another company about a merger or acquisition. The deal can often have a short decision-making period, involves complex legal, accounting and regulatory issues, and the employees may not be able to consider the benefit of the arrangement because of personal concerns about their jobs.

Pacesetting style

Leaders using this style set extremely high performance standards and then exemplify them. They challenge followers to achieve similarly high standards and can be critical of employees who fall short of high performance. Often this style alienates employees who don't appreciate the leaders' demonstrations of their competence and ability.

When, however, the employees are highly skilled and self-motivated, and are able to keep up with the leader's standards and high performance, the pacesetting style can be useful. This leadership approach is sometimes used by sport team captains, who attempt to inspire others to follow their lead and "do as I am doing" through, for example, adopting a rigorous and demanding work, conditioning, or practice schedule.

Coaching style

Leaders using this style spend much time helping employees identify their unique skills and weaknesses and encouraging their success. These leaders make agreements with individual employees about their personal growth and their success within the organization. Most leaders do not have time for this level of interaction with their employees, but it is an effective approach when the organization has some key employees who are aware of their weaknesses and who are interested in self-improvement. It also has considerable utility in team sports, where the number of followers or participants is relatively small and an important aspect of team success is the personal improvement of the weaker members of the team.

Goleman contends that these styles are all appropriate and useful depending on the leader's strengths and the circumstances. Moreover, he argues that effective leaders often use these styles in tandem or in conjunction with other styles. His research shows that the two most effective styles of leaders are the authoritative and affiliative, but also that leaders who have mastered four or more of the styles (especially the authoritative, democratic, affiliative and coaching styles) have the very best workplace climate and business performance.

DEEPER INSIGHTS INTO LEADERSHIP: TWO PERPETUAL QUESTIONS REGARDING LEADERSHIP

Nearly all the contemporary literature on leadership addresses two perpetual questions about leadership and the ability of exceptional leaders to exert a significant impact on their followers. These additional insights into leadership will help you get a better, broader sense of the nature and importance of leadership in many areas and how leaders function to lead others.

Question 1: Are leaders born or can leadership be taught?

One of the great practitioners of sport leadership was Vince Lombardi, the long-time, successful coach of the Green Bay Packers. Lombardi said: "Leaders are made, they are not born. They are made by hard effort, which is the price which all of us must pay to achieve any goal that is worthwhile."

The conventional wisdom today, contrary to the "great man" theory of leadership, is that leadership skills and attributes can be acquired by education, by personal initiative and by opportunities to develop the ability to lead. Indeed, from the plethora of books on the subjects of leadership and becoming a leader, it appears that leadership can be for everyone. Developing leadership competencies in men and women results in more willing and prepared leaders to move our society forward.

As a practical matter, successful organizations, whether they are sport organizations, or Fortune 500 companies, or a branch of the armed forces, cannot simply wait for a situation to occur and passively hope that a leader will step up and lead. They must, in order to survive and prosper, anticipate the challenges and needs of the organization and develop leadership talent that will be available to lead when the need arises.

Question 2: Are leadership and management the same?

People often confuse, or conflate, leadership and management. They are different abilities. Some leaders are also effective managers; others are not. Some skilled managers have excellent leadership abilities; many do not. Warren Bennis, a great thinker on the subject of leadership, explained the distinctions between managers and leaders as follows:

> The manager administers; the leader innovates. . . .
>
> The manager has a short-range view; the leader has a long-range perspective.
>
> The manager asks how and when; the leader asks what and why.
>
> The manager has his or her eye always on the bottom line; the leader's eye is on the horizon. . . .
>
> The manager does things right; the leader does the right thing. . . .
>
> (Bennis, 2002, in Rhode & Packel, 2011)

Of course, there is no stigma in being a capable and conscious manager. Organizations need effective management to permit them to achieve their mission. However, if an organization needs to change, achieve new goals, or articulate and pursue a vision of a new future, then it needs a leader.

In the context of sport, the need for both effective managers and effective leaders is evident. Determining where management ends and leadership begins (or vice versa) is less important than understanding how individuals advance the interests and success of teams and sports organizations. Some coaches, for example, stick to strategy and tactics, whereas others, like John Wooden and Vince Lombardi, occupy iconic positions in society at large.

LEADERS' ATTRIBUTES: HOW FOLLOWERS RATE LEADERS' ABILITIES AND TALENTS

Contemporary leadership literature often describes leadership in terms of the close relationship between leaders and their followers or constituents. A great deal of this literature focuses on the behaviors of leaders and how followers respond to those behaviors.

Barry Posner and Jim Kouzes, authors of *The Leadership Challenge*, have surveyed thousands of people across six continents and asked them to identify the top characteristics of exemplary leaders. The results of the top characteristics and the percent which each was identified by respondents is as follows:

1. honesty: eighty-nine percent (89%);
2. forward-looking: seventy-one percent (71%);
3. inspiring: sixty-nine percent (69%);
4. competent: sixty-eight percent (68%);
5. intelligent: forty-eight percent (48%).

(Kouzes and Posner, 2014)

Another thoughtful description of an effective leader's abilities and strengths identifies five categories:

1. values (such as integrity, honesty, trust, and an ethic of service);
2. personal skills (such as self-awareness, self-control, and self-direction);
3. interpersonal skills (such as social awareness, empathy, persuasion, and conflict management);
4. vision (such as a forward-looking and inspiring); and
5. technical competence (such as knowledge, preparation, and judgment).

(Rhode, 2013)

The highly valued characteristic of honesty is really about the leader's credibility and followers' sense of trust in the leader. The interwoven characteristics of credibility and trust raise the issue of the ethical foundations for a leader's actions. Leadership devoid of an ethical compass is not true leadership. Hitler or Stalin, for example, had strong personalities but led their followers to disaster.

Creative, effective leadership in sports organizations

The world of sport provides extraordinary opportunities to study exemplary leadership and, conversely, examples of failed leadership. The notoriety and exalted status given to athletes and coaches and their teams by media and fans can catapult them into superstar status rapidly, even if they do not aspire to such a highly visible status.

Adults look to athletes to provide examples of life skills and values to young people. Many young people idolize athletes for their skills and attributes as players and competitors. Such athletes as Derek Jeter, LeBron James, and Payton Manning have the ability to inspire young fans to become not only great athletes but also great adults and citizens.

Athletes also provide the opportunity to disappoint fans or confuse young athletes when aspects of their behavior are inconsistent with their role as team leaders or ethical participants in sport competition. For example, some fans of Derek Jeter were highly disappointed by his failure to step forward and criticize his teammate, Alex Rodriguez, for not apologizing until 2009 for his long-time doping. One *New York Times* columnist wrote that Rodriquez's:

> Yankee teammates didn't speak up or urge Major League Baseball to punish him more severely. No, they just sat stone-faced at Rodriguez's news conference and listened to an admitted cheat. Good guy, Derek Jeter, the long-time team captain, was front and center in the audience to show his support, even though Rodriguez's confession tainted him and every other player in the game. In baseball, it was called having Rodriguez's back.

(Macur, 2013)

In many respects, sport is a microcosm of society with all of the challenges, complexity, and complications of our world. Issues of poverty, discrimination, corruption, human rights, and social justice also are evident in the world of sport and competition. Leaders in sport, similar to those in our political and social spheres, are critical to the success of our society.

Sport leadership begins at the top—for example, by a commissioner, university president, team ownership group CEO, or a coach. Often this person is the most visible representative of a sport organization and is the person to whom fans, players, governance organizations and the press look to in defining the culture and ethos of a team or organization.

Perhaps the most visible leadership position in this group is a league president or CEO, such as the Commissioner of Major League Baseball or the Commissioner of the National Football League. These individuals are charged with the essential leadership functions of providing a vision for the future success of the league, persuading others to move forward on that vision while addressing challenges and difficulties, providing the public face for the effective and ethical direction of the organization, and making hard decisions for the league or the sport.

There have been some very public examples of both effective and ineffective leadership by individuals holding these positions. For example, Adam Silver took over as Commissioner of the National Basketball League in February 2014, and within two months he banned club owner, Donald Sterling, from the National Basketball Association (NBA) for life for making public, racist comments about a current and former NBA player. Viewed by many observers, Silver's actions were unprecedented, but they quickly and decisively addressed the public concerns about an NBA franchise being owned and operated by a person making such comments.

Contrast that situation with one in 2011 involving the action of former president of Ohio State University, Gordon Gee, in dealing with then football coach Jim Tressel. Tressel lied to school administrators about his prior knowledge of his players' trading memorabilia for cash and tattoos. As allegations against Tressel began to mount in the press, Gee was asked about the allegations against Tressel and whether Gee would terminate Tressel for his conduct. Gee infamously answered at a press conference "I hope he doesn't fire me." President Gee's humor undermined his ethical leadership. Tressel did eventually resign under pressure, later followed by President Gee.

There are many other situations where the leadership of a team or organization has been suspect because the designated leaders have failed to inspire confidence and trust. For example, Sepp Blatter, president of the world soccer governing body, FIFA, for many years, has fended off multiple inquiries about influence buying, accepting bribes, and other breaches of his duty as a fiduciary for the organization (Borden, 2015). Another example is the Commissioner of the NFL, Roger Goodell, who has been criticized for the NFL's tardy and, in many respects, ineffective handling of major problems, such as claims by former players of concussion-related illnesses and the domestic abuse claims involving current players (Fermin, 2014). These examples emphasize the point that leadership at the top is critical to the success of these organizations and to the confidence that fans, athletes, and others have in those sport programs.

Although it is true that some of the most important leadership opportunities occur at the level of the team, the vision and ethical direction of the sport organization by people in leadership positions drive a great deal of public perception about the organization.

LEADERSHIP BEHAVIOR AND DEVELOPMENT IN SPORT

Athletic teams require effective leadership. One of the most important relationships in sport is between the coach and the players. Successful sports teams have strong and effective leaders, and there are several dimensions to the leadership demonstrated by the coach.

The role of coach as leader

An obvious measure of success is performance as reflected in a win–loss record. Another is the satisfaction of the players in terms of their experiences, such as heightened motivation to compete because of the skill and encouragement of coaches. Given these dimensions to the athletic team experiences, it is natural that sport experts have developed psychological and sociological theories and models for evaluating the coach-player relationship.

There are two main models or theories developed by experts in the field of leadership effectiveness by coaches: the behaviorally oriented approach of Smoll and Smith and a "multi-dimensional model of leadership" by Chelladurai and Saleh. Smoll and Smith studied behaviors of coaches and their athletes; they identified 12 behavioral categories that have an impact on the development of their athletes (Smoll & Smith, 1984, 1989).

Their comprehensive studies found that coaches with the most positive impact on athletes' development typically follow these guidelines or approaches: a high degree of positive reinforcement, encouraging athletes' correction after they have made a mistake, providing instruction on how to correct mistakes, and technical instruction. These approaches emphasize essential leadership attributes such as positive communication and respect for followers.

A second prominent approach to understanding the importance of coaches identified five types of leadership behaviors applicable to sports teams and groups:

1. Training and instruction: focusing behavior on improving the athletes' performance.
2. Democratic: allowing the team to make some decisions collectively.
3. Autocratic: giving the team leader personal authority.
4. Social support: showing concern for the well-being of others.
5. Rewarding: providing team members with positive reinforcement.

(Chelladurai and Saleh, 1980)

This approach emerged from surveys of several different cohorts of athletes and other students, including hundreds of physical education degree students and varsity athletes in four different sports. The researchers concluded that three factors significantly affect the behavior of the teams' leaders: situational characteristics (such as whether the opposing team is weak or strong), the experience and personality of the team leader, and the demographics (such as age, gender, experience) of team members.

The survey results showed that athletes seem most satisfied when their coaches emphasize training and instruction as well as providing positive feedback and reinforcement. Some athletes in some sports valued autocratic leadership approaches by a coach more than athletes in other sports.

Sport leadership experts contend that effective leadership in sport is dynamic and based upon a complex series of interactions between a team leader, team members and various situational constraints and influences. Their perspectives suggest that positive outcomes (performance and athletes' satisfaction) occur when there is alignment between the leader's actual behavior (e.g. organizing practices and training sessions or providing positive feedback to team members), the group members preferred leadership behavior (i.e. their preference for a highly organized, supportive leader) and the behavior that is required in relation to the situation.

There is also evidence that participants in highly interactive team sports (e.g. basketball, football, volleyball) prefer more autocratic leadership than do participants in "co-acting" sports such as swimming or bowling. Studies have found a relationship between poorer performing teams and the frequency of social support indicating that more affirming feedback is necessary on such teams in order to maintain motivation (Crust & Lawrence, 2006).

Athlete gender and importance of leadership development

There are more similarities than differences in the preferred leadership behavior of men and women. There is, however, some evidence that men prefer more instructive behaviors and a more autocratic style of leadership than women athletes.

Despite the similarities in leadership behaviors, it has also been shown that sport competition opportunities for groups, such as women, who are underrepresented in athletic roles, can have profound influences on their success, including their leadership roles, in life. A study by EY Women Athletes Business Network and espnW found that women executives reported that a sports background can accelerate a woman's leadership and career potential and has a positive influence on their hiring decisions (Female Executives, 2014). The survey of 400 women executives showed that a majority of women occupying executive level positions played sport at the university level compared to 39 percent of women at other management levels. Of the female executives, 75 percent reported that a job applicant's background in sport influences their hiring decision.

CONCLUSION

To sum up, a popular refrain about the importance to society of this subject is: "leadership matters." Leadership is equally important in sport, including how it is practiced, how it is made available to fans, how the public perceive its ethics and values. Sport clubs and teams not only are more successful if led by ethical leaders, but also the players, especially young athletes, can learn attributes and skills of ethical leadership by their participation on the team.

The values of sports—hard work, fair play, perseverance, dealing with setbacks—are communicated by its leaders on a daily basis. These values are essential to a strong and vibrant society.

ETHICAL LEADERSHIP CASE STUDIES

Case study #1

Alvin Executive is the athletic director at State University, a Division I powerhouse in men's football and basketball. He reports directly to the president of State U. (with "dotted line" reporting on financial matters to Vice President of Finance and

Administration) and enjoys a good working relationship with the President and her executive leadership team. Three years ago, Alvin hired Bob Maniac to serve as men's basketball team coach. Maniac came to State U. with an impressive record of successively greater wins at lesser programs over eight years.

However, there were a few reported episodes of unusual behavior by Maniac in dealing with his assistant coaches and with the media. Alvin told Maniac that State U. "really needs to turn the corner and become a perennial threat in the NCAA tournament and regular conference champion." Maniac's teams quickly ascended to the top two or three teams in the conference in his first two years, but Alvin has "heard through the grapevine" that Maniac's relationships with his players and coaches are not great. He hears rumors that Maniac is acerbic, crude, and demeaning to some of his players, occasionally pushing them into conditioning exercises that a former assistant coach described as "sadistic and counterproductive."

No players or former players have sought out Alvin to complain about Maniac's behavior. Also, during this time, Alvin is considering an early contract renewal for Maniac if the team gets a four or better seed at the upcoming NCAA tournament.

In mid-January of the current season, State U.'s men's basketball team is tied for the conference lead, with a high possibility of making it into the NCAA tournament. Alvin receives a telephone call from a reporter for ESPN News who tells him that a YouTube video was just uploaded that shows about 15 minutes of recent team practice sessions, in which Maniac is screaming at players, referring to them in homophobic terms and threatening them with physical violence, with throwing them off the team, and with revoking their scholarships. The reporter asks Alvin for his comments and reaction to the video and whether or not the university is sticking with its coach.

1. Alvin is called into a meeting with the President of State U. to discuss the breaking news story on ESPN News. As the perceived leader of the athletic program, what should Alvin be thinking about as his next steps and actions?
2. As the Athletic Department's leader and as a key university employee, to whom does Alvin owe his primary responsibility—the student-athletes? The president of the university? The university? The boosters? The athletic department? Where do his leadership responsibilities reside?
3. What are the next steps that Alvin should take as Athletic Director? As an employee responsible for the well-being of the players as well as the winning of games?
4. What ethical theories apply to this situation and why?

Case study #2

Shortly before the beginning of the NFL season, the *Miami Herald* publishes a story about Jim Sensitive, a rookie lineman on the local professional football team, who quit the team suddenly, leaving a voicemail message for the coach explaining his reasons. The message was that Sensitive was tired of, and somewhat frightened by, the ongoing behavior of another lineman, Ricky Ignition, toward him. Sensitive stated that Ignition told him in the locker room that his sister and mother "are whores and sluts," had left a voicemail message that he would kill Sensitive, and had encouraged other linemen to verbally abuse and ridicule him. Ignition, who is white, repeatedly referred to Sensitive in team meetings and practices using racial slurs. In an interview for the newspaper, Ignition defended himself, stating that his actions were just "hazing; you know, like a college fraternity . . . but maybe I carried it too far." Ignition also said that "this happens on all teams . . . you know, to break the rookies in. They wouldn't know that we want them to succeed if we just ignored them. Hell, the coach knows it too and so does the team owner. Everyone knows this is how teams welcome new players." Ignition's teammates seem to agree. The newspaper reported interviews with other players on the team who said that "all that is just Ricky being Ricky"; that is "just who he is"; that they were surprised that "Sensitive took it so hard" since "he was able to give it back sometimes to Ricky."

The Commissioner of the NFL, after learning of the newspaper story, insisted that Ignition be suspended until "an independent fact-finder" appointed by the league could investigate and report on the incidents between Sensitive and Ignition and the conduct of the team in managing the situation. The Commissioner acted quickly in responding to the Sensitive–Ignition situation.

1. Looking at the Ignition situation, why didn't other players intervene on Sensitive's behalf? Did the football team have a bad "culture" or "environment"? How would the players change that?
2. Many of the Sensitive–Ignition type situations cannot occur without the acquiescence of the coaching staff and club ownership. How would you assess the leadership competence at those levels? What would you suggest to turn it around from where the team culture permits such unethical behaviors? Could you conclude that the football team organization is led by ethical leadership in ownership? In the coaches' office?
3. Assess the quality of leadership in the Commissioner's Office. Obviously, the Commissioner is not in every team locker room, but can he claim that he was unaware of these types of situations if, indeed, as Ignition claims, "all the teams do this to break rookies in." Should supervisory responsibilities for all these negative practices reside in the highest level of the sport; or do they belong with the teammates and coaches?

STUDENT LEARNING EXERCISE

Prepare an essay on an ethical exemplary ethical leadership experience. The essay can describe a situation of the your own leadership (for example, by inspiring a team to success or overcoming a difficult common problem) or an example of someone else's exemplary leadership that inspired you. Be prepared to share your experiences with the class.

PROBLEMS/QUESTIONS

1. Which theories of leadership—transformational, servant, etc.—best describe the roles of the athletic director at your school in providing responsible direction to a team or program? Coach? University president?
2. Assess the notion that leadership skills can be taught and that they are "life-long skills" that benefit student-athletes long after they graduate.
3. Some athletic programs (amateur, collegiate, professional) have problems with ineffective or misguided leadership. Other programs suffer from management problems. How can you distinguish leadership shortcomings from management programs? Can you identify and describe examples of each type of inadequacy or problem?
4. Based on your personal experiences on teams and projects, what type of leadership practices are most effective in inspiring your participation? What are the least effective practices?
5. Identify an instance of an ethical problem in sports that was caused or exacerbated by a failure of leadership.
6. What is the relationship between leadership and ethics?

BIBLIOGRAPHY

Aaltio-Marjosola, Iiris & Takala, Tuomo, Charismatic Leadership, Manipulation and the Complexity of Organizational Life, 12 *Journal of Workplace Learning* 146 (2000).

Audas, Rick, et al., The Impact of Managerial Change on Team Performance in Professional Sports, 54 *Journal of Economics and Business* 633 (2002).

Belson, Ken, Brain Trauma to Affect One in Three Players, N.F.L. Agrees, *New York Times*, September 12, 2014.

Bennis, Warren, On Becoming a Leader, in Rhode, Deborah L. & Packel, Amanda K. *Leadership: Law, Policy, and Management* (2011).

Blanchard, Kenneth H., et al., *Leadership and the One Minute Manager: Increasing Effectiveness through Situational Leadership* (1985).

Borden, Sam, Sepp Blatter Withstands Scandal and Criticism to Secure a Fifth Term, *New York Times*, May 29, 2015.

Burns, James MacGregor, *Leadership* (1978).

Canter, Lee & Marlene Canter, *Assertive Discipline* (1993).

Charbonneau, Danielle, et al., Transformational Leadership and Sports Performance: The Mediating Role of Intrinsic Motivation, 31 *Journal of Applied Social Psychology* 1521 (2001).

Chelladurai, Packianathan, et al., Dimensions of Leader Behavior in Sports: Development of a Leadership Scale, 2 *Journal of Sport Psychology* 34 (1980).

Ciulla, Gini A. & Joanne B., *Ethics: The Heart of Leadership* (1998).

Crust, Lee & Lawrence, Ian, A Review of Leadership in Sport: Implications for Football Management, 8 Athletic Insight 24 (2006).

Cumbo, L.J., Ethical Leadership: The Quest for Character, Civility, and Community, 47 *Current Reviews for Academic Libraries* 726 (2009).

Danzig, Arnold, How Might Leadership Be Taught? The Use of Story and Narrative to Teach Leadership, 2 *International Journal of Leadership in Education* 117 (1999).

Day, David V. & Lord, Robert G., Executive Leadership and Organizational Performance: Suggestions for a New Theory and Methodology, 14, *Journal of Management*, 453 (1988).

Doh, Jonathan P., Can Leadership Be Taught? Perspectives From Management Educators, 2 *Academy of Management, Learning & Education* 54 (2003).

Female Executives Say Participation in Sport Helps Accelerate Leadership and Career Potential, *EY*, October 2014.

Fermin, Jeff, 3 Leadership Mistakes Roger Goodell Made That You Shouldn't, *Huffington Post*, September 12, 2014.

Goleman, Daniel, *Working with Emotional Intelligence* (1998).

Goleman, Daniel, Leadership That Gets Results, *Harvard Business Review*, March–April 2000.

Goleman, Daniel, et al., *The New Leaders: Transforming the Art of Leadership Into the Science of Results* (2002).

Greenleaf, R.K., Essentials of Servant Leadership, in Larry C. Spears & Michele Lawrence, *Focus on Leadership: Servant-leadership for the 21st Century* (2002).

Hamilton, Neil W., *Ethical Leadership in Professional Life*, 6, U. St. Thomas L. Rev., 380 (2009).

Heifetz, Ronald A., Anchoring Leadership in the Work of Adaptive Progress, in *The Leader of the Future: Visions, Strategies, and the New Era* (2006).

Heifetz, Ronald A. & Linsky, Marty, *Leadership on the Line* (2002).

Hickman, Gill R., *Leading Organizations: Perspectives for a New Era* (2009).

Jacobs, Melissa, The NFL Still Has a Domestic Violence Problem—and Ray Rice Could Help Solve It, *The Guardian*, May 26, 2015.

Johnson, Craig E., Meeting the Ethical Challenges of Leadership: Casting Light or Shadow, 28 *The Journal of Academic Librarianship* 81 (2002).

Kellerman, Barbara, *Bad Leadership: What It Is, How It Happens, Why It Matters* (2013).

Kouzes, James M. & Posner, Barry Z., *The Truth About Leadership* (2010).

Kouzes, James M. & Posner, Barry Z., *The Leadership Challenge* (2014).

Laios, Athanasios, et al., Leadership and Power: Two Important Factors for Effective Coaching, 7 *International Sports Journal* 150 (2003).

Leadership theories, *Changing Minds*, undated.

Macur, Juliet, For Want of Real Leaders, N.F.L. Culture Will Stay Lost, *New York Times*, November 10, 2013.

Manz, Charles & Sims, Henry, *Businesses Without Bosses* (1993).

Marcy, Richard T., et al., Thinking Straight: New Strategies are Needed for Ethical Leadership, 28 *Leadership in Action* 3 (2008).

Martinek, Tom & Hellison, Don, *Youth Leadership in Sport and Physical Education* (2009).

Monahan, Kelly, A Review of the Literature Concerning Ethical Leadership in Organizations, 5 *Emerging Leadership Journeys* 56 (2012).

Moreno, Carlos M., An Approach to Ethical Communication From the Point of View of Management Responsibilities, 1 *Journal of Applied Ethics* 97 (2010).

NCAA Student Athlete Leadership Forum, ncaa.org, undated.

Nekoranec, Wendell, Ethical Leadership and OD Practice, 41 *OD Practitioner* 2 (2009).

Northouse, Peter G., *Leadership: Theory and Practice* (2015).

Nye, Joseph S., Jr., The Powers to Lead (2008), in Rhode, Deborah L. & Packel, Amanda K., *Leadership: Law, Policy, and Management* (2011).

Plinio, Alex J., et al., The State of Ethics in Our Society: A Clear Call for Action, 7 *International Journal of Disclosure & Governance* 172 (2010).

Polden, Donald J., Leadership Matters: Lawyers' Leadership Skills and Competencies, 52 Santa *Clara L. Rev.*, 899 (2012).

Rhode, Deborah L., *Lawyers as Leaders* (2013).

Ryska, Todd A., Leadership Styles and Occupational Stress Among College Athletic Directors: The Moderating Effect of Program Goals, 136 *The Journal of Psychology* 195 (2002).

Scott, David, *Contemporary Leadership in Sport Organizations* (2014).

Smoll, Frank L., & Smith, Ronald E., Leadership Research in Youth Sports, in J.M. Silva III & R.S. Weinberg (Eds.), *Psychological Foundations of Sport* (1984).

Smoll, Frank L., & Smith, Ronald E., Leadership Behaviors in Sport: A Theoretical Model and Research Paradigm, 19 *Journal of Applied Social Psychology* 1522 (1989).

Souba, Wiley W., The Being of Leadership, 6, *Philosophy, Ethics & Humanities in Medicine*, 5 (2011).

Sullivan, Philip J. & Kent, Aubrey, Coaching Efficacy as a Predictor of Leadership Style in Intercollegiate Athletics, 15 *Journal of Applied Sport Psychology* 1 (2003).

Thompson, Jim, *Positive Coaching: Building Character and Self-Esteem Through Sports* (1993).

Ting, Sharon & Peter Scisco, *The CCL Handbook of Coaching: A Guide for the Leader Coach* (2006).

Ward, R., The Soul of Classical American Philosophy: The Ethical and Spiritual Insights of William James, Josiah Royce, and Charles Sanders Peirce, 45 *Current Reviews for Academic Libraries* 644 (2007).

Warner, Stacy, et al., The Football Factor: Shaping Community on Campus, 4 *Journal of Issues in Intercollegiate Athletics* 236 (2011).

Wooden, John & Steve Jamison, *Wooden on Leadership* (2005).

Yukl, Gary A., *Leadership in Organizations* (2005).

CHAPTER 4

The changing ethical landscape of amateurism

INTRODUCTION

With the global decline of support for amateurism in the Olympic Games during the last three decades, the last frontier for competitive amateur athletics resides in the popular intercollegiate model. Yet, within the context of the culturally significant role amateur athletics play in 21st century society, the modern-day definition of amateurism continues to shift from its original form, and the traditional definition faces a steady stream of challenges.

In the ethical context, amateurism is a classic case of virtue ethics because the purpose of amateur athletics is to generate good character along with a sound body. This chapter presents a foundation for understanding the concept and ethics of amateur athletics, with particular focus on intercollegiate athletics and the evolution of the model as it relates to how sports are played, viewed, and promoted.

DEFINITION AND HISTORY OF AMATEURISM

Merriam-Webster Dictionary defines the word *amateur* as "a person who does something (such as a sport or hobby) for pleasure and not as a job." The derivation of *amateur* comes from a Latin term *amator*, defined as "lover of." The term *amateur* as it relates to athletics began in the ancient Greek Olympic Games. The Greek root of the word *athlete* means "one who competes for a prize," and participants in the early Olympic Games received prizes worth large sums of money and other material goods for winning athletic contests. By today's standards, the ancient Greek Olympians were professional athletes. As modern athletics suggests, the desire for money has the potential to undermine the ethical aspects of amateurism.

In 1865, entrepreneur John Chambers founded London's Amateur Athletic Club (McNabb, 2014). Adamant that people take up an active lifestyle, Chambers developed popular competitions as a means of fostering leisure activity and community spirit. As interest in athletic participation grew, the aristocracy in 19th-century England set the sporting pace for the country with the notion of "people at play" as the guiding principle. Local elites initiated games, which became associated with seasonal and religious occasions

(Gorn & Goldstein, 2004). Soon games grew more sophisticated, morphing from contests such as cock-fighting to events that tested the human physique.

The foundations of today's popular sports such as football and baseball extend from this period of heightened physicality. The result of these games, though often unrecorded, was the satisfaction gained from participation and the character building associated with that satisfaction, furthering the acceptance of virtue ethics.

A firmer understanding of amateurism evolved during the Olympic Games in the late 1800s. For competing athletes, the concept of amateurism meant that competitors would participate for the love of sport, which showed good character, and not for the promise of compensation for performance. Strictly enforced, this premise banned athletes from competition if they had received any monetary prize for athletic achievements. Also, athletes could not work as sport coaches nor perform against professional athletes, even as unpaid competitors.

In the most famous example of the enforcement of this rule, Olympic legend Jim Thorpe had his medals from the 1912 Olympic Games revoked in 1913 because the International Olympic Committee discovered that he had played two summers of semi-professional baseball with pay during college.

In the mid to late 19th century in the United States, competitive amateur athletics grew in popularity as the final scores in intercollegiate contests became news. Contrary to earlier views that amateurism promoted character, school authorities initially frowned upon these seemingly frivolous and often violent competitions, with many faculty members and school presidents calling for the end of athletic participation by students.

Nevertheless, prestige came from winning intercollegiate contests, and the visibility of sports teams provided the colleges with valuable notoriety. Institutions soon realized a revenue source from these contests by charging admission to spectators. Ironically, given the initial character issues related to the intercollegiate athletes, prestige, visibility, and money transformed intercollegiate athletics into a permanent fixture on university campuses by the turn of the 20th century. Large stadiums with thousands of seats began to be built (Flowers, 2009).

Administrators concluded that students participating in athletics and winning games could help a school obtain more prestige, visibility, and money. They also determined that for their teams to win more games, they should recruit the best players (Miller, 2012). To that end, schools began accepting marginal scholars as student-athletes.

As early as the 1870s, universities "began to offer both graduates and undergraduates financial assistance in the form of room and board, jobs, and even small cash considerations in exchange for athletic participation" (id.). Not surprisingly, these practices would lead to ethical problems.

THE RISE OF THE NCAA

In 1906, in response to the "dangerous and exploitive athletics practices of the time," authorities from 62 college institutions joined together to form the Intercollegiate Athletic Association of the United States (IAAUS), which would change its name to the National Collegiate Athletic Association (NCAA) in 1910 (NCAA official website). At the request of President Theodore Roosevelt, this association emerged in a time of crisis to develop policies to protect the participants in the sport of football, because from 1905 to 1910, football competition had led to 79 deaths and more than 500 serious injuries (Frederickson & Ghere, 2015).

Subscribing to the ethical framework of utilitarianism by promoting the greatest good for the greatest number, the actions of the newly founded governing body officially legitimized college athletics and primarily the game of football in an effort to generate harmony and safety among participants and university faculty and administrators. Using this utilitarian approach, the founders worked to establish a formal set of bylaws to enhance safety, to control the admission of athletes to schools, to regulate athletic participation by students, and to preserve the amateur model. Nevertheless, with the growing popularity of competitive sport and its increasing production of revenue, several schools blatantly paid students to compete (Kahn, 2007).

For example, in the late 1920s Claude Passeau intended to attend Louisiana State University in Baton Rouge. Instead, an interested alumnus offered Passeau a $20 bill (approximately $275 in today's value) to board a train to visit Millsaps College in Jackson, Mississippi, with the promise that Passeau could keep the money even if he decided to attend school at LSU. Ultimately deciding upon Millsaps, Passeau lettered in four sports in college and became a professional baseball player upon graduation (Mitchell, 2003).

Realizing amateur intercollegiate athletics had come to resemble professional sports, the NCAA amended its rules in 1956 to allow schools to offer scholarships to any undergraduate athlete, therefore legitimizing the idea of "paying" student-athletes. Hewing to virtue ethics, however, the NCAA coined the term "student-athlete" to describe students who participated in athletics, reaffirming the amateur code (Byers, 1997).

Today's NCAA membership has shaped intercollegiate athletics into a multi-billion dollar industry with mega-million dollar operating budgets for athletic departments, million dollar coaching salaries, lavish amenities for participants in the name of student-athlete welfare, and an escalated and seemingly never-ending "arms race" highlighted by state-of-the-art facilities and equipment. Still abiding by the code of 1956, the NCAA has continued to protect amateurism through an elaborate and often ambiguous set of regulations. Athletic departments employ numerous officials to protect the amateur status of their student-athletes. The NCAA manual has grown from its 6-page edition of 1906 to a publication of nearly 500 pages in 2017. At every turn, the NCAA has protected the ideal of amateurism, yet the assault on the organization itself and on the general concept of the amateur athlete (and the virtuous character of that athlete) continues.

The composition of the NCAA

With amateurism as its most prominent value, the NCAA comprises more than 1,000 colleges and universities across three divisions and sponsors 89 championships in 23 sports. Choosing to voluntarily join the NCAA, active member institutions participate in association-sponsored competition, including championships; develop and vote on legislation; and enjoy the benefits of affiliation, including receiving a share of revenue.

According to the NCAA's website, Division I institutions sponsor at least seven sports for men and seven for women or six for men and eight for women. Contest and participant minimums exist for each sport in addition to scheduling criteria.

For sports other than football and basketball, Division I schools must play 100 percent of the minimum number of contests against Division I opponents. Men's and women's basketball teams must play all but two games against Division I teams. For men, they must play one-third of all their contests in the home arena.

Schools with football classify either as Football Bowl Subdivision or NCAA Football Championship Subdivision. Football Bowl Subdivision teams have to meet minimum attendance requirements (average 15,000 people in actual or paid attendance per home game), which must be met once in a rolling two-year period.

Ticket sales, television contracts, and endorsement opportunities produce enormous revenue. Some Division I schools generate sufficient revenue to operate self-sufficiently and independently of any university subsidy, although many schools do depend on institutional subsidization.

Division I schools also must meet minimum financial aid awards for their athletic program, with maximum financial aid awards for each sport (NCAA official website). All of these rules are aimed to develop the character of student-athletes fostered by amateurism.

Division II institutions sponsor at least five sports for men and five for women, or four for men and six for women. The character development generated by amateurism has, in turn, generated a set of rules for Division II schools different from the rules for Division I schools.

Football and men's and women's basketball teams must play at least 50 percent of their games against Division II or Division I opponents. Sports other than football and basketball have no scheduling requirements. Football has no attendance requirements, nor does basketball have attendance requirements for home games.

Division II schools have maximum financial aid awards for each sport. Many Division II student-athletes pay for school through a combination of scholarship money, grants, student loans, and employment earnings. Division II athletic programs receive financial allocations in each institution's budgets, the same as the academic departments. Revenue generation is less important and less probable in Division II (NCAA official website).

Division III institutions have yet a different set of amateurism rules to generate good character. They must sponsor at least five sports for men and five for women with minimum contest and participant requirements for each sport. Division III athletics feature student-athletes who receive no financial aid related to their athletic ability, with athletic departments staffed and funded like any other department in the university.

Division III athletic departments place special importance on the impact of athletics on the participants rather than on the spectators. Division III athletics encourages participation by maximizing the number and variety of athletics' opportunities available to students, placing primary emphasis on regional in-season and conference competition. Division III athletic departments depend almost exclusively on university subsidization for operating expense (NCAA official website).

The impact of the NCAA on amateurism

The NCAA passes legislation at annual conventions to foster and protect amateurism. Committees and cabinets, comprised of representatives from institutions, divide oversight of championships, academics, compliance, and other specializations throughout the association. As a result of the complexity of the structure, the legislative process sometimes takes two or more years for the refining and passing of proposals.

All of these systems are in place to help the organization focus on ensuring the recognition of student-athletes as students first. The NCAA regulates its sponsored sports to create equitable opportunities for participants by protecting the integrity of competition while ensuring the core role of the participants as students.

Promoting virtue ethics, the NCAA describes amateurism as a "bedrock principle" of college athletics:

> Maintaining amateurism is crucial to preserving an academic environment in which acquiring a quality education is the first priority. In the collegiate model of sport, the young men and women competing on the field or court are students first, athletes second.
>
> (NCAA official website)

In fact, the typical mission statement of a collegiate athletic department reiterates these principles and expresses a commitment to the development of the student-athlete's character academically, athletically, and socially. For example, Duke University's athletic department mission statement, which is a clear example of virtue ethics, reads as follows:

> The guiding principle behind Duke's participation in Division I athletics is our belief in its educational value for our students. Intercollegiate athletics promotes character traits of high value to personal development and success in later life. These include the drive to take one's talents to the highest level of performance; embracing the discipline needed to reach high standards; learning to work with others as a team in pursuit of a common goal; and adherence to codes of fairness and respect.
>
> (Duke Athletics official website)

According to the NCAA, its "membership has adopted amateurism rules to ensure the students' priority remains on obtaining a quality educational experience and that all student-athletes are competing equitably" (NCAA official website). To foster character, the NCAA mandates that, in general, amateurism requirements do not allow student-athletes to:

- have contracts with professional teams;
- take a salary for participating in athletics;
- accept prize money above actual and necessary expenses;
- play with professionals;
- participate in tryouts, practice or competition with a professional team;
- accept benefits from an agent or prospective agent;
- enter into an agreement to be represented by an agent; or
- delay initial full-time collegiate enrollment to participate in organized sport competition.

Arguably, however, the ideal of the amateur athlete, whose priority is a quality education as defined by the NCAA, no longer seems to exist (Frederickson & Ghere, 2015). Modern-day student-athletes, and certainly the most elite, perform in an arena in which the sport outcome definitely matters. Wins and losses impact institutional revenues—revenue can ebb and flow with each final score—and more money goes toward support of student-athletes in an effort to improve performance.

Student-athletes receive housing, meals, and books with their scholarships. Institutions also provide student-athletes with athletic gear, transportation to and from games, and access to highly trained coaches. Although these high-performing amateur athletes are not commercially paid, some of them make significant personal investments of time and effort with a goal of developing a more professional level of expertise; their institutions commit resources to assist in this effort (id.).

The increased wealth and status associated with intercollegiate sport arise primarily from two NCAA Division I sports: football and men's basketball. The Southeastern Conference, for example, amassed $455.8 million in revenue in 2015, resulting in each member institution receiving a $31.2 million share.

Additionally, according to the U.S. Department of Education, the 65 universities that comprise the Power Five conferences (ACC, SEC, Big 10, Big 12, and PAC 12) totaled $6.3 billion in revenue during 2014–2015. Even the casual fan understands the high stakes involved and may not care about the virtue ethics aspects of amateurism.

Coaches of elite NCAA Division I football and men's basketball programs receive compensation far more than state or university officials, and the intense attention leads to little job security. For example, Jim Harbaugh, who serves as the head football coach at the University of Michigan, reportedly makes over $8 million a year, nearly ten times the annual compensation of Michigan president, Mark Schlissel.

In many cases, the base pay for a coach comes from a nominal university payment with the remaining dollars coming from the generosity of donors. These benefactors exert significant influence by offering funds to supplement a coach's pay and by helping to buy out contracts for coaches. It is difficult for some to believe that such astronomical salaries are consistent with amateurism or virtue ethics. The pressure on coaches and administrators is to win and win now. Consistent victory generates increased visibility and generates significant revenue. Winning leads to increased donor giving, corporate sponsorships, and ticket sales, all critical revenue streams.

This emphasis on winning exposes tensions and limits on amateurism in the areas of recruitment and retention of athletes, services of sport agents and advisers, academics, and commercialism. This emphasis undermines the character development associated with virtue ethics.

RECRUITING, RETENTION, AND AMATEURISM

Successful recruiting provides the lifeblood for college athletics. To produce winning sport programs, coaches and administrators must find student-athletes with outstanding athletic abilities. During this fast-paced, stressful recruiting process, coaches seek to entice high school students to join their programs, often operating with few roster spots and a limited amount of athletically related financial aid, while prospects have a narrow window of opportunity during which to sign offers to play sports in exchange for some form of a scholarship. The resulting pressure has led to cheating in recruiting. Stories about that cheating date back to the inception of formal intercollegiate athletic competition and persist to this day, with numerous associated ethical problems.

To help control recruiting from being a win-at-all-costs free-for-all, the NCAA's manual of bylaws devotes hundreds of pages to the rules and regulations pertaining to the permissible recruitment of student-athletes. Although some of the adopted rules protect the prospective student-athlete during the recruitment process, most of the legislation limits the actions of overzealous coaches seeking to gain an advantage in getting commitments from highly talented prospects (Lumpkin, 2009).

Such limitations include those on the timing and frequency that coaches can contact prospective student-athletes. The absence of such regulations would create the effect of coaches constantly contacting recruits, which would violate the principles of care ethics.

Nevertheless, impermissible contacts continue, because the regulatory function of college athletic departments often inadequately monitors every action that a coach may take. Promoting an atmosphere of compliance helps athletic departments limit rule infractions and presents a significant step toward an ethical mode of operation that is in conformity with deontology in that it is universalizable.

To assist further in controlling recruiting (and with international recruiting becoming more common), the NCAA has adopted a process for all incoming Division I and Division II student-athletes to ensure a status of amateurism prior to the student-athletes being eligible for competition. All incoming student-athletes must be certified as amateurs.

According to the NCAA, since 2007, the amateurism certification process has ensured that incoming Division I or II student-athletes meet NCAA amateurism requirements regarding core course enrollments, test scores, and core grade point averages, which provide some indication of character. The NCAA has established the certification process "to bring about national uniformity and fairness" (NCAA official website).

The prospects register with the NCAA Eligibility Center at www.eligibilitycenter.org, where prospective student-athletics provide information about their amateur status. Most prospective student-athletes who fully complete the process receive certification.

The amateurism certification staff and the institutions must agree upon the particular set of facts about prospective student-athletes before interpretive inquiries, appeals, or reinstatement requests may be made to the NCAA. Prospective student-athletes, including international students, must abide by NCAA amateurism rules, which have at their core the character-building traits associated with virtue ethics.

Data suggests, however, that almost 25 percent of prospective student-athletes receive offers of impermissible benefits during recruiting (Recruiting Confidential Poll, 2012). Boosters may enhance tightly scheduled recruiting visits with side trips to lavish restaurants, parties, and strip clubs, all of which violate NCAA rules and virtue ethics.

After athletic departments successfully recruit student-athletes and after the athletes receive NCAA Eligibility Center clearance, retaining student-athletes becomes the next challenge. College coaches often promote the concept of never-ending recruiting to keep student-athletes happy by attempting to lavish student-athletes with athletic gear, extravagant travel arrangements on road trips, fancy locker rooms and amenities, and an unlimited meal plan.

Boosters may, as occurred at the University of Miami from 2002 to 2010, try to wield their influence by improperly providing benefits to student-athletes in the form of cash, cars, meals, clothes, and special visits to properties such as hotels, beach homes, and extravagant yachts. Student-athletes have also received free goods and services such as tattoos, which occurred at Ohio State University in 2010.

Other impermissible benefits for student-athletes include significant cash payments for personal memorabilia (rings, uniforms, balls, and equipment), which occurred at Texas A&M University in 2013. Obviously, none of these practices are consistent with the virtue ethics that was the moving force behind the establishment of amateurism in 19th-century England.

Moreover, in the heightened "win now" marketplace, coaches often turn to the increasingly popular transfer student market for athletic talent. Because the most talented athletes in the sports of football and men's basketball attend a limited number of schools, the desire of student-athletes to play for a winning team leads some of the student-athletes to transfer to another program, where the prospect of winning more may lead to better professional opportunities in the future. Again, transferring schools solely to better one's position is inconsistent with virtue ethics.

AGENTS AND ADVISERS IN AMATEURISM

Only between 1 and 3 percent of elite college football, baseball, and basketball players should expect to have a career playing professional sport. With a small pool of potential professional talent, professional scouts and advisers—pursuing substantial money both by advising student-athletes to turn professional and later by representing them as their agents—target student-athletes. For those students who legitimately have an opportunity to succeed as professional athletes, navigating the complexity of the professional sport landscape necessitates having appropriate assistance. This need presents another ethical challenge to amateur status and virtue ethics.

Using the principles of care ethics to protect the welfare of student-athletes, the NCAA regulates interaction between agents or advisers and student-athletes. Association bylaws prohibit student-athletes with eligibility remaining from agreeing, either orally or in writing, to be represented by an agent or organization in the marketing of their athletic abilities or reputations. The idea is that such representation undermines amateurism and fair play, although it also puts the athletes at a tremendous disadvantage in determining how to enter the world of professional sports.

NCAA rules prohibit student-athletes from receiving preferential benefits or special treatment because of the students' reputations, skills, or potential as professional athletes. Some examples of impermissible benefits include free or reduced cost services; free or reduced cost rent; cash, loans, or co-signing on a loan; use of automobiles; gifts; and free or discounted clothing and equipment (NCAA official website). On the other hand, student-athletes may enter into agreements for future representation with an agent or organization. Again, these rules preserve the virtue ethics that was the foundation of amateurism.

For sports such as football, basketball, baseball, soccer, and hockey, NCAA rules also allow student-athletes with remaining eligibility to secure legal advice regarding proposed professional sport contracts, as long as the lawyers do not represent the student-athletes in negotiations for such contracts. The lawyers may not be present during discussions of contract offers with professional sport organizations, nor have any direct contact (in person, by telephone, or by mail) with professional sport organizations on behalf of the student-athletes.

The distinction made by the NCAA between receiving advice about turning professional and having a professional negotiate on one's behalf is difficult to associate with any theory of ethics. It seems to be a distinction without a difference. Is it, for example, a rules violation for a student-athlete to negotiate with a professional team in one room while his lawyer is in an adjacent room to give the student-athlete advice?

Finally, if student-athletes utilize the services of lawyers regarding proposed professional sport contracts, the student-athletes must pay the lawyers the going rate for such services. The NCAA considers the receipt of such services free-of-charge or at a discounted rate as impermissible benefits to the student-athletes, which undermine amateurism and virtue ethics. This is particularly important for baseball and hockey student-athletes, who may be drafted out of high school and seek to protect their amateur status in the event that they want to attend college and compete in intercollegiate athletics.

ACADEMICS AND AMATEURISM

The overriding questions concerning the significance of academic study for many intercollegiate athletes include whether the students attend the universities primarily to play sports and whether the structure of athletics limits the ability for students to earn their degrees (Lumpkin, 2009). Perhaps to curb the attacks from critics who argue that intercollegiate athletics is becoming more professionalized, the NCAA and member schools purport to emphasize, consistent with virtue ethics, the role of athletes as students more than ever before.

For example, the NCAA has designed and implemented legislation to improve graduation rates of student-athletes. The association requires that student-athletes make satisfactory progress toward earning their degrees every academic year to maintain athletic eligibility. Virtue ethics requires no less.

Moreover, the NCAA has implemented a program called the Academic Progress Rate (APR), which measures the success of all student-athletes in an athletic program in making progress toward graduation. The athletes' failure to meet satisfactory benchmarks results in the NCAA imposing penalties on the institutions and teams, which are, according to the NCAA, not sufficiently developing the academic character of the student-athletes. Penalties include post-season participation bans and/or a reduction in scholarship offerings to ensure that the focus of the student-athletes and of the institutions remains on academic achievement, which is one foundation of character. To help foster such focus, athletic administrators usually assign employees to oversee academic success programs for student-athletes.

Some critics view the academic progress of these athletes only as a means of their maintaining eligibility for athletic participation and nothing more—the opposite of virtue ethics. However, most university officials vehemently discredit that suggestion and instead offer athletic eligibility as a byproduct of successful scholastic achievement, claiming that the student-athletes have earned their opportunities to represent the institutions and display their unique talents.

In fact, to represent their institutions in intercollegiate competition, student-athletes must meet initial eligibility requirements as well as make satisfactory progress toward their degree every academic year. Specific to Division I athletics, to receive a scholarship, practice, and compete in the first year of college, student-athletes must satisfy a series of academic requirements, including successfully completing 16 core courses in high school, ten of which must be completed before the beginning of the senior year of high school. Of the ten core courses, seven must be in English, math, or science.

Student-athletes must earn a 2.3 grade point average in the 16 core courses and must meet the sliding scale requirement of Grade Point Average (GPA) and test scores on the American College Test (ACT) or Scholastic Aptitude Test (SAT) exams (NCAA official website). The student-athletes also must graduate from high school and must be admitted to the college institutions for which they intend to play. All of these requirements reflect not only virtue ethics but also utilitarianism, because they produce the greatest good for the greatest number of students.

Despite academic requirements to bolster the virtue ethics underpinning amateurism, there are other developments in the opposite direction. Athletic conferences have expanded geographically, requiring more time away from school for student-athletes. Television requirements have caused more games to be played on school nights. The plethora of football bowl games and the college football playoff have extended seasons and curtailed study time. All these developments generate more revenue—the antithesis of amateurism—for the universities.

COMMERCIALISM AND AMATEURISM

The concerns about amateurism in athletics arise from the increasingly commercialized aspects of intercollegiate sport (Lumpkin, 2009). What has increased this commercialization is the expansion of the athletic conferences. Initially, these conferences were composed of universities "with similar enrollments, missions, [and] a geographical proximity" (id.). The proximity of these schools helped to lessen the number of missed classes by student-athletes and to reduce costs.

Conference commissioners and athletic directors support the idea of increased revenue generation through conference expansion, although faculty and university presidents often bristle at the idea because of the potential for additional missed class time and increased travel for student-athletes (id.).

However, today's conferences seek to obtain the widest geographical reach for the purposes of broadening the conference footprint and generating higher revenues from network television because of the increased size of the viewing audience. In recent years, football's biggest conferences have poached teams from each other in a race for more money (Waldron, 2013). Since the University of Miami, Virginia Polytechnic Institute and State University, and Boston College chose the Atlantic Coast Conference over the Big East in 2004, ten schools have left one of football's six major conferences for another. Financial motivation has ruled: bigger conferences with teams in better television markets mean more lucrative television packages from networks like ESPN, CBS, and Fox Sports (id.). Television packages have not been shown to increase the virtue ethics that is the basis of amateurism.

Additional revenue sources derive from the cultivation of relationships by athletic department employees with corporate sponsors, who pay significant premiums in exchange for advertising. New and creative opportunities to showcase corporate logos continue to emerge.

New terminology such as in-arena time-and-space inventory suggests that the sponsors' need for ample space to highlight their company logos results in the building or refurbishing of facilities. For example, the evolution of the digital ribbon boards provides rotating advertising for which corporate sponsors pay per minute of impression time during athletic contests. Obviously, these practices bear little relationship to virtue ethics or to amateurism.

This commercialism fuels the on-going "arms race" in intercollegiate athletics. Institutions now devote substantial resources to enhance or to build new facilities; to install new technology in locker rooms for student-athlete convenience and entertainment (Apple TV, video gaming systems, high-speed internet connectivity, and large TVs); and to intensify the game-day atmosphere with enormous video displays and eye-catching video ribbon boards.

The outsourcing of marketing, promotions, and ticket sales to professional agencies also indicates a new trend in intercollegiate athletics. Those agencies, including IMG College, Learfield Sports, Van Wagner Sports Entertainment, and The Aspire Group, generate revenue worth hundreds of thousands to millions of dollars for athletic departments.

These agencies sell intercollegiate sports programs to corporate sponsors and broadcast partners. Additionally, apparel companies such as Nike, Adidas, and Under Armour provide cash considerations to the schools in exchange for exclusive advertising rights and offer contracts to outfit the institutions' sports teams. Essentially, athletes become walking and running "billboards" for these apparel companies, in contravention of true amateurism and unrelated to virtue ethics.

THE EXPLOITATION DILEMMA AND PAY FOR PLAY

The corrupting influence of money in athletics has existed since at least the mid-1800s. The unrelenting attack on amateurism today comes from the direction of the popular media and centers on Division I football and men's basketball. The basic argument suggests that universities benefit from national visibility and enhanced prestige from having their teams appear on national television and radio with significant revenue generated as a result (Frederickson & Ghere, 2015). That revenue, in turn, provides good salaries for coaches, athletic administrators and other departmental personnel.

In essence, universities gain from the arrangement, as do the television and broadcast companies, but what do the student-athletes gain, considering their amateur status and considering that only approximately 1 percent of them will become professionals? More pointedly, in this present system, college football and basketball players are expected to consider themselves amateurs and students when—given the huge cash flows—they are simply unpaid professionals (id.), which is a violation of care ethics.

In his popular article entitled "The Shame of College Sports," author and civil rights historian Taylor Branch argues that the biggest challenge in college athletics is not that the athletes go unpaid. Rather, it is that they are voiceless about whether they should be compensated or whether the scholarships that they may receive offer a fair exchange for their efforts as active players on their respective teams (Branch, 2011). Some former college athletes have begun to take action on this idea by challenging the NCAA in court, arguing that the organization is exploiting them in a way that is contrary to deontology because it is not universalizable.

The professionalization of college sports was an issue in a legal case that centered on the commercialized use of names, images, and likenesses (NILs) of elite Division I football and men's basketball players in videogames. In 2014, the trial court determined that the NCAA's rules "unreasonably restrain trade in the market for certain educational and athletic opportunities offered by Division I schools" (*O'Bannon v. NCAA*, 2009).

This ruling, in effect, allowed scholarships to cover the full cost of attending college for student-athletes and permitted deferred payments to players for use of their NILs for every year the athletes remain academically eligible. In the ruling, the NCAA could cap the deferred payments at no less than $5,000 per year in 2014 dollars.

On appeal, the NCAA relied heavily on the argument that Judge Wilken failed to apply the 1984 Supreme Court ruling that the NCAA protects amateurism in college sports. This 1984 *NCAA v. Oklahoma Board of Regents* case, which ended the NCAA's monopoly on television contracts, includes this passage from the Supreme Court: "in order to preserve the character and quality of the (NCAA's) 'product,' athletes must not be paid, must be required to attend class and the like" (*NCAA* v. *Board of Regents of the University of Oklahoma*, 1984).

The NCAA successfully has used this passage in court cases for decades. On the other hand, the O'Bannon plaintiffs said the NCAA inconsistently applied amateurism and offered new evidence that has accumulated since 1984 that the commercialism of football and men's basketball "has eroded and undermined the relationship between athletics and academics" (Berkowitz, 2015).

Although the Ninth Circuit spent much of its decision in the appeal explaining why the NCAA's amateurism rules are not exempt from antitrust scrutiny, the ruling did eliminate the $5,000 trust fund component. The three-judge panel expressed hesitation that "offering cash sums untethered to educational expense—such as $5,000 a year for NIL rights—would transform NCAA sports into 'minor league status' and would not 'preserve amateurism'" (*O'Bannon v. NCAA*, 2015). With this decision, the court is therefore espousing amateurism as a manifestation of virtue ethics.

Another related development undermining amateurism and virtue ethics is the attempt to classify student-athletes as employees. Northwestern University became the focal point of the labor fight in January 2014, when a handful of football players called the NCAA a "dictatorship" and announced plans to form the first U.S. labor union for college athletes. In a decision, a regional National Labor Relations Board director ruled that Northwestern football players who receive scholarships fit the definition of employees under federal law and therefore should be able to unionize.

On appeal, the full five-member National Labor Relations Board reversed the ruling with a unanimous decision holding that the prospect of union and non-union teams could disrupt the competitive balance in college football. Again, amateurism and virtue ethics—

at least in theory—trumped commercialism.

The legal war has just begun with this torrent of litigation. The eventual outcomes of these cases and others will determine the significance of the shift in the current landscape. The rules of the sports have changed little over the years despite the fact that the financial context in which they operate is changing dramatically from millions to billions. Amateurism and the virtue ethics it represents are under assault. The U.S. Supreme Court declined to review the O'*Bannon* case, but there are numerous other cases in process that will present other opportunities for Supreme Court review.

REDEFINING AMATEURISM AND IDEAS TO IMPROVE THE INTERCOLLEGIATE MODEL

The virtue of amateurism has been questioned since the inception of the NCAA. Although sometimes slow to adjust, the organization routinely has enacted rules to protect and to preserve what it defines as amateur status. Today, the landscape of intercollegiate athletics and its amateur model presents concerns about student-athletes' well-being, fiscal responsibility on campus, unsustainable economic models, and organizational and legal reform. Amateurism and the intercollegiate sports model will continue to evolve as the NCAA and its member institutions adjust to social forces that determine the popularity of amateur sports. Virtue ethics and utilitarianism will, hopefully, be the guiding lights.

Legal and ethical reasons dictate changes to the model to enhance student-athletes' educational and athletic experiences. An increased emphasis should be placed on academic success. Commitment to the role that student-athletes play as students preserves the model of intercollegiate athletics. The universities, conferences, and the NCAA should institute strong programs that promote academic success and that advance career development opportunities consistent with virtue ethics and utilitarianism. Athletic departments that fail to graduate student-athletes should be penalized by a loss of scholarships.

Coaches forcing student-athletes to transfer should also be the cause for a reduction in scholarship allocations. Restricting travel time should limit missed class time. Providing workshops for career planning, such as classes for resume writing, interview skill development, and etiquette training, should complement the educational experience and should reinforce the concept of student-centered athletic programs, while simultaneously allowing student-athletes to develop athletic skills.

Limitations should be placed on athletically related activity, which would shift the present model significantly. NCAA rules permit student-athletes to participate in no more than 20 hours of training and competition per week and no more than 4 hours of training per day while requiring at least one day off from all activity per week. Activities such as strength and conditioning training, practice, competition, and film review all count toward applicable limits.

Athletic departments should ensure that student-athletes do not train in excess of this time limit. However, at present, the number of hours spent training or participating in some form of countable activity routinely passes the 20-hour threshold, and enforcement of this requirement has been lax. For example, competition counts as 3 hours, regardless of how long a game actually lasts, and the time does not include pre-game warm-ups.

Moreover, pressure on student-athletes to attend the so-called voluntary film review has been widely reported.

Anecdotal accounts from student-athletes suggest that their actual time spent participating in countable activities sometimes is more than 30 hours per week. For example, a baseball student-athlete can play as many as 5 games in a week, in addition to a day of practice. Assuming the practice lasts 4 hours and the games count as 3 hours per contest, coaches would log a total of 19 hours for their athletes' participation. However, considering that baseball usually entails a lengthy pre-game warm-up routine that requires players to arrive up to 3 hours prior to the start of the game, the actual time spent in a week approaches 30 hours.

Limiting countable athletic activities on competition days should begin with a realistic counting of the hours involved. Limiting daily practice activity to no more than 3 hours should also alleviate some of the time pressure on student-athletes and should allow them to have more time for taking classes and studying so they can develop their character in accord with virtue ethics.

Refinements should be made to financial aid rules to allow both athletic and institutional aid. The NCAA has long maintained that student-athletes who receive any amount of an athletic scholarship cannot also accept any form of institutional need-based aid without the institutional aid also counting as part of an athletic award. For sports other than football, basketball, ice hockey, women's volleyball, and women's tennis—which all may offer a prescribed amount of full scholarships–the number of athletic grants-in-aid may be divided among several student-athletes.

Yet, if one student-athlete receives both an athletic award and an institutional award, the total amount counts against the athletic scholarship and thereby reduces the amount of athletic aid available for distribution to other student-athletes. In the best interest of student-athletes, if the students qualify for institutional aid and also accept offers of athletic aid, the students should collect both awards. Furthermore, only the athletic award should count against the applicable athletics aid cap. Current proposed NCAA legislation may change this unfair practice, which lessens incentives for academic-based or need-based scholarships.

Care ethics warrants that cost of attendance stipends should be paid to student-athletes. A full scholarship covers tuition, room and board, and books. However, the cost for student-athletes to attend the institution exceeds the value of the scholarship award in many cases. Institutions publish a cost-of-attendance figure, which includes travel costs and other expenses for daily life. New NCAA rules allow some schools to provide this gap award, which now bears the name of "cost of attendance" award. Awarding student-athletes with this additional financial aid exhibits a positive step toward increasing student-athlete welfare as students now have more resources to cover expenses to gas money, an occasional movie outing, and buying essential products for quality living. This additional money is particularly important for athletes, because their demanding athletic schedules leave no time for part-time employment. Not providing this money is contrary to care ethics; nor would it violate virtue ethics, because it would simply provide basic living expenses.

CONCLUSION

Amateur college athletes can no longer fairly be described simply as students who enjoy spending free time in recreation. Rather, the lives of these "amateur" athletes involves strenuous athletic preparation and generates billions of dollars.

Although evolving, amateurism in the intercollegiate model continues to impact both the student-athletes and the universities. Challenges to the amateur model call for student-athletes to be paid for their participation and for the student-athletes to benefit from the development of their own personal brand. These changes in turn pose a challenge to the virtue ethics that have formed the foundation of amateur athletics since the 1800s. A new ethical basis for amateurism has not yet emerged. Such a basis, adapted to 21st-century circumstances, is a critical need.

ETHICAL LEADERSHIP CASE STUDIES

Case study #1

A football student-athlete enrolled at an NCAA member institution. The institution provided rules education to the student-athlete, including informing him that he would be ineligible to compete in college football if he signed an agreement with an agent. The student-athlete had been at the institution for four years, but had competed in only two seasons because of academic issues. An agent made contact with the student-athlete and told him that he would check with the institution to determine whether the student-athlete had eligibility remaining. The agent later informed the student-athlete that the institution reported that the student-athlete had no remaining eligibility. This information was incorrect.

The student-athlete had attempted to contact an academic advisor during Christmas break regarding whether he had any remaining eligibility, but he did not receive a response verifying this for approximately one week. In the meantime, the agent had provided the student-athlete with a National Football League Players Association (NFLPA) Standard Representation Agreement (SRA) and had told the student-athlete that the deadline to sign with the agent in order to enter the NFL draft was quickly approaching. The student-athlete did not verify the deadline to enter the NFL draft with the NFL league office nor did the student-athlete confirm his NCAA eligibility status with the institution but rather signed the SRA. In early January, the student-athlete had a change of heart and asked the agent to tear up the SRA, and the agent complied. At the end of January, the agent sent a letter to the student-athlete confirming that he had terminated his services and that the SRA was void.

Has the student-athlete jeopardized his eligibility to compete in college? What ethical issues are implicated in this situation? What leadership issues?

Case study #2

A men's basketball student-athlete attended an NCAA Division I member institution for one year before withdrawing. After withdrawing, the student-athlete traveled with a friend to New York City, where he met with a sports agent. The agent paid $175 of the student-athletes travel and meal expenses during the trip. Several months later, the sports agent paid travel expenses of approximately $700 for the student-athlete to participate in a five-day NBA pre-draft showcase. Later, the agent paid approximately $500 in travel expenses for the student-athlete to participate in a professional league tryout.

The year after withdrawing, the student-athlete permitted the agent to enter his name for the NBA draft, but the student-athlete was not drafted. The agent then paid approximately $1,500 in expenses for the student-athlete to participate in a tryout with a professional team. After the professional team declined to sign the student-athlete, he enrolled at an NCAA Division II member institution and sought to compete on the men's basketball team. The student-athlete asserted that he had no oral or written agreement with the sports agent.

May the student-athlete's eligibility be reinstated? What are the ethics implicated in this situation? Has the NCAA provided ethical leadership on this issue?

Case study #3

Brett, a lawyer, has been advising Will, a baseball prospective student-athlete. Will is a junior in college and was recently selected in the Major League Baseball draft. Will has asked Brett to help him determine the value of the contract he could expect to be offered based upon his draft slot so that he can decide if he wants to pursue professional baseball or to return to college and play baseball.

Explain how Brett may help Will without jeopardizing Will's collegiate eligibility. What may Brett do according to NCAA regulations? According to ethics? How can Brett provide ethical leadership to Will?

STUDENT LEARNING EXERCISE

Prepare a short paper framing the redefinition of amateurism within the context of the intercollegiate athletic model. Support your redefinition with ethical theory. Formulate a leadership plan for the NCAA regarding this redefinition.

PROBLEMS/QUESTIONS

1. As the definition of amateurism changes, do the ethical theories supporting it also change?
2. What ethical questions would a shift in amateur status for college athletes present?
3. Would the popularity of intercollegiate athletics increase or decrease if the present status of amateurism was replaced by a more professionalized model? How does this increase or decrease relate to ethics?
4. Would the popularity of intercollegiate athletics increase or decrease if the present format of Division I and Division II athletics were replaced with the pure amateur status of Division III athletics? How does this increase or decrease relate to ethics?
5. What ethical leadership actions, if any, should leaders in higher education take to protect the integrity of education as it relates to intercollegiate athletics?

BIBLIOGRAPHY

Berkowitz, Steve, NCAA Files Reply in O'Bannon Appeal, *USA Today*, February 11, 2015.

Branch, Taylor, The Shame of College Sports, *The Atlantic*, October 2011.

Byers, Walter, *Unsportsmanlike Conduct: Exploiting College Athletes* (1997).

Duke Athletics official website, www.goduke.com.

Flowers, Ronald, Institutionalized Hypocrisy: The Myth of Intercollegiate Athletics, 36 *American Educational History Journal* 343 (2009).

Frederickson, George & Ghere, Richard, *Ethics in Public Management* (2015).

Gorn, Elliot & Goldstein, Warren, *A Brief History of American Sports* (2004).

Kahn, Lawrence, Markets: Cartel Behavior and Amateurism in College Sports, 21 *Journal of Economic Perspectives* 209 (2007).

Lumpkin, Angela, *Modern Sports Ethics: A Reference Handbook* (2009).

McNabb, Tom, *Athlos: A Website Dedicated to Athletics Literature* (2014).

Merriam-Webster Dictionary, Definition of Amateur, undated, www.merriam-webster.com/dictionary/amateur.

Miller, Anthony, NCAA Division I Athletics: Amateurism and Exploitation, *The Sport Journal*, January 3, 2012.

Mitchell, Jeff, The Man With the Golden Arm, *Millsaps Magazine*, Winter 2003.

NCAA Eligibility Center official website, eligibilitycenter.org.

NCAA official website, ncaa.org.

NCAA v. Board of Regents of the University of Oklahoma, 468 U.S. 85 (1984).

O'Bannon v. NCAA, No. CV 09–3329 (N.D. Cal. July 21, 2009).

O'Bannon v. NCAA, No. 14–16601, 14–17068 (9th Cir., 2015).

Recruiting Confidential Poll, *ESPN Magazine*, January 9, 2012.

Waldron, Travis, Is the Outrageous Exploitation of College Athletes Finally Coming to an End?, *Alternet*, January 25, 2013.

CHAPTER 5

Fan behavior

Ethics, responsibilities, and expectations

INTRODUCTION

Although fan behavior, or misbehavior, is frequently chronicled and discussed, the connection between fan behavior, on one hand, and ethics and leadership, on the other hand, is not immediately apparent. Ethics and leadership are typically thought of in connection with a player's obligations to his or her team, or an organization's duties to its members. However, if one views the sport fan experience from the two perspectives of the fan's responsibilities and the fan's expectations, the ethics-leadership connection becomes more evident. The "responsibilities" lens brings into focus the fan-to-fan or fan-to-participant relationship rather than the role of fan as simply a sports consumer; the "expectations" lens focuses on the more traditional issue of fan safety.

The duty imposed by law on management to provide a safe environment for its fans is long-standing. Although what actually constitutes a safe environment may vary from sport to sport, the traditional rules of negligence law have long been applied to sports venues. As with many aspects of the law, judicial definition of fan safety standards is easier than real-world application, particularly in the rapidly changing modern sports world. Notwithstanding the fact that screens behind home plate were once sufficient to satisfy the legal duty of reasonable care in baseball (what a reasonably prudent person would do in the same or similar circumstances), modern decisional authority has trended toward imposing greater responsibility on management, such as the positioning of concession stands so as to minimize the dangers of foul balls, and requiring management to have emergency medical and other assistance policies and procedures. In part because of this legal trend, professional sports leagues have re-evaluated their standards for fan protection, leading to the implementation of such safeguards as nets behind the goals in the National Hockey League (NHL), and Major Leagues Baseball's (MLB) consideration of banning maple bats, which tend to dangerously splinter.

Also affecting fan safety is the increasing incidence and severity of fan misconduct. As more and more heated, if not violent, interactions between fans and players, and fans and other fans, occur (or are more visible because of the ubiquitous modern media), the questions of what ethical duties fans owe others and how responsible leadership shapes those duties loom larger.

Traditionally, fan misbehavior has been seen in terms of criminal conduct: fights among fans, trespass onto the field of play, offensive heckling. But fan conduct must be seen in the broader context of ethical behavior before leadership that brings about such behavior can be instituted. It is far simpler to be reactive, for example, to have security guards intercede when fan fights break out or when a fan runs onto the field of play, but it is another, more difficult, task to define and identify what is ethical and unethical fan behavior and then, through thoughtful leadership, influence and shape fan behavior. Without such leadership, the fan experience, and in turn, the overall sport experience, are diminished.

HISTORY

The word "fan" itself suggests passion and exuberance. Whether its derivation, as many believe, dates from the 19th-century shortening of the word "fanatic" or, as others contend, an even older corruption of the word "fancy" or "fancier" (as in a person who fancies sports), the term has long been used to describe a fervent and enthusiastic aficionado of a sport or team (Dickson, 2011).

Whatever the origin of the word, examples of passionate fan behavior are as old as sports themselves. Intense fan support for competing teams of chariot racers in 500 AD led to Constantinople's Nika riots which, by some accounts, resulted in 30,000 fatalities. Such staid sports as cricket and cycling experienced fan riots in Europe in the late 19th and early 20th centuries. The emergence of baseball as America's national pastime in the early 1900s set the stage for numerous examples of overly enthusiastic and sometimes violent fan behavior in baseball as well as, more recently, in other sports.

In the early 1960s, the courts acknowledged that passionate fan behavior had become an important part of the sports experience:

> For present day fans, a goodly part of the sport in a baseball game is goading and denouncing the umpire when they do not concur in his decisions, and most feel that, without one or more rhubarbs, they have not received their money's worth. Ordinarily, however, an umpire garners only vituperation – not fisticuffs. Fortified by the knowledge of his infallibility in all judgment decisions, he is able to shed billingsgate like water on the proverbial duck's back.
>
> (*Toone*, 1964)

Recently, however, the frequency and severity of incidents of fan misbehavior seem to be on the rise. Riots by fans of championship winning as well as losing teams are not uncommon. Soccer hooliganism is well documented and has led teams to use state-of-the-art technology such as facial recognition systems to combat it by allowing management to identify troublemakers in the stands. Some incidents, although not violent, are certainly unethical, such as those that have the potential to interfere with the competition itself—e.g. the nightly setting off of fire alarms at the New England Patriots' hotel prior to Super Bowl XLIX.

Other incidents are violent and tragic. The case of San Francisco Giants' fan Bryan Stow captured national headlines. Stow was severely beaten in the parking lot of Dodgers Stadium after a game between the rival Giants and Dodgers teams.

We read reports, seemingly every day, of violent fan encounters, such as what has been dubbed the Malice at the Palace, a massive fight involving players and fans at a Pacers-

Pistons NBA game that resulted in nine players being suspended and five players and five fans being charged with assault. Yet another example is the University of Alabama football fan who shot and killed another Alabama fan simply because the latter did not seem sufficiently upset over Alabama's loss to Auburn in the Iron Bowl.

There are no statistics on whether such incidents have increased proportionate to the rise in prominence of sports in our culture, or whether the apparent increase in incidents may also be partially a function of greater awareness of incidents resulting from the prevalence of cameras, both media and private, and the opportunity for celebrity that the cameras provide. Regardless, unethical fan behavior as well as management's failure to address its ethical obligations to its fans, adversely impact the spectator experience (whether by delays in the game, concerns over personal safety, or even longer, slower lines because of enhanced security measures), increase costs to the industry, and tarnish the images of teams, leagues and associations.

SAFETY

Fan expectations

When a fan purchases a ticket to a sporting event, a relationship is created between the fan and the franchise. One consequence of that relationship is that by purchasing the ticket the fan is agreeing to accept certain risks that are inherent in attending the sporting event. For example, fans attending a golf tournament accept the inherent risk that they may get hit by an errant shot, baseball fans may encounter foul balls, and hockey fans always need to keep an eye on the puck. Virtually every professional sporting event ticket in the last 50 years or more has contained language to the effect that management is not responsible for injuries resulting from the sporting contest as well as the warning that disruptive fans will be ejected from the venue. An example of the language on a Wilkes-Barre/Scranton Penguins hockey ticket is as follows:

PENGUINS TICKET DISCLAIMER

Warning! – Despite enhanced spectator shielding measures, pucks still may fly into the spectator area. Serious injury can occur. Stay alert at all times including during warmup and after the play stops. If struck, immediately ask usher for directions to medical station. The holder of a ticket assumes all risk and danger of personal injury and all other hazards arising from or related in any way to the event for which this ticket is issued, whether occurring prior to, during or after the event including specifically (but not exclusively) the danger of being injured by hockey pucks and sticks, other spectators or players, or by thrown objects. The holder agrees that the arena, the league, its officers and employees, the participating clubs, their officers, players, employees and agents are expressly released by the holder from claims arising from such causes. . . .

Management reserves the right to refuse the admission or to eject any person whose conduct management deems disorderly, obnoxious or unbecoming. No bottles, cans, flasks or alcoholic beverages are permitted to be brought into this facility. Violators will be ejected from the premises. Event opponents, dates, times and promotions subject to change without notice. – No money refunded. No exchanges accepted. Ticket fraud includes, but is not limited to, misrepresentation of a disability and/or the production and use of counterfeit or stolen tickets to the Wilkes-Barre/Scranton Penguins. Wilkes-Barre/Scranton Penguins considers ticket fraud to be extremely serious and will take appropriate action to prevent such usage. Guests holding fraudulent tickets or misrepresenting a disability in an attempt to purchase ADA designated seats are subject to ejection without reimbursement or restoration and many may be subject to criminal prosecution as allowed by law.

The risks inherent in spectating, however, do not completely relieve management of taking reasonable precautions to protect the fan. Another consequence of the fan-franchise relationship is that management is required to provide a reasonably safe environment for the fan or, in other words, to protect the fan from an unreasonable risk of injury (Hylton, 2003). In its simplest form, sport managers have a legal duty not to be negligent with respect to their patrons.

In general, management must act as a reasonably prudent operator would act in the same or similar circumstances (Champion, Jr., 2004). This is the same legal standard that the law imposes in most situations, whether sports-related or not: a driver must exercise reasonable care not to increase the risks of the road; a store owner must act in a reasonably prudent manner to make sure that, for example, products are shelved in a manner that they are not likely to fall onto a customer; and a residential landlord should not allow frayed wiring and leaky gas pipes to imperil tenants.

In sport, however, this obligation goes beyond just having basic safety features that the owner of any premises is expected to provide; the sport and the fan's relationship to the sport must be considered. The most obvious reasonable precautions managers in sport must take are the nets present behind home plate in baseball, behind the goals in hockey, and behind the goalposts in football. But what is enough safety?

The legal duty does not require management to protect the spectator from every risk or guarantee the safety of fans from every possible danger. Not only does the standard of care require only reasonable conduct, but the very nature of the sport the fan goes to enjoy affects management's duty to safeguard the fan. Just as participants in a sport assume certain risks inherent in the sport (a boxer will get punched, a football player blocked or tackled, and a hockey player checked), so must the sports fan assume certain risks inherent in watching live sporting contests.

Although the legal standard imposed on management of protecting fans from unreasonable risk has been present for well over a century (Hylton, 2003), management's obligations in meeting the standard have changed, particularly over the last few decades (Neymeyer, 1996).

Baseball, because of its long-standing role as the national pastime, and because of the constant danger to fans presented by flying bats and balls (as opposed to the relatively safe fan experiences of football and basketball), has long been the subject of lawsuits brought by injured fans (*Crane*, 1913). For these reasons, the body of law regarding fan safety in the context of the sport of baseball is particularly well developed and illustrative of the evolution of the legal and ethical duties related to fan safety.

One of the most common dangers to baseball fans, and historically one of the most litigated, is that of the foul ball. It was long held that in order for a baseball team, for example, to meet its legal duty to its fans in the case of foul balls, the team needed only to provide reasonably maintained netting behind home plate and just up the baselines where foul balls and errant pitches are most prevalent and dangerous. Courts deciding foul ball cases would exonerate the team from liability by simply determining that the location of the netting and its height were similar to the netting provided by teams in the league or similar leagues, and that the netting was not in a state of disrepair.

Because foul balls leaving the playing field at high rates of speed are so common in baseball, fans were charged with the knowledge that this risk existed in every game attended. In other words, fans were deemed to have assumed the risk of injury from foul balls, which were held to be a risk inherent in every baseball game.

Courts therefore routinely found in favor of the teams and against injured fans, for example in baseball:

> Before 1992, nearly all cases (brought by spectators injured by foul balls while attending professional baseball games) were decided in favor of the defendants. The basis for the decisions was that fans assumed the risk for their own personal safety when seated in an unprotected area and that the stadium operator, having provided reasonable protection, was not the insurer of the patron's safety.
>
> (Neymeyer, 1996)

The same rationale was used to defeat fan injury claims in other sports as well: hockey fans assume the risk of being hit by a flying puck; NASCAR fans assume that debris from a crash may leave the track and enter the stands. In one sense, the sports spectator is treated no differently than, say, a movie patron who can potentially trip in a darkened theater—each assumes certain risks inherent in the very nature of the activity they are enjoying.

In another sense, however, sports fans are in a somewhat unique position since they trade certain levels of safety in order to enhance their spectating experience. A NASCAR fan may consider the excitement of sitting trackside more important than the increased dangers associated with being so close to the action. Baseball fans typically prefer to be close to the field and may often view protections such as safety nets as obstructions to their enjoyment of the game. The balancing act of the fan who weighs the risks against the level of enjoyment is a variant of the one that management and courts engage in when determining if the sporting venue is operated in a reasonably prudent manner.

Since 1992, however, the tide has been turning. Courts have been more willing to find franchises liable despite traditional precautions such as screens, nets, and ticket warnings, warning signs, and announcements. Although these precautions still provide a measure of protection, and in some cases may be sufficient, they are no longer necessarily adequate. For instance, the courts have shown a willingness to look beyond the protections provided in the stands and consider those in the other areas where fans congregate at sporting events. In *Maisonave v. The Newark Bears Professional Baseball Club, Inc.*, the court noted:

> In respect of areas other than the stands, the Court recognizes that a different standard of care is appropriate, in part because of transformations in the game of baseball that have enabled players to hit baseballs harder and farther. Additionally, fans foreseeably and understandably let down their guard when they are in other

areas of the stadium. In the areas outside of the stands, including concourses and mezzanines such as the one in this appeal, a commercial sports facility is no different than any other commercial establishment and courts do not hesitate to apply general negligence principles in virtually all other tort situations and the specialized business invitee rule to commercial enterprises. To apply the limited duty rule to the entire stadium would convert reasonable protection for owners to immunity by virtually eliminating their liability for foreseeable, preventable injuries to their patrons even when the fans are no longer engaged with the game. The Court does not impose strict liability for owners in areas outside of the stands, however. It simply applies traditional tort principles and concludes that the proper standard of care for all other areas of the stadium is the business invitee rule, which provides that a landowner owes a duty of reasonable care to guard against any dangerous conditions on his or her property that the owner either knows about or should have discovered.

(*Maisonave*, 2005)

Another possible reason for the franchise becoming more liable for fan safety is that injured fans have become more creative in asserting their claims in ways designed to circumvent the broad protections afforded management by the assumption of the risk doctrine. Fans injured by a foul ball might sue not because they were hit, but because the venue had inadequate medical response policies or personnel, leading to greater injury and pain. Fans struck by an errant hockey puck while walking down the aisle to their seats, in recognition of the fact that they assumed the basic risk of being hit by a puck, might assert that management violated its own policies by letting them walk down the aisle while the puck was in play.

The erosion of management's protection from fans' claims of negligence is largely attributable to the evolution and changes in all areas of negligence law, but other factors have contributed. In fact, management itself has contributed to this trend by introducing distractions during games such as roving mascots, high-definition viewing screens showing constant replays, advertisements, and in-game amusements, all of which serve to distract the spectator from the action on the field of play. These distractions, well established in modern professional sporting events, have even provided a new legal approach for fans seeking greater protection from the games they attend: liability based on management's creation of risks rather than management's failure to reasonably protect fans from the risks inherent in the sport. One federal class action suit seeks to require MLB to provide foul ball safety nets from foul pole to foul pole, and to implement an ongoing evaluation program to determine what other precautions should be taken now and in the future (Waldstein, 2015).

Leadership and keeping fans safe

Discussion of purely legal protections, however, addresses only a part of the fan safety ethics issue for, to slightly paraphrase former Supreme Court Justice Earl Warren, laws float in a sea of ethics. Whether (or to what extent) enhanced fan safety has been driven by the fear of legal liability, as opposed to more "ethical" considerations related solely to the well-being of the patron, is difficult to determine.

Professional sports leadership has taken different approaches regarding legal protections. For example, in 1992, on the heels of a judicial decision holding management liable for a spectator's foul ball injury, the Chicago Cubs and Chicago White Sox pushed for and obtained legislative protection in the form of the Illinois Baseball Facility Liability Act, or "foul ball law." That law, followed by similar laws in Colorado and Arizona, required a fan injured by a batted ball or thrown bat to demonstrate that the bat was defective or the player engaged in reckless conduct. Illinois passed a similar law in 1995, the Hockey Facility Liability Act, to insulate hockey venues from activity-related liability.

It was not until a young fan who was seated above and behind a goal was killed by a puck in 2002 that the NHL required each team to place netting above the glass behind the goal areas (Taylor, 2002). Although this move was not dictated by a specific legal decision or a change in the law, it was nonetheless made only after a tragic event.

Whether to avoid lawsuits and liability or the bad publicity of an ugly incident, or both, the sports industry has become more forward-thinking regarding fan safety. The frequency and severity of spectator injuries from foul balls (nearly 100 fans reported foul ball injuries at major league games in the last half of the 2015 season) has caused MLB to make safety recommendations to each of its teams. While encouraging teams to extend netting to protect all field-level seats between the ends of the dugouts and home plate is the primary recommendation, MLB has offered other suggestions: encouraging teams (and on line ticket sellers) to state which seats are behind netting and to explore new ways to educate fans about the dangers of flying bats and balls.

These recommendations followed the filing by baseball season ticket holders of a class action suit against MLB in which they contended that MLB was not meeting its standard of care owed to fans—that is, that MLB has been negligent by not taking greater steps to minimize the danger of foul balls and flying bats (*Payne* et al., 2015). MLB stated that it began reviewing its safety standards before the filing of that suit. Whether or not litigation was the mechanism that forced MLB to make its recommendations, or whether MLB was attempting to stay in front of legal action is debatable.

What is not debatable, however, is that by recommending that each team take steps to enhance fan safety beyond the minimum currently required by legal decisional authority, MLB has changed the standard of care in baseball in this context and acted in a more ethical manner, which comports with both the utilitarian theory of the greatest good for the greatest number and care ethics. The courts today, just as those of 100 years ago, apply the same negligence analysis: did the team act as a reasonably prudent team in the same or similar circumstance would have acted? Because MLB itself has suggested enhanced precautions, and because at least some teams will immediately adopt those suggestions, any team that is dilatory in doing so will likely be seen as violating their standard of care to their fans at least ethically if not legally.

FAN RESPONSIBILITIES

Incidents of fan-on-fan violence have led management to provide security personnel in larger numbers and greater presence, including screening upon venue entry and video surveillance of the venue and parking facilities. As noted above, however, the ethical duty does not lie solely with management. Recognizing, which frequently means defining, ethical fan behavior is a predicate to embracing leadership strategies to promote it.

Defining unethical fan behavior

Defining ethical fan behavior is no easy task. It is, in some ways, even more elusive than Supreme Court Justice Potter Stewart's famous "definition" of pornography ("I know it when I see it."). When it comes to unethical fan conduct, however, not everyone seems to know when they see it.

When does playful banter among rival fans at a game become offensive or worse? Why do many sport enthusiasts view favorably the collective volume of Seattle Seahawks fans, which is designed to and does interfere with opponents' ability to hear their quarterbacks' audibles, whereas they view a single fan, who heckles and screams near the bench of an opposing NBA team so as to disrupt the coach's strategizing during a time out, as improperly interfering with the game?

Obviously, it is not enough to simply say that any fan behavior that interferes with the game itself is unethical. Nor is it sufficient to define such behavior as that which interferes with another fan's enjoyment of the game—while many find the volleying of beach balls at Dodgers games to be an annoying intrusion on their spectating, an equal number seem to enjoy the activity. A fan who stands up in the excitement of a goal or a home run might obstruct another's view and thus diminish his or her spectating experience, but such conduct is not generally considered unethical.

Even though an all-purpose definition of unethical fan behavior might not be possible, any working definition must have both subjective and objective elements. It must also go beyond legal definitions and concepts in part because, although all criminal or tortious (wrongful) conduct would be seen as unethical, the converse is not necessarily true, as noted in Chapter 1.

A good definitional starting point is to determine the duty a fan owes and to whom it is owed. All would agree that every fan has an ethical duty to obey the law. Running onto the field of play, throwing objects at players, and fighting are all easy cases, because they are examples of criminal or at least tortious conduct. Examining this legal foundation makes it clear that fans have legal duties to other fans, players, and management.

These legal duties reflect ethical duties as well. Under such theories as utilitarianism and deontology, ethical fans would not unduly interfere with another fan's enjoyment of the game; would not interfere with the participants' ability to play the game; nor would they create problems for management or the stadium operator. What is ethical fan behavior, however, requires more and goes beyond legal duty.

The fact that unethical fan conduct is relative (to the general culture and a sports' particular traditions, for example) further hampers the ability to define it. What is acceptable fan conduct today is often different than what was acceptable 50 or 100 years ago. Today, fans rushing onto the diamond after an MLB game would be considered a transgression, yet it was a very common occurrence a hundred years ago. Reaching from one's seat into the field of play to catch a foul ball or home run is a natural instinct that might have implications for the teams (turning an apparent home run into an out or a single into a ground rule double, etc.), but the act itself is generally not considered unethical (as opposed to, for example, actually going onto the field during play). In fact, the same act is just as likely to make one a goat (Cubs fan Steve Bartman) as a hero (Yankee fan Jeffrey Maier), as described below.

In Game 6 of the 2003 playoffs between the Chicago Cubs and the Florida Marlins, the Cubs were protecting a 3 to 2 game lead in the series. In the eighth inning, the Cubs were ahead 3–0, and seemingly on their way to their first World Series appearance in almost 60 years.

A Marlins player hit a pop-up into left field foul ball territory. As the Cubs left fielder positioned himself to catch the ball, Steve Bartman, and several other fans seated in the front row also attempted to catch the ball. Bartman did not succeed, but he did manage to deflect the ball away from the irate Cubs fielder.

The Marlins proceeded to score eight runs to win that game and went on to win the next game and the pennant. Despite the fact that the umpire ruled that there was no fan interference, Bartman had to be escorted from the stadium for his own safety, and his life was never the same. He received countless threats from Cubs fans, was placed under police protection, changed his phone number, and strove to be anonymous, declining interviews, paid commercial offers, and public appearances of all kinds.

A few years earlier, New York Yankee fan Jeffrey Maier was sitting in the first row of the right field stands at Yankee Stadium during the first game of the American League Championship Series between the Yankees and the Orioles. The Yankees trailed the Orioles by a run in the bottom of the eighth inning when Derek Jeter hit a fly ball to right field in the direction of Maier. Maier reached over the fence separating the field from the stands and caught the ball. Notwithstanding the Orioles' claims of fan interference on a ball that their right fielder would have caught but for Maier, the umpire ruled the ball a home run, and the game was tied. The Yankees went on to win the game and the series. Unlike Steve Bartman seven years later, Maier instantly became a hero to Yankee fans everywhere.

Both Bartman and Maier were diehard fans of their respective teams, both were in their home parks to root for their teams, and both did nothing more than try to catch a ball that flew toward their seats. The circumstances were very similar, but the effect on their lives quite different. Although neither interfered with the games according to the umpires, Bartman will forever be reviled by Cubs fans and blamed for the team's failure to reach the World Series, while Maier received adulation.

What is deemed to be ethical behavior is clearly situational. Spectators do not expect the fans in front of them to remain seated the entire game, yet very few fans would consider it acceptable for these people to stand constantly and obstruct the views of anyone sitting behind them, which would not be universalizable conduct nor would it produce the greatest good for the greatest number. Some fan-held signs are considered acceptable. In fact, it is common for teams to give away such items as foam fingers, signs, rally towels and similar items to fans entering an event with the expectation that fans will wave them during the game. However, signs and other items that are particularly large or obtrusive might be banned or considered unethical pursuant to utilitarian or deontological theories.

Leaving one's seat while play is in progress during a basketball, football, or baseball game is common and accepted; however, leaving one's seat while a hockey puck is in play will immediately earn the ire of every neighboring fan. Even the time-honored tradition of heckling opposing players can go from acceptable to unethical if the hurled barbs are considered too offensive. Racial slurs, comments about sexual preferences, and similar taunts go beyond the pale and would be almost universally considered to be contrary to virtue ethics and care ethics. But simply using coarse language will rarely result in ejection or reprimand, despite the fact that it may be considered generally offensive in nature and not entirely consistent with virtue ethics.

Is it enough to say that unethical fan behavior includes criminal and tortious conduct as well as conduct that unduly or unreasonably interferes with the playing of the game or the reasonable spectating expectations of other fans? What is undue/unreasonable? Is a fan in the middle of a row who constantly disturbs her neighbors by leaving her seat to go up the aisle acting "unethically?" Does the fan with a particularly loud voice or shrill whistle unduly interfere with the enjoyment of those around him?

Attempts to implement the definition

The prevalence of fan codes of conduct is illustrative of the significance of fan ethics in modern athletics. Fan conduct is circumscribed at all levels of competition and with varying limits. Rather than try to list all offending conduct, one high school athletics association, in accord with virtue ethics and care ethics, defines improper fan conduct simply as any behavior that is not "positive, respectful and encouraging of the athletes, coaches, officials and the game" (Kent City School District, 2011). Another high school code sets out both positive and negative conduct as follows:

Encouraged

Enthusiastic support of your team
Good sportsmanship
Family friendly atmosphere
Commitment to safety
Welcoming attitude to all fans and visitors

Unacceptable Behaviors

Disruptive, unruly or intoxicated behavior
Foul or abusive language or obscene gestures
Rudeness to fellow fans or . . . personnel
Use of alcohol or tobacco . . .
Visibly intoxicated or disruptive fans

(Heritage Hills, 2016)

Most major professional sports leagues and teams have some form of fan code of conduct. These codes, although illustrative of types of ethical and unethical behavior, are neither exhaustive nor precisely definitional, and they serve to highlight the fact that defining ethical fan behavior is difficult. Nevertheless, they do set some boundaries and provide a framework for evaluating proper fan behavior. An example of text from the Denver Broncos NFL team follows.

Fan Code of Conduct

Sports Authority Field at Mile High and the Denver Broncos are committed to creating a safe, comfortable and enjoyable experience for all fans, both in the stadium and in the parking lot. Therefore, a Fan Code of Conduct exists for all guests.

The following behaviors will not be tolerated at Sports Authority Field at Mile High:

- Behavior that is unruly, disruptive or illegal in nature.
- Foul, obscene, offensive or abusive language, gestures or actions.
- Interfering with the progress of the game or throwing any object onto the field or in the stadium premises.
- Failing to follow the instructions of stadium personnel.
- Verbal or physical harassment of opposing team fans.
- Smoking, except in designated areas.
- Fighting.
- Indecent exposure or the wearing of obscene or indecent clothing.
- Conduct that endangers spectators or participants.
- Ethnic intimidation.

Event patrons are responsible for their conduct as well as the conduct of their guests and/or persons occupying their seats. Event patrons and guests who violate these provisions will be subject to ejection without refund, potential loss of ticket privileges for future games, and possible revocation of their season ticket account.

Prior to entering stadium gates, all patrons will be subject to screening, including pat downs, and inspection of all bags and other items carried in. Please refer to *www.sportsauthorityfieldatmilehigh.com* for the most detailed information.

For Fan Behavior Concerns, Text "RESPECT" & your message & Your Location to 78247.

(Denver Broncos NFL, undated)

LEADERSHIP AND FAN BEHAVIOR

Despite the difficulty in defining fan ethics, the issue of fan behavior is nevertheless paramount to the fan enjoying an event, to participants engaging in their athletic activities without outside interference or disruption, and to management avoiding the expense, inconvenience, disruption, and notoriety of fan misconduct. Arriving at a working under-standing—if not an all-encompassing definition—of ethical fan behavior necessarily leads to the issue of the role of leadership in framing and nurturing it.

In many ways, sport industry leaders have a poor track record when it comes to promoting ethical behavior, and punishing and deterring unethical behavior. Too often those leaders have ignored unethical behavior, particularly on the part of players and coaches, so long as the players performed well and the coaches produced wins. Examples of college coaching staff recruiting violations, use of performance-enhancing drugs by athletes, and management's willingness to overlook that use have often been met with silence or lip service—provided the players and coaches produced results.

It can be argued that the sport industry's willingness to accept improper behavior on the part of the participants and management has created a culture of acceptance, which has trickled down to the fans. At the same time, the phenomenon of fan as "part of the game" has grown. The spread of media coverage of sporting events, the 24–7 nature of sports news in the last few dozen years, and the current ubiquity of smartphone cameras and online venues for videos such as YouTube have likely contributed to the acceptance of exaggerated, if not unethical, fan conduct designed to gain the fan camera time and temporary celebrity.

No sporting event broadcast is complete these days without numerous shots of fans in costume, painted faces, or holding signs. The difficulty in measuring the impact of the media on fan behavior does not disprove such a link. It is worth noting that the media and the industry accept that there is such a link, which is demonstrated by their refusal to broadcast fans running onto fields of play—i.e. deterrence by ignoring.

The evolution of the sports industry into a more sophisticated and media-savvy enterprise has also resulted in a deeper inquiry into the issue of fan behavior. The cost to a team or a league of incidents like the Malice at the Palace or the Bryan Stow beating at Dodgers Stadium is no longer simply the cost of some additional security personnel. The adverse public perception may result in lower ticket sales and also results in a damaged public image. Given teams' and leagues' close connections with and reliance on sponsors, advertisers and broadcasting deals, they must be sensitive to anything that would mar their images.

Although one might prefer that the industry's leaders promote proper fan behavior for ethical reasons, economics and legal liability appear to remain the primary driving forces. When fan behavior is examined from the perspective of criminal or tortious conduct alone, then leadership need only take measures such as security cameras and additional security personnel. When viewed in a purely economic context, if there is no impact on revenues, then management might hesitate to take measures, particularly those with costs attached, to address certain fan behaviors.

Leadership, however, whether motivated by self-interest, ethics, or the promotion of the sport or team, can attempt to shape fan behavior and take a proactive approach to managing unethical fan behavior. The growth in the implementation of fan codes of conduct has already been discussed. Although once content to simply have such a code of conduct on record in an office or in the back of a program, professional and collegiate sports leaders are pushing the fan ethics agenda in new and more creative ways.

In this regard, most professional teams now show pre-game and in-game videos describing unacceptable behavior. The NBA's Atlanta Hawks have even won the IDEA's Golden Matrix Award for Best In-Game Feature for the creativity of its fan code of conduct videos (Vivlamore, 2014). The videos parody popular songs "Blurred Lines" and "Wrecking Ball", and warn against improper language, interrupting play, throwing objects, fighting, and so forth. They also notify fans about possible ejections or legal consequences and remind fans to call security if they observe any misconduct.

Most teams also have phone or text "hotlines," and fans are encouraged to report offensive language or behavior. Teams have for some time barred the sale of alcohol after a certain point in the game, and they routinely prohibit fans from bringing to events potentially dangerous objects, or similar items that might interfere with other fans' enjoyment of the contest.

Management's increasing awareness of the importance of prevention has not diminished the value of enforcement. Ejection and prosecution may be the ultimate weapons, but industry leaders have employed other, less severe ways to discourage poor fan behavior. As part of its fan conduct policies, the NBA has prepared red warning cards to be handed to disruptive fans ahead of and hopefully instead of ejection. These cards read as follows:

WARNING

You are being issued a warning that the comments, gestures and/or behaviors that you have directed at players, coaches, game officials and/or other spectators constitute excessive verbal abuse and are in violation of the NBA Fan Code of Conduct.

This is the first and only warning that you will receive. If, after receiving this warning, you verbally abuse any player, coach, game official or spectator, you will be immediately ejected from the arena without refund.

(Traina, 2013)

This discreet device (compared to immediate ejection or public admonishment by an usher) serves not only as a warning, but as a tool to educate fans about the behaviors that the league expects from them.

The importance of prevention and enforcement is obvious, but sport leaders have also recognized the value of rehabilitation. One company, the AJ Novick Group, offers a form of "traffic school" for boorish fans. The company provides programs to the NFL and Major League Soccer as well as many colleges and universities. The programs—consistent with care ethics, utilitarianism, and deontology—require that fans ejected for non-violent infractions (such as abusive language or intoxication) complete the fan behavior course and obtain a certification showing completion before they are allowed to attend another game (Bondy et al., 2013).

The online course of instruction at www.fanconductclass.com covers the following areas:

- Introduction, purpose and benefits of Fan Conduct Class.
- Stadium "Code of Conduct" policies.
- Alcohol abuse and public intoxication (intoxication or other signs of alcohol or substance impairment that results in irresponsible behavior).
- Alcohol education and risk reduction.
- What is disruptive fan behavior? (Behavior that is unruly, disruptive, or illegal in nature).
- Gaining control of ourselves (interference with the progress of the game, including throwing objects onto the field).
- Skills in improving empathy toward other fans.
- Skills for becoming less impulsive and improving judgment.
- Skills for better managing stress and learning new ways of staying in control during the game day experience.
- Communication skills as prevention (Foul or abusive language or obscene gesture).
- Verbal or physical harassment of opposing team fans.
- Smoking policies.
- Skills in improving the game day experience for oneself and others.
- Review of stadium code of conduct and course skills.

CONCLUSION

Whether or not they are being pushed by increasing legal liability, economics, and public relations, or pulled by an ethical desire to provide fans with the best possible sports experience, sports leaders are recognizing and embracing the importance of fan ethics to the spectating experience and the health of the sports industry in general. The movement toward establishing codes of conduct and pursuing different methods of conveying to fans the specifics and intent of those codes reflect an evolution of ethical leadership parallel to the evolution of modern sports.

ETHICAL LEADERSHIP CASE STUDY

Neo Phyte has never attended a hockey game before. A friend gives him a ticket to a professional game. Neo arrives before the game, and, during the player warmups, he starts down the aisle to his seat, which is in the lower level of the arena. On the way down the aisle, he notices that the brand new, giant state of the art video board is showing some amusing hockey bloopers. As he nears his seat, he sees that the team's mascot is blocking his entry into his row and a crowd of people have left their assigned seats to gather around the mascot to enjoy the antics. While Neo is standing in the aisle near his row, unable to easily get to his seat, and alternately enjoying the video board and the mascot's clowning, he is hit in the head by an errant puck from the ice. He is knocked unconscious and requires several stitches.

1. Does the fact that the incident occurs before the game preclude the team from asserting an assumption of the risk defense if Neo sues?
2. Is the level of the fan's experience relevant or should all fans be treated equally?
3. Does the team have an ethical duty to try to educate fans about the dangers of the game before they enter the venue? Is a warning on the back of a ticket that pucks may fly into the stands simply a legal precaution or an acknowledgment by management that some level of education is necessary for some fans?
4. Is it unethical for a team to potentially put a fan's safety in jeopardy by creating diversions?
5. Does it matter ethically if the team has a written policy that states that fans should not congregate in aisles and should not sit in other fans' seats or obstruct the access of other fans to their assigned seats?
6. What leadership steps might the team's ownership take to reduce the likelihood of similar incidents in the future without eliminating mascots and video boards? What would be the most effective way to implement these leadership steps?

STUDENT LEARNING EXERCISE

Given the design of a baseball stadium, concession stands can either be situated such that all fans in line are protected from foul balls, but they cannot see the game while in line, or they can be placed such that all fans in line can still watch the game, but only some of the fans are protected. Formulate an ethical solution.

PROBLEMS/QUESTIONS

1. What factors should an ethical baseball team owner consider when balancing fan enjoyment of the proximity of bullpens located near the field of play in foul territory with the safety provided by bullpens that are sequestered well off the field?

2. Although foul balls in the stands are common, flying bats are not so common. Are flying bats nevertheless fan risks inherent in the sport of baseball? What about wild pitches and errant throws? Regardless of their frequency, should an ethical team leader seek to eliminate the risks these dangers pose to fans? Do team leaders have any ethical duty to the numerous other fans who would have their views obstructed if such protective measures were taken?

3. Based on a football team's revenues, it can afford to either install improved lighting in its parking lots or increase the number of security personnel and ushers inside the stadium. How would an ethical team owner decide?

4. A basketball team has determined that while alcohol sales greatly increase their revenues and are wanted by most fans, a number of fights and incidents involving abusive and disruptive fans are related to alcohol sales. Therefore, the team has designated certain sections to be non-drinking sections. Ethically, what should the team do if a fan or fans wish to sit in the non-drinking sections, but those sections are sold out? How should the team provide ethical leadership on this issue?

BIBLIOGRAPHY

Applebaum, Lindsay, *This Year in Fan Behavior, 2014 Edition*, si.com, December 31, 2014.

Bearman v. University of Notre Dame, 453 N.E. 2d 1196 (1983).

Benejam v. Detroit Tigers, Inc., 246 Mich. App. 645 (2001).

Bondy, Filip, Leonard, Pat & Abramson, Mitch, Now There's a School for Unruly Fans, *New York Daily News*, March 23, 2013.

Bonsignore, Vincent, Sports Fans' Behavior Has Gone Over the Top, *Los Angeles Daily News*, October 8, 2012.

Boston Globe Staff, Notable Fan Injuries During Sporting Events, *Boston Globe*, June 7, 2015.

Buckner, Candace, As "Malice at the Palace" Brawl Turns 10, Impact Lasts, *USA Today*, November 18, 2014.

Champion, Jr., Walter, *Fundamentals of Sports Law* (2nd ed. 2004).

Cincinnati Base Ball Club Co. v. Eno, 112 Ohio St. 175 (1925).

Crane v. Kansas City Baseball & Exhibition Co., 168 Mo. App. 301 (1913).

Curtis v. Portland Baseball Club, 120 Ore. 93 (1929).

Denver Broncos National Football League, Fan Code of Conduct, undated, www.sportsauthorityfield atmilehigh.com/stadium-information/fan-code-of-conduct.

Dickson, Paul, *The Dickson Baseball Dictionary* (3rd ed. 2011).

Dusckiewicz v. Jack Carter dba Jack Carter Enterprises, 115 Vt. 122 (1947).

Fan Conduct Class, www.fanconductclass.com, 2016.

Gil de Rebollo v. Miami Heat Associations, Inc., 137 F. 3d 56 (1st Cir. 1998).

Henne, Ricky, San Diego Sports Commission Promotes Fan Code of Conduct, www.chargers.com/news/2013/08/28/san-diego-sports-commission-promotes-fan-code-conduct, August 28, 2013.

Heritage Hills (Indiana) High School, Fan Code of Conduct, www.hhpatriots.com/athletics/fancodeof conduct, 2016.

Hopkins v. Connecticut Sports Plex, LLC, 2006 Conn.Super. LEXIS 1710 (2016).

Hylton, J. Gordon, A Foul Ball in the Courtroom: The Baseball Spectator Injury as a Case of First Impression, *38 Tulsa Law Review*, 485 (2003).

Iervolino v. Pittsburgh Athletic Co., 212 Pa.Super. 330 (1968).

Illinois Baseball Facility Liability Act, 745 Illinois Compiled Statutes 38.

Illinois Hockey Facility Liability Act, 745 Illinois Compiled Statutes 52.

Jasper v. Chicago National League Baseball Club, Inc., 309 Ill. App. 3d 124 (1999).

Jones v. Three Rivers Management Corp., 483 Pa. 75 (1978).

Kent City School District (Ohio), Fan Code of Conduct, www.kentschools.net/files/2011/10/NewFan CodeofConduct2011 (2011).

Kling, Bill, What Makes Fans Crazy About Sports, *Sports Business Daily*, April 19, 2010.

Lapointe, Joe, NHL Arenas To Add Netting to Protect the Fans From Pucks, *New York Times*, June 21, 2002.

Lowe v. California League of Professional Baseball, 56 Cal. App. 4th 112 (1997).

Maisonave v. The Newark Bears Professional Baseball Club, Inc., 185 NJ 70 (2005).

Maytnier v. Rush, 80 Ill. App. 2d 336 (1967).

Morrissey, Rick, MLB Must Play Fair With Hard Foul Balls, *Chicago Tribune*, May 12, 2002.

Nemarnik v. The Los Angeles Kings Hockey Club, LP, 103 Cal. App. 4th 631 (2002).

Neymeyer, Robert, Fans Strike Out With Foul Ball Litigation, *Sports and the Law* (1996).

NFL Teams Implement Fan Code of Conduct, www.nfl.com/news/story/09000d5d809c28f9/article/ nfl-teams-implement-fan-code-of-conduct, August 5, 2008, updated July 26, 2012.

Nocera, Joe, Danger at The Ballpark (And In a Baseball Ticket's Fine Print), *New York Times*, November 21, 2015.

Payne, et al. v. Office of the Commissioner of Baseball (d/b/a Major League Baseball), et al., Case No. 3:15-cv-03229-SC, U.S. District Court for the Northern District of California, San Francisco Division (July 13, 2015).

Pearson, Rick, "Foul Ball" Law Restricts Suits, *Chicago Tribune*, September 25, 1992.

Ratcliff v. San Diego Baseball Club of the Pacific Coast League, 27 Cal. App. 2d 733 (1938).

Sciarrotta v. Global Spectrum, 194 NJ 345 (2008).

Stampfl, Karl & Janega, James, Ballpark Safety Is About Keeping Your Eye On The Ball, *Chicago Tribune*, July 15, 2008.

Strauss, Ben, Ten Years Later, Infamous Cubs Fan Remains Invisible, *New York Times*, October 13, 2013.

Taylor, Phil, The Death of a Fan, *Sports Illustrated*, April 1, 2002.

Taylor v. The Baseball Club of Seattle, LP, 132 Wash. App. 32 (2006).

Tierney, Ted J., Heads Up!: The Baseball Facility Liability Act, 18 *Northern Illinois University Law Review* 601 (1998).

Toone v. Adams, 262 NC 403 (1964).

Traina, Jimmy, NBA "Bad Behavior" Warning Cards to Fans Is a Real Thing, foxsports.com, December 5, 2013.

Vivlamore, Chris, Hawks Code of Conduct Videos Win Award, *Atlanta Journal Constitution*, July 28, 2014.

Waldstein, David, Fan Injuries Spur MLB to Call for Netting At Stadiums, *New York Times*, December 10, 2015.

Wells v. Minneapolis Baseball & Athletic Association 142 NW 706 (1913).

Wong, Edward, Fan Safety and Liability Debated In Puck Death, *New York Times*, March 22, 2002.

Wyshynski, Greg, Ten Years After Death of Brittanie Cecil, Recalling Backlash Over NHL Safety Netting, yahoo.com, March 15, 2012.

Wyshynski, Greg, Young Fan Sues Hockey Team, Seeks Record Damages for Getting Hit by Puck, yahoo.com, March 19, 2014.

Yates v. Chicago National League Baseball Club, Inc., 230 Ill. App. 3d 472 (1992).

CHAPTER 6

The ethical costs of medical issues

INTRODUCTION

Sports concussions have been widely reported in the media and featured in the popular film, *Concussion*, released in 2015. But concussions have been around since time immemorial, so what is the source of the spike in public interest?

First, concussions are a major ethical issue. Risking one's mental health for a sporting event implicates utilitarianism, deontology, virtue ethics and care ethics. Second, there is an increased understanding of the causes, effects, and costs of certain contact sports because of concussions, costs which, throughout most of history, have been borne by individuals or by tax revenues from society at large. Both the historical ways of paying for concussions and the potential new ways—perhaps best exemplified by the approximately $1 billion the NFL will pay to settle the more than 4,000 lawsuits about concussions by former players—have been reflected in the U.S. legal system. The relation of this legal process to the ethics of concussions in sport will be explored in this chapter.

The U.S. legal system has moved from decisions on concussions favoring the assumption of the risk by the individual to an imposition on sport administrators of legal duties to create the environment most conducive to protecting athletes from concussions. Driving this shift is the universalizable ethical principle that those institutions that are benefiting financially or otherwise from a concussion-causing sport—not individuals or society at large—should be financially responsible for the consequences of the injuries.

A less publicized but probably more widespread medical, ethical, and legal problem in sport is injury from overuse of a particular part of the body (depending on the sport). Such overuse is a relatively recent phenomenon among youth because of the proliferation of year-round travel teams dedicated to one sport. This overuse, which raises issues of care ethics, is particularly problematic because it can affect children, who are unable to give informed consent to such overuse.

Related to overuse is the problem of burnout. Continual efforts to succeed in one sport, usually accompanied by pressure from parents and coaches, have caused a large number of youths to drop out of sports altogether. Chronic muscle or joint pain, elevated resting heart rate, and fatigue are medical issues that may manifest as a result, raising issues of care ethics and virtue ethics.

THE HISTORICAL LEGAL DOCTRINE OF SPORTS INJURIES: ASSUMPTION OF THE RISK

The legal doctrine "assumption of the risk" has governed sport injuries for many years. Put in terms of universalizability, one would not expect to collect damages for taking a known risk, like playing sports, which inherently carries with it risk, and one would not pay someone if he or she were injured for taking a known risk. In the context of sport, assumption of risk is the defense most prevalently discussed in cases of negligence liability.

Like most legal doctrines, however, assumption of the risk is not without its complexities, which will be discussed in the section below. As some risks became more known, however, and as professional leagues arguably were increasing some risks unnecessarily, the assumption of risk defense has come under increasing pressure, especially in the cases of football, soccer, and hockey.

The legal doctrine of assumption of the risk is divided into primary assumption of the risk and secondary assumption of the risk. In a typical lawsuit involving this legal doctrine, the plaintiff is the individual who assumed the risk (i.e. engaged in a sport where injuries occur) and brought the suit against the defendant (i.e. the person or entity that facilitated the plantiff's engaging in the sport). Primary assumption of the risk means that the defendant in the case owes no duty of care to the plaintiff because the plaintiff undertook a known risky activity.

Secondary assumption of the risk includes cases in which the defendant does have a duty to the plaintiff because, for example, the defendant has increased the risks inherent in the sport. Secondary assumption of the risk has been merged into the concept of comparative negligence, which means that fault can be allocated between the plaintiff and the defendant.

The best way to illustrate the doctrine of assumption of the risk is to describe an actual sport case involving that issue, of which there are many. *Balthazor v. Little League Baseball, Inc.*, a 1998 California state court case provides an illustrative example of the way courts traditionally have decided these cases. In that case an 11-year-old boy was batting against a 15-year-old pitcher on an unlighted field three minutes before sunset. The pitcher had already hit two batters, his first pitch narrowly missed the plaintiff, and his second pitch hit the plaintiff in the face and caused serious injury.

The court considering this case stated that, in order to decide it, the court had to determine "the nature of the . . . sport in which the defendant is engaged and the relationship of the defendant and the plaintiff to that . . . sport." The court decided that the relationship of the league (the defendant) to the player (the plaintiff) was the same as that of teacher–student or coach–player. Given this relationship, the court found that the league had a duty not to increase the risks of the sport over and above those inherent in the sport but also that the league was not an insurer of the plaintiff's safety.

With these principles in mind, the court considered the first argument of the plaintiff, that the game should have been stopped three minutes before sunset because the diminished lighting increased the risks that a batter would be hit by a pitch. The court rejected this argument for two reasons. First, the court asserted that changing lighting conditions are inherent in the game. Second, the court observed that the batter was able to dodge the first pitch, which showed that there was sufficient visibility. Therefore, the court held, getting hit by a pitch is a risk inherent to baseball, which means that the league had no duty of care based on this first argument.

The plaintiff's second argument was that the league was negligent not to remove from the game the obviously wild pitcher, who had hit two previous batters. The court also held that this risk was inherent in the game of baseball, which historically has allowed many wild pitchers to play. Eliminating wild pitchers from the game, the court reasoned, would change the nature of the game and would stifle some pitchers. Therefore, the league owed no duty to the batter on this issue.

The third argument of the plaintiff was that the league increased the risks of the game by not providing faceguards with the batting helmets that are required. In response, the court stated that the league's duty under the assumption of the risk doctrine was not to increase the risks of the game, which did not include a duty to *decrease* the risks inherent in the game:

> Here, the face guard which [plaintiff] argues should have been required was not part of the normal safety equipment used by the League. The League's failure to require additional equipment did not increase a risk inherent in the sport: that a player might be struck by a carelessly thrown ball.
>
> (*Balthazor*, 1998)

The case described above was very typical of the assumption of the risk cases in sport until recent times: the plaintiff was almost always sympathetic, and the plaintiff almost always lost because, ethically speaking, the doctrine of assumption of the risk was thought to be universalizable and to produce the greatest good for the greatest number. As more has been learned about risks to player safety, however, and about when professional leagues may have learned of these risks, the law has started to change. Those changes, and the ethical support for them, both of which will no doubt be evolving over the next decade, are described below as they relate to concussions in football, soccer and hockey.

CONCUSSIONS

The word "concussion" comes from the Latin word *concutere*, which means to shake violently. Such shaking, which is common in sports, is all that it takes to cause a concussion (Cantu & Hyman, 2012). A concussion occurs when the brain moves within the skull in such a way as to impair alertness. The brain floats in the skull and can keep moving in the same direction that a person has been moving after the motion of that person stops suddenly, such as when a runner with the ball in football is tackled.

The brain can actually come in contact with the skull in such a way as to cause injury without the loss of consciousness (Cantu & Hyman, 2012). The Centers for Disease Control website (cdc.gov), for example, defines a concussion as follows:

> A concussion is a type of traumatic brain injury – or TBI – caused by a bump, blow, or jolt to the head or by a hit to the body that causes the head and brain to move rapidly back and forth. This sudden movement can cause the brain to

bounce or twist in the skull, stretching and damaging the brain cells and creating chemical changes in the brain.

(Centers for Disease Control and Prevention, 2017)

Although loss of consciousness was once central to the definition of concussion, this is no longer true. In 2013, the American Academy of Neurology broadened the definition "to include a variety of possible symptoms caused by mild head trauma, including headaches, amnesia and sensitivity to light and sound—but not necessarily loss of consciousness" (Rothman, 2015).

Given this definition, it is not surprising that there are millions of sport concussions reported every year, and probably many more are not reported. Football is probably the sport most closely connected with concussions, but any sport can generate them, particularly hockey, rugby, lacrosse, and soccer.

Many concussions in soccer, for example, result from the common practice of heading the ball. Not only does heading itself have the potential to cause concussions, but collisions often occur between opposing players who are trying to head the ball. The impact can cause a concussion even in the player who was prevented by an opponent from heading the ball.

Given how concussions occur, helmets provide little protection against them because helmets do not stop the motion of the brain within the skull. Helmets have been very effective in protecting against skull fractures, but no helmet has yet been developed that protects against concussions with any degree of certainty.

Not every concussion is the same. Aside from differing in severity, numerous symptoms are associated with concussions, some or all of which can occur in any given case. In addition to the symptoms mentioned above, others include nausea, vomiting, depression, irritability, memory problems, and difficulties with sleep.

Concussion protocols

Protocols of what to do when a player has, or is suspected to have, a concussion have been formulated by prestigious medical organizations and conferences. The protocols, which are consistent with care ethics, deontology and utilitarianism, call for the player to come out of the game immediately upon experiencing symptoms. Furthermore, the player is not to return to play until the symptoms disappear, and he or she can demonstrate certain cognitive skills like counting backwards.

If the player's symptoms persist after the game, the protocols state that he or she should not return to play or practice unless and until the symptoms disappear. A step-by-step process is recommended before an individual's return to play or practice, including a medical evaluation, frequent monitoring, and complete rest while symptoms are occurring. After the symptoms disappear, the steps back to practice and play include light aerobic exercise, non-contact training drills, full contact drills and, lastly, game play.

The NCAA Concussion Guidelines (found on ncaa.org) are illustrative, having many similarities, for example, with the guidelines of the National Federation of State High School Associations (National Federation of High School Associations, 2014). The NCAA guidelines mandate, consistent with care ethics and deontology, that their member institutes implement the following (NCAA, 2015):

1. An annual process that ensures student-athletes are educated about the signs and symptoms of concussion.
2. A process that ensures a student-athlete who exhibits signs, symptoms or behaviors consistent with a concussion shall be removed from athletics activities and evaluated by a medical staff member with experience in the evaluation and management of concussion.
3. A policy that precludes a student-athlete diagnosed with a concussion from returning to athletic activity for at least the remainder of that calendar day.
4. A policy that requires a medical clearance for a student-athlete diagnosed with a concussion to return to athletics activity as determined by a physician or the physician's designee.

The NCAA also has a protocol regarding the return to academic activities (return-to learn) after a concussion as follows (NCAA, 2015):

1. If the student-athlete cannot tolerate light cognitive activity, he or she should remain at home or in the residence hall.
2. Once the student-athlete can tolerate cognitive activity without return of symptoms, he or she should return to the classroom, often in graduated increments.

Of course, protocols such as these would seemingly be easier to implement in a professional league of adults, where competent trainers and doctors are readily available, than in youth leagues, where generally no such expertise is readily available. Concussion protocols are not mandatory, however, in most situations.

For example, concussion protocols are not mandatory at the highest levels of the world's most popular sport, soccer. Indeed, limitations on substitutions in the rules of soccer can give a coach an incentive to keep a concussed player in a game, contrary to care ethics, virtue ethics, utilitarianism, and deontology.

Concussions in professional sports

Boxing

Boxing has had serious, well-known problems with these injuries for years. Since at least 1928, the medical profession has been aware of *pugilistica dementia*, more commonly known as punch-drunkenness. A stereotype of boxers developed from this condition, and, unfortunately, there are all too many real-life examples.

Little, however, can be done or has been done to protect the boxers. Headwear, which is not required at the professional level, does not, as noted above, prevent the brain movement that causes concussions. State boxing commissions have not done much to ameliorate the inherent violence of the sport.

Referees can declare a technical knockout when a boxer is obviously seriously impaired, and there are trained medical personnel on hand for some fights, but the problem of concussions persists. Indeed, mixed martial arts are now more popular than boxing, and that sport has the potential to expose the fighters to a greater risk of concussion. Kicks to the head, for example, are permissible in mixed martial arts, and such kicks present an obvious concussion risk.

Football

In football, medical knowledge on concussions was rather sparse until the 1980s. Initially, the long-term damage from these injuries was denied by the National Football League, but now it is widely recognized by that league and others. Although football is an inherently violent game, concussions did not become a focus of the NFL until 2009.

In the sport's early years, there were some deaths each year in football games, in large part because of a formation known as the flying wedge, where teammates linked arms on kickoff returns. Early in the 20th century, President Theodore Roosevelt convened the major football powers and threatened to ban the game unless reform occurred. The Intercollegiate Athletic Association of the United States (IAAUS), which became the NCAA, was then formed to enact reforms (Barr, 2012).

On October 19, 1905, a *New York Times* article was headlined "Abolish Football, Says Harvard Bulletin" ("Abolish," 1905). It reported that a well-known surgeon who had coached football teams stated that "the human body is not fitted to endure the game as it is played in the American colleges."

The January 5, 1906 edition of the *Harvard Crimson*, in an article "The Physical Side of Football," reported on the work of the Harvard team doctor on concussions and on the reactions of the team members to that subject:

> Cases of concussion were frequent, both during practice and games. In fact but two games were played during the entire season in which a case of concussion of the brain did not occur. . . . Frequently the fact that a man had received a serious injury was noticed by the surgeon from the sidelines before it was recognized by the players. . . . The mental state of the players who had concussion was variable, some being highly excitable and hysterical, others merely confused, and in a few cases, knocked completely unconscious. In every case there was a certain loss of memory. . . . Concussion was treated by the players as a trivial injury and rather regarded as a joke.
>
> ("The Physical Side," 1906)

After the flying wedge was eliminated from college football in 1906, nothing was done about concussions for many years, although from time to time there were articles about the dangers of concussions in football. In 1939 helmets became required at the college level and in 1943 at the professional level. Helmets, however, as noted above, were and are designed to, and do, protect from skull fractures, not from concussions.

Many claim that helmets actually increase the chance of concussions because helmets give an offensive player an incentive to use his head as a weapon. Comparisons have been made with rugby, a sport which is played without helmets, which some claim has fewer concussion problems than American football.

The reason for so little concussion reform until 2009 was the lack of definitive scientific evidence linking football-related concussions to cognitive impairment and other mental and emotional problems, although distinguished physicians clearly were raising alarms about further participation by injured players in a game. For example, in 1986 the respected sports neurologist, Robert Cantu, wrote the following in a medical journal:

[i]nitial treatment of a mild concussion requires the player to be removed from the game and observed on the bench. . . . Before such a player is allowed to return, he should be asymptomatic not only at rest but also after demonstrating that he can move with his usual dexterity and speed during exertion. If an athlete has any symptoms during either rest or exertion, continued neurological observation is essential.

(Cantu, 1986)

Because this position was not widely accepted, however, there was room for debate and denial on the part of those who profited from football, primarily the NFL. Because of the leadership position of the NFL, reform did not occur.

As players became larger and impacts harder, however, undeniable problems started to emerge. Some NFL players committed suicide or died homeless on the street, drawing more attention to the issue. In 2002, the Hall of Fame center of the Pittsburgh Steelers, Mike Webster, died homeless and demented. The doctor, a Nigerian immigrant named Bennet Omalu, who subsequently examined slides of Webster's brain tissue, discovered that Webster had a brain in the condition of someone many years older than he was. In 2005, Omalu published his findings, diagnosing a new disease—chronic traumatic encephalopathy (CTE). The NFL initially vilified Omalu and denied his findings. The league even commissioned its own study allegedly demonstrating that the effects of concussions were unknown.

Findings from the research of the NFL's Committee on Mild Traumatic Brain Injury began to be published in a series of articles in *Neurosurgical Focus* (Pellman & Viano, 2006). Some of the conclusions the committee reached were not shared by other concussion researchers. These unshared opinions included the following:

- Because a majority of concussed NFL players returned to the same game in which they were injured, concussions in professional football were "not serious injuries."
- If an NFL player's concussion symptoms went away, and if he could pass a medical exam, there was no reason he couldn't resume play in the same game he was injured. It "might be safe" for concussed high school and college players to return on the same day too.
- Concussed NFL players who lost consciousness weren't at increased risk for another concussion, or for the lingering symptoms of post-concussion syndrome.
- The widely used guidelines for grading a concussion's severity and determining how long a player should rest and recover were unreliable. Team doctors should use their best judgment and make case-by-case decisions rather than following an "arbitrary, rigid" concussion management system.
- NFL players with three or more concussions showed "no evidence of worsening injury or chronic cumulative effects." That included "no signs" of CTE in the active players.

(Mangels, 2012)

Subsequently, in August 2007, the NFL distributed a pamphlet to players that noted that concussions should be taken seriously, while at the same time contending that research "has not shown that having more than one or two concussions leads to permanent problems if each injury is managed properly" (id.).

As the number of suicides increased, however, that denial became untenable. Although the chances of an average person contracting CTE are close to zero, the vast majority of the brains of deceased NFL players that were studied had this disease.

Finally, in 2009, the NFL changed its position and recognized the seriousness of concussions and the need for strict protocols to deal with them. Even after the NFL's change in position, however, the doctor who had been the co-chair of the NFL's Committee on Mild Traumatic Brain Injury wrote an article for *Neurology Today*, "Do the Facts Really Support an Association between NFL Players' Concussions, Dementia and Depression," in which he stated:

> Many also believe that all retired players who have dementia and depression are suffering as a result of multiple head injuries sustained during their NFL careers. This 'false fact' implied that retired NFL players are somehow immune to the multiple risk factors and diseases that are associated with dementia and depression in the general population.
>
> (Casson, 2010)

The NFL's acknowledgment of the seriousness of concussions in 2009 came too late to avoid litigation, which can often be a side effect of unethical actions. Thousands of players filed numerous class actions against the NFL, and the cases were all consolidated in a federal court in Philadelphia.

The NFL made a motion to dismiss the case, but before the motion was decided, the parties announced a settlement, which was ultimately amended to amount, potentially, to over $1 billion for injuries that had already been sustained and for a medical monitoring program lasting decades. Some players have opted out of the settlement in order to bring individual cases, not class actions, guaranteeing a continuous stream of concussion-related litigation for the NFL for years to come.

Riddell, the helmet manufacturer with the largest sales, was also named in the class action lawsuit filed against the NFL. Riddell claimed, reportedly based on a University of Pittsburgh Medical Center study, that its Revolution helmet decreased the incidence of concussions by 31 percent.

The claim was challenged at a hearing of the U.S. Senate Commerce Committee in 2011 by the chair of the American Academy of Neurology's sports neurology section. Although Riddell has since ceased making the 31 percent claim, it was sued as a result of that claim. As of late 2016, although the NFL has settled the class action, Riddell is still actively litigating the class action.

Hockey

The NHL has made some improvements in concussion protocols, but it is also fighting lawsuits that attempt to connect concussions and brain disease. More concussions began appearing in hockey games in recent years as the players got bigger and faster, but the size of the ice remained the same.

Concussions have been a particular problem for those players known as "enforcers" who engage in numerous collisions and fights. Although "enforcer" is not an official role, the players who act in this capacity often instigate or respond to violent play. Numerous retired players have alleged mental impairment as a result of the NHL's alleged misconduct regarding concussion education, prevention, and treatment.

In response, the NHL has changed some rules on checking, in particular banning so-called "blind-side checks," a check delivered to the body from behind or beside a player who is unable to see it coming. The NHL has also adopted concussion protocols. As often happens, these reforms have trickled down to the lower levels of hockey. In particular, numerous youth hockey leagues go further than the NHL and actually prohibit checking, which is also prohibited in women's hockey at the Olympic level.

But the NHL has denied the connection between concussions and brain disease, and it has continued to allow fighting. Those positions, plus a legacy of denying the problem and denying care to players, have generated a major class action lawsuit that—unlike the NFL lawsuit discussed above and the soccer lawsuit discussed below—shows no signs of settling as of late 2016. Because ethical questions regarding concussions are being litigated in the courts and because lawsuits should be avoided by sports managers if at all possible, it is instructive to analyze this lawsuit and its ethical implications in some detail (*In Re National Hockey Players Concussion Injury Litigation*, 2015).

In the case, the players/plaintiffs start out by alleging that, inconsistent with care ethics and deontology, NHL players sustain close to 1,000 or more hits to the head in one season. Although it would be hard to document a precise number, the number of hits per season is clearly not a trivial number, especially when one considers the intensity of some of these blows. The plaintiffs then attempt to turn seemingly positive actions by the NHL against the league. One such action was the requiring of helmets starting in 1979 and a so-called "Concussion Program" to research and study brain injuries.

According to the plaintiffs, the NHL, with these acts, assumed a duty, consistent with virtue and care ethics, as a guardian against head trauma in players. They further claim that this duty was not carried out by the NHL because helmets do not protect against concussions and because the Concussion Program was a fraud, taking seven years to complete, another seven years to issue, and concluding only that more research was needed.

The conclusion of the Concussion Program was unacceptable, according to the plaintiffs. It ignored the bulk of the scientific work that had been done (some of which is cited above) concerning the dangers of concussions and the medical protocols (some of which are also cited above), concerning how to treat concussed players.

The plaintiffs seek to hold the NHL responsible for this knowledge but excuse themselves from knowing it. They allege, in order to make this claim consistent with universalizability, that players are generally not well educated and are trained to do unquestioningly what their coaches and other authorities tell them, so that they, consistent with care ethics, should not be expected to know the medical history and details about concussions. One of the players, an enforcer named Randy Poeschek, gives a quote in the Complaint on this subject that many players echo: "I did what I had to do to get into the league. But you're oblivious. You're young. You don't think you're going to have these issues. Nobody tells you" (Waldron, 2015).

In addition to the concussion dangers inherent in hockey plays, the plaintiffs allege that the fighting allowed in the NHL poses significant concussion danger. The complaint lists literally hundreds of fights engaged in by the so-called enforcers. The complaint also describes the tragic deaths of some enforcers, who were posthumously diagnosed with CTE. These include Rick Rypien and Wade Belak, who apparently committed suicide.

A lawsuit filed by the relatives of another enforcer, Derek Boogaard, who died at age 28 from a pill overdose and who was posthumously diagnosed with the serious brain disease CTE, has been allowed to move forward by a federal judge in Illinois. The lawsuit claims that "the NHL promoted violence and implied that head trauma was not dangerous" (Zagger, 2016). The NHL claimed that the suit should be dismissed because these subjects were covered by the collective bargaining agreement between the NHL and the NHL Players Association. The lawsuit therefore belonged in arbitration rather than in court. The court rejected that argument.

Nonetheless, fighting continues to be permitted in the NHL. The Commissioner of the NHL has stated publicly that there are no plans to stop fighting:

> I don't think it's sensible right now to have a debate . . . that's very emotional on both sides. If there comes a point here that's on the table and that enough people feel needs to be changed, then it'll get considered. But according to the last poll I saw from the players, something like 98 percent of the players like it the way it is. And if you're going to make a change, you need consensus.
>
> (Proteau, 2013)

Fighting, of course, is not necessary to the game of hockey, nor is it consistent with virtue ethics and care ethics. It is not permitted in the NCAA nor in the Olympics, and seldom occurs in the NHL playoffs. Ken Dryden, who is in the NHL Hall of Fame as a goalie and was later a member of the Canadian Parliament, is quoted in the Complaint against the NHL as follows: "The model of an NHL without fighting is right there in front of us . . . the playoffs . . . enforcers don't play [because] teams and coaches can't afford anything stupid and unpredictable" (id.).

Reports of medical findings have also shown chronic brain injuries in current NHL players. Dr. Paul Echlin, a sports concussion specialist, who reported the findings from research done by Harvard Medical School and Western University of Canada, was quoted in *The New York Times* as follows:

> We've seen evidence of chronic injuries later in life from head trauma, and now we've seen this in current players . . . How many more studies do we need before we realize significant changes are needed in the way we play the game?
>
> (Klein, 2014)

Compared to football, the problem in the NHL is much more serious because the NHL regular season is five times longer than the football season, 82 games versus 16 games. The NFL's own studies show that almost one-third of retired players will develop long-term cognitive problems and that these problems will occur at a much younger age than in the general population (Belson, 2014). Given the extra 66 games the NHL plays, the problem is likely greater than it is in the NFL.

It is reasonable, therefore, to expect that hockey's longer season will produce more long-term cognitive problems than the NFL and, therefore, that there will be a hockey settlement along the lines of the NFL settlement. The expense of these settlements sends a strong message to all sports administrators, consistent with care ethics, deontology, and virtue ethics, to be proactive about concussions in order to protect the players from their strong desire to compete when it is medically indicated that they should be following a concussion protocol.

Soccer

Soccer also has a problem with concussions, but it has not yet been thoroughly addressed. Unlike the NFL and the NHL, soccer's highest body, FIFA, has taken only limited action to prevent and treat concussions. Indeed, restrictive rules about substitution often require a concussed player to stay in the game for some period after the injury. FIFA rules allow only three substitutions per game, which makes coaches reluctant to use these substitutions for head injuries.

This situation happened with a member of the German team in the 2014 Men's World Cup. Midfielder Christoph Kramer played for an additional 14 minutes after being hit on the left side of his head. Clearly, he was injured, as he asked Italian referee Nicola Rizzoli: "Is this really the World Cup final?" As a result of Kramer's injury, FIFA did agree to introduce guidelines, consistent with care ethics, developed by the Forum on Concussion in Sport and Physical Education (Cross, 2015).

CONCUSSIONS IN YOUTH SPORT

Pre-adolescent children have particular characteristics that make concussions more likely to occur and more likely to be serious. First, the size of a child's head is much greater in proportion to the child's neck than is the case with adults. This creates a "bobblehead" effect with more movement of the brain within the skull. This effect lessens as the child becomes an adolescent (Cantu, 2012).

Second, adults develop a substance in their brain called myelin, an insulating sheath around many nerve fibers, which helps to protect from concussions. Pre-adolescent children have much less myelin than adults, and their nerve fibers can be torn apart more easily (id.).

Third, children are also much less likely to recognize a concussion than an adult. They are also much less likely to request help, such as being taken out of a game. Children may blindly follow the instruction of a coach to head the ball even when such an instruction is not in the best interests of the child. Children are legally incapable of giving informed consent to facing the concussion risks that come with all contact sports. Fortunately, increased awareness of concussion risks in professional sport has carried over to youth sport, especially the contact sports of football and soccer.

Youth football

Once the NFL changed its position on concussions lower levels of football—college, high school, and youth—began taking this problem more seriously. Now, at all levels, there is a greater consciousness of the problem, although the lower levels of football do not have the resources that the NFL has, such as having a neurologist on duty at games.

Regardless of the level of resources, the question arises about whether, considering care ethics, tackle football can be safe for a 5-year-old, which is the minimum age at which a child is allowed to participate in the well-known Pop Warner football program. Indeed, Pop Warner football has had to pay out substantial sums of money in a youth concussion litigation that resulted in permanent injury.

At the youth sport level in particular, legislation is playing an important role in lessening concussions. In 2009, the state of Washington, for example, passed the Zackery Lystedt Law, also known as the "shake-it-off law," which requires, consistent with care ethics and utilitarianism, non-profit organizations utilizing school facilities and school districts to implement policies regarding concussion management. This law requires that any young athletes suspected of sustaining a concussion be examined and cleared by a licensed healthcare provider before resuming practice or play. The law was named after a 13-year-old boy who, when playing junior high football, sustained an obvious head injury in the first half of a game. Nonetheless, the boy shook it off and kept playing in the second half, after which he collapsed on the field.

He then endured many medical procedures, was in a coma for three months and was not able to stand for three years. His father eloquently critiqued the "warrior mentality" that is prevalent in contact sports, even youth sports:

> Sometimes players and parents wrongly believe that it shows strength and courage to play injured. Battling pain is glamorized. Zack couldn't swallow or hold his head up [after collapsing]. Strength is seeing Zack stand up out of his wheelchair and learning to walk again.
>
> (Centers for Disease Control and Prevention, 2014)

All 50 states and the District of Columbia have now enacted laws protecting youth from concussions, most modeled on the Lystedt Law. Concussion protocols at the high-school level have included such requirements as having:

- coaches sign a statement that they have received instruction on the nature and risk of head injuries;
- parents review and sign an annual concussion and head injury information sheet before their children can play football; and
- youth athletes sign an annual concussion information sheet encouraging them to report suspected head injuries for themselves or for a teammate.

On the other hand, in Canada, as of mid-2016, only one province, Ontario, had a law relating to youth concussions: Rowan's Law, which is named after a 17-year-old rugby player named Rowan Stringer, who died after she suffered two sports concussions within a week.

Second concussions are particularly dangerous, and often fatal, if they occur before the first concussion has healed. This is a condition known as Second Impact Syndrome. A Canadian neurosurgeon was quoted as follows:

> Would knowledge of concussions have prevented her death? I think there's a good chance it would have, if she had been clued in. . . . One of her texts indicated that she had Googled 'concussion.' But she didn't read enough, or it didn't sink in enough, to prevent her from playing in that final game that took her life.
>
> (Hall, 2015)

After Rowan Stringer's death, Canada's Minister of Sport and Persons with Disabilities, Carla Qualtrough, began advocating for youth concussion laws everywhere in Canada, not just in Ontario. She was quoted as follows:

> You think of the scenario where your team has made finals and your star player was concussed two weeks ago. He seems fine. The coach wants him in, the parents want him in, the athletes want him in, and he wants to be in. . . . You need a protocol or a process that protects that athlete from all that external pressure. If he sprained his ankle instead of his brain, he wouldn't be on the field.
>
> (id.)

Youth soccer

Although many parents have preferred to have their children play soccer rather than football on the grounds that they believe soccer is safer, this assumption is not necessarily true. As mentioned earlier, many concussions occur in soccer, in particular from heading the ball or from collisions. This is particularly a problem because soccer is by far the world's most popular sport, with literally millions of youth players. Unless FIFA and soccer organizations at lower levels take action similar to that taken in football, these young players are at risk. As stated above, youth players are particularly vulnerable because their bodies do not have the protection of an adult body and they are unable, contrary to care ethics utilitarian and deontology, to give informed consent to the risk they are being asked to take.

According to world-class players like Brandi Chastain of the first U.S. team that won the Women's World Cup in soccer, rules that limit heading the ball would not impede the development of soccer skills. On the website safersoccer.org, she states:

> As a parent, I won't allow my children to head the ball before high school, and as a coach I would prefer my players had focused solely on foot skills as they develop their love of the game. I believe this change will create better and safer soccer.

Again, a lawsuit, not leadership, has created positive change for youth soccer in the United States. In 2014, because—contrary to care ethics, deontology, and utilitarianism—there had been no recognition by soccer organizations of the scientifically documented dangers from heading in soccer to the brains of children under 14, a proposed class action lawsuit was brought by several minors and their parents against FIFA; the United States Soccer Federation, Inc.; U.S. Youth Soccer Association, Inc.; American Youth Soccer Organization; National Association of Competitive Soccer Clubs, Inc. DBA U.S. Club Soccer; and California Youth Soccer Association. Initially the lawsuit was dismissed on technical grounds.

In 2015, however, the United States Soccer Federation, which controls U.S. soccer youth national teams and academies, including Major League Soccer youth club teams, settled the case. The settlement provides much more regulation than previously existed regarding heading the ball for children under the age of 14.

Under the new rules, players under the age of 10 will not be allowed to head the ball, and players 11 to 13 years old will be allowed only limited heading in practice. This is a substantial improvement over the current situation, in which players as young as 6 years have been allowed to head the ball. Therefore, fewer injuries will occur, and insurance costs should eventually decrease as a result.

The significance of this settlement is that it affects millions of youth players in the United States. According to the Center for Injury Research and Policy in Columbus, Ohio, in 2010 female soccer players suffered 25,953 concussions and male players 20,247. It is estimated that one-third of these concussions were caused by heading. Concussions can lead to extensive school absences, memory problems, headaches and social isolation (Cantu, 2012).

The settlement, however, has not been met with universal acclaim. For example, the sports editor of a small Louisiana newspaper, who also coaches a youth team, spoke for advocates of cultural relativism when he editorialized as follows:

> The U.S. Soccer Federation needs to do one of two things. It needs to either ban headers from the game forever or it needs to suck it up, accept that injuries sometimes happen in sports and let the rules of the game be the same—just as it's been for the past 150 years. Sometime here in the near future, we have to understand and realize that bad things can happen to people in sporting activities. It's part of the risk that is involved with calling oneself an athlete.
>
> (Gisclair, 2015)

A more scientific argument for traditionalists appeared in an op-ed article in *The New York Times*, written by a pediatric neurologist advocating moral subjectivism. The article claims that the definition of concussions has become too broad: "We've gotten into this [concussion] 'crisis' in part because a concussion has acquired a looser definition over the years" (Rothman, 2015). According to this pediatric neurologist, the result of the broadened definition is that many young people ("who are exposed to far less concussion danger than professional athletes because young people play less and play against smaller, slower competitors") – are kept out of competitive sports:

> There is a way to exercise such caution without exaggerating the scope of concussions. The American Academy of Pediatrics and the American Academy of Neurology should redefine mild head trauma that produces only headaches as a 'noncussion.' The definition should emphasize that symptoms go away within seven to 10 days, and children should withdraw from full play for at least two weeks. If the athlete, family and coaches all agree that the child has fully recovered, it would not be necessary to consult a pediatrician or neurologist.
>
> (Rothman, 2015)

On the other hand, a recent alarming Mayo Clinic study, published in the December, 2015 issue of the peer-reviewed journal *Acta Neuropathologica*, found that approximately one-third of males who had participated in amateur contact sports suffered from a significant amount of CTE. Of 1,721 cases in the Mayo Clinic Brain Bank, there were 66 males who had documented participation in youth contact sports like football, boxing, wrestling, and rugby. Of those, 32 percent had CTE pathology, compared with zero in the 198 brains without documentation of participation in contact sports (Punksy, 2015).

The head of this study, realizing its potential implications, was quoted as follows:

> The purpose of our study is not to discourage children and adults from participating in sports because we believe the mental and physical health benefits are great. It is vital that people use caution when it comes to protecting the head. Through CTE awareness, greater emphasis will be placed on making contact sports safer, with better protective equipment and fewer head-to-head contacts.
>
> (id.)

OVERUSE INJURY AND BURNOUT

Overuse

Overuse injuries and burnout are subtler ethical problems than concussions, which, as described above, have been through the crucible of litigation in recent times. Overuse injury and burnout have not been susceptible to litigation; the ethics in these situations therefore remain less developed.

Overuse and burnout became more apparent when youth sport moved from a participation model to a more professional model. In the not too distant past, youth sport focused on the participation of all. Many baseball little leagues, for example, had rules requiring the participation of all players for a minimum number of innings.

In high schools, top athletes often participated in a different sport each season, usually football in the fall, basketball in the winter, and baseball in the spring. These so-called three-letter athletes not only were respected for their ability, but also benefited from the fact that these different sports involve different parts of the body. Therefore, no one body part was being stressed on a year-round basis.

The situation has now dramatically changed, probably because parents often have unrealistic expectations about the prospects of their children for athletic scholarships to college and even for a lucrative professional sports career. These expectations are often encouraged by coaches of so-called elite youth travelling teams, which cost parents thousands of dollars per year in the hope that this constant travel to play other elite teams will improve the skills of their child. What often results instead—inconsistent with care ethics and utilitarianism—are stress injuries from overuse.

It is also not surprising that, in addition, the continual strain on the same body parts from playing one sport year-round (making the seasons longer than any professional sport season), the pressure from parents who invest thousands of dollars per year in their athletic children and from coaches who financially benefit from receiving this money combine to cause burnout in many young athletes. The athletes often respond to this pressure by dropping out of the particular sport and out of sport in general, thereby losing benefits such as exercise, teamwork, persistence, and sportsmanship.

The medical definition of overuse injury is straightforward. A position statement of the American Medical Society for Sports Medicine (AMSSM) defines overuse as occurring "due to repetitive submaximal loading of the musculoskeletal system when rest is not adequate to allow for structural adaptation to take place," i.e. continual use of trauma-tized muscles, tendons, bones, and the like without giving them time to heal (DiFiori et al., 2014).

Burnout

Burnout is defined as occurring "as a result of chronic stress that causes a young athlete to cease participation in a previously enjoyable activity." Burnout has also been called "overtraining syndrome," which may manifest in "chronic muscle or joint pain, personality changes, elevated resting heart rate . . . decreased sports performance . . . fatigue, lack of enthusiasm about practice or competition, or difficulty with successfully completing usual routines" (Brenner, 2007).

The exposure and rewards at the top for youth sport have become much greater in recent years. A well-known example of this trend is the televising of the Little League World Series on ESPN. Recently, one of the participants, Mo'ne Davis, a girl who success-fully competed with the boys, became a national celebrity, with her picture on the August 25, 2014 cover of *Sports Illustrated* and appearances on national television shows and in professional competitions.

Although such extraordinary benefits go to only a few children, the adults responsible for those children often go to great lengths for the slim chance of gaining such benefits. The result is not only the overuse injuries and burnout discussed in this chapter, but also cheating scandals, including the illegal use of performance-enhancing drugs. Moreover, such conduct toward children raises issues concerning deontology, care ethics, and utilitarianism.

The amount of overuse injury and burnout is substantial and growing. The AMSSM estimates that "3.5 million children are injured annually playing sports or participating in recreational activities" and that 45.9 to 54 percent of these are overuse injuries (DiFiori et al., 2014). This data indicate that over 1.5 million overuse injuries occur every year. These numbers are particularly alarming, the report notes, because such injuries, on one hand, are under-reported and, on the other hand, are increasing.

Regarding burnout, precise figures are not possible because burnout is not easily identified. A proxy for such figures, however, is the dropout rate from sports. That rate has been reported by organizations such as Safe for Kids to be as much as 70 percent by age 13 (Feldman, 2015). It is notable that that figure is not just for dropping out of one sport, but rather dropping out of sports altogether. As one commentator notes: "That number is simply staggering, and we need to do something about it" (DiFiori et al., 2014).

Although many parents, contrary to care ethics, are motivated to invest in youth sports by a possible college scholarship or professional sports career for their children, the odds are heavily stacked against those benefits. One of the most graphic depictions of these low odds appears on the website of the NCAA. It goes over a number of sports (some of the more popular of which include football, baseball, men's/women's basketball, hockey, and soccer) and gives the daunting shrinkage of numbers from high school to college to the professional ranks.

Each section of the NCAA website is prefaced by the same language: "When we survey NCAA student-athletes about their expectations of moving on to professional athletics careers, the results indicate surprising confidence in that possibility. The reality is that very few go pro."

The website gives detailed statistics, starting with the number of high school students who get scholarships to Division I NCAA schools. For football, for example, there are approximately 1 million high school participants, 2.5 percent of whom compete in Division I college football.

The numbers of college sports participants who are drafted into the professional leagues is, not surprisingly, even smaller. The NFL draft, for example, has approximately 250 slots, which can accommodate 1.6 percent of the participants in NCAA football. Because, as noted above, only 2.5 percent of high school football players participate in Division I NCAA football, taking 1.6 percent of that number, only a miniscule percent of high school football players will get drafted into the NFL, a percentage which would be reduced if we considered as the denominator lower levels of youth football like Pop Warner. The percentage goes even lower when one considers that not every player who is drafted in the NFL ends up playing on a team, and, of those that do, the average career length is 3.5 years.

The numbers work out similarly for every sport. Rationally speaking, it would be more economic to take the money invested in youth travel sports, which amounts to thousands of dollars per year, and invest it in a college fund. In that way there would be a certain return on the investment rather than the low-percentage chance of getting an athletic scholarship.

The costs for youth sports travel teams are not trivial. One cost, of course, is for the coach. Generally, they are paid for their time, which can amount to payments in the four-figure range per player (Butler, 2011). This cost also can, contrary to virtue ethics and deontology, create conflicts of interest because the coach financially benefits from the willingness of the parents to keep making these payments. Such a conflict could cause a coach to overrate the chances of an athlete to get an athletic scholarship, which, as described above, are low.

Then there are substantial youth sports travel costs, including transportation and lodging. That, of course, includes transportation and lodging for the coaching staff. Often children are sent to specialized summer sports camps. These can cost from hundreds to thousands of dollars.

Some of these camps are highly specialized, with track records of producing professional athletes. Some are more than camps; they are academies with months- or years-long programs, which include sports psychologists and chefs on staff. For example, a golfing academy in Fort Worth, Texas, provides a nine-month program and costs approximately $40,000 for commuters and $60,000 for residents (Smith, 2014).

Emotional and psychological costs are, of course, imprecise, but they clearly exist. Investing thousands of dollars in a youth athlete, for example, can put financial pressure on a family. This financial pressure may, in turn, cause the parents to put more pressure to perform on the youth athletes, or the youth athletes may simply put that pressure on themselves because they know the financial pressure they are putting on their parents.

The parents may also suffer from so-called "achievement by proxy" syndrome, in which, contrary to care ethics, the child becomes an instrument of an adult's goals, despite what is beneficial for the child (Tofler & DiGeronimo, 2000; Reed, 2015). This syndrome can start with simple pride in the accomplishments of one's child, but can then progress to increasing investment, involvement, and control.

The problems may also spread to non-athletic siblings of the young athlete. These non-athletes may be deprived of family resources (including parental time). Or they may be forced to spend time travelling with the family to athletic events about which they are, at best, indifferent.

Much of this intensive training for youth on travel teams may result from the common belief that 10,000 hours of practice are needed to perfect a skill (Gladwell, 2008). In fact, this widely held belief, which, of course, is irrelevant if sports are played just for fun, has been challenged: "I can appreciate the value of the deliberate practice framework . . . popularized by Gladwell. . . . But equally, the realization that certain individuals have innate abilities that will help them achieve elite levels is crucial." In other words, "In high performance sport, there is no such thing as alchemy—you do not make gold out of other metals. If you want to produce a champion, a gold medal, then you must start out with the right raw materials" (Tucker, 2011).

Contrary to the emphasis on intensive training in one sport, studies indicate that sport diversification, consistent with virtue ethics, leads to more athletic success than does sport specialization. In August 2015 the NFL, MLB, the NHL, the NCAA, the U.S. Olympic Committee and three dozen other leading sports organizations placed an advertisement in a prominent sports publication advocating against early, single-sport specialization. The virtue ethics message in the advertisement was loud and clear: "EARLY SPECIALIZATION DOES MORE HARM THAN GOOD" and "MULTI-SPORT PARTICIPATION CAN LEAD TO BETTER PERFORMANCE, LESS BURNOUT, LESS SOCIAL ISOLATION, AND, MOST IMPORTANTLY, MORE LIFELONG ENJOYMENT IN SPORTS" (Wallace, 2015).

The scientific studies supporting this position include a survey of 708 minor league baseball players on when they started to specialize. Only 25 percent specialized before 12 years of age, and 15 was the mean age of specialization. Significantly, those who specialized later were more likely to have received a college scholarship (Ginsburg et al., 2014). Similarly, a UCLA study of 296 NCAA Division I athletes reported that 88 percent participated in two or three sports as children, and 70 percent did not specialize in one sport until after they were 12 (American Medical Society for Sports Medicine, 2013).

Sports managers, athletes, athletes and parents should seriously consider the following medical recommendations, consistent with care ethics, designed to avoid and/or alleviate overuse injury and burnout (Brenner, 2007; DiFiori et al., 2014). These include the following:

- take one to two days off a week to recover physically and psychologically;
- do not increase training regimes by more than 10 percent per week;
- take at least two to three months per year away from the sport;
- emphasize fun, skill acquisition and sportsmanship;
- participate in only one team per season;
- alert the athlete to symptoms of burnout like fatigue and lack of motivation;
- educate athletes, parents and coaches about the dangers of overuse.

CONCLUSION

There are numerous costs to society from concussions, burnout and overuse. Obviously, contrary to utilitarianism, injured people need medical care and become less productive in the short run and, in some cases, in the long run. Most of these expenses have been borne by the individual, by insurance companies, or—for those who are uninsured and unable to pay—by society. As noted above, the legal doctrine that dictated this result is called "assumption of the risk."

Now, however, with greater knowledge of the risks of these problems, the law is beginning, consistent with care ethics and utilitarianism, to impose duties on sporting organizations. This is especially true with organizations like the NFL, which denied the effects of concussions at a time when such knowledge was available.

Sporting organizations now have to act as a reasonable person would act under these circumstances. Although, as is clear from the descriptions of litigation above, the law is not fully settled yet, it appears that such reasonableness would include—consistent with care ethics, deontology, and utilitarianism—appropriate warnings about concussions and meaningful concussion protocols governing when a player can resume play.

Care ethics requires administrators, coaches, parents and players to recognize these dangers, educate players about them and make sure that procedures are in place to protect children, in particular, who do not have the knowledge and experience to protect themselves. In a December 17, 2015 op-ed article in *The New York Times*, Dr. Bennet Omalu, the hero of the movie *Concussion*, stated a very universalizable proposition:

> Our children are minors who have not reached the age of consent. It is our moral duty as a society to protect the most vulnerable of us. The human brain becomes fully developed at about 18 to 25 years old. We should at least wait for our children to grow up, be provided with the information and education on the risk of play, and let them make their own decisions. No adult, not a parent or a coach, should be allowed to make this potentially life-altering decision for a child.

On the subject of the early specialization in sport that can lead to overuse injury and burnout, hockey great Wayne Gretzky said: "One of the worst things to happen to the game [of hockey], in my opinion, has been year-round hockey and, in particular, summer hockey. All it does for kids, as far as I can tell, is keep them out of sports they should be doing in the warmer weather" (Feldman, 2015). In other words, care ethics, deontology and utilitarianism require that adult-type sports pressures not be imposed on children.

ETHICAL LEADERSHIP CASE STUDIES

Case study #1

Knute is the football coach at Champion High, which is a perennial football powerhouse, having won the state championship the last three years in a row. This year Champion is in the finals again, led by its running back, Gipper. By half-time, when Champion is leading by three points, Gipper complains to Knute that he has a headache and some dizziness. Although Gipper had sustained some hard tackles in the first half, he had never lost consciousness nor had he asked to come out of the game.

1. Do any ethical theories require Knute to seek a medical opinion? Does it matter to your answer whether a doctor is on duty at the game or not?
2. Ethically, is Knute required to give information about this situation to Gipper's parents, who are in the stands watching the game? Same question, but assume that Gipper's parents are not at the game.
3. Would or should it make any ethical difference if this were a regular season game against the weakest team in the league rather than the championship game?
4. Would or should it make any ethical difference if Gipper insisted that Knute keep this confidential? If Gipper insisted that he go back into the game?
5. How would you assess the leadership of the NFL, FIFA and the NHL on the issue of concussions?

Case study #2

Gogetter is the coach of a youth travelling baseball team. He is recruiting Berra, a talented 10-year-old catcher, for the team, which practices and plays games year-round. When Gogetter is discussing the team with Berra's parents, they express concerns about the repetitive stress on Berra's legs from catching year-round.

1. Ethically, how should Gogetter respond to the concerns of Berra's parents?
2. What ethical responsibility, if any, does Gogetter have to learn about the repetitive stress issues of a 10-year-old being a baseball catcher year-round?
3. What should Gogetter ethically suggest to ameliorate the concerns of Berra's parents?
4. Does the fact that Gogetter gets paid $10,000 per year to coach the team create a conflict of interest? How, if at all, can that conflict be ethically avoided?
5. Formulate a national leadership campaign on the issue of repetitive stress injuries in youth sports.

Case study #3

Berra from Case study #2 above persists playing year-round and becomes the top-rated college catching prospect in the U.S. He has, however, started feeling a constant dull pain in his thighs, and has become uncharacteristically irritable, plus he is not sleeping well at night.

1. What, if anything, is ethically required for Berra's coach to do or to suggest?
2. His parents?
3. His doctor?
4. How would the coach exercise effective leadership on this issue for the rest of the team?

STUDENT LEARNING EXERCISE

Prepare an essay about a concussion or concussions that you have sustained (or if you have not sustained one, a concussion or concussions of which you have knowledge). The essay should describe how the concussion occurred, your or the individual's reaction to it, the short-term and long-term effects, and the reactions of others: coaches, parents, doctors, teammates. Be prepared to discuss the ethical implications of the above and how ethical leadership could have played a role in preventing the concussion.

PROBLEMS/QUESTIONS

1. Ethically, to whom do doctors for the football team owe their loyalty: the team, the player, or the player's parents?
2. If a coach suspects that a player is downplaying or denying a concussion, can the coach ethically let the player go back in the game? Does it matter how important the game is?
3. What, if anything, is ethically owed by teams or leagues to players who sustained injuries before the dangers of concussions were known as well as they have been known since 2009?
4. If the dangers of concussions from contact sports are not yet fully known, what are the ethical arguments for and against continuing to allow those sports to be played?
5. To what extent is a "warrior mentality" of helping the team regardless of injury ethically helpful and when does it become ethically harmful? How should ethical leadership address the "warrior mentality?"
6. Ethically, what should be the penalty for contact with the head in baseball, football, basketball, soccer, and hockey?
7. What ethical effect, if any, should the scientific evidence that blows to the head are more harmful to children under 14 have on youth football, youth hockey, youth soccer?

BIBLIOGRAPHY

Abolish Football, Says Harvard Bulletin, *The New York Times*, October 18, 1905.
American Medical Society for Sports Medicine, *News Release*, April 23, 2013.
Balthazor v. Little League Baseball, 62 Cal. App. 4th 47 (1998).
Barr, Carol, History of Faculty Involvement In Collegiate Athletics, NCAA, 2012.
Belson, Ken, Brain trauma to affect one in three players, NFL agrees. *The New York Times*, September 12, 2014.

Bernstein, Amy, Into the Red Zone: How the National Football League's Quest to Curb Concussions and Concussion-Related Injuries Could Affect Players' Legal Recovery, 22 *Seton Hall Journal of Sports & Entertainment Law* 271 (2012).

Brenner, Joel, Overuse Injuries, Overtraining and Burnout in Child and Adolescent Athletes, 119 *Pediatrics* 1242 (2007).

Butler, Sarah, $4000 for youth baseball: Kids' Sports Costs Are Out of Control. *CBS Money Watch*, April 29, 2011.

Cantu, Robert, Guidelines for Return to Contact Sports after a Cerebral Concussion. 14 *The Physician and Sports Medicine* 75 (1986).

Cantu, Robert & Hyman, Mark, Concussions and Our Kids: America's Leading Expert on How to Protect Young Athletes and Keep Sport Safe (2012).

Casson, Ira, Do the "Facts" Really Support an Association between NFL Players'Concussions, Dementia and Depression? 10 *Neurology Today* 6 (2010).

Centers for Disease Control and Prevention, Heads Up, Brain Injury Prevention, www.cdc.gov/headsup/ basics/concussion_whatis.html (accessed May 24, 2017).

Centers for Disease Control and Prevention, The Lystedt Law: A Concussion Survivor's Journey (2014).

Cerra, David, Unringing the Bell: Former Players Sue NFL and Helmet Manufacturers over Concussion Risks in Maxwell v. NFL. 16 *Michigan State University Journal of Medicine and Law* 265 (2011).

Cross, John, Germany's Christoph Kramer Playing FOURTEEN Minutes of World Cup Final after Suffering Concussion Leads to FA Action, *Mirror Online*, June 24, 2015.

Diehl, Erica, What's All the Headache: Reform Needed to Cope with the Effects of Concussions in Football. 23 *Journal of Law and Health* 83 (2010).

DiFiori, John, et al., Overuse injuries and Burnout in Youth Sports: A Position Statement from the American Medical Society for Sports Medicine, 24 *Clinical Journal of Sports Medicine* 3 (2014).

Echlin, Paul, Editorial: A Prospective Study of Physician-observed Concussion during a Varsity University Ice Hockey Season, 33 *Neurosurgical Focus* 1 (2012).

Feldman, Justin, Diversification Prevents Injuries, Develops Skills in Kids. *Poughkeepsie Journal*, September 19, 2015.

Ginsburg, Richard et al., Patterns of Specialization in Baseball Players, 8 *Journal of Clinical Sports Psychology* 261 (2014).

Gisclair, Casey, Header Ban Will Hurt Soccer, *Houma Times*, November 25, 2015.

Gladwell, Malcolm, Outliers: The Story of Success (2008).

Goldberg, Daniel, Mild Traumatic Brain Injury, the National Football League, and the Manufacture of Doubt: An Ethical, Legal, and Historical Analysis 34 *Journal of Legal Medicine* 157 (2013).

Hall, Vicki, Rowan's Law: How the Death of One Teen is Surviving as a Wake-up Call for Canada on Handling Youth Concussions. *National Post*, November 25, 2015.

Hall, Vicki, Federal Government Won't "Drag Our Heels" on Concussion Issue. *Ottawa Sun*, December 3, 2015.

Hecht, Alexander, Legal and Ethical Aspects of Sports-related Concussions: The Merril Hoge Story, 12 *Seton Hall Journal of Sport Law* 17 (2002).

In Re National Hockey Players' Concussion Injury Litigation, MDL No. 142551, Case No. 15-CV-03904-SRN-JSM, United States District Court, District of Minnesota, October 20, 2015.

Keim, Twila, Physicians for Professional Sports Teams: Health Care Under the Pressure of Economic and Commercial Interests, 9 *Seton Hall Journal of Sport Law* 196 (1999).

Klein, Jeff, Study Finds Changes in Brains of Hockey Players Who Had Concussions, *The New York Times*, February 4, 2014.

Koloup, Elisabeth, Get Your Head in the Game: Legislation Addressing Concussions in Youth Sports and its Development in Maryland, 42 *University of Baltimore Law Forum* 207 (2014).

Lipsky, Bryan, Dealing with the NFL's Concussion Problems of Yesterday, Today, and Tomorrow, 18 *Fordham Intellectual Property, Media & Entertainment Law Journal* 959 (2007).

Malliaras, Peter, et al., Current Practices in Determining Return to Play Following Head Injury in Professional Football in the UK, 46 *British Journal of Sports Medicine* 1000 (2012).

Mangels, John, NFL Could Face Thousands of Lawsuits from Ex-players over Brain Damage from Concussions, *The Cleveland Plain Dealer*, May 12, 2012.

Marchie, Anthony & Cusimano, Michael, Bodychecking and Concussions in Ice Hockey: Should Our Youth Pay the Price? 169 *Canadian Medical Association Journal* 124 (2003).

National Federation of High School Associations, Suggested Guidelines for Management of Concussion in Sports, November 21, 2014.

NCAA, Concussion Guidelines (2015).

NCAA.org, Estimated Probability of Competing in Professional Athletics, www.ncaa.org/about/resources/research/estimated-probability-competing-professional-athletics (accessed March 10, 2017).

Partridge, Bradley, Dazed and Confused: Sports Medicine, Conflicts of Interest, and Concussion Management. 11 *Journal of Bioethical Inquiry* 65 (2014).

Pellman, Elliot & Viano, David, Concussion in Professional Football: Summary of the Research Conducted by the National Football League's Committee on Mild Traumatic Brain Injury, 21 *Journal of Neurosurgery* 12 (2006).

The Physical Side of Football, *Harvard Crimson*. January 5, 1906.

Polsky, Scott, Winning Medicine: Professional Sports Team Doctors' Conflicts of Interest, 14 *Journal of Contemporary Health Law & Policy* 503 (1997).

Proteau, Adam, Bettman Won't Rule Out Fighting Ejection for NHL in Future; Also says League Is Doing More for Retired Players, *The Hockey News*, December 8, 2013.

Punsky, Kevin, Evidence Suggests Contact Sports Played by Amateurs Increase Risk of Degenerative Disorder, *Mayo Clinic News Release*, December 2, 2015.

Reed, Ken, Youth Sports Burnout Driven by Achievement by Proxy Syndrome, *Huffington Post*, October 10, 2015.

Rothman, Steven, Parents, Stop Obsessing over Concussions, *The New York Times*, December 22, 2015.

Safer Soccer, Concussion Legacy Foundation, undated, https://concussionfoundation.org/national-initiatives/safer-soccer.

Shuttleworth-Edwards, Ann, et al., Ethically We Can No Longer Sit on the Fence—A Neuropsychological Perspective on the Cerebrally Hazardous Contact Sports, 19 *South African Journal of Sports Medicine* 32 (2009).

Smith, Corbett, Time and Money, *Dallas Morning News*, July 31, 2014

Tofler, Ian & DiGeronimo, Teresa, Keeping Your Kids Out Front Without Kicking Them from Behind: How to Nurture High-Achieving Athletes, Scholars, and Performing Artists, (2000).

Tucker, Ross, Training, Talent, 10,000 Hours and the Genes, *The Science of Sport*, August 11, 2011.

Valerio, Judy et al., Ethical Implications of Neuroimaging in Sports Concussion, 27 *The Journal of Head Trauma Rehabilitation* 216 (2012).

Waldron, Travis, Former NHL Enforcer Says the League is in "Denial" on Concussions, *Huffington Post*, December 15, 2015.

Wallace, Jennifer, Why Kids Shouldn't Specialize in One Sport, *Huffington Post*, August 19, 2015.

Zagger, Zachary, Judge Oks Derek Boogaard Kin's NHL Wrongful Death Suit, *Law360*, September 29, 2016.

CHAPTER 7

Social, legal, and ethical issues of performance enhancement in sport

INTRODUCTION

This chapter addresses issues about artificial enhancement of competitive abilities of athletes, specifically, the problems associated with the use of drugs that are designed and consumed to enhance athletic performance. Professional and amateur sports teams, leagues and international competitions, such as the Olympics, have experienced scandals about competitors' use of performance-enhancing drugs; these scandals have significantly harmed the reputation of all concerned.

Although performance-enhancing drugs are one of the most important topics in sports and sports ethics, there is little controversy about their use. Virtually everyone opposes them on ethical grounds because they undermine the very purpose of sports, which is to find out who is the best competitor on a level playing field. By definition, performance-enhancing drugs tilt the field in a way that helps the drug cheat.

The use of such drugs by professional athletes has materially contributed to the use of them by young athletes, with the result that some youth athletes are harming their health. The use of artificial enhancements in sports raises issues of integrity of competition, unfairness among competitors, and public health and safety.

As the rewards for successful athletic performance increase through prize purses, television coverage, sponsorships, and professional players' contracts, the demand for the latest and best performance enhancement has been growing. Athletes age and, over time, lose their competitiveness, so their resort to artificial enhancements is a common and growing problem in athletics. Further, drawing the line on what exactly is performance enhancement is difficult. As technology and medical innovation develop, it has become increasingly difficult to detect and punish drug cheats.

ISSUES AND PROBLEMS PRESENTED BY ATHLETES' USE OF PROHIBITED PERFORMANCE ENHANCEMENTS

This section of the book considers the effects of taking performance-enhancing, and some non-performance-enhancing, drugs by professional and amateur athletes. It addresses the questions of why athletes risk their health, reputation, and ability to compete by taking banned substances.

The reasons athletes resort to drugs to enhance their performance and remain competitive are varied. Often, however, the resort to illegal substances occurs because such athletes are aging and struggling to compete with younger athletes, because they fear the loss of esteem or financial gain accompanying their status in the sport, or because their competitors are using the performance-enhancing drugs.

The chapter also explores many of the issues facing leagues, teams, and youth coaches as they attempt to maintain the integrity of their sport and the health of their players in a national and international sports culture that encourages success and victory at any cost. This requires a consideration of the regulatory framework that has been created to prevent use of such substances. Given the prevalence of detected instances of illegal drug use by athletes, is the current regulatory apparatus—both nationally and internationally—sufficient or should more stringent enforcement regimes be implemented? If so, what agencies or organizations should be expected to create new enforcement mechanisms?

A PRIMER ON PERFORMANCE-ENHANCING SUBSTANCES

This section introduces the principal types and forms of performance-enhancing drugs, how they are used by athletes to enhance their competitive performance, and the associated health effects of the use of the substances. It will make clear that performance-enhancing drugs have more dissimilarities than similarities, and that their ability to affect performance depends on the demands of the sport.

Types and forms of performance-enhancing drugs

There are several types of performance-enhancing drugs and substances that are used by athletes expressly for the purpose of advancing their on-the-field performance or ability to compete better than their best. The substances include banned and illegal drugs, drugs that have a therapeutic and permitted purpose but are only prescribed by a physician, and substances that are sold "over the counter" and can add marginal benefit to an athlete's ability to compete.

Some athletes take forms of steroids, known as anabolic-androgen steroids, to increase their muscle mass and strength. These steroids attempt to duplicate the benefits of testosterone, a hormone produced naturally by the body. The anabolic effect of testosterone is to promote muscle building and the androgenic effect is to develop male traits such as hair growth and a deeper voice.

There are a variety of approved medical uses of synthetic forms of testosterone for both men and women. However, simply taking the drug for athletic performance enhancement is not an approved medical reason.

Androstenedione (andro) is a hormone produced by the human adrenal glands, ovaries, and testes and it normally converts to testosterone and estradiol in both men and women.

It is available for legal use only by prescription and in a medically determined form and dosages. It is a controlled substance under most countries' laws.

Andro has been promoted widely by drug manufacturers and bodybuilding magazines as a substance that will allow athletes to train harder and recover more quickly. According to the Mayo Clinic, scientific studies refute these claims and conclude that taking supplemental androstenedione does not increase testosterone and aid in enabling athletes to get stronger, quicker (Mayo Clinic Staff, 2004a).

A human growth hormone known at gonadotropin has a steroid-like effect and it has been taken by athletes who desire to improve muscle mass and performance. However, there are no definitive studies that demonstrate that taking gonadotropin substances will have that effect. It is a controlled substance and can be obtained only with a physician's prescription.

Some athletes, especially competitive cyclists and other endurance sport athletes, have taken epoetin, a synthetic form of erythropoietin to boost their performance and stamina. Erythropoietin (EPO) is a hormone that is used to treat anemia in people with severe kidney disease and it increases production of red blood cells and hemoglobin, which results in improved movement of oxygen to the muscles.

The injection of EPO or synthetic oxygen carriers or their introduction through blood transfusions by athletes is referred to as "blood doping." Synthetic oxygen carriers are chemicals that have the ability to carry oxygen to the body. They have some appropriate uses—for example, in emergency medical situations—but are banned if used to boost athletic performance. All blood-doping substances and techniques are banned by the World Anti-Doping Agency (WADA) and other anti-doping agencies and organizations.

Diuretics—drugs that change the body's natural balance of fluids and salts—have been used by athletes to induce dehydration to "make weight." Some diuretics have the effect of diluting the user's urine and are used by unscrupulous athletes to mask the presence of illegal substances in their urine and permit them to pass a drug test.

Many competitive athletes take nutritional supplements to recover from hard workouts and rebuild muscle mass. These substances can be purchased over the counter and are unregulated in many sports. The most common type of supplement used by athletes is creatine, which also is a naturally occurring compound that helps muscles release energy.

Finally, some athletes use stimulants to stimulate their central nervous systems and increase heart rate and blood pressure in order to enhance their performance levels, reduce fatigue, suppress appetite, and increase their awareness and aggressiveness. The major forms of stimulants are caffeine and amphetamines. Amphetamines, such as ephedrine and pseudoemhedrine hydrochloride, are often found in cold medicines.

The foregoing summary of the major types of performance-enhancing drugs is not exhaustive. Moreover, the list of banned substances is subject to great volatility, with new performance-enhancing drugs and techniques coming out for athletes' use with great frequency.

Health risks of performance-enhancing drugs

Nearly all the substances taken by athletes to enhance their performance have side effects and present potential health-related problems. These potential and actual health problems are the chief costs of the use of performance-enhancing substances by athletes.

The following list describes some of the principal costs, especially health risks, of particular types of performance-enhancing drugs:

- Steroids, especially the so-called "designer steroids," can result in physical side effects (in men: growth of breasts, infertility, shrunken testes and impotence; in women: increased body hair, baldness, infrequent or absent menstrual periods). Steroids have also been found to contribute to depression, aggressive behavior, liver abnormalities and tumors, and, in younger users, inhibition of growth and development, leading to greater health problems in the future.
- Use of growth hormones such as gonadotrophin can induce a variety of adverse effects including heart problems, high blood pressure, diabetes, vision problems and carpal tunnel syndrome.
- Use of erythropoietin among competitive cyclists allegedly contributed to the deaths of 18 athletes in the 1990s and has been linked to heart attacks, strokes and pulmonary embolisms.
- Athletes who use diuretics, even in medically indicated levels, are predisposed to gout, dehydration, dizziness, blood pressure problems and rashes.
- Possible side effects of creatine include stomach cramps, muscle cramps and weight gain; high-dose creatine use has been linked to damage to kidneys and liver functions.
- The effects of the use of stimulants are well documented because of their use in the drug culture as well as in the sports culture. Commonly seen effects are heart problems (rhythm abnormalities and palpitations), tremors, weight loss, high blood pressure, strokes, hallucinations, and anger outbursts. Many stimulants are addictive to frequent users.

It is important to remember that the chief public health danger with most of these performance-enhancing drugs is that they are not regulated by a medical authority and are often manufactured by illegal sources. For example, the so-called "designer steroids" are manufactured by individuals who may, or may not, have any medical or technical competence, have never been tested for safety aspects (e.g. purity, toxicity, unintended side effects like conflicts with other drugs taken by the user), and are being sold illegally by individuals who are violating criminal laws.

Further, some substances like nutritional supplements, are not classified as drugs so they are not regulated or monitored by the Food and Drug Administration. Their manufacturers are not required to adhere to the same standards of production and sale as regulated drugs, so it is possible for the supplement to have contaminants in the dosages, which, in some instances, has led to an athlete's positive test for performance-enhancing drugs.

The use of performance-enhancing drugs by young athletes is a matter of special significance and concern. The Mayo Clinic reports that one in 20 teenagers reported taking steroids to increase muscle mass for the purposes of improving appearance (such as by bodybuilding regimes), to make a team, or to become more competitive in a sport (Mayo Clinic Staff, 2004b).

The adverse side effects of steroid use (and other performance enhancements) can be more severe in young athletes than in adult athletes. There are campaigns to better educate parents and coaches of the prevalence of this drug use among teenage athletes.

HOW ATHLETES' USE OF PERFORMANCE-ENHANCING DRUGS HARMS THE SPORT

In the 1990s and early 2000s, United States' sports fans were transfixed with the spectacle of criminal indictments of great professional sports figures for performance-drug-related offenses, subpoenaed testimony in Congress about their drug use while playing a professional sports and repeated public confessions by athletes about their "cheating" the sport and their fans by their use of performance-enhancing drugs. Some of professional baseball's most notable figures of that time—Mark McGwire, Barry Bonds, Keith Hernandez, and others—were interrogated and, in some instances, charged criminally with illegal drug use.

One star athlete, Roger Clemens, was indicted for lying to a Congressional committee examining steroid use in professional baseball. This public exposure of drug use while playing a professional sport and repeatedly denying use of performance-enhancing drugs caused great skepticism by fans as to the integrity of baseball.

Perhaps the greatest scandal occurred in professional cycling, in which Lance Armstrong repeatedly denied taking performance-enhancing substances while publicly ridiculing his accusers, concocting elaborate methods of evading detection and vilifying the individuals and agencies charged with detecting drug use and cheating in international cycling. When he was stripped of his title, it was discovered that most of his competitors were also taking performance-enhancing drugs.

A short history of performance-enhancing drug use in amateur and professional sports

One of the foundations of competition in sports is that the best athlete should win the contest or match through exemplary skills and abilities demonstrated on a fair field—i.e. "May the best man (or woman) win" but not "at all costs." That is, it is expected of every athlete to act under the same code of conduct and restrain themselves from taking an unfair advantage in competition.

However, there is no all-encompassing definition of "fair play" and "a level playing field" to guide all the difficult decisions on fairness and cheating. Similarly, there is no definitive guide to the distinction between performance-enhancing drugs and substances that perform a restorative function, just as there are no clear delineations between an athlete's natural abilities and his or her acquired and enhanced abilities to perform at a higher level of skill, strength, or ability.

Athletic skills and performance-enhancing drugs have evolved together over many years. The origin of the word "doping" is the Dutch word "doop" which is a viscous opium juice. According to some historical sources, it may have been used by athletes competing in the early Olympics, perhaps as early as 776 BC (Bowers, 1998). In addition to "doop", ancient Olympic athletes were also known to ingest animal hearts and testicles to gain strength and endurance (Jenkins, 2007).

Efforts to constrain cheating by taking unnatural supplements or performance-enhancing drugs have a long history. In 1928, the International Association of Athletics Federation (IAAF) set forth in its Handbook the first articulated rule against doping:

Doping is the use of any stimulant not normally employed to increase the power of action in athletic competition above the average. Any person knowingly acting or assisting as explained above shall be excluded from any place where these rules are in force or, if he is a competitor, be suspended for a time or otherwise from further participation in amateur athletics under the jurisdiction of this Federation.

After World War II, the U.S. Congress passed the Food Additives Amendment which would allow for certain substances that are generally added to food to skip the pre-market review of the Food and Drug Administration. This statutory amendment led to the formation of the first list of substances generally recognized as safe.

The 1968 Olympics provided a watershed moment for enforcement of anti-doping efforts. During those games, for the first time, the International Olympic Committee (IOC) began testing athletes participating in the Olympics for prohibited substances and identified one athlete, Hans-Gunnar Liljenwall, a participant in the modern-day pentathlon, who tested positive for a prohibited substance. The Swedish Modern Pentathlon team was stripped of its bronze medals.

At the same time, there was great public awareness of the problems of performance-enhancing drugs being used on race horses. May 1968 was the first instance of a horse being disqualified from the Kentucky Derby, the premier American thoroughbred horse race, for use of a banned substance.

The Olympics again provided a testing ground for identifying and disciplining athletes who used banned or illegal substances to enhance their performance. At the 1988 Olympics in Korea, Ben Johnson, a Canadian 100-meter world record holder, was stripped of his gold medal because he tested positive for the anabolic steroid, stanozolol.

In 2003, a Northern California lab, BALCO, was raided by federal investigators who found performance-enhancing substances that had been sold to professional athletes, including Barry Bonds, who had won the Most Valuable Player Award several times and was one of the greatest home run hitters in baseball history.

The BALCO scandal led to a Congressional enactment, The Anabolic Steroid Control Act, which was signed by President George W. Bush on October 22, 2004. The Act led to numerous steroid-based substances being added to the list of anabolic steroids banned from over-the-counter sales. This, in turn, led to the creation of a list of steroids banned by Major League Baseball.

The Anabolic Steroid Control Act is part of a comprehensive national legislative framework to combat illegal use of dangerous steroids and similar substances. The Act defines anabolic steroid to mean any drug or hormonal substance, chemically and pharmacologically related to testosterone.

The Act authorized the Attorney General to exempt from regulation under the Controlled Substances Act any compound, mixture, or preparation that contains any anabolic steroids that are intended for administration to a human being or an animal, and that does not present any significant potential for abuse because of its concentration, preparation, formulation, or delivery system. The Act also directed the U.S. Sentencing Commission to review the criminal sentencing guidelines with respect to anabolic steroids and to amend them as appropriate to increase criminal penalties for their sale or possession and use.

TEAM, LEAGUE, AND GOVERNMENTAL ATTEMPTS TO REGULATE ILLEGAL USE OF PERFORMANCE-ENHANCING SUBSTANCES

The professional sports leagues also took the position that taking illegal drugs was inconsistent with the integrity of the game, as well as constituting a potential health problem for players. Perhaps the most well-known statement came from the then Commissioner of Major League Baseball, Fay Vincent, in June 1991. The statement articulated MLB's new drug policy which consisted of several key parts: a prohibition on use of illegal substances, a testing program, enhanced punishment for violation of the policy, creation of an employee assistance program to assist athletes who use illegal substances and tighter controls over prescription drugs used by athletes during the playing season.

Other professional leagues followed baseball's lead on illegal substance use, although the policies are not uniform either in content or enforcement. Indeed, the National Basketball Association was accused by Congressional investigators in 2005 and 2008 of having a policy with gaps that prevented the rigorous enforcement of illegal drug use by players. It has also been argued that the benefit of performance-enhancing drugs, especially steroids, is greater for some athletes than others, which may explain why some professional sports, like golf, have had fewer highly publicized scandals involving athletes using illegal drugs.

The creation of drug use policies by professional sports leagues also occurred in an environment of collaboration and conflict between the teams (largely the owners and team managers) and the players' unions. The drug testing and enforcement policies of the North American professional sports organizations are negotiated between the league (representing team owners) and the respective players' unions. Although the unions have professed the importance of having drug-free competition, they are often motivated to protect their member-athletes from invasion of privacy and public notoriety as a drug user or "cheater."

The NBA's policy, which was negotiated in 2011 with the players' union, provides for periodic testing of athletes (in both the regular season and the off-season) to be done by an independent testing laboratory. However, the NBA has been criticized for its policy being too general and too lenient on offenders of certain performance-enhancing drugs, such as steroids, which are vigorously prosecuted in other professional sports. The NBA has reasoned that steroid use is not a significant problem in professional basketball, as it is, for example, in football and in baseball, where torque or physical force is more important to player success.

The conflict between the players' associations and the owners and leagues is, according to some observers, counter-intuitive because both the players (whose interests and viewpoints are represented by the players' unions) and the teams (owners and league) share concerns about player health and safety, the integrity of the game in the eyes of fans, and the overall negative efforts on the game caused by performance-enhancing drug use.

International enforcement of performance-enhancing substance bans has proven to be particularly difficult, especially with respect to competitions such as the Olympics, because of the influence of governments on enforcement agencies. There are several agencies of international sports and athletics that are concerned and exert some control or regulation over use of performance enhancements.

The chief agency is WADA, which was created in 1999 in the wake of scandals about international cycling competitions being inundated with doped athletes. The agency was conceived at the World Conference on Doping, convened in 1999 by the IOC. The goals of the agency are to promote and coordinate the fight against doping in sport internationally. Its governance group of 38 members draws equally from representatives from the Olympic Movement and from public authorities such as national anti-doping organizations like the U.S. Anti-Doping Agency (USADA).

The agency draws its funding from the athletic organizations (like the IOC) and from governmental support. WADA's annual budget funds a number of initiatives and activities, including public outreach on the harms of performance-enhancing drugs by athletes, educational programs for athletes, doping testing facilities and the mechanics of drug testing throughout the world. For example, WADA accredits 30 laboratories worldwide to perform testing of athletes.

WADA's reach and significance has grown considerably since its founding. It evolved quickly into the pre-eminent quasi-governmental watchdog over doping in sports. Its decisions can be reviewed by the Court of Arbitration for Sport (CAS), based in Lausanne, Switzerland. The internal operation and international reach of WADA is set out in the World Anti-Doping Code, which articulates prohibited practices and substances and sanctions for violation of the Code. In 2007, a revised Code was adopted unanimously by more than 600 sports organizations worldwide, including the IOC, several professional sports leagues, and several national anti-doping agencies.

The activities of WADA have generated controversies and legal disputes. One of the most controversial areas of WADA activities is its methodologies and policies for drug testing of athletes. Several players' unions and associations have complained about the invasion of athletes' privacy occasioned by drug testing policies and procedures. For example, several athletes and their association have complained about WADA's "where-abouts" system of drug testing. Under this system, athletes are required to select one hour per day, seven days a week at which time they may be tested (urine, blood, etc.), without notice, for use of performance-enhancing drugs. Another controversy arose when WADA criticized the National Football League for its lax policies on blood testing for human grown hormones, and blamed the NFL Players Association for stonewalling the implementation of such testing in U.S. professional football.

On another front, WADA has been criticized by organizations that seek to eliminate doping in sports as being lax on enforcement, especially concerning the activities of national (often Olympic) sports organizations in some countries. The complaint has been that there is an inherent (and sometimes operational) conflict within WADA, whose governing board includes sports officials from many countries whose athletes are tested by WADA for drug use. These governmental organizations can influence the funding that goes from those countries to WADA to support its activities. The criticism is that WADA has backed off from vigorous enforcement in some instances in order to avoid angering leaders of those national sports' authorities.

However, WADA acted dramatically in the 2016 Rio Olympics, banning most of the Russian track and field team because of alleged state-sponsored doping. The Russian government denied the allegation of state-sponsored doping and complained that athletes who never failed a drug test were banned. The Russian government also confirmed, as virtually everyone does, that it supports clean competition.

A follow-up to this scandal is that many athletes have now been stripped of medals awarded at the 2008, 2012, and 2014 Olympics. This delayed-reaction discipline results from two facts: 1) bodily fluid samples must be preserved for 10 years; 2) drug detection technology is constantly improving.

Testing for performance-enhancing drugs and other substances is here to stay. The economic, reputational, and other stakes in professional and amateur sports are too high to permit athletes' performance to go unregulated. WADA, and similar national drug-testing and enforcement agencies, are the first tranche of such efforts, but it is unlikely that they will be the last or the only such organisations. As the stakes for competitive success become greater, and the pharmacological and technological opportunities become more sophisticated and difficult to detect, we can expect more doping in sports and more scandals.

WHY DO ATHLETES TAKE PERFORMANCE-ENHANCING DRUGS?

This is a recurring and, perhaps, a foolish question because these drugs are referred to as "performance-enhancing," so the desire to use them is self-evident. However, the pertinent questions really are, first, how much doping is occurring in competitive athletics and, second, what is so performance-enhancing about these drugs that athletes would risk public shame, being banned from competition, and/or possible criminal conviction?

Studies have shown that doping is much more prevalent than many fans and sports' observers realize. For example, in one report on two studies of elite German athletes on national squads, the authors report that between 25.8 percent and 48.1 percent of the athletes used at least one doping technique. Fairly stated, 51.9 percent of the athletes in one of the studies never used a doping technique while in the other study, 61.3 percent of the athletes competed without using illegal substances during the one season (Pitsch & Emrich, 2012).

The challenging question presented by these substantially consistent studies is: what percentage of competitive athletes would you expect to have competed without using any illegal substances? Many observers of competitive sport would think that 61 percent is shockingly low, while more cynical observers would not be surprised that such a high percentage of those athletes would be taking illegal substances to enhance their performance.

These findings are consistent with other studies of the prevalence of doping in sports. However, conclusions about doping use in sports are complicated by several variables. First, there is a lower incidence of use of steroids—a "strong" drug with serious health side effects that is heavily regulated—than other illegal performance-enhancing drugs. Second, the use of illegal drugs varies by the sport, with some sports, like bodybuilding, reporting much higher usage of drugs (especially steroids) than other sports. Third, there are distinct differences in the use of illegal performance substances between men and women athletes, with men athletes much more likely to use those substances to enhance their performance than women.

One study of the use of anabolic androgenic steroids reported that millions of boys and men, principally in Western countries, have abused those illegal drugs while the prevalence in use among women is much lower (Kanayama et al., 2010). The study also reports that the long-term medical effects on younger athletes are particularly pernicious, with users experiencing higher rates of dependency on those drugs (i.e. addiction) and being much more prone to use opioids in addition to the steroids.

The answer to the second question—why?—is twofold: competitive power and the restoration of athletic power. According to one expert, "Steroids don't make someone a good athlete or a bad athlete; they make you stronger, but they don't make you a better athlete" (Scruggs, 2009). In sports, such as football and baseball, where physical power over opponents or pitched balls is a critical aspect of the game, the ability to quickly gain torque power through artificial means heightens performance. Indeed, the case studies of athletes who acknowledged the use of steroids demonstrate the effectiveness of artificial enhancement of power in hitting home runs, winning cycling races, and other competitive endeavors.

OTHER PERFORMANCE ENHANCEMENTS

Some examples may be helpful to frame the issues of other performance enhancements. Suppose Johnny, a 20-year-old rising star in Triple A baseball, during the off-season, gets Lasik surgery on his eyes in order to sharpen his vision and see the fastball at an earlier point after the pitcher's delivery and, the next day, he gets "Tommy John" ligament surgery on his pitching arm elbow. The surgery is expected to permit him to compete several years longer (if the surgery is, in fact, successful) and may increase the velocity of his fastball. On game day, he takes a couple of over-the-counter stimulants (mainly caffeine-based) and, to further sharpen his focus in the game, takes some cognitive-enhancing drugs (such as Ritalin or Adderall). Do the concerns about competitive fairness and "level playing field among athletes" that were presented in the discussion about performance-enhancing drugs also apply to any or all of Johnny's activities? If so, how do you draw the line between those performance enhancements that are permitted from those that are banned?

Many of the non-drug enhancements are even more mundane that the ones described in this paragraph. Should our concerns about performance enhancements also apply to studying film of our techniques (our jump-shot, for example, in basketball) or the use of a squat suit or lifting belt for weightlifting competition? Or, how about if scientists discovered that the chief enhancing quality of blood doping was not increased oxygenation in an athlete's body but, rather, a dramatic increase in the athlete's motivation to train? Do sport observers and fans also feel that motivation-enhancing, like cognitive-enhancing, substances are also forms of cheating that should be prohibited?

Experts in the field of performance enhancement are beginning to consider the problem in broader terms and are looking at it in terms of ergogenic enhancement. The term refers to the application of any physical, mechanical, nutritional, psychologic or pharmacologic procedure or aid that improves physical work capacity or athletic performance (Katch et al., 2007).

The underlying questions remain: When should such applications be considered cheating? How do we draw the line between such applications that are beneficial to the sport and to the athletes, and those that harm the integrity of the sport? Will the growing prevalence of such applications affect fan interest in the sport, or will fans simply adjust their understanding and acceptance of the ergogenic enhancement as a usual and customary aspect of the sport?

One expert in the field, Hugh Herr, a biomechanical engineer at Massachusetts Institute of Technology, has been studying how technology is increasingly adapted to address biomechanical and other constraints on human performance, and he foresees the possibility that performance-enhancing technologies will advance to the point that they will not only extend human limits but will demand an Olympics all of their own (Thompson, 2012).

APPLICATION OF ETHICAL THEORIES TO PERFORMANCE ENHANCEMENT

The most important ethical theories to apply to the use of performance-enhancing drugs are utilitarianism, care ethics, and virtue ethics. Under any of those theories, the use of performance-enhancing drugs is not ethical. A brief review of each follows.

The standards of utilitarianism, with its espousal of the greatest good for the greatest number, would clearly not be met by the use of performance-enhancing drugs. It clearly produces *no* good for an athlete to win a competition based on performance enhancement by drugs. Such conduct defeats the purpose of the competition—i.e. to determine who is the best athlete on a level playing field with uniform rules—while also harming the athlete's health, setting a bad example for those who admire the athlete and defrauding the fans. Therefore, non-performance-enhanced competition is clearly what produces the greatest good for the greatest number.

Similarly, the standards of care ethics, with its emphasis on interpersonal relationships, community and caring, would clearly not be met by the use of performance-enhancing drugs. No interpersonal relationship can be based on drug use for a non-medical reason, which is inimical to the user's health. Similarly, an athlete cannot have an honest relationship with his or her competitors if he or she is covertly using drugs to gain an advantage over the competitor.

Regarding community, it is impossible to create community if some in the community are secretly trying to gain an unfair advantage over others. Indeed, the opposite of community would result from such misconduct, because the essential community element of trust—by competitors, fans, and officials—would be missing.

With respect to caring, one would have not to care for another's welfare if one were dispensing performance-enhancing drugs to him or her, because such drugs are unhealthful. Nor could one possibly care about one's competitors if one were cheating them by gaining an unfair advantage. Lack of caring would also extend to the fans, because they would not be seeing fair competition but rather an artificial entertainment.

Finally, the standards of virtue ethics, with its emphasis on character and moral disposition, would clearly not be met by the use of performance-enhancing drugs. This is perhaps the clearest case, because the use of performance-enhancing drugs is against the rules of competition—i.e. cheating—and cheating is incompatible with good character. The person of good character would not resist the temptation of using performance-enhancing drugs—he or she would not be tempted in the first place.

IS TAKING PERFORMANCE-ENHANCING DRUGS CHEATING?

In considering the overarching question of how athletes taking performance-enhancing substances and treatments harm sport and athletic competitions, it is necessary to address the ethical issue of cheating. In these modern times, there are significant questions about the lengths that individuals can go to in order to be successful. This is true with respect to business practices (e.g. marketing a product, discriminating in price between different customers, salary levels for employees, and others) as well as success on the field of athletic competition.

It has become common to see both athletes and the average business person take any inch they can in the mastery of their craft or in getting an advantage over a competitor. Each business, profession, trade or craft has its own ways of gaining these extra inches or their secret advantage.

But what denominates an improper "cutting corners" from a "smart business practice?" For the businessman, this could involve insider trading; for the doctor prescribing drugs to people not in need; for the lawyer protecting a client they know is wrong; and for the professional athlete, taking performance-enhancing substances. As was discussed in Chapter 2, there are important insights into an ethos-based approach to athletic competition that are raised by performance-enhancing activities that contravene the rules and norms of the competition or sport. An individual's decision to cheat is commonly thought of as never being the "right way" to gain an edge in mastery but many people— athletes and business persons alike—take this route.

The discussion about cheating in sports is similar to discussions about dishonest business behavior. However, for many observers, they are different because sports and athletic contests are merely "entertainment" and so why should we worry about improper behavior by one athlete or a group of athletes who "cut corners" and cheat in the sport? Some of the arguments against cheating in sports are:

- Sports is a big business that generates billions of dollars per year.
- Although sports contests are largely for entertainment of the fans and spectators, that does not mean that fans don't care about the integrity of the game or contest. When a player cheats and acts in a dishonest way compared to the other athletes and contestants, it shatters the fans' beliefs in the sport and the game itself, not just the particular player. This argument is widely used when people discuss rigged sports contests—e.g. the referee or official has taken money to call the game in favor of one contestant or team—and they often conclude that such games are not real, but fake and dishonest.
- Sports contests often involve one competitor against another competitor. So if one competitor is assisted by an extraneous factor, then the contest is not truly between two men (or women); it becomes like a contest between a man and a machine. The contest is inherently dishonest; it is not what it purports to be.
- Over the long run of the sport, it becomes impossible to compare the best or greatest athletes or performances if some athletes are artificially benefited. Their records of performance cannot accurately and fairly be compared with other athletes who did

not use the artificial performance enhancement. For example, this issue was very significant to many baseball fans when Roger Maris, the New York Yankees' great home run hitter, had his one-season home run record of 61 home runs bested by athletes who had used steroids to enhance their performances. The baseball record book for home runs in a season had some athletes whose performances were foot-noted or marked with an asterisk that noted their use of performance-enhancing drugs.

THERAPEUTIC USE EXEMPTIONS

WADA allows the use of performance-enhancing drugs if a competitor has a medical reason for taking the drug, a so-called Therapeutic Use Exemption (TUE). Some—particularly Russia—have called this practice into question. The reasoning is that, regardless of medical necessity, the drug being taken is, by definition, performance-enhancing, so it undermines the level playing field which is the foundation of sporting competition.

Furthermore, the argument goes, there is no transparency in the TUE process so that competitors and fans are not aware that a competitor is being permitted to take a performance-enhancing drug. For example, U.S. star gymnast, Simone Biles, won numerous medals at the 2016 Rio Olympics, but, while she was achieving that, it was not publicly known that, in fact, she was taking a performance-enhancing drug pursuant to a TUE. After the Olympics, this fact was revealed when WADA records were hacked.

Although, generally, individuals have a right of privacy over their health and drug records, a question arises whether that right extends to sport competitions. One does not have a right to compete in sporting events. A question arises whether one should forfeit some privacy for that right. The alternative is that a competitor is taking a performance-enhancing drug without the knowledge of his or her competitors or of the fans. That fact seems highly relevant to a sports competition. Virtue ethics and utilitarianism would seem to dictate disclosure of TUEs that are granted. Otherwise, some competitors have an undisclosed advantage.

INSTITUTIONAL FAILURES: LAPSES OF ETHICS AND FAILURES OF LEADERSHIP

Although the inappropriate and often unlawful use of performance-enhancing drugs has been evident throughout much of the history of sports, there have been some significant and recent scandals that permit a close-up examination of the legal, societal, and economic costs of performance-enhancing drug use. More significantly, these scandals have deeply and negatively affected the sports themselves, including incurring fan or spectator disgust and long-term harm to the culture of competition in those sports. These scandals illuminate several levels of failures and flaws by athletes, by leagues and teams, by regulatory authorities charged with policing the integrity of competition in the sports, and to some degree by the fans and spectators themselves.

The "Bash Brothers": Mark McGwire, Jose Canseco, and Barry Bonds, and the harm to major league baseball

One of the greatest scandals in professional sports occurred in major league baseball in the United States in the 1980s to late 2000s. Dozens of professional baseball players were discovered to have used a variety of performance-enhancing drugs to increase their recovery time and their performance on the field. Several of them were the most popular and admired players, and the disclosures of their illegal use of the drugs harmed their reputations and that of professional baseball. Many of their records for home runs now have an asterisk or other notation that their performance was enhanced and should, therefore, not be compared to players who performed at a high level but without drugs.

Roger Maris, an All Star outfielder with the New York Yankees, set the Major League record for most home runs in a season with 61 home runs in 1960. Some 37 years later, two players—Sammy Sosa and Mark McGwire—were battling to break that record. McGwire hit 70 home runs and Sosa hit 66 home runs. The year before, in the 1996 season, McGwire hit 52 home runs and Sosa hit 40. Why the significant increase in home runs hit by two players? Indeed, during the 1997 season in Major League Baseball, 13 different players hit 40 or more home runs. What incredible changes occurred in professional baseball since 1960 that can account for the significant increase in home runs? The answer to the question was obvious to the Commissioner's Office, to the team owners, to the team managers, and to the players: doping by use of steroids was rampant in baseball and beefed up, more powerful players were knocking the ball out of the ball parks with much greater frequency. In 1998, Sosa and McGwire shared *Sports Illustrated* magazine's "Sportsman of the Year" award. That same year, McGwire finally admitted to using andro to enhance his performance and to permit faster rejuvenation of his playing ability. At the time, andro was banned by the NFL and the NCAA, but not Major League Baseball.

The scandal reached its peak in 2001 when Barry Bonds hit 73 home runs in one season, even though he had never hit more than 50 home runs in any prior season. The incredible enhancement of performance (as well as dramatic changes in his physiology) led many to conclude that he was using performance-enhancing drugs.

The "history" of major league baseball's great heroes and performers became tainted due to the significant drug use among modern players. One example is the famed "500 Home Run Club"—listing players who, during their careers, hit 500 or more home runs. In 1996, Eddie Murray became just the 15th player to join the club which dated back almost 100 years. However, between 1998 and 2009, ten more players joined the club and six of those ten had documented ties to performance-enhancing drugs.

Like many of the doping scandals in professional and amateur athletics, there was clear and unambiguous evidence that athletes were competing at significantly higher levels of performance within a short period of time. Yet, the many monitors of the sports and competitions—coaches, league directors and commissioners, and fellow athletes—failed to publicly intervene and call attention to the inappropriate and often illegal use of the substances.

Some commentators argue that the excitement and fan appeal of the home run race between Sosa and McGwire, and the run-up to Bonds' home run season created financial incentives for managers and the Commissioner to look the other way. But, ultimately, it was the media that blew the whistle on these practices—for example, by encouraging the U.S. Congress to investigate, because they considered it cheating and debasing the game.

The Lance Armstrong scandal and its harm to international cycling

Born in Plano Texas in 1971, Lance Armstrong is one of the most widely known cyclists in the history of the sport. Rising quickly as a child athletic prodigy, Armstrong was the U.S. National Amateur champion by age 20 and five years later became the number one cyclist in the world. Unfortunately, at this time, he also was diagnosed with testicular cancer that had spread to his lungs and his brain. However, making a miraculous comeback, Armstrong was back on a bike the following year and only two years later won the Tour de France.

With his story of beating cancer and taking the cycling world by storm, Armstrong had become the ideal All-American Boy, capturing the hearts of many Americans. Before his run was over, he won eight consecutive Tour de France, the most prestigious cycling competition in the world. With his success also came a skyrocketing market brand, through endorsement deals, signing bonuses, and appearances, among other things, Armstrong became worth roughly $125 million.

However, criticism also followed. Much of the criticism surrounded the increasingly widespread suspicion that he used performance-enhancing substances. There was greater suspicion with respect to Armstrong's situation, especially following publication of a book by David Walsh and Pierre Ballester in 2004 (which came out just before Armstrong's sixth consecutive Tour victory). The authors conceded that the evidence in their book was "circumstantial," but they had assembled considerable evidence of doping by Armstrong and his U.S. Postal Service Pro Cycling Team. At that point, Armstrong had no reason to come forth. Had he come clean to the sport and the public, the gravity of the consequences of his doping would likely not have been as grave.

Instead, Armstrong continued to publicly deny any illegal drug use and lashed out at his critics, many of whom were concerned about the rumors of increased drug use across the sport as Armstrong's competitors began to use banned substances to remain athletically competitive. He continued to race on the international level, picking up his sixth and seventh tour victories, including becoming the first cyclist in history to win the mountain stages three consecutive times.

Following his seventh tour victory, Armstrong retired from the sport for a year before returning in 2006, the year when his former teammate Floyd Landis won the Tour but tested positive for synthetic testosterone and was stripped of the title. Amid his retirements, Armstrong would not return to the top three until 2009. However, his superstar brand continued to grow, as reflected in his selection to *Time Magazine*'s 100 Most Influential People ranking in May 2008. With his public image growing, allegations began to arise again that Armstrong had taken performance-enhancing substances and amid these allegations he finally stepped away from cycling in 2011. This was the beginning of the end for Armstrong because of a grave mistake he made in 2012.

In 2012, USADA filed suit against Armstrong charging him with the use of performance-enhancing substances—principally steroids and blood boosters—from 1999 to 2005, and of leading a complex doping program on his cycling team. USADA insisted that Armstrong either subject himself to arbitration in the Court of Arbitration for Sport or accept sanctions imposed by a cycling authority or by USADA. Armstrong chose not to contest the charges, citing the potential toll on his family. He received a lifetime ban from competing in all sports that follow the WADA code—effectively ending his athletic career. He was also stripped of all of his achievements after 1998, including his seven Tour de France titles.

The international cycling organization (UCI) upheld USADA's decision, also stripping his cycling wins but determining that his titles would not be allocated to other competitors, many of whom were also suspected of using performance-enhancing drugs. Armstrong chose not to appeal the decision to the CAS and later, in a 2013 television interview, Armstrong confessed that some of the allegations of his persistent and significant drug use were true.

Armstrong's fall from the pinnacle of his sport was one of the most protracted and wrenching episodes in international sports. He essentially refused to admit that he used banned drugs, but stated that he would not challenge doping charges. He was subsequently banned for life from the sport of cycling by the international cycling agency, was stripped of all seven of his Tour de France titles, lost several lucrative endorsements—including Nike and Anheuser-Busch—and, finally, was forced to step down from his position as chairman of the "Live Strong" foundation, which he founded.

Some experts have suggested that if Armstrong had come out and told the truth about his drug use, it was likely that he would have been able to escape with a much lesser punishment, perhaps just one of his tour titles being stripped, but because of his lies and the fiasco he caused in the courtroom, he lost much more. By that time, he had already done the damage and could not fix his image before the government painted a negative picture of him.

He tried to fix his image on the popular Oprah show, but that did not work. Had Armstrong confessed to taking performance-enhancing substances following the 2004 Walsh and Ballester book, the consequences may not have been as grave for him personally and for the professional cycling sport.

Russia's organized and systematic doping of its athletes

The three scenarios—one in professional baseball, one in international cycling, and one in international amateur athletics—share some common aspects. First, professional athletes at the "top of their games" become enmeshed in the need to remain competitive and continue to win, either because they accepted what they thought was the norm in the sport ("everyone else is doing it, so I can") or because they became corrupted by their success in competition, with its attendant wealth and fame. Second, the permission to cheat by taking performance enhancements was widespread and came from a number of sources, such as other athletes, a team manager or coach or from social media and blog postings of fans.

In at least one exceptional case, the impetus to cheat by taking performance-enhancing drugs came from the athlete's government and that country's international competition group. This fact alone raised a significant question of the integrity of governmental agencies involved in international sports' competition. This situation also cast doubts on the watchdog anti-doping agency, WADA, which did not detect dozens of doping athletes at the time they were competing.

In 2012, WADA received an email from an Olympic athlete from Russia, Darya Pishchalnikova, a world-class female discus thrower and Olympic medal winner, claiming that she had taken banned drugs at the direction of Russian sports and anti-doping authorities, and that she had reliable information on systematic doping in her country. She stated that she wanted "to cooperate with WADA." Her allegations in the email were precise and detailed, including names and facts, and they coincided with other investigative reporting of widespread doping of Russian athletes competing in the Olympics. For example, the lab director of the 2014 Sochi Olympics reported to a newspaper investigating allegations of a Russian doping scandal that at least 15 Russian medal winners at those games had used banned substances "as part of a state-run program." WADA eventually, after several years of receiving and investigating evidence of Russian Olympic team doping, acted and banned several Russian teams from competing in the 2016 summer Olympics.

The fallout from the WADA investigation and its seemingly reluctant enforcement was considerable. WADA's governing body is made up of IOC officials and government officials and the charge has been made that the composition of this body presents inherent, and demonstrated, conflicts of interest with the enforcement responsibilities of WADA. WADA's $28 million budget is funded equally by sports bodies (such as the IOC) and by governments (the United States is the single largest contributor to that budget). Those organizations have strong reasons to avoid drug scandals in the competitions and matches they sponsor and on their national teams.

The national teams are organized and operated to win international titles and this motivation, as was demonstrated in the Russian doping scandal, influenced the national anti-doping agency to facilitate the doping cover-up that persisted for years in Russia. The result is an international sports scandal in which many of the people and agencies and sports authorities are considered to be protecting cheating athletes, fostering a climate of cheating among athletes on national teams, or covering up cheating scandals in their countries.

CONCLUSION

The prevalence of performance-enhancing substances and practices is challenging the integrity and ethical norms of athletic competition and the "rules of the game." The many reported instances of the use of the substances and practices have eroded public confidence in both the "best team wins" perspective of competitions and the ability of leagues to control the use of the substances and practices.

The use of performance-enhancing drugs also constitutes significant public health problems, especially as young athletes attempt to emulate their idols in the professional leagues and become even more powerful, physically resilient, and desired by teams and coaches. Like many public health issues, the growing, acceptable use of performance-enhancing substances must be addressed by education of athletes, coaches and fans and by elimination of the competitive benefits sought by athletes when they use the substances.

Although the use of performance-enhancing substances and techniques goes back to the early Olympics, the current day has witnessed an enormous increase in the types of such drugs and devices and in the difficulty of detecting them when used by athletes. This trend toward greater use of substances and greater difficulty in banning them and preventing their use is likely to escalate as technology and science add sophistication to the drugs and complexity to the roles of detection and prohibition.

It may well turn out that social standards defining what is fair and what is cheating may evolve as the forces of science and technology advance in many areas other than sport and competition. As for now, however, the use of performance-enhancing drugs is inconsistent with the major ethical theories of deontology, utilitarianism, care ethics, and virtue ethics.

ETHICAL LEADERSHIP CASE STUDIES

Case study #1

The "history" of major league baseball's great heroes and performers became tainted due to the significant drug use among modern players. One example is the famed "500 Home Run Club"—listing players who, during their careers, hit 500 or more home runs. In 1996, Eddie Murray became just the 15th player to join the club which dated back almost 100 years. However, between 1998 and 2009, ten more players joined the club and six of those ten had documented ties to performance-enhancing drugs. How can Major League Baseball exercise ethical leadership to address the situation? Specify types of leadership that the Commissioner of MLB should have considered and why?

Case study #2

Bicycling was rocked by a scandal involving its most famous competitor. That scandal was followed by the revelation that most of the top cyclists had been doping. How could the bicycling authorities have exercised ethical leadership to have prevented this situation? How should they have exercised ethical leadership to repair the situation?

Case study #3

The World Anti-Doping Agency uncovered credible evidence of state-sponsored doping by an important country. Because WADA believes that it is incapable of detecting all of this doping, it enacts a mass ban on athletes from this country regardless of whether they actually failed a drug test. Is such a ban ethical, and why?

STUDENT LEARNING EXERCISES

1. In considering the total ban of Russian athletes from the Rio 2016 Paralympics regardless of whether they failed a drug test, outline an ethical leadership program that would protect the integrity of the Paralympics without the necessity of a mass ban.
2. Consider the situations involving use of cognitive-enhancing substances (e.g. Ritalin), performance-sustaining procedures (e.g. "Tommy John" surgery), and biomedical enhancements (such as Oscar Pistorius's artificial limbs) and prepare a "statement

of fair competition" defining when it is ethically proper and improper in international competition for athletes to use these substances, procedures and enhancements. In drawing the appropriate lines between what is cheating with respect to these situations, describe why the enhancement is or is not in accord with deontology, care ethics, virtue ethics, and utilitarianism.

PROBLEMS/QUESTIONS

1. What ethical leadership roles should governmental authorities take to address doping in sports? Coaches and league officials?
2. Do coaches and team owners, such as those employing Barry Bonds or Mark McGwire have an ethical responsibility to the public to prevent doping in sport? How should they have acted once it became obvious that their players were using unhealthy, possibly illegal, substances to hit that many home runs?
3. Who should be held ethically responsible for an athlete mistakenly taking a performance-enhancing drug and why? Doctors? Trainers? Players?
4. What is the proper role of team physicians in detecting improper drug use by players and what should they ethically be required to do when they have evidence or a strong factual basis for believing that athletes are doping? Is the team trainer in a different position than the team physician when considering evidence that members of the team are abusing banned substances?
5. Is the primary purpose of the ban on performance-enhancing drugs the health and safety of players? Or to maintain the reputation for integrity of the sport?
6. What are the ethical arguments why a player who took performance-enhancing drugs should get into the Hall of Fame of his sport?
7. Some performance-enhancing drugs such as Adderall are routinely prescribed for individuals with cognitive processing issues such as ADD or ADHD. There are individuals who can apply for a Therapeutic Use Exemption that allows them to compete in sporting events despite their use of a performance-enhancing drug. Is this ethically permissible, and why? Ethically, should such use be disclosed?

BIBLIOGRAPHY

Abbott, Henry, *The Gaps in NBA Drug Testing*, TrueHoop, January 11, 2013.

Albergotti, Reed & O'Connell, Vanessa, Cycling Legend Loses Titles, *Wall Street Journal*, August 24, 2012.

Aschwanden, Christie, The Future of Cheating in Sports, *Smithsonian Magazine*, July, 2012.

Bloom, Barry, *Mitchell Report Proposes Solutions*, MLB.com, December 13, 2007.

Bowers, Larry D., Athletic Drug Testing, 17 *Clinics in Sports Medicine* 299 (1998).

Jenkins, Sally, Winning, Cheating Have Ancient Roots, *Washington Post*, August 3, 2007.

Kanayama, Gen, et al., Illicit Anabolic-Androgenic Steroid Use, 58 *Hormones & Behavior* 111 (2010).

Katch, Frank, et al., Exercise Physiology: Energy, Nutrition, & Human Performance (2007).

International Association of Athletic Federations, Drugs in Sport/Doping Control, *IAAF Medical Manual* (2012).

International Association of Athletic Federations, Handbook, p. 55 (1927-8).

Mayo Clinic Staff, Performance-Enhancing Drugs: Know the Risks, www.mayoclinic.org/healthy-lifestyle/fitness/in-depth/performance-enhancing-drugs/art-20046134 (2004a).

Mayo Clinic Staff, Performance-Enhancing Drugs and Teen Athletes, www.mayoclinic.org/healthy-lifestyle/tween-and-teen-health/in-depth/performance-enhancing-drugs/art-20046620 (2004b).

Nightengale, Bob, Reasons for Bonds' Bad Image Split Between Steroids and Racism, *USA Today*, April 6, 2006.

Office of National Drug Control Policy Reauthorization Act of 2006, U.S. Government Publishing Office (2006).

Peters, J. The Man Behind the Juice: Fifty Years Ago, a Doctor Brought Steroids to America, slate.com, February 18, 2005.

Pitsch, Werner & Emrich, Eike, The Frequency of Doping in Elite Sport: Results of A Replication Study, *47 International Review for the Sociology of Sport 559* (2011).

Schmidt, Michael S., Inside a Tempting World of Easy Steroids, *New York Times*, April 11, 2009.

Schmidt, Michael, Inside A Tempting World of Easy Steroids, *New York Times*, April 11, 2009, quoting Dr. Ramon Scruggs.

Thompson, Helen, Superhuman Athletes, *487 Nature 289* (July 19, 2012).

Verroken, Michele & Mottram, David, Doping Control in Sport, in Mottram, D. (ed.), *Drugs in Sport* (2002).

Weinbaum, William & Schaap, Jeremy, *The Final Hours of Ken Caminiti's Life*, espn.com, November 3, 2004.

World Anti-Doping Agency, The Agency's History, undated, www.wada-ama.org.

World Anti-Doping Agency, Blood Doping, undated, www.wada-ama.org/en/questions-answers/blood-doping#main-content.

CHAPTER 8

The ethics of race discrimination in sport

INTRODUCTION

The business and entertainment of athletics has long held a spot at the center of American popular culture. Although the benefits of sport abound, a darker side exists because racial tension has had a major impact on sports and on sport organizations. Arguments about racial superiority have focused on innate genetic differences among certain groups of people and how these differences impact athletic prowess. More broadly, these concerns stem from the larger societal issue of racial discrimination.

Sport, as a microcosm of society, helps reveal attitudes regarding race relations in the United States. This chapter explores racial discrimination in sport, with particular focus on African-Americans, and examines the role that sport has sometimes played in society promoting racial equality. From an ethical standpoint, this chapter considers why a certain group of people (African-American) have not always been given the same opportunities as another group of people (Caucasian) within the framework of sport.

A BRIEF HISTORY OF RACE IN THE UNITED STATES

Black Africans arrived in colonial America in 1619, soon after the establishment of the English settlement at Jamestown. By the mid-17th century, the colonial economy prospered under a slave-based economic system orchestrated by plantation owners, and, during the 18th century, black African slaves provided the primary source of labor for the colonial agricultural society. As the colonists' relationship with England became strained late in the 18th century, leading to revolution and eventual independence, a system of racism became integrated into the American way of life. The establishment of slavery led to the denial of all rights of citizenship for African-Americans, who represented approximately 20 percent of the population of the new nation; slavery also drove the development of racial classification systems (Hoberman, 2002).

These classification systems and ideas about the meaning of race arose as colonists sought to explain why the whites of the new world looked and acted differently from the black Africans. The colonists assumed that their own appearance and actions were normal and that any variations of behavior were abnormal, divergent, dishonest, illogical, and/or primitive. In this way, whiteness became the standard against which all other people were assessed and evaluated.

Through the lens of cultural relativism, this concept of race logic suggested that people of color were simple beings driven by strength rather than intellect, instincts rather than ethical codes, and compulsion rather than prudence. These beliefs were part of an over-simplified Darwinian model of human evolution, in which mental attributes were seen to be superior to physical qualities among humans and other primates. This approach led to the erroneous conclusion that white-skinned people were superior beings who deserved to be in positions of power (id.).

Prior to the Civil War, whites in the United States in the colonized areas used this race logic to justify slavery and the physical mistreatment of African-Americans. A predominant attitude of racial superiority guided this era even in sport participation. As a result of the institution of slavery, African-Americans were afforded little time to participate in recreational activity, and even when given time, few sporting opportunities were available to them. Caucasian Americans viewed themselves as in control so that African-Americans played a subordinate role (Franklin, 1994). For example, Caucasian plantation owners selected slaves to participate in boxing matches and to serve as jockeys for horse racing. In horse racing, African-Americans were permitted to ride as jockeys because horse riding was deemed a "mechanical exercise," which Caucasians had no interest in performing (Davis, 2008).

After the Civil War, widespread changes in the social, political, and economic status of African-Americans created a shift toward increased access for African-Americans to gain medical care and to receive educational opportunities. Legal and political structures promoting equality were implemented, and African-Americans began to obtain voting power. Mirroring these developments, the Reconstruction era provided a period of increased inclusion for African-Americans in sport.

In the aftermath of the Civil War, African-Americans began to achieve notable acclaim in sports such as boxing, baseball, horse racing, and cycling (id.). In the mid-1880s, African-Americans Moses "Fleetwood" Walker and Weldy Walker signed baseball contracts with the Toledo Mudhens of the now defunct American Association although they were ridiculed both on and off the field (Hylton, 1998). Moreover, Isaac Murphy, who some consider the best jockey of all time, became the first African-American to win the Kentucky Derby in 1884 (Davis, 2008).

Social justice slowed near the end of the 19th century as racial repression increased. Efforts to disenfranchise African-Americans and the development of "black codes" effectively excluded them from many areas of American society during this post-Reconstruction era. Legal maneuvering by way of state statutes, municipal codes, and judicial decisions played a role in the creation of segregation. As laws upheld the practice of segregation, the treatment of African-Americans in sport deteriorated (id.).

For example, strong social forces in the United States eventually led to the complete disappearance of African-American jockeys in horse racing. Owners stopped hiring them, and the Jockey Club systematically prevented African-American jockeys from joining. Furthermore, the participation of African-Americans in the sport of baseball declined and disappeared. By 1900, African-Americans and dark-skinned Latinos were completely excluded from professional baseball (id.).

The turn of the 20th century represented a new era for African-Americans as they adapted to a segregated American society. African-Americans established separate organizations like the National Bar Association for African-American lawyers (Hylton,

1998). Other separate organizations that emerged included the National Medical Association and the National Negro Press Association for African-American doctors and journalists respectively (Davis, 2008). In the world of sports, African-Americans created different sports leagues, mirroring the segregation in American society. The National Negro Baseball League and the American Negro League became the foundation of African-American professional baseball in the 1930s and 1940s (Wiggins, 2005).

By the 1950s and 1960s, the Civil Rights era marked the weakening of deep-seated beliefs about racism. Examples of progress for African-Americans included improvement in education; prohibition of racial discrimination in employment; increased political power; the decision of *Brown v. Board of Education*, which ended legal segregation in public schools; and the economic boost for wage-earners of color. In sport, the enhanced commercialization of collegiate and professional competition contributed to decreasing discriminatory practices. Sport leaders realized that disallowing African-Americans from participating in athletics was not financially optimal (Davis, 2008).

Although in the post-Civil Rights era most overt forms of racial discrimination have ended, African-Americans continue to suffer prejudice, which impacts their professional advancement. For example, a disproportionate number of African-Americans are unable to move beyond middle management in private industry in the United States (Sage, 2007). Moreover, wide gaps persist in education for African-Americans and also with regard to income (Harris, 2006). Even in the sports world, for example, implicit bias continues. The integration of players is more prevalent than the integration of coaches and administrators across most sports, and minority candidates filling open managerial positions remains low (Davis, 2008).

In the 21st century, racism in the United States still exists. Although the legal and civil reforms of the last century made strides in bettering race relations and ended *de jure* discrimination (discrimination according to law), *de facto* discrimination (discrimination in fact) and inequality still exist. African-Americans and other minority groups remain affected by racism. High profile incidents of white-on-minority violence, many times involving police activity, contribute to racial tension, reopen old wounds, and further racial stereotyping. Sport, because of its prominence and popularity, has the potential to provide an opportunity to lessen the impact of harmful stereotypes. For example, in 2016, a number of NFL players refused to stand for the national anthem before games in protest of racial problems. This symbolic act received extensive national attention.

HISTORY OF THE LAW REGARDING DISCRIMINATORY CONDUCT

The modern legal history of racial discrimination begins with the post-Civil War passage of three constitutional amendments designed to confer certain basic civil rights on African-Americans and to nullify the Supreme Court's holding in the Dred Scott Decision of 1857 that African-Americans were not United States citizens (Finkelman, 2015).

The Thirteenth Amendment, enacted in 1865, effectively abolished slavery; however, it did not address the legal status of former slaves. The constitutional authority of Congress to pass such a law was unclear, providing Congress with the opportunity to deny citizenship status to former slaves. Moreover, the emergence of Black Codes enacted by many Southern states diminished the benefits of citizenship for former slaves. These codes restricted the activities of freed African-Americans, thus ensuring their availability as a labor force. For example, many states required African-Americans to sign yearly labor contracts. Refusal meant risk of being arrested as a vagrant and fined or forced into unpaid labor.

The only way to be certain of Congressional authority on this subject and to ensure permanent citizenship was to again amend the Constitution, which Congress accomplished with the ratification of the Fourteenth Amendment in 1868. Known then as the "Recon-struction Amendment," it provided citizenship to African-Americans with guaranteed equal protection under the law. Then, in 1870, the Fifteenth Amendment was adopted and provided voting rights for African-Americans and other persons of color.

A few years later, Congress attempted to enforce the protections of the Fourteenth Amendment and extend the civil rights of African-Americans to include equal access to public accommodations, such as hotels and trains, by passing the Civil Rights Act of 1875. It did not succeed because in 1883 the Act was declared unconstitutional by the U.S. Supreme Court as part of the so-called "Civil Rights Cases" (*Civi Rights Cases*, 1883).

In those cases, the Supreme Court combined five similar cases testing the constitu-tionality of the 1875 Act. In an 8–1 decision, the Supreme Court invalidated the Act on the grounds that the enforcement clauses of the Thirteenth and Fourteenth Amendments did not empower Congress to enact legislation to enforce those amendments with private citizens. The majority held that only if a state enacted laws that infringed on the rights of African-Americans could Congress intervene. Passive conduct by the states, such as tolerance of discrimination, the court stated, was beyond the power of Congress to address (*Civil Rights Cases*, 1883).

In the late 1800s, judicial setbacks continued. In 1896, the Supreme Court endorsed the "separate but equal doctrine" in the landmark case of Plessy v. Ferguson (*Plessy*, 1896). The facts in this case were that Homer Plessy, who alleged that he was one-eighth African and seven-eighths Caucasian, attempted to board a whites-only train car in New Orleans in violation of Louisiana's "Separate Car Act." Under the ethical framework of moral subjectivism, he contended that the statute violated the Thirteenth and Fourteenth Amendments.

The Supreme Court rejected Plessy's contentions and held that the Thirteenth Amendment merely abolished slavery, but did not prohibit racial classifications or segregation. More importantly, the Supreme Court, perhaps examining the case through the lens of cultural relativism, adopted the concept of separate but equal, holding that the Fourteenth Amendment required equality of the races, but that "it could not have been intended to abolish distinctions based upon color, or to enforce social, as distinguished from political, equality, or a commingling of the two races upon terms unsatisfactory to either" (id.).

As a result of *Plessy*, Jim Crow laws—state and local racial segregation laws—flourished for nearly 60 years. During that period, the Supreme Court upheld the wartime detention of Japanese-American citizens, accepted the separate but equal doctrine in public schools, permitted segregation in private enterprises and allowed separate but equal public accommodations. During that same period, however, some gains were also made. For example, President Truman established a Committee on Civil Rights and ended segregation in the military and civil service.

The Supreme Court did not reject the doctrine of separate but equal in public education until 1954, finally turning the tide against segregationist practices and laws (*Brown*, 1954). In *Brown v. Board of Education*, African-American students who sought admission to non-segregated public schools challenged the separate but equal doctrine on the grounds that segregated schools could not be equal. The court unanimously answered in the affirmative the question: "Does segregation of children in public schools solely on the basis of race, even though the physical facilities and other 'tangible' factors may be equal, deprive the children of the minority group of equal educational opportunities?" (id.).

The decision in *Brown* opened the floodgates for judicial rejection of separate but equal and other segregationist practices in areas other than public schools. Racial segregation in the context of public transportation, public parks, restaurants, and other areas was soon successfully challenged. Sport organizations were part of this trend. The Supreme Court rejected the separate but equal doctrine for public golf courses and sporting events, striking down a Louisiana law banning interracial prizefighting.

Congress passed the Civil Rights Act of 1964, which incorporated language from the Civil Rights Act of 1875, to prohibit discrimination in public accommodations, education, and employment. Title II of that Act forbids discrimination in places of public accommodations, which include hotels and motels, restaurants, movie theaters, concert halls, and sports arenas and stadiums, and Title VII prohibits discrimination in the employment context.

The Civil Rights Act of 1964 is the single most significant legislative enactment designed to address "institutional" racial (and other) discrimination in the areas of public accommodation, education, and employment. However, mere statutory enactments cannot eliminate cultural and social biases, or completely level the playing field. As President Lyndon Johnson said after the passage of the Civil Rights Act of 1964 and the Voting Rights Act of 1965:

> You do not take a person who, for years, has been hobbled by chains and liberate him, bring him up to the starting line of a race and then say, 'you are free to compete with all the others,' and still justly believe that you have been completely fair. Thus it is not enough just to open the gates of opportunity. All our citizens must have the ability to walk through those gates.
>
> (Johnson, 1965)

RACE IN INTERCOLLEGIATE ATHLETICS

Racial integration

In the post-Jim Crow era, the pivotal moment for integration in intercollegiate athletics came during the NCAA men's basketball championship in 1966, just two years after the passage of the Civil Rights Act of 1964. On March 19 at the University of Maryland, basketball powerhouse University of Kentucky played upstart Texas Western University (now known as the University of Texas, El Paso).

Close examination of the event would have revealed an all-Caucasian crowd, all-Caucasian NCAA officials, and all-Caucasian referees, coaches, cheerleaders and sportswriters.

Led by Hall of Fame coach, Adolph Rupp, Kentucky fielded an all-Caucasian roster. Across the court, Texas Western dressed four Caucasian players, seven African-American players, and one Hispanic player.

At tip-off, history was made as the Texas Western Miners became the first major college team to start five African-American players in a championship game. Moreover, earlier in the season, the Don Haskins-led Miners started five African-American players for the first time in any game in major college basketball (Fitzpatrick, 2003).

Just 15 years earlier, the concept of an intercollegiate team starting an all-minority lineup would have been inconceivable, especially when in-game violence was the norm any time a person of color stepped on the field. For example, a football contest between Oklahoma A&M (now Oklahoma State University) and Drake University in 1951 highlighted the struggle for African-American equality in sport. The game featured an undefeated Drake team, which was led by the nation's top rusher, African-American running back Johnny Bright. Although a gifted athlete, Bright was not allowed to live on campus because of his African-American heritage (Lapchick, 2008).

On the opposite side was Wilbanks Smith, an Oklahoma A&M star defensive tackle and white. At the time, segregation was legal in Oklahoma, and Smith violently pursued Bright two times during the game. The second time, Smith broke Bright's jaw with a punch to the face, an incident which was captured by a newspaper photographer. Oklahoma A&M went on to defeat Drake, which had to play the rest of the contest without its star player. Neither Smith nor Oklahoma A&M was punished as a result of the assault (id.).

Although deliberate in-game violence lessened after the Bright incident, blatant racism persisted. Of note, the Southeastern Conference (SEC) was the last major conference in the United States to abandon practices of segregation. Many member schools fought diligently to keep African-Americans off their own teams and also refused to compete against other teams that included African-Americans.

For example, in 1956, the state of Louisiana passed a law banning interracial sport competitions, which forced the Harvard basketball team to cancel a trip to New Orleans because of the Ivy League team's history of African-American participation (Pennington, 2012). In Mississippi, legislators threatened to cease school funding for institutions that competed against integrated teams. For that reason, Mississippi State did not participate in the NCAA men's basketball tournament in 1959, 1961, and 1962 (Lapchick, 2008).

As stated previously, in 1954, the U.S. Supreme Court mandated the integration of public schools in the landmark *Brown v. the Board of Education* case. Although the University of Kentucky had admitted its first African-American students five years earlier, Kentucky fought integration in athletics another 17 years before Nat Northington and Greg Page, two African-American football players, played on the 1966 Kentucky team.

In fact, Northington and Page are documented as the first African-American student-athletes to participate in any SEC sport. Not until 1971–1972 did every SEC school have at least one African-American student-athlete. Three decades later, in 2004, Sylvester Croom was hired at Mississippi State University as the SEC's first African-American head football coach and University of Georgia's Damon Evans became the SEC's first African-American athletic director (id.).

Today, perhaps because of a better understanding of race through the lens of virtue and care ethics, intercollegiate sport enjoys the benefit of a diverse student-athlete population. Data comparison of the 1999–2000 academic year and the 2014–2015 academic year suggests significant improvement in diversity across multiple sports. For example, in the sport of football in 1999–2000, Caucasian student-athletes comprised 51.3 percent of all Division I football participants, while minorities represented a total of 49.7 percent of participants, of which 39.5 percent were African-American. In 2014–2015, Caucasian student-athletes totaled 40.2 percent of those who played football, and the percentage of minority participants registered 59.8 percent, of which 47.1 percent identified as African-American (ncaa.org).

In the sport of men's basketball, Caucasian student-athletes represented 34.6 percent of the sport's Division I contestants in 1999–2000 compared to 25.2 percent in 2014–2015. African-American participation improved from 55 percent in 1999–2000 to 58.3 percent in 2014–2015, while other minority representation increased from 10.4 percent in 1999–2000 to 16.5 percent in 2014–2015 (id.).

Even in a sport like gymnastics, often characterized by its large percentage of Caucasian athletes, the diversification of participation has trended positively. In 1999–2000, 84.9 percent of Division I male gymnasts identified as Caucasian, while 85.3 percent of women gymnasts identified as Caucasian. In that same period, only 1.9 percent of male athletes and 3.3 percent of female athletes registered as African-American. In comparison, in the 2014–2015 season, Caucasian male gymnasts accounted for 69.1 percent, and Caucasian female gymnasts accounted for 70.2 percent, while African-American male participation jumped to 5.3 percent and African-American female involvement increased to 8.6 percent.

Although diversity of the athlete population has increased in college sport, racial diversity among coaches and administrators lags behind. In a 2015 study conducted by Dr. Richard Lapchick of the Institute of Diversity and Ethics in Sports, African-American men represented only 10 percent of Division I coaches and about 10 percent of Division I athletic directors. Moreover, this lag also extends to the university administrative ranks, leaving African-American athletes with few African-American professors or administrators from which to seek guidance, because nearly 90 percent of faculty athletics representatives are white (New, 2016).

The academic divide

Attendance at college for many minority students comes through participation in athletics. Since the 1960s, the increase of minority student involvement in sport, in particular among African-Americans, has resulted in part from the *quid pro quo* relationship in which student-athletes receive scholarships in exchange for participating in intercollegiate sport as an extracurricular activity while enrolled in academic coursework. However, the academic emphasis in the "contract" routinely becomes lost, and the reforms to ensure better scholastic results sometimes have had negative consequences for minority student-athletes.

The NCAA began implementing significant changes in the regulation of academics for student-athletes with the development of Proposition 48 in the 1980s, a time in which African-Americans and other minority student-athletes were changing the landscape of college sport. The Proposition required that entering freshmen would be eligible for scholarships and participation only if they had achieved a grade point average of

2.0 in 11 required high school classes. The Proposition also required that a student achieve a minimum score of 700 on the SAT or a 15 on the ACT. Many critics of Proposition 48 argued that it represented a way to devise a regulatory structure that permitted only some minority participation in sport while preserving the tradition of predominately white participation (Wilson, 2014).

Although NCAA leaders argued that the new rules were not based on racial concerns, the racially disparate impact was significant. In a study, Dr. Richard Lapchick, Director of the Institute for Diversity and Ethics in Sport, revealed that, if Proposition 48 had been in effect in 1981, 69 percent of the males entering college on an athletic scholarship would have been rendered ineligible for competition and more than two-thirds of African-American male freshmen athletes would have been denied an opportunity to attend college on athletic financial aid (id.). Since the implementation of Proposition 48 in 1986, the NCAA has revised these academic initial eligibility rules four more times with each iteration making the rules more rigorous.

Despite the changing rules, diversity among athletes has continued to increase; however, the ultimate measurement of collegiate academic success—graduation rates—shows a gap between white athletes and African-American athletes. For example, of the 70 institutions that competed in football bowl games in 2012, more than half had a gap of at least 20 percent between the graduation rates of Caucasian athletes and African-American athletes. One quarter of the competing teams had a 30 percent gap (Bimper, 2013).

Furthermore, when comparing the academic performance of athletes to that of the general student body, a study conducted by the University of Pennsylvania determined that between 2007 and 2010, among NCAA Division I colleges and universities, 96.1 percent graduated African-American male student-athletes at rates lower than student-athletes overall. Also, 97.4 percent of all Football Bowl Subdivision (FBS) institutions graduated African-American male student-athletes at rates lower than undergraduate students overall (Harper, 2013).

With billions of dollars on the line and with increasing pressure to win, college sport is marred with cheating scandals in the form of academic misconduct, scandals which have adversely affected the reputation of some institutions and, to some extent, tarnished the reputation of intercollegiate sport as a whole. When African-American students are involved in these scandals, the scandals have a racial dimension as well.

EXPLOITATION OF STUDENT-ATHLETES

In general, the percentage of African-American males in the student body of most universities is low, while the percentage of African-American males participating in the revenue-generating sports of football and basketball at these institutions is high (Grantham, 2015). Central to intercollegiate sport is the concept of amateurism. However, as intercollegiate sport has become big business, particularly in sports like football and men's basketball, many people ask whether student-athletes should be paid an amount in addition to the scholarship money they receive.

The exploitation of student-athletes, particularly African-American athletes, has been a controversial issue since the late 1900s. Sociologist Harry Edwards summarized the status in 1985 by stating that:

universities and athletic departments have gained huge gate receipts, television revenues, national visibility, donors to university programs, and more, as a result of the performances of gifted basketball and football players, of whom a disproportionate number of the most gifted and most exploited have been [African-Americans].

(Edwards, 1985)

The same argument can be made today.

Since former executive director of the NCAA Walter Byers coined the term "student-athlete" in the 1950s, university administrators have weighed in on the student-athletes as amateurs controversy, debating the commercialization of intercollegiate sport (Byers, 1995). Faculty and university administrators worry about the advancement of the business of college sport at the expense of academic priorities and the mission of higher education. Most believe that student-athletes recruited to compete in revenue-generating sports like football and basketball present an ethical dilemma, because these students are often the most academically at risk relative to their peers.

As the flow of money continues to university athletic departments, the question about whether student-athletes should be paid cannot be avoided. The business of college sport is larger than ever, with student-athletes that are stronger and faster than ever before. Holding firm to its philosophy of amateurism, the NCAA shows no signs of changing its position that athletes are students first taking part in non-academic programs that enhance the mission of higher education.

The history of amateurism has not demonstrated inherent racism. In fact, the ethos of amateurism at its onset was classist. Upper-class aristocrats in England developed a method to avoid competing against lower-class factory workers by instituting a no-pay-for-play explanation. As the concept of amateurism evolved into American intercollegiate sport, the values of no-pay-for-play were upheld (Hruby, 2016).

Even today, the principles of amateurism remain race-neutral. The NCAA expressly prohibits student-athletes from accepting any compensation beyond the fixed value of a scholarship. This understanding applies equally to white and African-American student-athletes. White student-athletes, like the former Texas A&M quarterback Johnny Manziel, are prohibited from selling autographed pictures no differently than African-American student-athletes like former Auburn quarterback Cam Newton, who was denied the opportunity to capitalize on his marketability (id.). However, critics of amateurism argue that its rules restrain student-athletes from earning income, and because a disproportionate number of athletes in sports that generate the most revenue are less affluent African-Americans, such restraint rises to the level of exploitation.

The NCAA must address several ethical situations to avoid the continued perceived exploitation of student-athletes of color. From which ethical lens will an examination of amateurism in college sport yield more benefits for student-athletes? Who should be paid and why? Will compensation be used to help with academic initiatives? If only scholarship athletes in revenue-producing programs (i.e. football and men's basketball) are compensated, then the NCAA will have to be prepared to justify excluding other athletes, including the non-scholarship athletes in football and men's basketball.

RACIAL DISCRIMINATION IN PROFESSIONAL SPORTS

Although the NCAA, through the leadership of university presidents, has taken the lead in creating more inclusive and diverse participation in amateur sports, the issue of race and minority opportunities in professional sports has a somewhat different history. Professional sport in America, like intercollegiate sport, is a reflection of the society as a whole, and desegregation in sport has paralleled the desegregation of other major institutions in the country.

However, the motivations for action and change in professional sports are different than those in amateur sports, especially those within college and university structures. Many professional sport organizations are owned by wealthy families, some of whom have been somewhat less receptive to societal and cultural changes nationally and in their own communities. At times, this patriarchal management of professional sports, especially in the United States, has resulted in resistance to greater inclusiveness in hiring, retention and advancement of minority employees such as coaches and executives. The following sections will describe two major points in the integration of racial groups into the mainstream of professional sports.

Jackie Robinson and the integration of professional baseball

Until 1945, professional baseball in the United States was segregated: the Major Leagues were composed of white players and owners and, to a large extent, a white fan base. In the Negro Leagues, African-American players could compete. There was virtually no overlap between the leagues—that is, they did not engage in such activities as competing against each other for national championships or trading players. African-American fans did follow white players and white teams in the major leagues. In many ball parks, African-American patrons had to sit in "colored only" sections in the period of "Jim Crow" America.

From 1920 to 1944, the Commissioner of Baseball, Kenesaw Mountain Landis, was a federal judge brought in as commissioner following the Black Sox cheating scandal in the 1920s. However, Landis was a segregationist, perhaps due to the prevailing "separate but equal" doctrine articulated by the U.S. Supreme Court, and resisted efforts to integrate the game of baseball.

In August 1945, Branch Rickey, president and general manager of the Brooklyn Dodgers, signed a very promising baseball player, Jackie Robinson, who had previously played in the Negro League, to a minor league contract. Robinson was assigned to a Dodger farm team in Canada where he had a notable year in 1946 as a young prospect. Rickey then brought Robinson up to the major leagues for the 1947 season. Robinson had an exceptional rookie year, earning the first "rookie of the year" award in the National League.

Rickey had begun working on the integration of major league baseball as early as 1943 with the approval of the Dodgers' board of directors. Apparently, Rickey's desire to integrate major league baseball was a combination of an idealistic sense of social justice, thoughtful business acumen, and a confluence of societal changes working toward integration of sport teams and competitions. Rickey's conduct was a strong example of virtue ethics.

At that time, there were many outstanding baseball players in the Negro League teams, and Rickey believed that it would be a matter of time before other clubs began hiring black players away from those teams. Moreover, many African-American men had fought for the United States in World War II and were returning home to, among other things, resume following baseball. Just prior to the war, Olympic sports and boxing had been integrated by great athletes like Jesse Owens and Joe Louis, so the idea of African-Americans and whites playing on the same teams and against each other was not unheard of.

One of the most intriguing aspects of Rickey's integration of major league baseball was his "compact" or understanding with Jackie Robinson. According to several sources, Rickey strongly counseled Robinson that he should not lose his temper when confronted by racist taunts from fans and white players, including players from his own team. Robinson agreed to Rickey's terms and withstood considerable racist hate-speech during his early years in the major leagues. Such conduct was utilitarian in that ultimately it produced the greatest good for the greatest number. Such conduct was also a strong example of virtue ethics.

Larry Doby, an African-American player who, like Robinson, had played in the Negro Leagues prior to World War II, also began his major league career in 1947, when he signed with the Cleveland Indians. Doby played many years in the major leagues and later became the second African-American manager (Chicago White Sox) in 1978; the first was the legendary Frank Robinson.

Following the desegregation of major league baseball, increasing numbers of African-American players were hired by teams. Baseball became a game that helped define the national character of the United States as a "melting pot" of races, ethnicities, and religions.

In more recent times, however, African-American participation in baseball has declined. To address this decline, Major League Baseball launched its Diversity Task Force in 2014 in an effort to attract more African-American youths to the game. At the time, only 8.3 percent of major league players self-identified as "black," so there has been a significant decline in black players since Jackie Robinson first broke the "color line" in 1947. The Task Force considered several reasons why so few African-Americans play major league baseball, including the post-Little League cost of improving baseball skills by attending private academies, the much smaller college scholarship amounts provided to baseball players, and the paucity of opportunities to play baseball in poorer communities in the U.S.

The Task Force has recommended that MLB expand its baseball initiatives to urban areas, implement novel coaching initiatives to support minority players' goals, and use current and former baseball players to promote the game to urban, minority populations. These recommendations exemplify care ethics and utilitarianism.

Compared with the low percentage of African-Americans in MLB, about 27 percent of players self-identify as Hispanic (including Mexican, Dominican, etc.). However, many of these players have immigrated to American baseball from clubs, organizations, and training facilities in the Caribbean and Central America, rather than from U.S. urban communities.

The "Rooney Rule" and equal opportunity in professional football

The Rooney Rule was adopted by the NFL in 2003 following the 2002 season, in which two successful African-American coaches were fired at the end of the season. It also followed the release of a study by two leading class action lawyers, Johnny Cochran and Cyrus Mehri.

The study showed that, despite better win–loss records, African-American coaches were more likely to be terminated or not hired. The study recommended that professional football teams hire more minority coaches. The study's recommendation was based on the fact that "between 1986–2001, black coaches averaged 9.1 wins per season and white coaches averaged 8.1" and the belief that "America's game should 'represent America's diversity and the best values in society'" (Cochran, 2002).

In response, the NFL Commissioner announced the formation of a committee on workplace diversity to be chaired by Pittsburgh Steelers owner, Dan Rooney. By December 2003, the committee issued a set of guidelines for teams to follow during the interviewing process for senior football operations positions, such as head coaches and general managers. The results of the implementation of the Rooney Rule have been significant and positive in relation to the goals established by the NFL and the committee. The Rooney Rule exemplifies care ethics, utilitarianism, and deontology.

As a result of the implementation of the Rooney Rule, teams, such as the Pittsburg Steelers, have hired coaches like Mike Tomlin, an African-American who may not have been considered but for the Rooney Rule. Equally significant, two great African-American coaches, Tony Dungey and Mike Tomlin, have coached their respective teams to Super Bowl victories since the implementation of the Rooney Rule.

The Rooney Rule was subsequently amended to apply to Hispanic/Latino coaches and managers and, since the Rule was initiated, seventeen NFL teams have had either an African-American or Latino head coach or general manager. In 2016, five of the thirty-two head coaches were African-American, and one was Latino. Some argue that a problem with the rule is that some minority candidates are interviewed only to comply with the rule, and are not legitimate job candidates.

Within the framework of care ethics and utilitarianism, the principles underlying the creation of the Rooney Rule include equality of opportunity, enhancement of diversity within professional football, and the creation of greater inclusiveness in professional sports. These principles can also be applied to females and to sports other than professional football. Indeed, women are now a part of some NBA and NFL coaching staffs.

The NFL Commissioner announced on February 4, 2016 that the Rooney Rule would be extended to females at the executive level, and at least one female will have to be interviewed for any executive opening in the NFL.

MASCOT RACIAL CONTROVERSY

Many sport teams employ the use of mascots, which are usually people dressed in a costume depicting the origin of the team or its logo. Online searches of sport mascots are replete with images of animals adorned with team colors and anthropomorphic characters dressed as banana slugs (UC Santa Cruz), cayenne peppers (University of Louisiana-Lafayette) and okra (Delta State University).

Mascots play the important role of influencing younger fans to become and remain interested in the team and to generate game-time excitement for fans of all ages. The San Diego Chicken, the Notre Dame Leprechaun, and the Stanford Tree are examples of iconic mascots that have established a bond between the team and its fans.

However, in modern-day sport, there has been a public outcry against certain mascots that seem racist or culturally insensitive. The most notable examples are team names, logos, or mascots relating to Native Americans. Consistent with deontology, virtue ethics, and care ethics, many college and high school teams have changed their mascots and team names from the likes of Injuns, Fighting Chippewas, Redskins, and Indians because of sensitivities of Native American groups and other fans.

Some teams, however, have resisted the calls for greater thoughtfulness and sensitivity to racial or ethnic groups. These teams—perhaps the most prominent example is the Washington Redskins—have insisted that their team name and mascot are reflections of the team's history rather than images of a derogatory nature. Yet other teams argue that they do not mean to disparage Native Americans by use of a Native American name or image, but rather as a means to honor the Native Americans.

However, because of cultural awareness, many teams have changed their logo. Some examples include the Kansas City Chiefs and the Atlanta Braves, which replaced logos depicting Native American warriors with the letters KC and the script A, respectively. Stanford changed its mascot from an Indian to the Stanford Tree.

As of spring, 2017, the Washington Redskins controversy is winding its way through the courts. That case is discussed further in Chapter 12 on intellectual property rights. Because of the freedom of speech aspect of that case, it raises issues relating to utilitarianism and deontology.

ATHLETES, SYMBOLIC SPEECH, AND RACIAL INJUSTICE

Athletes, like other popular public figures such as actors and politicians, can influence public opinion on prominent topics and issues. Athletes often use their reputations and public recognition to highlight these topics and issues, including the racial divisions in the United States or the world.

At the 1968 summer Olympics, two African-American runners, John Carlos and Tommie Smith, won medals in the 200-meter sprint and during the medal award ceremony put on black gloves and delivered a "Black Power" salute from the podium. It was a powerful and galvanizing moment in sports, in which these athletes used their victories to make a highly political statement to an international audience on television and in the press.

Prior to the 1968 Olympics, John Carlos had attempted to form a boycott of the Olympics. The boycott was to last until several matters of perceived racial injustice were remedied, including an insufficiency of African-American coaches, the restoration of boxer Muhammad Ali's heavyweight boxing title, and the withdrawal of South Africa and Rhodesia from the Olympics.

The Olympic race was won by Smith with a white Australian taking silver and Carlos winning a bronze medal. The Australian, Peter Norman, supported the gestures and protest by wearing a button for the Olympic Project for Human Rights, which had been founded by Carlos.

Subsequent to their actions, Carlos and Smith were disciplined by the IOC; Smith and Carlos were barred from the Olympic Village and thrown off the U.S. Olympic track team. The athletes received a great deal of public support for their political gestures, but they also received death threats and vilifying comments from others.

In 2016, another athlete, professional football player Colin Kaepernick, created a public controversy about the treatment of African-Americans in the United States when he refused to stand at attention when the national anthem was played before NFL games. In the spirit of virtue ethics and care ethics, Kaepernick claimed he was "not going to stand up to show pride in a flag for a country that oppresses black people and people of color. To me, this is bigger than football, and it would be selfish on my part to look the other way." Then, he referred to several tragic events in 2016 that involved police officers in Ohio, Wisconsin, and other states shooting unarmed African-American men, stating that "There are bodies in the street and people getting paid leave and getting away with murder" (Giwargis, 2016).

Some, also in the spirit of virtue and care ethics, have opposed Kaepernick's action. Their argument is that disrespecting the national anthem is disrespectful to the country, particularly to men and women serving in the military.

CONCLUSION

Racism may never completely end. People will not change without sacrifice, and education is necessary to change the racist perceptions and attitudes that people hold. In search of a remedy, the leaders in sport must continue to recognize the existence of racism and discrimination. Next, leaders must assist in the transition to a period where racial diversity is the norm. Arguably, progress is being made. The problem of racism in sport may one day no longer exist so prominently, and if sport is still a reflection of society, the problem of racism in society may also improve.

Collegiate and professional athletes of all races, ethnicities and of both genders are capable of piercing through the public consciousness on matters of public concern and opinion, and can impact the national discussion in ways that ordinary citizens cannot. Many of these athletes, like highly popular entertainers, have attempted to use their public image and notoriety to advance political and society grievances and issues of equality, opportunity and fair treatment. However, in doing so, they subject themselves to criticism from those parts of the population that disagree with the political or societal issue being raised. Because the critics also believe in the ethics of their cause, society must find ways to resolve these differences of opinion. The universal appeal of sports is one avenue to such a resolution of differences.

ETHICAL LEADERSHIP CASE STUDY

Ricky Metal owned a professional sports team. A veteran businessman, Metal had owned his team for decades. One evening, in the privacy of his own home, Metal was recorded making racially insensitive remarks about African-Americans and persons of color. The recording was released to the media and a firestorm erupted. Upon hearing the comments on the recording, media personalities called for Metal to step down from his role as team owner. The commissioner of the league called for an investigation, the results of which found that Metal was in fact the person recorded.

The commissioner condemned the remarks, and the league then immediately ordered a lifetime ban for Metal, effectively disassociating him from the league and forcing Metal to sell the team.

1. Did the commissioner act ethically in addressing the concern? By what theories?
2. What impact would the league's decision have on bridging the perceived racial divide? What further ethical leadership can/should the league provide on this issue?

STUDENT LEARNING EXERCISE

1. Research the actions, motivations and explanations of Branch Rickey in desegregating major league baseball. What ethical theories support his actions? What types of leadership was he exercising?
2. Students should articulate which issues of diversity rise to the level of concern for sport and whether those issues are also prevalent in society. Students should offer ethical leadership solutions for methods of establishing equality.

PROBLEMS/QUESTIONS

1. What are some racial and ethnical stereotypes that exist about athletes or sport? Are such stereotypes ethical? Why?
2. How can sports exercise ethical leadership to challenge the views of racist logic and help to transform racial and ethical relations?
3. Is using a team name such as the Fighting Sioux or the Redskins an ethical problem? What Is the ethical solution? What is the best way to exert ethical leadership on this issue?
4. If a poll results in a majority of respondents stating that use of the Washington Redskins name isn't offensive, does that change the ethics of the situation and make it acceptable to use the name? Why?

BIBLIOGRAPHY

Anderson, Paul M., Racism in Sports: A Question of Ethics, 6 *Marquette Sports Law Journal* 357 (1996).

Belson, Ken, NFL Will Require Interviews of Women for League Executive Positions, *New York Times*, February 4, 2016.

Bimper, Albert, Kansas State Scholar Examines the Classroom Experiences of Black Student Athletes, Research & Studies, *The Journal of Blacks in Higher Education*, May 2, 2013.

Brown v. Board of Education, 347 U.S. 483 (1954).

Byers, Walter, *Unsportsmanlike Conduct: Exploiting College Athletes* (1995).

Civil Rights Cases, 109 U.S. 3 (1883).

Clark, Robert, Do BCS National Championships Lead to Recruiting Violations? A Trend Analysis of NCAA Division I (FBS) Infractions, *Journal of Sport Administration and Supervision*, April 2009.

Cochran, Johnnie, *Black Coaches in the National Football League: Superior Performance, Inferior Opportunities* (2002).

Davis, Timothy, Race and Sports in America: An Historical Overview, *Virginia Sports & Entertainment Law Journal*, June 2008.

Edwards, Harry, *Educating Black Athletes, Sport and Higher Education*, edited by Donald Chu, et al., (1985).

Finkelman, Paul, How the Civil War Changed the Constitution, https://opinionator.blogs.nytimes.com/2015/06/02/how-the-civil-war-changed-the-constitution/ (2015).

Fitzpatrick, Frank, Texas Western's 1966 Title Left Lasting Legacy, espn.com, November 19, 2003.

Franklin, John, *From Slavery to Freedom: A History of African Americans*, 7th ed., (1994).

Freeman, Mike, The Rooney Rule 10 Years Later, *Bleacher Report*, October 24, 2013.

Giwargis, Ramona, Bay Area, Nation Divided on Kaepernick Anthem Controversy, *San Jose Mercury News*, September 1, 2016.

Grantham, Charles, With College Sports at Crossroads, Unspoken Problem Facing NCAA is Race, si.com, May 19, 2015.

Harper, Shaun, Black Male Student-Athletes and Racial Inequities in NCAA Division I College Sports, Center for the Study of Race and Equity in Education (2013).

Harris, Cheryl, Whitewashing Race: Scapegoating Culture, 94 *California Law Review* 907 (2006).

Hoberman, John, *Mortal Engines: The Science of Performance and Dehumanization of Sport* (2002).

Hruby, Patrick, Four Years a Student-Athlete: The Racial injustice of Big-Time College Sports, sports.vice.com, April 4, 2016.

Hylton, J. Gordon, American Civil Rights Laws and the Legacy of Jackie Robinson, 8 *Marquette Sports Law Journal* 387 (1998).

Johnson, Lyndon B., Commencement Address at Howard University: To Fulfill These Rights lbjlib.utexas.edu, June 4, 1965.

Lapchick, Richard, Breaking the College Color Barrier: Studies in Courage, espn.com, February 20, 2008.

McManus, Jane, Roger Goodell: Women Will Interview for Open Executive Jobs, abcnews.com, February 4, 2016.

Minority Coaches Push for NCAA to Adopt Rooney Rule, si.com, January 6, 2016.

NCAA official website, Sport Sponsorships, Participation, and Demographics Search, web1.ncaa.org (2016).

New, Jake, *No Rooney Rule for Colleges*, insidehighered.com, September 22, 2016.

Pennington, Bill, In 1956, a Racial Law Repelled Harvard's Team, nytimes.com, March 14, 2012.

Plessy v. Ferguson, 163 U.S. 537 (1896).

Sage, George, Introduction to Diversity and Social Justice in College Sports, Fitness Information Technology (2007).

Sanders, Libby, Have Money Will Travel: The Quest for Top Athletes, *Chronicle of Higher Education*, August 1, 2008.

Thornton, Patrick, The Increased Opportunity for Minorities in the National Football League Coaching Ranks: The Initial Success of the NFL's Rooney Rule, 6 *Willamette Sports Law Journal* 45 (2009).

Two Hawks, John, Mascots–The Damaged Defined, nativecircle.com, April 9, 2016.

Waldron, Travis, Federal Judge Delivers Another Legal Blow to "Redskins" Team Name, huffingtonpost.com, July 8, 2015.

Wiggins, David, The Unlevel Playing Field: A Documentary History of the African American Experience in Sport (2005).

Wilson, Delgreco, Black Athletes, Race, and the Rise of NCAA Eligibility Requirements, delgrecowilson.com, September 18, 2014.

CHAPTER 9

The ethics of gender discrimination in sport

INTRODUCTION

As stated in Chapter 1, one of the principal differences between law and ethics is that ethics prescribes what should be done, whereas law prescribes what must be done. For example, ethics prescribes that like cases be treated alike. Our law prescribes such like treatment in certain specific situations, but not in all situations—for example, not until recently did the principle of treating like cases alike apply in the field of gender equity in sports. That situation has now changed. The law now definitely prescribes that like cases be treated alike in the area to which this chapter is devoted: gender.

Before 1964, gender discrimination was not generally prohibited, and initially was not included with categories like race. In that year, however, with the passage of the Civil Rights Act, the law started prescribing that like cases regarding gender be treated alike.

In sports, the primary legal prescription regarding gender started with some important legislation in 1972. The history of the development of the ethics of this situation, therefore, largely tracks the legislative and judicial development of that legislation. Given that females comprise 50 percent of humanity, the ethical support for the legislative and judicial actions in this arena is definitely utilitarian. Support is also derived from care ethics, virtue ethics, and deontology.

There has been discrimination against women in sports since ancient times, when they were not allowed to participate in the Olympic Games. The discrimination continued unabated until the passage by the U.S. Congress of Title IX of the Education Amendments of 1972. That law has gone through numerous court challenges, which will be discussed below, but it has survived stronger than ever. The ethics of treating like cases alike—a version of universalizability—has been reflected in Title IX to dramatic effect, greatly increasing the participation of women in sports.

Title IX continues to develop, with recent cases in the area of sexual orientation and transgender rights. The importance of Title IX is such that anyone connected with sports should be knowledgeable regarding the law, the regulations, and ethics related to it.

A BRIEF HISTORY OF WOMEN IN SPORTS BEFORE TITLE IX

In the ancient Olympic Games in Greece, participation was open to all free male Greek citizens, but not to females. Indeed, married females were not even permitted to attend the games. An exception was made for the daughter of the king of Sparta in 392 and 396 BC, because she was the owner (not the driver) of the winning chariot in the four-horse chariot race.

When the modern Olympic Games started in 1896, women were still not allowed to participate. The founder of the modern Olympic Games is quoted as saying that such participation would be "impractical, uninteresting, unaesthetic and incorrect" (Mansell & Foster, 2013).

Females in 19th-century United States were constrained in sports and many other areas of endeavor, because it was widely believed that a woman's main role was child-bearing and that athletics might impair that ability. Even when women began to participate in sport after women's colleges were established, sport was not competitive but rather consisted of so-called "play days." Because competition was considered too stressful for females, the different colleges did not compete with one another but rather created combined teams composed of players from different colleges.

One of the best examples of the baselessness of this fear about the fragility of women is Joan Benoit Samuelson, the winner of the first women's Olympic marathon in 1984. She was quoted in April, 2016 on the 50th anniversary of women competing in the Boston Marathon: "It was thought that running would do us bodily harm, and we would never bear children. Now here I am: 150,000 miles and two children later, I'm still running. And I'm cheering on a daughter" (Associated Press, 2016).

The dates that women were allowed to participate in certain Olympic sports are as follows:

1900	golf, croquet, lawn tennis, and sailing
1904	archery
1908	tennis, figure skating
1912	swimming
1924	fencing
1928	gymnastics
1936	alpine skiing
1948	canoeing
1952	equestrian sports
1960	speed skating
1964	volleyball, luge
1976	basketball, handball
1980	field hockey
1984	shooting, cycling
1988	table tennis, sailing
1992	biathlon
1996	softball
1998	curling, ice hockey

2000	weightlifting, pentathlon, taekwondo, triathlon, water polo
2004	free-style wrestling
2008	BMX
2012	boxing
2014	ski jumping

By the 2012 London Olympic Games, women were competing in all Olympic sports, and women outnumbered men on the U.S. team 269 to 261.

Ironically, the Olympic Games were a part of the legislative history that led to the Title IX legislation that has opened up sports for women very successfully. The Games were going on while Congress was debating one of the precursors to Title IX, the Civil Rights Act of 1964. The history of that debate illustrates just how retrograde the views on gender were at that time.

The debate occurred in February, 1964, at the time of the Innsbruck, Austria Winter Olympic Games. With the Olympic Games half over, the U.S. had won no medals, until a woman named Jean Saubert won two medals in skiing events. This fact was noted by Congresswoman Frances P. Bolton after Southern Congressman Howard W. Smith introduced an amendment to the Civil Rights Act inserting "sex" as a prohibited category of discrimination, alongside race and religion.

The amendment adding sex was apparently an attempt to derail the legislation. For example, a congressman from South Carolina, Mendel Rivers, stated in support of the amendment, "It is incredible to me that the authors of this monstrosity [the civil rights bill] . . . would deprive the white woman of mostly Anglo-Saxon or Christian heritage equal opportunity before the employer. I know this congress will not be a part to such an evil" (Roth, 1993; see also Blanchard, 2015). Rivers thought that adding women to the law would kill it, but instead the law, including "sex," was passed. The "sex" language therefore resulted from an unlikely cooperation between female and Southern legislators.

Not much was done about gender until Title IX was passed in 1972. Indeed, in 1986, when then-Associate Justice William Rehnquist of the U.S. Supreme Court first commented on the legislative history of the "sex" amendment discussed above, he said: "[T]he bill quickly passed as amended, and we are left with little legislative history to guide us in interpreting the act's prohibition against discrimination based on 'sex'" (*Meritor*, 1986).

TITLE IX

The passage of the Civil Rights Act energized the movement for women's rights. The Civil Rights Act focused on employment discrimination, not sports. The Act led to Executive Order 11375, signed by President Lyndon Johnson in 1967, which prohibited any entity receiving federal contracts from employment discrimination on the basis of sex.

This Executive Order in turn led to discrimination complaints to the Department of Labor against universities and colleges, which had numerous federal contracts. These complaints led to the proposal for Title IX, co-authored by the late Congresswoman Patsy Mink of Hawaii. Title IX is part of the United States Education Amendments of 1972, 20 U.S.C., Sections 1681–1688.

Senator Birch Bayh of Indiana was co-author of Title IX. He stated during the debate on the bill that:

> We are all familiar with the stereotype of women as pretty things who go to college to find a husband, go on to graduate school because they want a more interesting husband, and finally marry, have children, and never work again. The desire of many schools not to waste a "man's place" on a woman stems from such stereotyped notions. But the facts absolutely contradict these myths about the "weaker sex" and it is time to change our operating assumptions.
>
> (Congressional Record, 1972)

Clearly, Senator Bayh thought, in the spirit of utilitarianism, that the greatest good for the greatest number precluded discrimination against women. He clearly also believed, in the spirit of care ethics, that such discrimination did not exhibit a sense of caring and relationship.

At the time Title IX was passed in 1972, the organization for women's collegiate athletics was the Association of Intercollegiate Athletics for Women (AIAW). That organization was founded in 1971 and at first prospered, as women's collegiate athletics grew on the strength of Title IX. Ultimately, because of that selfsame prosperity, the NCAA became interested in women's athletics, which it had previously ignored.

The NCAA and the AIAW began to compete to put on women's athletic events, a competition which the NCAA dominated. This situation became so difficult for the AIAW that it sued the NCAA on antitrust grounds in 1982. After it lost the case, the AIAW ceased to exist in 1983, becoming a footnote to history. Ironically, the same ethical theories that ended discrimination against women in sports precluded the need for a special women's sports organization.

The legislative development of Title IX

By the time its co-author, Patsy Mink, passed away in 2002, which resulted in Title IX being renamed the "Patsy Takemoto Mink Equal Opportunity in Education Act," the Act had undergone significant legislative development. In 1972, for example, when it was passed, sport was not mentioned.

The key language was utilitarian, attempting to expand rights for one half of the population: "No person in the United States shall, on the basis of sex, be excluded from participation in, be denied the benefits of, or be subjected to discrimination under any education program or activity receiving Federal financial assistance." As is often the case with legislation, further regulations must be published in order to provide the necessary detail on enforcement.

In the case of Title IX, these further regulations were promulgated in 1975 by the cabinet department then known as the Department of Health, Education and Welfare. It was these regulations that made clear the impact that Title IX would have on college athletics. In 1980, the Department of Health, Education and Welfare was split in two, and the enforcement of Title IX was given over to the Office for Civil Rights in the newly created Department of Education.

Ironically (given the NCAA–AIAW conflict described above), the NCAA opposed the implementation of Title IX. Senator John Tower of Texas proposed an amendment that would have exempted revenue-producing sports (football and men's basketball) when determining if equitable athletic opportunities are provided for men and women. This proposed amendment would have had a dramatic effect on Title IX because football in particular has the greatest number of athletes and is the most expensive sport to support. Both of these efforts by the NCAA and Senator Tower, which would have ethically undermined Title IX, failed.

Title IX was dealt a temporary judicial and ethical setback in 1984, when the U.S. Supreme Court ruled that it applied only to the specific college programs that received direct federal assistance. Because athletic departments did not receive such assistance, this decision made Title IX ineffectual until Congress passed the Civil Rights Restoration Act of 1987. This Act made it clear that Title IX applied to all programs of any educational institution that received any federal money, including student loans.

Finally, in 1994, Congress passed the Equity in Athletics Disclosure Act. This Act made enforcement of Title IX easier by requiring educational institutions receiving federal aid (which includes nearly all of them) to disclose annually sport roster sizes and budgets for recruiting, scholarships, coaches' salaries, and other expenses.

Judicial development of Title IX

As with any controversial, complex piece of legislation, Title IX has required considerable interpretation by the courts. The result—bolstered by the ethics supporting Title IX—has been that Title IX has become stronger with virtually every case.

Mentioned in the section above was the one U.S. Supreme Court setback, which was remedied by the Congress with subsequent legislation. The U.S. Supreme Court more than made up for this setback, however, by ruling in 1992 that private suits for damages (and attorneys' fees) could be brought under Title IX. Sports managers and administrators must take these cases seriously, because they have resulted in both damage awards and injunctive relief. The ethics of the situation now has the full backing of the law.

Courts have determined how athletic resources must be allocated under Title IX. A well-known case involving Brown University addressed the tests, which are set out by the Office of Civil Rights of the Department of Education in order to determine whether gender discrimination in sports exists at an educational institution. The appellate court deciding the case set out these utilitarian tests as follows:

1. Whether intercollegiate level participation opportunities for male and female students are provided in numbers substantially proportionate to their respective enrollments; or
2. Where the members of one sex have been and are underrepresented among intercollegiate athletes, whether the institution can show a history and continuing practice of program expansion which is demonstrably responsive to the developing interest and abilities of the members of that sex; or
3. Where the members of one sex are underrepresented among intercollegiate athletes, and the institution cannot show a continuing practice of program

expansion such as that cited above, whether it can be demonstrated that the interests and abilities of the members of that sex have been fully and effectively accommodated by the present program.

(*Cohen*, 1993)

The court had to apply these standards to a factual situation in which Brown had 14 women's varsity teams and 16 men's teams. There were, however, only 37 percent of the women enrolled who were participating in varsity sport versus 63 percent of the men enrolled. The total enrollment of Brown was 48 percent women and 5 percent men. Therefore, Brown was out of compliance with the first standard above requiring participation proportional to gender enrollment (and also out of compliance with utilitarianism).

This lack of compliance required the court to construe the remaining two standards as they applied in a situation where Brown attempted, in a cost-cutting move, to cut two women's teams (volleyball and gymnastics) and two men's teams (water polo and golf), saving $61,000 and $16,000 respectively. Amy Cohen, a gymnast, filed suit.

Because Brown also did not meet standard two above (expanding programs), the court focused on the third standard. Brown argued that it had been fully and effectively accommodating females because, as the court stated, Brown "allocates athletic opportunities to women in accordance with the ratio of interested and able women to interested and able men" (id.). The court rejected this argument in a utilitarian way, holding that Brown read the word "fully" out of the third standard above.

Rather, the court held, the third standard "requires not merely some accommodation, but full and effective accommodation" (id.). Therefore, the court went on, "If there is sufficient interest and ability among members of the statistically underrepresented gender, not slaked by existing programs, an institution necessarily fails this [the third] prong of the test" (id.). Obviously, such accommodation was not being made by Brown because Amy Cohen and the other gymnastic and volleyball team members were demanding varsity teams in their respective sports.

A later appeal of the *Brown* case, *Cohen v. Brown University* (1996), strengthened Title IX even more. The 1993 appellate decision described above related to a preliminary injunction in the case. After a full trial, won by the plaintiffs, the appellate court ruled again in 1996.

The court made it clear in 1996 that Title IX was not an affirmative action statute, but rather an anti-discrimination statute. As such, according to the court, it is remedial and does not establish quotas:

Title IX operates to ensure that the gender-segregated allocation of athletics opportunities does not disadvantage either gender. Rather than create a quota or preference, this unavoidably gender-conscious comparison merely provides for the allocation of athletics resources and participation opportunities between the sexes in a non-discriminatory manner.

(*Cohen*, 1996)

The above holding is reflective of deontology, i.e. it is not possible to universalize a system that discriminates against a whole gender.

Brown complained that its unbalanced male/female sports participation simply reflected lesser female interest in sports. The court categorically rejected this argument, stating that the argument ignores "the fact that Title IX was enacted in order to remedy discrimination that results from stereotyped notions of women's interests and abilities" (id.). Even if it could be demonstrated that women were less interested in sports than men, the court held, this would provide "only a measure of the very discrimination that is and has been the basis for women's lack of opportunity to participate in sports" (id.). This language strongly reflects the concerns of care ethics.

Cutting back on male teams to comply with Title IX is not reverse discrimination. This proposition was established by yet another appellate court, which was ruling on the decision of the University of Illinois to cut its men's swimming team, but not its women's, because of concerns about Title IX *(Kelley,* 1994). Like Brown, the University of Illinois had problems with the first standard regarding proportionality: at the time the case was decided in 1994, 23 percent of its women were varsity athletes despite a female enrollment of 44 percent.

The men on the swimming team complained that they were victims of reverse discrimination under Title IX and that they were not receiving the equal protection of the law guaranteed by the U.S. Constitution. The court described their claims as follows:

> Plaintiffs contend . . . that the applicable regulation and policy interpretation pervert Title IX. Title IX, plaintiffs contend, 'ha[s] through some alchemy of bureaucratic regulation been transformed from a statute which prohibits discrimination on the basis of sex into a statute that mandates discrimination against males . . .' Or, as plaintiffs put it later: 'If a university is required by Title IX to eliminate men from varsity athletic competition . . ., then the same Title IX [sh]ould require the university to eliminate women from the academic departments where they are over[-]represented. Such a result would be ridiculous.'
>
> (id.)

Despite the above arguments, the court stated that the university's decision not to terminate the women's swimming team was "prudent" (id.).

The court went on to hold that the men's equal protection rights were not violated:

> Congress has broad powers under the Due Process Clause of the Fifth Amendment to remedy past discrimination. . . . Even absent a specific finding that discrimination has occurred, remedial measures mandated by Congress are 'constitutionally permissible to the extent that they serve important governmental objectives . . . and are substantially related to achievement of those ends.'
>
> (id.)

That finding led to the conclusion that Title IX was also not violated:

> Title IX's stated objective is not to ensure that the athletic opportunities available to women increase. Rather its avowed purpose is to prohibit educational institutions from discriminating on the basis of sex. And the remedial scheme

established by Title IX and the applicable regulation and policy interpretation are clearly substantially related to this end.

(id.)

Yet again, a court is in effect ruling that gender discrimination is not universalizable.

Despite its positive effect on athletic participation opportunities for women, Title IX case law has not been helpful to them in achieving equity in athletic administration or coaching positions. Indeed, Title IX has had an unintended consequence regarding sports administration: it has made women's athletics more remunerative, thus attracting more men into positions that women had held when women's sports were less lucrative, e.g. women's basketball.

As mentioned above, before Title IX, women had their own athletic association, the AIAW. As also noted above, that association and all its jobs disappeared after the NCAA started competing with it.

Universities and colleges often had separate athletic programs for men and women before Title IX. Now these programs have been integrated, usually headed by a male. As of 2012, only five out of 120 athletic directors of Division I NCAA schools were females (President's Council, 2012).

Prior to Title IX, although a very few women coached male teams, over 90 percent of women's teams were coached by women. As of 2012, that number is down to 43 percent, and only 2 percent of men's collegiate teams are coached by females (President's Council, 2012).

The leading case on equality of male and female coaching salaries also came out poorly for women. In 1994, a case involved a female coach of the women's basketball team at the University of Southern California, who received 40 percent of the compensation that the male coach of the men's basketball team received (*Stanley*, 1994). When USC offered her a 20 percent increase in pay, she rejected it as "an insult." Nonetheless, despite what appeared on its face to be unequal treatment, the court ruled against her claim.

The USC female basketball coach lost her case for several reasons. Her suit was brought under the Equal Pay Act, 1963, which the court held did not prohibit "unequal wages that reflect market conditions of supply and demand" (id.). The court further held that "An employer may consider the marketplace value of the skills of a particular individual when determining his or her salary" (id.). The market conditions in this case were that men's college basketball generated more revenue than women's college basketball. Therefore, the situation regarding the male coach receiving more money could be universalized.

The female coach argued that differences in spectator interest and revenue generation resulted from USC's "disparate promotion of men's and women's basketball teams" (id.). The court also rejected this argument, holding that "societal discrimination in preferring to witness men's sports in greater numbers cannot be attributed to USC" (id.).

THE IMPACT OF TITLE IX

The statistical impact of Title IX is transformational. In the first 35 years after Title IX was enacted, the number of female high school athletes increased from 294,015 to

2,953,355, an increase of 904 percent. At the same time, male high school athletes increased 15 percent (Wade, 2012). Ethical behavior works!

Regarding college athletes, the increase for females was from 29,977 to 166,728, an increase of 456 percent. At the same time, male college athletes increased 31 percent (*The Society Pages*, 2012).

This dramatic increase in numbers of female athletes has also resulted in improved results in competition. At the 2012 Summer Olympic Games, for example, females won 68 percent of all the medals won by the U.S. team.

Non-statistical change resulting from Title IX, though more difficult to measure, also appears to have been dramatic. As stated—completely consistently with virtue ethics— in a publication of the Leadership for Healthy Communities program of the respected Robert Wood Johnson Foundation:

> Being active can help prevent childhood obesity while also contributing to positive youth development. A report from California State Parks found that youth who participate in recreation programs that included physical activity increase their self-esteem, experience less depression, and interact more often with positive role models and authority figures. By increasing the availability, affordability, and quality of youth recreation programs that include a physical activity component, policymakers can advance a win-win approach of improving health and promoting positive youth development.
>
> (Robert Wood Johnson Foundation, 2015)

Celebrating 40 years of Title IX, the National Coalition for Women and Girls in Education notes that "sports participation decreases a young woman's chance of developing a range of . . . diseases, including heart disease, osteoporosis, and breast cancer" (National Coalition, 2012). Furthermore, that organization observes that youthful female athletes are less likely to smoke, to use drugs, or to get pregnant (id.). These findings are directly in line with care ethics.

Educational benefits listed by the National Coalition from female sport participation include a higher likelihood of graduating from high school, higher grades (especially in science), and higher scores on standardized tests. These benefits accrue particularly to females of color: "female Hispanic athletes are more likely than non-athletes to improve their academic standing, graduate from high school, and attend college" (id.).

Female athletes—consistent with virtue ethics—also benefit from sport in their careers. According to the National Coalition, "82 percent of female business executives played sports, with the majority saying that lessons learned on the playing field contributed to their success" (id.).

Two researchers have found what they call a "Chastain Effect," named after the female soccer player who was on the first U.S. women's soccer teams to win the World Cup and the Olympic Games. The research shows that an increase in female sports participation makes women more confident and independent (Clarke, 2014).

Other research, performed under the auspices of the prestigious National Bureau of Economic Research, suggests that Title IX is responsible for an approximately 4 percent increase in the female labor force. More significantly, the percentage of women in traditionally male jobs has increased (Stevenson, 2010).

Defining a male occupation as one in which two-thirds of the workers under the age of 50 are male, the number of females in male occupations jumped almost 10 percent from 1980 to 2000. Similarly, defining a female occupation as one in which two-thirds of the workers under the age of 50 are female, the number of females in female occupations declined 2.5 percent in the same time frame. These numbers are economically meaningful because those in male occupations earn approximately twice what those in female occupations earn (Stevenson, 2010), a ratio which is clearly not universalizable.

THE NCAA RECOMMENDATIONS REGARDING TITLE IX DEMONSTRATE THE BREADTH OF THAT LEGISLATION

The NCAA has published a practical guide for colleges and universities on gender equity in intercollegiate athletics. These recommendations are not theoretical: in 2016, a jury awarded the former women's basketball coach of San Diego State University $3.35 million because she was retaliated against for complaining about unequal treatment of the men's and women's teams (Zeigler, 2016). The breadth of the NCAA guide, which is consistent with utilitarianism and deontology, is impressive, covering, among other things:

- athletic scholarships;
- provision and maintenance of equipment and supplies;
- scheduling of games and practice times;
- travel and per diem expenses;
- opportunity to receive tutoring and assignment and compensation of coaches;
- provision of locker rooms, practice and competitive facilities;
- provision of medical and training services and facilities;
- provision of housing and dining services and facilities;
- publicity; support services; and recruiting.

(NCAA, 2008)

The NCAA guidelines also state that athletic scholarships must be "substantially proportionate" for both genders. In response to 25 lawsuits about unequal financial aid filed against college athletic departments by the National Women's Law Center on the 25th anniversary of Title IX, the Office of Civil Rights of the Department of Education issued a Clarification Letter on Financial Aid dated July 23, 1998.

The NCAA urges compliance with this letter, which requires no more than a 1 percent difference between the amount of scholarship aid given to a gender and the overall athletic participation of that gender. For example, if men composed 65 percent of the participation in athletics, financial aid to men should be between 64 percent and 66 percent of financial aid given. This recommendation is consistent with utilitarianism and deontology.

There are some nuances to this seemingly straightforward rule. For example, if a student receives non-athletic scholarship money in addition to an athletic scholarship, that non-athletic scholarship money does not count in this calculation.

If an institution deviates from this rule, it must provide a legitimate, non-discriminatory reason. The Clarification Letter, consistent with care ethics, lists such legitimate reasons as:

- actions taken to promote athletic program development;
- differences in in-state and out-of-state tuition;
- unexpected fluctuations in the participation rates of males and females;
- phasing in of athletics scholarships pursuant to a plan to increase participation; and
- unexpected last-minute decisions by scholarship athletes not to enroll.

These exceptions also have some nuances, consistent with deontology. For example, as stated by the Clarification Letter regarding more expensive out-of-state scholarships: "[I]f a college consistently awards a greater number of out-of-state scholarships to men, it may be required to demonstrate that this does not reflect discriminatory recruitment practices" (Office for Civil Rights, 1998). Regarding the phasing in of scholarships for a new team, the Clarification Letter states that "the university may be required to demonstrate that the time frame for phasing-in of scholarships is reasonable in light of college sports practices to aggressively recruit athletes to build start-up teams quickly" (Office for Civil Rights, 1998).

The questions that the NCAA urges its members to consider regarding the provision of equipment and supplies include such universalizability factors as 1) why there exist any differences between men's and women's teams, 2) is the quality of the equipment the same, and 3) is the equipment replaced on the same schedule? Budgets should be carefully perused for equality and, if the students are asked to provide any of their own equipment, the reasoning for that should be clear and persuasive.

Regarding scheduling of games and practices, the NCAA recommends, pursuant to universalizability, that five areas be explored. The first of these is how many competitive events are scheduled. If both genders are not receiving equal opportunities for prime-time games, there should be an explanation.

The second area is equivalence of practice times. Questions include length and time of practices and the ability to practice when school is not in session. If a men's sport like football has no female equivalent, the NCAA suggests that the school take into account a bigger picture.

Equivalence of pre- and post-season competition is another important area, according to the NCAA. For example, if the men's baseball team gets to practice in Florida, the women should have the same opportunity.

Travel and per diem allowance contain many traps for the uninformed, according to the NCAA. First, the respective sizes of the travel teams must be considered. If not equal, there must be a rational reason why.

The mode of transportation is sometimes handled by the players themselves, with carpools and similar informal arrangements. The NCAA recommends that travel policies be formalized in order to avoid Title IX problems.

Housing must also be equivalent when on the road. How many people must share a room is an important factor. Also, if some teams get housing the night before a home game, that perquisite should be offered to both genders.

Length of stay is also important. Policies should be uniform regarding arrival and departure times, which should depend on the distance traveled.

Per diem and dining arrangements should also be regulated by uniform policies. If one gender is regularly eating at sit-down restaurants and the other is regularly eating fast food, that indicates a problem.

The opportunity to receive academic tutoring is another significant area. An important threshold question is whether the same proportional number of tutors is available to both genders. According to the NCAA, the school should have a formal policy regarding the provision of tutors, the assignments of the tutors, and the compensation of the tutors.

The NCAA also makes recommendations regarding the opportunity to receive coaching, and the assignment and compensation of the coaches. The number of full-time and part-time coaches should be compared on an apples-to-apples basis—i.e. they should be universalizable. The number of part-time coaches may affect the accessibility of the coaches to the players, which is a factor. The qualifications of coaches should not be grossly different.

As noted above, during the discussion of the lawsuit brought by the University of Southern California's female basketball coach, Title IX has not been particularly helpful in the area of coaching salaries because setting salaries is a complex matter. The NCAA is therefore not too emphatic on this subject, although the NCAA suggests uniform policies where possible. For example, if some teaching assignments are handled by coaches, the school should beware of situations where the females are consistently teaching more substantive (and therefore time-consuming) courses than the males.

Regarding the provision of locker rooms, practice facilities and game facilities, the most important factor is accessibility. This should be equal (universalizable) unless there are compelling reasons to the contrary. Facilities should look more or less the same, taking into account that older facilities generally do not look as good as the newer ones. In this regard, however, it is helpful to have a master plan for all the facilities.

Playing surface should also be considered. Artificial turf for one gender and natural grass for the other would be a red flag. In the professional context, the U.S. women's soccer team has made an issue of this.

Size and number of lockers is something that is readily discernible. The same is true for the size and quality of the shower stalls and the restroom facilities. Team rooms with amenities like flat-screen televisions should also be factored into the assessment.

The equivalency of medical and training facilities and services is another area that must be assessed. For example, both genders must have equivalent access to strength and conditioning coaches, and the weight rooms in which they operate.

Access to team doctors and trainers is also important. One problem to beware of is the assignment of certified athletic trainers to the men and student trainers to the women.

Housing and dining facilities and services is yet another area which the NCAA believes is significant. The location and quality of the housing must be equivalent—i.e. universalizable. The meal plans must be uniform for both genders.

Publicity is another area on which the NCAA focuses. There should be equivalence in the availability and qualifications of sports information personnel. For example, the men should not have access to paid professionals while the women are consigned to students in this field.

Team publications should also be equivalent—i.e. universalizable. For example, the men's basketball team should not have a hardbound media guide while the women's is soft cover. The fact that some sports like football receive more coverage than others, like field hockey, is not an excuse to deviate from equivalence. Similarly, outsourcing marketing and public relations does not absolve the institution from equivalent treatment of the genders.

Administrative support is another area covered by the NCAA. This measures things like access to the athletic director and the number of administrative assistants that the various teams have. Equal access to computers and video equipment is also included in this category.

Payment of student-athletes

Lawsuits regarding paying NCAA student-athletes may well have Title IX consequences. As of late 2016, a major lawsuit is pending that would require the payment of NCAA athletes. The basis for the lawsuit is that football and men's basketball in particular generate billions of dollars in which the student-athletes in those sports do not share because of the NCAA's position on amateurism.

No women's sports are considered revenue-generating. Therefore, if this lawsuit succeeds, a determination will have to be made how to comply with Title IX. The idea that football and men's basketball players would be paid but women athletes would not be paid certainly raises serious questions under Title IX and under the concept of deontology.

GENDER DISCRIMINATION IN PAY AT THE PROFESSIONAL LEVEL

A more recent example of a situation regarding equal pay occurred at the professional level of women's soccer. The women filed a complaint in April, 2016 to the Equal Employment Opportunity Commission that the United States Soccer Federation paid them less than the male soccer players, even though in 2015, by virtue of winning the Women's World Cup, the women generated far more income than the men. That case was resolved in April 2017 by a new collective bargaining agreement that improves the pay, bonuses and travel provisions of the women and that gives them some control of licensing and marketing rights.

UNISEX TEAMS

Some courts have considered how "separate but equal" and "unisex" teams fit in with Title IX. Although "separate but equal" has been prohibited by the U.S. Supreme Court in matters relating to race, the concept has been explicitly accepted by the 1975 federal regulations for Title IX:

  (b) *Separate teams.* Notwithstanding the requirements of paragraph (a) of this section, a recipient may operate or sponsor separate teams for members of each sex where selection for such teams is based upon competitive skill or the activity involved is a contact sport. However, where a recipient operates or sponsors a team in a particular sport for members of one sex but operates or sponsors no such team for members of the opposite sex, and athletic opportunities for members of that sex have previously been limited, members of the excluded sex must be allowed to try-out for the team offered unless the sport involved is a contact sport. For the purposes of this part, contact sports include boxing, wrestling, rugby, ice hockey, football, basketball and other sports the purpose or major activity of which involves bodily contact.

The reason for this is simple. In some cases, a unisex team would exclude women entirely because women might not be able to effectively compete with bigger and stronger men. Having separate teams for men and women, many believe, increases athletic opportunities for women. Therefore, it is utilitarian and universalizable.

As stated above, the regulation makes an exception for contact sports. One case, however (*Mercer*, 1999), created an exception to this exception once a woman is allowed to try out for a contact sport. That case involved a female place-kicker, who had played that position in high school; who was told by the coach that she had made the Duke University football team; and who then was not allowed to participate in games. The jury awarded her $1 in actual damages and $2 million in punitive damages, the latter of which was reversed because the court ruled that Title IX did not permit punitive damages.

Although the punitive damages were reversed, their amount gives an indication of how the jury felt about the ethics of gender discrimination in sports. As mentioned above, sports administrators who take these cases lightly do so at their peril.

The unisex issue has not been decided at the collegiate level, but there has been a case at the high school level (*Hoover*, 1977). A woman in the junior class was prohibited from trying out for the soccer team because of advice from a medical committee that playing on a mixed-gender soccer team was a health and safety risk for females. The risk was generated by the fact that, because of various physical differences, on average women are less capable of sustaining a collision than men.

The court disposed of this reason summarily:

[W]hile males as a class tend to have an advantage in strength and speed over females as a class, the range of differences among individuals in both sexes is greater than the average differences between the sexes. [Defendant school district] has not established any eligibility criteria for participation in interscholastic soccer, excepting for sex. Accordingly, any male of any size and weight has the opportunity to be on an interscholastic team and no female is allowed to play, regardless of her size, weight, condition or skill.

(*Hoover*, 1977)

Allowing the female to try out for the soccer team, the court was quite emphatic: "Any notion that young women are so inherently weak, delicate or physically inadequate that the state must protect them from the folly of participation in vigorous athletics is a cultural anachronism unrelated to reality" (*Hoover*, 1977). In other words, such discrimination is not universalizable.

SEXUAL ORIENTATION AND TRANSGENDER ISSUES

Sexual orientation and Title IX

Whether sexual orientation discrimination is covered by Title IX has yet to be definitively decided by the courts. A case in California, *Videckis and White v. Pepperdine University*, was brought by two female basketball players at Pepperdine University who alleged that they were discriminated against because of their sexual orientation (*Videckis*, 2015).

As of late 2016, the case is at an early stage. Pepperdine argued in a motion to dismiss the case that sexual orientation was not covered by Title IX. The court did not accept this argument, ruling, consistent with deontology, that:

> [S]exual orientation discrimination is a form of sex or gender discrimination, and . . . the 'actual' orientation of the victim is irrelevant. It is impossible to categorically separate 'sexual orientation discrimination' from discrimination on the basis of sex or from gender stereotypes; to do so would result in a false choice. Simply, to allege discrimination on the basis of sexuality is to state a Title IX claim on the basis of sex or gender.
>
> (*Videckis*, 2015)

You Can Play is an organization advocating for the rights of LGBTQ athletes, with a website at www.youcanplayproject.org. Its mission statement is as follows:

> You Can Play works to ensure the safety and inclusion of all in sports—including LGBTQ athletes, coaches and fans.
>
> You Can Play works to guarantee that athletes are given a fair opportunity to compete, judged by other athletes and fans alike, only by what they contribute to the sport or their team's success.
>
> You Can Play seeks to challenge the culture of locker rooms and spectator areas by focusing only on an athlete's skills, work ethic and competitive spirit.

Transgender facilities

Transgender issues are likely to become more predominant in sports. The State of North Carolina in 2016 prohibited transgender people by law from using restrooms of the gender that is not their biological heritage, but in 2014 liberalized that law after the NBA and NCAA took the position that the original law would cause NBA and NCAA events not to be held in North Carolina. The U.S. Department of Justice has challenged this law, and the Office for Civil Rights of the Department of Education and the Civil Rights Division of the U.S. Department of Justice issued a letter on May 13, 2016 regarding, among other things, locker rooms and athletics.

Regarding locker rooms, the letter states:

> A school may provide separate facilities on the basis of sex, but must allow transgender students access to such facilities consistent with their gender identity. A school may not require transgender students to use facilities inconsistent with

their gender identity or to use individual-user facilities when other students are not required to do so. A school may, however, make individual-user options available to all students who voluntarily seek additional privacy.

(Office for Civil Rights, 2016)

Regarding athletics, the letter states:

Title IX regulations permit a school to operate or sponsor sex-segregated athletics teams when selection for such teams is based upon competitive skill or when the activity involved is a contact sport. A school may not, however, adopt or adhere to requirements that rely on overly broad generalizations or stereotypes about the differences between transgender students and other students of the same sex (i.e. the same gender identity) or others' discomfort with transgender students. Title IX does not prohibit age-appropriate, tailored requirements based on sound, current and research-based medical knowledge about the impact of the students' participation on the competitive fairness or physical safety of the sport.

(id.)

This letter was issued during the Obama administration, and it may change with the Trump adminsitration. Schools across the nation are struggling with this issue, and there are court cases pending in this area. Is it universalizable that transgender students should be treated equally or are there other factors that make such discrimination non-universalizable?

FEMALE SPORTSCASTERS

Treatment of female sportscasters raises serious questions of gender discrimination. Up to now, most of these questions have been raised at the professional level. Some female sportscasters, for example, have brought cases alleging that they were fired because of their age and appearance. Although student sportscasters are not paid, some of the issues affecting the professionals may also affect them, and the courts may not consider such discrimination to be universalizable.

A Google search for "female sportscasters" turns up in the first four entries the following: "10 of the Sexiest Female Sportscasters," "75 Hottest Female Sportscasters on TV—Busted Coverage," "The Top 50 Hottest Woman Sportscasters," and the "40 Hottest Female Sports Reporters." A search under "male sportscasters" turns up nothing analogous (Katz, 2015).

Such discrimination has been noted in academic work—for example, a 2005 thesis in communication submitted at Virginia Polytechnic Institute and State University entitled "Public Perceptions of Credibility of Male and Female Sportscasters" by Heather Michelle Toro. She states that:

Even the most attractive and most knowledgeable female sportscaster can't overcome the stereotype of another pretty face who cannot talk sports. Her sex prevents her from being judged as credible as the least attractive and least knowledgeable male sportscaster.

(id.)

These attitudes can lead to legal problems at the collegiate level. Administrators should make sure that sportscasting opportunities are provided on merit, not on stereotypes.

CONCLUSION

As a result of Title IX, women have made tremendous and ethical progress in sports since 1972. It would be naive, however, not to note discrimination that still exists. Centuries of discrimination cannot be eliminated in a few decades. For example, women for the most part do not make nearly as much money from sports as men do. The numbers of women coaches and sports broadcasters are small compared to men in those professions. One thing is certain: after over four decades of Title IX, the law is still evolving. This will result in many ethical problems that sports administrators will have to continue to confront.

ETHICAL LEADERSHIP CASE STUDIES

Case study #1

Oldschool is the athletic director at State University, which has a student body equally split between men and women: 50 percent of the men participate in varsity athletics but only 40 percent of the women do, up from 25 percent five years ago. Oldschool is informed that the Office of Civil Rights of the Department of Education will be auditing his department for compliance with Title IX.

1. Is State University in compliance with Title IX?
2. What ethical significance, if any, does the increasing rate of women's participation have?
3. Can Oldschool ethically comply with the audit by reducing men's participation to 40 percent?
4. Oldschool takes an email survey of the students, which shows that no more than 40 percent of the women have an interest in athletic participation. Does this make any ethical difference? How can/should Oldschool provide ethical leadership with regard to this low interest level?

Case study #2

State University's football and men's basketball teams are very profitable, generating over $10 million for the university. After the NCAA settles a lawsuit, the NCAA now permits the compensation of college athletes. State University wants to reward its players for their hard work that generates profits and sets aside $1 million to compensate the football and men's basketball players.

1. What are the ethical arguments that the female athletes at State University should also be compensated?
2. Ethically, how much should the compensation for women be and how should it be distributed?

3 Using ethical principles, how much compensation, if any, should be given to the male athletes on teams other than football and men's basketball?

4. How should State University provide leadership regarding the goal of equal payment to all of its student-athletes?

Case study #3

One of the students at State University, Pat, was born a male but considers herself a female. She wants to try out for the women's basketball team and to shower and change in the women's locker room.

1. Ethically, should Pat be allowed to try out for the women's basketball team?
2. Ethically, should Pat be allowed to shower and change in the women's locker room?
3. If so, what accommodations should be made for Pat when the team travels to another college for a game?
4. If Pat sets any records, what are the ethics of her birth sex being noted in the record book?
5. What sort of leadership should State University provide on the issue of equal facilities for transgender individuals?

STUDENT LEARNING EXERCISE

Prepare an essay about how you (or someone you know or know of) have been harmed by or have benefited from gender discrimination in sports. The essay should describe the discrimination, how/if it was resolved, and the ethical aspects of it. The essay should consider how, if at all, the situation would have been different before the advent of Title IX and how ethical leadership could have been applied to prevent the discrimination.

PROBLEMS/QUESTIONS

1. Why is it ethically important to eliminate gender discrimination in sports?
2. What have been some of the negative ethical impacts of such discrimination?
3. What are some of the misperceptions about females that have contributed to gender discrimination in sports?
4. Does gender discrimination ethically apply to discrimination against gay or transgender individuals?
5. Do males whose teams have been eliminated so that their college or university can comply with Title IX have an ethical claim for reverse discrimination? Why or why not?
6. Why are there so few female sportscasters? How can ethical leadership be applied to remedy this situation?
7. If courts rule that football and men's basketball players must be paid, what ethical impact, if any, will that have on female college athletes?

BIBLIOGRAPHY

Associated Press, Celebrating 50 years of women in the race, *San Francisco Chronicle*, April 17, 2016, p. B 13.

Blanchard, Paul, Insert the Word Sex-How Segregationists Handed Feminists a 1964 "Civil Rights" Victory Against the Family, *The Family in America*, Winter 2015.

Clarke, Phoebe, Title IX's Other Effects: Do Sports Make Women Less Religious?, *Deadspin*, March 4, 2014.

Clarke, Phoebe, The Chastain Effect: Using Title IX to Measure the Causal Effect of Participating in High School Sports on Adult Women's Social Lives, *The Journal of Socio-Economics*, February, 2014.

Congressional Record, Vol. 118, p. 5804 (1972).

Cohen v. Brown University, 991 F. 2d 888 (First Circuit, 1993).

Cohen v. Brown University, 101 F. 3d 155 (First Circuit, 1996).

Holden, Dominic, Department of Education Issues Guidelines to Protect Transgender Students in Single-sex Classrooms, Buzzfeed, December 1, 2014.

Hoover v. Meiklejohn, 430 F. Supp. 164 (D. Colorado, 1977).

Katz, Ron, Gross Gender Discrimination in Sportscasting, forbes.com, November 28, 2015.

Katz, Ron, Legal Precedent May Create an Uphill Battle for Women's Soccer Claims, forbes.com, April 1, 2016.

Kelley v. University of Illinois, 35 F. 3d 265 (Seventh Circuit, 1994).

Mansell, Pam & Foster, Rebecca, *The Girls of Southend High School 1913–2013* (2013).

Mercer v. Duke University, 190 F. 3d 138 (Fourth Circuit, 1999).

Meritor Savings Bank, FSB v. Vinson. (1986). 477 U.S. 57, 63–64.

National Coalition for Women and Girls in Education, *Title IX at 40: Working to Ensure Gender Equity in Education* (2012).

NCAA, *Gender Equity in Intercollegiate Athletics* (2008).

Office for Civil Rights, the U.S. Department of Education, Dear Colleague Letter: Bowling Green State University, July 23, 1998.

Office for Civil Rights, U.S. Department of Education, Dear Colleague letter from Gerald Reynolds, Assistant Secretary for Civil Rights, July 11, 2003.

Office for Civil Rights, Department of Education and Civil Rights Division of U.S. Department of Justice, Dear Colleague Letter from Catherine E. Lhamon, Assistant Secretary for Civil Rights and Vanita Gupta, Principal Deputy Assistant Attorney General for Civil Rights, U.S. Department of Justice, May 13, 2016.

President's Council on Fitness, Sports & Nutrition, 40th Anniversary of Title IX: Status of Girls' and Women's Sports Participation, September, 2012.

Robert Wood Johnson Foundation, Making the Connection: Physical Activity and Positive Youth Development (2015).

Ross, Terrance, What Gender Inequality Looks Like in Collegiate Sports, *The Atlantic*, March 18, 2015.

Roth, Elizabeth, The Civil Rights History of "Sex": A Sexist, Racist Congressional Joke, *Ms. Magazine*, March/April, 1993.

Stanley v. University of Southern California, 13 F. 2d 1313 (Ninth Circuit, 1994).

Stevenson, Betsey, Beyond the Classroom: Using Title IX to Measure the Return to High School Sports, National Bureau of Economic Research, Working Paper 15728 (2010).

Videckis and White v. Pepperdine University, 2015 WL 8769974 (C.D. Cal., Dec. 14, 2015).

Wade, Lisa, The Effect of Title IX on Sports Participation, *The Society Pages*, June 23, 2012.

You Can Play, Our Cause, Our Mission, www.youcanplayproject.org/pages/mission-statement (accessed May 24, 2017).

Zeigler, Mark, Beth Burns Wins Wrongful Termination Lawsuit vs. SDSU, *San Diego Union–Tribune*, September 28, 2016.

CHAPTER 10

Violence and hazing in sport

INTRODUCTION

Sports often parallel and reflect the society in which they are played. They are rules-based, competitive, and increasingly inclusive. They diverge in one key aspect: societal goals involve peaceful resolution of conflicts, whereas in many sports, violence is part of the game.

In fact, sport performance and achievement are often measured by the level of violence. Hockey would not be hockey without body checks. Bone-jarring tackles are a part of football. Rugged physical play is necessary in rugby, water polo, and even in "non-contact" sports, such as basketball. The question is not how to end on-field violence in sports, for that would mean an end to many sports. The questions are: how much violence is too much violence on the playing field, what should be done to punish and deter such excess, and who should regulate the sport and administer such punishment?

An issue related to violence in the context of organized sports is hazing. Hazing used to be considered an acceptable, if not desirable, ritual, which promoted team unity and bonding. Society and sport culture are becoming less tolerant of hazing; however, both face the same obstacles in addressing this issue. Identifying and defining hazing is often difficult. The extent to which teams and athletic organizations should self-police versus the role of statutes and criminal liability is an equally difficult issue.

PHILOSOPHICAL CONSIDERATIONS OF VIOLENCE AND CONSENT IN SPORT

Before looking more thoroughly into the legal issues and specific cases of violence in sport, it is important to consider the unique ethical status of violence in sport. Attitudes toward violence in sport differ from attitudes toward violence outside the sporting realm. As discussed briefly in Chapter 1, consent and assuming the risks inherent in each sport play key roles when considering the ethics of violence in sport. Clearly, if someone were to deliberately run into another person walking down the sidewalk on a neighborhood street, this would be considered wrong, both legally and ethically. Yet, this exact instance occurs on the football field hundreds of times during games. We permit this behavior because of the implied consent among those who participate in football: by agreeing to play football, one consents to the possibility that others may knock them over and tackle them. Similarly, implied consent to certain types of violent acts exists in various other sports such as boxing and ice hockey.

Consent and its relation to violence in sport come into question, though, in various ways. First, the exact behavior being consented to must be clear. Hockey players, for example, consent to being checked into the boards. Although players certainly try to avoid being checked, checking is considered good ice hockey. Additionally, players consent to the fact that they will occasionally be fouled—that is, that they may be on the receiving end of an illegal check or a high stick, although illegal maneuvers are not generally considered to be good hockey, anyone who participates in the game understands that penalties do happen quite frequently. Players thus consent to and assume the risk of such actions as part of the sport.

Additionally, how does one player's or team's consent relate to the intent of one's competitors? For example, audio of a 2012 pre-game talk by the NFL's New Orleans Saints' defensive coach, Gregg Williams, showed him commanding his players to harm players on the competing team, even offering money in the form of a bounty for those who did so. He repeatedly encourages his players to inflict head trauma on opponents with statements like "Kill the head and the body will die" and "Make sure we kill Frank Gore's head . . . we want his head sideways." He urges players to hit opposing quarterback Alex Smith in the chin, offering to pay the first player who does so. He incites violence: "Every single one of you, before you get off the pile, affect the head. Early, affect the head. Continue . . . hit the head;" "[Receiver, Crabtree] becomes human when we . . . take out that outside ACL." (Darlington, 2012).

Certainly, violence is allowed, legitimate and even expected in the game of football. Even legal hits can induce injuries. Within any given game, however, illegal hits also occur, often unintended, as a result of either poor defensive play or of strong offensive play that causes the defender to be in a poor position to tackle legally. But when the sole intent becomes to induce harm and injury, then the play crosses an ethical line, whether that line is created by virtue ethics, care ethics, deontology, or utilitarianism.

Another issue of concern regarding violence in sport involves minors playing the game. In these cases, because minors cannot legally (or ethically) give full consent, or knowingly accept the risks inherent in the activity, the consent must be given by parents. To what extent can parents rightly consent to their children's participation in potentially harmful activities? Different answers to this question would be generated by, and even within, care ethics, virtue ethics, deontology, and utilitarianism.

Third, and connected with the above issues, is the question of whether there are—or ought to be—limits to violence to which adults can ethically consent. To take an extreme example, even if participants willingly consent to professional gladiator fights-to-the-death, the "sport" would clearly not be sanctioned in an ethical society because it is clearly not universalizable. Given that we are willing to draw a line limiting violence in sport, the question becomes, where and at what point do we draw it?

Sport philosophers have been asking such a question about the sport of boxing for years and now, with the advent of mixed martial arts (MMA) cage fighting, the issue has become even more pressing. To what extent should we allow people to consent to various levels of violence and then, to what extent ought we to sanction them for exceeding those levels?

Consent has also been called into question because those athletes who choose to participate in such extremely violent and harmful sports are often from lower socio-economic classes; in many cases, these individuals have fewer options and see these sports as a way to earn a living, which may result in a less voluntary consent.

One can make a rough analogy to prostitution. Although prostitutes may be said to give their consent to participate, we must question to what extent this consent is freely chosen and at what cost to both the participants and to society.

Finally, if one agrees that the violence is too overt in sports such as football, boxing, MMA, and others, that agreement calls into question the viewing of such activities. In a sense, by viewing and/or attending such contests, the viewer is complicit, because sports leagues thrive in many senses only as a result of the support of those who enjoy watching the competitions.

ATTEMPTS TO CONTROL VIOLENCE IN SPORTS

Everyone has heard the joke about "going to see a fight when a hockey game broke out." Although a humorous quip, it is also a telling one. Society does not condone body checks on the sidewalks or fistfights in the street. Such violence, however, is an integral part of hockey, just as blocking and tackling are part of football, and hard fouls part of basketball. And it is acceptable—to a point. Leaders in both sport and society struggle with locating the point of acceptability on the violence spectrum. They also grapple with how best to deal with situations when the point is crossed.

There is debate over whether or not the overall incidence of excessive on-the-field violence has increased, or if it simply appears so because of ubiquitous video cameras and sports media. It cannot be debated, however, that the problem, even if it is not increasing, must be addressed. When a survey of coaches, parents, and young athletes aged 9 to 15 disclosed that roughly 13 percent of those young athletes had tried to hurt an opponent, and when another researcher determined that 8 percent of coaches "had encouraged their athletes to hurt an opponent," it is clear that the issue cannot and should not be avoided (*USA Today*, 2005). There is no perfect solution for controlling violence in endeavors that are inherently violent. Self-regulatory, judicial, and legislative approaches have been tried, with varying degrees of success.

Sport self-regulation

Sports are rules-based. It is one of their defining features. All sports have rules prescribing proper play and conduct, and proscribing improper activity. Even the most violent of sports-like mixed martial arts have rules prohibiting certain acts such as eye-gouging. Referees and officials are charged with enforcing the rules during games and matches. They can award foul shots, order a player off the playing field to serve a penalty, or take away points. This sort of in-game, self-policing, often coupled with oversight by athletic associations and governance organizations, has been the traditional way athletic violence was regulated.

As professional and amateur sports participation grew, from youth soccer to adult recreational leagues to the highest level of professional athletics, the need to remove over-sight of athletic violence outside of sport to redress excessive violence on the playing field also grew. The ethical question of what on-field acts ought to be redressed off the field has no easy answer.

Efforts by the judicial system

Historically, the courts have rarely been called upon to determine the outcome of disputes involving violence by sports participants. A primary reason was "the infrequency with which professional athletes avail(ed) themselves of" their civil tort remedies (Carlsen, 2006). In addition to the "keep it in the clubhouse" mentality, players were reticent to seek criminal or civil tort redress because of "the tremendous pressure players feel from teammates, opponents, coaches, and management to resolve disputes without recourse to external sanctions." These "pressures include ostracism and retaliation by fellow players, the threat of being traded, and manipulation of salary and benefits by management" (id.).

However, the traditional reluctance of participants to seek reparation outside the sport has eroded in the last half-century. Sports no longer exclusively act as their own police force and judicial system, free from outside intervention. The courts, both civil and criminal, have been increasingly called on to adjudicate on-field incidents. The courts have, often reluctantly, attempted to answer the call, recognizing that while "the law should not place unreasonable burdens on the free and vigorous participation in sports . . . organized, athletic competition does not exist in a vacuum. Rather, some of the restraints of civilization must accompany every athlete on the playing field" (*Nabozny*, 1975).

Greater reliance on the court system, although it affords participants access to monetary remedies and criminal justice, imposes on the courts the extremely difficult job of determining how much to intrude in the sports domain. Striking "the balance between encouraging vigorous and free participation in recreational or sports activities, while ensuring the safety of the players" is a formidable task (*Marchetti*, 1990). To describe that task as formidable is an understatement. In addition to having to apply laws that do not lend themselves to the sports context, the courts adjudicating such matters have to be careful not to render decisions that might significantly alter the way the sports themselves are played or rules enforced.

Civil courts

Most civil cases that have made their way to the judicial system involved claims of negligence (Champion, 2004). Negligence can be defined as engaging in conduct that is unreasonable under the circumstances, such as carelessly hitting a golf ball toward another golfer, an overzealous check from behind in hockey, or a softball player who runs into a fielder rather than sliding to avoid contact. In the absence of showing a wanton disregard for the safety of other participants or reckless conduct, or specific intent to injure or harm, recovery in most sport injury cases based on the conduct of another player has been barred, as also discussed in Chapter 6, by the doctrine of assumption of the risk: a person who voluntarily engages in a sport accepts the risks ordinarily associated with that sport.

One court's discussion of the assumption of the risk doctrine as applied to football accurately reflects the prevailing traditional judicial sentiment toward claims of co-participant inflicted injuries:

The playing field is a body-contact sport. The game demands that the players come into physical contact with each other constantly, frequently with great force. The linemen charge the opposing line vigorously, shoulder to shoulder. The tackler faced the risk of leaping at the swiftly moving legs of the ball-carrier and the latter must be prepared to strike the ground violently. Body contacts, bruises, and clashes are inherent in the game. There is no other way to play it. No prospective player needs to be told that a participant in the game of football may sustain injury. That fact is self-evident.

(*Vendrell*, 1962)

Invoking the doctrine of assumption of the risk was successful, for the most part, in keeping the courts from judicially regulating violence in sport. The doctrine was less successful, however, in deterring inappropriate violence in sports or clarifying the boundaries as to the degree and type of violence that are acceptable aspects of each game.

Even though certain concepts such as assumption of the risk find their way into most judicial discussions of sport violence, there are no uniform definitions or methods of applying those concepts to individual cases. If the interpreters of laws—the judges—could not easily differentiate acceptable from unacceptable playing field violence, neither could they expect the contestants to differentiate:

A tort standard which clearly guides a judge, a jury, and most importantly, an athlete vigorously competing on the field of play, has yet to be found. How does one distinguish the legally acceptable from the unacceptable? Conduct that is negligent, conduct that is reckless or intentional, and conduct that exceeds the risks inherent in the sport are all standards that require consideration of both the subjective awareness of a game's risks by those who play it and the objective practices that are part of the culture of the sport.

(Richardson, 2004)

Two well-known cases, arising at about the same time in two separate professional sports, were responsible, in large part, for the expansion of the role of the civil courts in addressing on-field violence, and in the utilization of legal theories beyond that of negligence, and its nullifier, assumption of the risk.

During the game between the Los Angeles Lakers and the Houston Rockets on December 9, 1977, Lakers forward Kermit Washington punched Rockets forward Rudy Tomjanovich in the face, resulting in skull damage, broken jaw and nose, and other life-threatening injuries. The National Basketball Association later suspended Washington for 60 days and fined him $10,000—the largest monetary fine in sport history at that time.

The sport's internal mechanisms had addressed the incident, but Tomjanovich sought redress through the civil court system. Tomjanovich recognized that if he sued only Washington, even the deliberate punch that severely injured him might have been deemed protected by the doctrine of assumption of the risk. It was part of a skirmish during the game as well as an ongoing dispute between the teams.

Tough physical play, scuffling, and even some brawling were considered risks inherent in the sport. Tomjanovich, therefore, filed a lawsuit against the Lakers, Washington's employer, for promoting an environment in which violence was an acceptable tactic in the pursuit of winning games, a tactic that embraced "enforcers" such as Washington. The parties settled after the 1979 $3.2 million jury verdict in favor of Tomjanovich was appealed.

At about the same time as the *Tomjanovich* case, former Denver Broncos player Dale Hackbart sued the Cincinnati Bengals and Bengals player Charles "Booby" Clark for injuries he sustained in an exhibition game between those teams. In that game, Denver's Hackbart fell in an attempt to block Clark after the Broncos intercepted a pass. As Hackbart knelt on the ground watching the play move further upfield, Clark, "acting out of anger and frustration, but without specific intent to injure," used his right forearm to hit Hackbart in the back of the head, injuring Hackbart's neck (*Hackbart*, 1977).

The trial court acknowledged that football is "a contest for territory" and that the "most obvious characteristic of the game is that all of the players engage in violent physical behavior." From the pre-game psychological and emotional buildup, to the extreme aggression and reckless abandonment needed to play the game, to the contribution of noisy and animated crowds, the end result in professional football, according to the trial court, was "the spectacle of savagery." The trial court also noted that the primary method for policing on-field behavior was through the officials' and league's enforcement of the rules of the game.

Hackbart, cognizant of the assumption of the risk defense, contended that Clark's foul was "so far outside of the rules of play and accepted practices of professional football that it should be characterized as reckless misconduct." In ruling that the doctrine of assumption of the risk precluded Hackbart from recovering, the trial court considered conflicting testimony by two former NFL coaches and players who testified, on the one hand, that the incident was neither customary nor acceptable and, on the other hand, that it was "part of the game."

The most interesting part of the trial court's decision is that it did not focus on the question of whether or not Clark engaged in reckless misconduct. Instead, the trial court addressed "the larger question of whether playing field action in the business of professional football should become a subject for the business of the courts." The court concluded that tort principles are not easily applied to sports, in particular football, and that the courts are ill-equipped to regulate violence in professional football. The trial court's decision against Hackbart was reversed on appeal. The reviewing court found that recklessness was the viable middle ground between claims of negligence, which are easily stated, but which fall to the doctrine of assumption of the risk, and intentional tort claims such as battery, which require a showing of actual intent to cause the particular harm.

The *Hackbart* case, among others, illustrates the difficulty in applying traditional negligence concepts to sports, the problem of defining in sports what is merely negligent and what is reckless or intentional, and the role of social policy in determining the role the courts should assume in such matters at all. The fluid concept of assumption of the risk ("so apt to create mist that it is better banished from the scene" (*McGrath*, 1963)), the different athletic cultures in each sport, and the conflicting opinions about the very role courts should play in circumscribing the written and unwritten rules of sports, have created a lack of clarity for participants, officials, administrators, management, and the judiciary.

Criminal courts

For many of the same social policy reasons that discourage courts in the United States from fully embracing the application of civil law concepts to claims of sports violence, the judicial system has also been slow to utilize criminal laws and penalties in that context. Unlike civil cases, which involve the adjudication of suits, typically monetary, between private litigants, criminal law invokes the power of the government to punish wrongful conduct. Often, the same conduct can be the subject to both civil and criminal actions: a fight between two people on the street might result both in civil suits for assault and battery brought by the participants against each other seeking monetary compensation, and criminal charges of assault and battery brought by the government. Because of the government's substantial resources, and because life or liberty are often at stake, criminal cases are subject to more stringent rules, including the standard for conviction of certainty beyond a reasonable doubt.

Criminal prosecutions of on-the-field acts of violence face the same difficulties—inherent in the assumption of the risk doctrine—as civil suits. When legislators wrote the laws proscribing violence in society at large, they did not contemplate the laws' application to inherently violent activities. Consequently, the courts that must apply those laws to violent athletic conduct frequently have difficulty.

The task of determining what level of violence is acceptable and what is actionable (or, synonymously, "excessive" or "illegitimate") is difficult even in "non-contact" sports. When, for example, is an inside fastball in the non-contact sport of baseball reckless or wanton? When is a flagrant basketball foul too flagrant? When is a hard slide into second base negligent or worse? In answering such questions, it is not enough that an official did or did not mete out on-field punishment, eject a player, or award a penalty. When called upon, the courts must review such cases not just within the context of the rules of the game and the punishments the officials are authorized to impose, but within the concept of criminal (as well as civil) law not designed to regulate such conduct.

Canadian courts seem more inclined to apply criminal laws to sport violence cases. Some Canadian prosecutors and courts, for example, have not shied from using criminal laws to punish violence committed by sport participants. In the related cases of *Regina v. Maki* (1970) and *Regina v. Green* (1970), charges of assault were brought against NHL players Wayne Maki of the St. Louis Blues and Ted Green of the Boston Bruins after Green punched Maki in the mouth and Maki hit Green in the head with his stick.

Although Maki and Green were both acquitted, the court in its decision did not rely on the doctrine of assumption of the risk, as its U.S. counterparts have tended to do. Rather, the court found them not guilty because it could not be shown beyond a reasonable doubt that either party intended to injure the other.

The first criminal conviction resulting in a jail sentence for a participant's conduct during a game also involved the Canadian courts and ice hockey. In 1989, Minnesota North Stars player Dino Ciccarelli was convicted of criminal assault for punching and hitting opposing player Luke Richardson with his stick. According to the judge who sentenced Ciccarelli, "It is time now that a message go out from the courts that violence in a hockey game or in any other circumstances is not acceptable in our society" (Associated Press, 1988). As prosecutors and judges have become less inclined to let the sport industry police itself, the frequency of convictions is increasing; however, they remain the exception. In the case of Ciccarelli, the charges were in addition to his ejection from the game and ten-game suspension by the National Hockey League.

In another notorious example of on-ice violence that ended with NHL and criminal penalties, NHL enforcer Marty McSorley was convicted of assault with a weapon for hitting opponent Donald Brashear on the head with his stick during an NHL game. McSorley, who was suspended by the NHL for one year, was placed on 18 months' probation by a Canadian court.

The repercussions from Vancouver Canucks' Todd Bertuzzi's blind-side punch to the head of the Colorado Avalanche's Steve Moore in 2004 involved the judicial systems of two countries, as well as league-imposed civil and criminal punishment. After the incident, the NHL suspended Bertuzzi for 17 months, but he missed only 20 games because his suspension overlapped with the league's work stoppage in 2004–2005. The Vancouver Attorney General also took action against the player and filed charges of assault causing bodily harm. Bertuzzi pled guilty as part of a plea bargain to avoid jail time.

In addition, Moore filed a civil suit against Bertuzzi in Colorado state court, which was dismissed by the judge on jurisdictional grounds. Moore then filed a civil suit in Ontario alleging assault, battery, negligence, and outrageous conduct. That suit settled before trial.

Despite the involvement of the sport's governing bodies and the civil and criminal courts of two countries in the Bertuzzi incident, little light was shed on the basic question: when does a body check, permitted by the rules of the sport and assented to by the participants, become unacceptable violence that goes beyond the scope of on-ice sanctions and league regulations, and into the courtroom?

In one infamous incident in the 1993 NHL playoffs, Dale Hunter delivered a ruthless check to Pierre Turgeon after Turgeon had scored a goal and was celebrating. Turgeon suffered a concussion and a separated shoulder. By all accounts, the hit was late and overly aggressive. Hunter was suspended by the NHL for 21 games. Yet Hunter faced no criminal prosecution or civil suit. It is difficult to substantively distinguish the McSorley and Moore incidents from the Hunter incident, or from the hundreds if not thousands of high-sticks, hard checks, and boardings that occur every day at every level of play during hockey season. Care ethics would dictate the same result as the law: body checks, for example, should be appropriate, not excessive.

The difficulty in distinguishing between acceptable and unacceptable athletic violence is often cited as one of the primary reasons criminal laws are rarely invoked:

> Relying on criminal prosecution of violent players to control the culture of the sport is not fruitful, according to . . . many. . . . Negligence or reckless conduct may be tortious but in the context of a sports contest, it is usually not criminal. Criminal battery is the charge available to a prosecutor when one athlete violently injures another, but prosecutors rarely bring the charge. Commentators list numerous reasons: an act unlawful on the street is seen as lawful on the playing field, consent to a reasonably foreseeable act of sports violence is a defense under the Model Penal Code, prosecutors are reluctant to bring charges because the injured player will not file a complaint, and prosecutors believe that sports violence is controlled sufficiently by league rules and sanctions.
>
> (Richardson, 2004)

Legislative regulation

Legislative solutions have also failed to resolve the problem adequately or offer the courts guidance. Following closely on the heels of *Hackbart* and *Tomjonavich*, the United States Congress sought to address the issue and give the criminal courts a clearer mandate to intervene than the application of broad criminal laws such as assault and battery.

The Sports Violence Act of 1980 would have criminalized "excessive violence" by participants in professional sports. The Act defined excessive force as that which:

> has no reasonable relationship to the competitive goals of the sport; is unreasonably violent; and could not be reasonably foreseen, or was not consented to, by the injured person, as a normal hazard to such person's involvement in such sports event.

The Act was predicated on the fact that the traditional crimes of assault and battery were rarely invoked in the context of professional sports because they did not adequately address the violence inherent in sports and the application of the doctrine of assumption of the risk. The Act did not pass.

Three years after the Sports Violence Act was defeated, Congress proposed the Sports Violence Arbitration Act of 1983 to "reduce the number and costs of injuries resulting from the use of excessively violent conduct during professional sports events." The Sports Violence Arbitration Act would have required every professional sports league to create an "arbitration system" to address claims by players, clubs, and officials who "sustain injury as the result of excessively violent conduct." The Sports Violence Arbitration Act, which also failed to pass, would have allowed the leagues to continue to self-regulate under legislatively mandated guidelines.

SELF-REGULATION VERSUS OUTSIDE REGULATION

In light of the failings of the legal system, both legislative and judicial, have we come full circle to the point where the best regulation is self-regulation? Although the teams, leagues, and associations were traditionally the first line of defense, sanctions imposed by the leagues had little effect on curbing the incidence of sports violence (Reschly, 1999). Despite fines and suspensions meted out by teams, leagues, and associations, the excessive violence continues.

The failure of the leagues to effectively handle incidents "in house" is one of the factors that has led to greater judicial involvement in matters of on-field violence. Players, at first individually and later through the players' associations, often challenged the decisions of the league commissioners. These challenges typically were based on the severity of the sanction or punishment and, frequently, the role of the commissioner as judge, jury, executioner, and appellate tribunal. These challenges also often led to the very thing the leagues, and many times the players, sought to avoid: judicial intervention.

In 1971, the National Football League Players Association filed an unfair labor practices charge against the NFL because of fines imposed by the NFL to curb on-field violence. The labor practices claim ended up before the federal court of appeal, where the court opined favorably upon the right of the commissioner to sanction players whose conduct was detrimental to the NFL. Essentially, the court ruled that the commissioner may engage in virtue ethics.

In the National Basketball Association, player Latrell Sprewell was suspended in 1997 by the commissioner for a full year as punishment for choking his coach during a practice. After appealing to an arbitrator, his suspension was reduced.

The increased bargaining power of the players' unions and the concomitant increase in the sophistication of the collective bargaining agreements they negotiate with the leagues have neither removed the need for judicial intervention nor reduced the incidence of sports violence in the professional ranks. Depending on one's point of view, the leagues either do too much, imposing punishments far exceeding the severity of the transgression, or too little, tolerating, to the point of fostering, improper behavior.

The National Football League's "Bountygate" scandal in 2012, "represent(ed) a frighteningly public example of not just normalized, but also institutionalized violence in professional sports" (Roser-Jones, 2013). Between 2009 and 2012, players and coaches of the New Orleans Saints offered to pay "bounties" to players in amounts based on the severity of hits made on opposing players. Individual opposing players were sometimes targeted, most prominently Vikings quarterback Brett Favre, who was worth a bounty of $50,000 to any Saints player who knocked Favre out of the 2010 NFC Championship game.

The NFL levied stiff sanctions after the fact, including a one-year suspension to head coach Sean Payton. However, "[a]ll of this happened in what was believed to be a new era in the NFL, where the players' union and the league's commissioner were emphasizing player safety above all else" (id.). Virtue ethics was not working in the NFL, nor were care ethics, deontology, or utilitarianism.

It can be argued, nonetheless, that self-regulation, however imperfect, is the best approach to avoid the doctrinal and practical problems the courts have in coherently addressing the problem of excessive sports violence. Proponents of self-regulation contend that defining unacceptable play and punishing it are best left to insiders:

> The players and executives, themselves often former players, who negotiate the collective bargaining agreements in professional sports and who shape the rules of the game are best suited to determine the inherent risks of their sports. They have the opportunity to review violent plays that cause injury immediately, and the means to act expeditiously. Suspension is perhaps the greatest deterrent. While money and fame attract athletes to the dangers of a violent sport, the love of playing dwarfs all other reasons for assuming the risks of playing the game.
> (Richardson, 2004)

To many, self-regulation, combined with criminal or civil legal intervention in the most egregious cases, offers the best opportunity to control inappropriate sports violence while limiting the encroachment of outside forces that would change or even destroy the games to which we are drawn.

HAZING: INITIATION RITE OR SIMPLY WRONG?

Hazing is not a new phenomenon, nor one confined to college fraternities and sororities. Plato disapproved of the hazing and practical jokes of Athens's youth in 387 BC (Nuwer,

1999). Barely two decades after the founding of Harvard in 1636, the school's administration held disciplinary hearings on the subject, and in 1874 Congress enacted a law subjecting those who hazed at the Naval Academy to court martial.

Although quaint rituals in the first half of the 20th century, such as requiring college freshmen to wear beanies, have long ago become history, hazing continues to flourish. It has been estimated that 1.5 million high school students are hazed each year (Lipkins, 2006), 79 percent of college athletes have been hazed (Hoover, 1999), and in 95 percent of hazing cases, the college students who were hazed did not report it (University of Maryland, 2016).

Physical contact is an inherent part of many sports; in order to compete, one must assume certain risks of physical violence. Hazing in sports, however, has nothing to do with the way the game is played, and typically occurs off the playing field. Why, then, has hazing been accepted in sports? What behaviors constitute hazing? Are some forms of hazing acceptable while others are not? What can and should be done to prevent and punish hazing?

Hazing has long been accepted as a rite of initiation into various groups—including the military, fraternities and sororities, sports teams, fraternal organizations, scholastic societies, and gangs—because of the belief that it fostered a sense of camaraderie and unity within a group, and made each group, and membership therein, special, distinctive, and selective. "New initiates into a group may come from a wide variety of backgrounds, having little in common. The process of initiation gives all the members a common experience, something that they share only with other members of the group" (Radford, 2008).

The secrecy in which hazing is shrouded, and the reluctance of those who have been hazed to report such behavior, are corollaries of those beliefs. Those subjected to hazing want to belong to and be accepted by the group, and are reticent to betray it.

Definition of hazing

There are almost as many definitions of hazing as there are incidents of hazing. One definition is "any activity expected of someone joining a group that humiliates, degrades, abuses or endangers, regardless of the person's willingness to participate" (Hoover, 1999). California, one of the 44 states with some form of criminal anti-hazing law, defines it as initiation conduct that "is likely to cause, bodily danger, physical harm, or personal degradation or disgrace resulting in physical or mental harm" (California Education Code Section 32050).

The statutory definitions in some jurisdictions focus on endangering the physical well-being of a student: Georgia, Indiana and Missouri, for example. Some state laws even provide that the victim's consent operates as a defense (e.g. Wisconsin, Missouri and Maine).

The National Federation of State High School Associations defines hazing as "any humiliating or dangerous activity expected of a student to belong to a group, regardless of their willingness to participate" (Caudill, 2014). Under that definition, hazing includes: "(T)attooing, piercing, head-shaving, branding, sleep deprivation, physical punishment . . . 'kidnapping,' consuming unreasonable/unacceptable foods or beverages, being deprived of personal hygiene and/or inappropriate sexual behavior" (id.).

The definition suggested by Mothers Against School Hazing (MASH) "does an excellent job at defining the acts that constitute hazing" but does not address the notion that hazing and initiation are two separate things (Peluso, 2006).

MASH states that:

> [H]azing is a broad term encompassing any action or activity which does not contribute to the positive development of a person; which inflicts or intends to cause physical or mental harm or anxieties; which may demean, degrade or disgrace any person regardless of . . . consent of participants; . . . for admission into or affiliation with any student organization.

The concepts of consent and humiliation make it even more difficult to distinguish between hazing and harmless rites of passage. Does the seemingly innocuous requirement that freshmen wear pins that designate them as freshmen actually set them apart from other students and invite teasing, taunting, and other forms of humiliation? Is it degrading to require the members of a junior varsity team to carry the varsity player's equipment off the field after practice? Is it improper to require team members to stand and sing the school song in the cafeteria? Some would argue that these are benign initiation practices, while others would see them as subjecting the participant to ridicule, abuse, and embarrassment, in contravention of virtue ethics and care ethics.

Although one typically thinks of hazing in the context of high school, college, and other amateur athletics, professional sports are not immune. Nor does the fact that professional sports typically involve adult athletes eliminate the physical and emotional effects of hazing.

Two New Orleans Saints players were injured in training camp hazing activities, which included having to run through "a gantlet of players who hit the rookies with bags of coins" (Farrey, 2003). More recently, Miami Dolphins players, including lineman Richie Incognito, attempted to help "toughen up" fellow lineman Jonathan Martin. The "help" included "racial slurs and vicious sexual taunts about his mother and sister amounting to a pattern of harassment" (espn.com, 2014). Although Incognito's bullying of Martin was not associated with formal acceptance into an organization, it was predicated on the belief that he needed to "toughen up" in order to be accepted by his teammates.

Civil courts and hazing

Most civil cases related to hazing are based on the torts of assault and battery, and are brought against the perpetrators themselves. In such cases, the victim must prove that the hazers acted intentionally in causing harmful or offensive contact to the victim and, more importantly, that the victim did not consent to the act. Because hazing typically involves voluntary participation in the ritual by the victim, consent can be a difficult hurdle to clear. The courts have been slow to find tort liability when the victim knew of the group's hazing practices, subjected himself or herself to them, and, in many cases, helped to conceal those practices.

In *Jones v. Kappa Alpha Order, Inc.* (1998), Jones, a fraternity pledge who was repeatedly subjected to a variety of hazing acts sued the fraternity for, among other offenses, assault and battery. The fraternity, however, contended that Jones had voluntarily participated in the acts. The Alabama Supreme Court agreed with this defense, finding that Jones continued to endure the hazing by his fraternity, which began on his second day as a pledge, for a full academic year. The court also noted that Jones helped to "cover up the hazing by lying about its occurrence to school officials, his doctor, and even his own family" (id.). Consequently, the court held that Jones had knowingly and voluntarily subjected himself to the hazing conduct.

The court rejected Jones's argument that he was in a "coercive environment (that) hampered his free will to the extent that he could not voluntarily choose to leave the fraternity" (id.). In addition to the fact that Jones "voluntarily chose to continue his participation in the hazing activities," the court noted that Jones refused to seek assistance from the school and his parents and, in fact, lied to both when they asked if he was being hazed.

Finally, the court pointed out that Jones "realized that 20 percent to 40 percent of his fellow pledges voluntarily chose to leave the fraternity and the hazing, but he chose to stay" (id.). Accordingly, as "a responsible adult in the eyes of the law, Jones cannot be heard to argue that peer pressure prevented him from leaving the very hazing activities that, he admits, several of his peers left" (id.).

Imposing civil liability on teachers, coaches, and athletic organizations has been even more difficult. Unless the coach or teacher was actually involved in the hazing activity, a victim must establish that the supervisor was negligent—that is, that the supervisor did not act as a reasonably prudent person would have acted in "failing to intervene to stop dangerous hazing activities from taking place" (Sharp et al., 2014).

Adding to the difficulty is the fact that in some cases, teachers, coaches, and school officials are immune from personal civil liability when acting in their official capacities and without malice or any intent to cause injury to a student. In one case, a freshman football player was beaten by teammates in an initiation ritual at the team's summer football camp. The player sued, among others, the school principal and the football coach (*Caldwell*, 1998).

Although older players would "initiate" younger players each year by shaving their heads, trashing their rooms, and engaging in other such "horseplay," there was no evidence of beatings or other violent attacks. Since the principal and coach did not condone or take part in the initiation, they were immune from the civil claim.

Criminal courts and hazing

Criminal laws have been nearly as ineffective as civil laws in addressing and deterring hazing in sports. Even in states that have criminal anti-hazing statutes, the issues of consent, the reluctance to report infractions, and the belief that some conduct is initiation rather than hazing, render enforcement difficult. "Relatively few prosecutions have occurred under the statutes, partly because of the definitional difficulties in what is considered to be hazing" (Sharp et al., 2014).

What acts are hazing as opposed to what are harmless antics remains a difficult determination. State criminal laws also do not always address all of the issues that hazing cases present. Only 9 of the 44 state criminal anti-hazing statutes make it a crime to fail to report a hazing incident. Many state laws—Arizona, Idaho, and Virginia, for example—also provide that a victim's express or implied consent or voluntary willingness to be hazed is a defense to the crime. State laws are not even consistent in their application, with some applying only to public schools, some only to institutions of higher education, and some to any organization, educational or otherwise.

Current and future efforts to address hazing

Given the limitations of civil and criminal law to control and deter hazing, the role of schools, districts, athletic organizations, and even professional leagues in changing the culture of hazing is paramount. David Westol, a former assistant prosecuting attorney and football referee had this to say about eliminating hazing in high school and college sport: "Change comes from a change in culture – what is acceptable and what is not acceptable – on a team. Those dynamics are set in play by the athletic director, the coaches, and university administrators" (Nuwer, 2014). The culture can be changed when administrators realize that hazing doesn't promote bonding and team unity in the long term.

In December, 2016, the leadership of Major League Baseball instituted an Anti-Hazing and Anti-Bullying Policy designed to change the hazing culture in professional baseball. As part of the collective bargaining agreement, the MLB Players Association accepted the policy that, among other things, "prohibits 'requiring, coercing or encouraging' players to dress up as women or wear costumes that 'may be offensive to individuals based on their race, sex, nationality, age, sexual orientation, gender identity or other characteristic'" (Associated Press, 2016).

Norm Pollard, Dean of Students at Alfred University and co-author with the NCAA of a study on collegiate hazing, stresses that hazing "deprives the hazed and hazers alike of true, valid team-building." He states: "[p]art of the process is connecting with 'elders'— older adults with wisdom who can help the team with effective team-building and bonding" (Nuwer, 2014).

Only 16 of the state anti-hazing statutes require schools to promulgate anti-hazing policies and/or methods of educating students, teachers, and administrators about the state's anti-hazing law. In the absence of any federal anti-hazing statute, uniform state statutes with more severe penalties (over half of the state statutes classify hazing as a misdemeanor), and improved institutional policies, hazing in sports will continue undeterred. Among other proposals is a NCAA uniform conduct policy that classifies hazing as an "improper behavior", in order to "bring clarity, consistency and standardization to its member institutions" (Gutshall, 2008).

CONCLUSION

On-field excessive sports violence and off-field sports violence in the form of hazing have more in common than physicality. Neither civil nor criminal laws have effectively addressed either. Moreover, both involve elusive definitions of just what is inappropriate, policing both is hampered by the clubhouse mentality and the reluctance of victims to seek redress, and the crazy-quilt of state laws and rules of private institutions prevent the establishment of a clear and bright line between proper and improper behavior. Virtue ethics and care ethics have the potential to solve the problems, but the public has yet to demand their use.

ETHICAL LEADERSHIP CASE STUDIES

Case study #1

The proposed Sports Violence Act of 1980 defined excessive violence as:

> force that has no reasonable relationship to the competitive goals of the sport; is unreasonably violent; and could not be reasonably foreseen, or was not consented to, by the injured person, as a normal hazard to such person's involvement in such sports event.

This Act failed to become law. Which ethical theories apply to this formulation? What sort of ethical leadership would have been required to get this Act passed?

Case study # 2

Your state's proposed anti-hazing law has adopted the Mothers Against School Hazing (MASH) definition of hazing as:

> A broad term encompassing any action or activity which does not contribute to the positive development of a person; which inflicts or intends to cause physical or mental harm or anxieties; which may demean, degrade or disgrace any person regardless of consent of participants; and which must be endured for admission into or affiliation with any student organization.

The proposed law is currently being debated in the legislature. What are the ethical theories supporting this definition? How can MASH execute an ethical leadership plan to get legislative support for the law?

STUDENT LEARNING EXERCISE

Formulate a program to make coaches, administrators, and athletic organizations more sensitive to the problems of hazing.

PROBLEMS/QUESTIONS

1. What are the ethical issues related to excessive violence during a sports event by a participant?
2. What ethical theories support the legal doctrine of assumption of the risk?
3. What are the ethical differences between civil and criminal cases?

4. What are some of the ethical reasons that criminal cases charging excessive on-field violence are rarely prosecuted?
5. What ethical theories, if any, support hazing?
6. What are the ethical arguments for and against sports self-regulating to control on-field violence?
7. Is there ethical support for the proposition that voluntarily agreeing to be hazed prevents the victim from pursuing a civil claim against his or her hazers? Why or why not?

BIBLIOGRAPHY

Associated Press, Baseball Outlaws Hazing Ritual That Forces Rookies to Dress As Women, *New York Times*, December 13, 2016.

Associated Press, Ciccarelli Cited for Assault, *New York Times*, August 25, 1988.

Bad Behavior Cited in Youth Sports Study, *USA Today*, November 29, 2005.

Beitman, Hayley, Next Wave: Anti-Hazing Laws, *Michigan State University School of Journalism News*, April 6, 2012.

Caldwell v. Griffin Spalding Board of Education, 232 Ga App. 892 (1998).

California Education Code Section 32050, http://law.justia.com/codes/california/2005/edc/32050-32051.html (accessed May 24, 2017).

Carlsen, Chris J. in *Law of Professional and Amateur Sports*, edited by Uberstine, Gary (2006).

Caudill, Kathy, What Is Hazing?, National Federation of State High School Associations, July 24, 2014.

Champion, Jr., Walter, *Fundamentals of Sports Law* (2004).

Darlington, Jeff, Gregg Williams' Speech Takes Saints Scandal to Another Level, www.nfl.com/news/story/09000d5d8281a52a/article/gregg-williams-speech-takes-saints-scandal-to-another-level, April 5, 2012.

Farrey, Tom, Athletes Abusing Athletes, espn.com, June 3, 2003.

Gutshall, Brandon, Note: A New Uniform: NCAA Policy and Student-Athlete Misconduct, 76 *University of Missouri at Kansas City Law Review* /2/ (2008).

Hackbart v. Cincinnati Bengals, Inc., 435 F. Supp. 353 (D. Colo. 1977).

Hackbart v. Cincinnati Bengals, Inc., 601 F. 2d 516 (10th Cir. 1979).

Hoover, Nadine C., National Survey: Initiation Rites and Athletics for NCAA Sport Teams, www.alfred.edu/news/html/hazing_study.html, August 30, 1999.

Incognito, Others Tormented Martin, espn.com, February 15, 2014.

Jones v. Kappa Alpha Order, Inc. (Ex parte Barran) 730 So.2d 203 (Ala. 1998).

Lestina v. West Bend Insurance Company (501 N.W. 2d 28 (Wis. 1993).

Lipkins, Susan, www.insidehazing.com/statistics_25_high.php, 2006.

Mandarelaro, Jim, Hazing Continues Despite Efforts To Change, democratandchronicle.com, January 12, 2014.

Marchetti v. Kalish, 559 N.E. 2d 699, 703 (Ohio 1990).

McGrath v. American Cyanamid Co., 41 N.J. 272 (1963).

Meeker v. Edmundson, 415 F. 3d, 317 (4th Cir. 2005).

Nabozny v. Barnhill, 334 N.E. 2d 258, 260 (Ill. App. Ct. 1975).

Nuwer, Hank, *Broken Pledges* (1990).

Nuwer, Hank, Wrongs of Passage: Fraternities, Sororities, Hazing and Binge Drinking (1999).

Nuwer, Hank, Stopping Hazing in College And High School Athletics, Athletic Business, July, 2014.

Parks, Gregory S. & Southerland, Tiffany F., The Psychology and Law of Hazing Consent, 97 *Marquette Law Review* 1 (2013).

Peluso, Alyson, Hazing in Sports: The Effects and Legal Ramifications, U.S. Sports Academy – *The Sport Journal*, January 7, 2006.

Radford, Benjamin, Hazing: Why Young Men Do It, *Live Science*, May 14, 2008.

Regina v. Ciccarelli, 54 C.C.C. 3d 121 (Ontario Dist. Ct. 1989).

Regina v. Green, 16 D.L.R. 3d 137 (Ont. Prov. Civ. 1970).

Regina v. Maki, 14 D.L.R. 3d 164 (Ont. P.C. 1970).

Reschly, Steven D., *Tortious Impact, Sports and the Law*, edited by Charles E. Quirk (1999).

Richardson, Dean, Player Violence: An Essay on Torts and Sports, 15 *Stanford Law & Policy Review* 1 (2004).

Roser-Jones, Courtlyn, A Costly Turnover: Why the NFL's Bounty Scandal Could Change the Current Legal Standard of Deferring to Internal Disciplinary Sanctions in Instances of Game-Related Violence, 20 *The Sports Lawyers Journal* 1 (2013).

Sharp, Linda A., Moorman, Anita M. & Claussen, Cathryn L., *Sport Law: A Managerial Approach* (2014).

University of Maryland, Hazing Prevention, http://hazingprevention.umd.edu/HazingPrevention/HazingStatistics.aspx, 2016.

Vendrell v. School District No. 26C, Malheur County, 233 Or. 1 (1962).

Waldron, Travis, Why Do We Tolerate Hazing in Professional Sports?, *Think Progress*, November 6, 2013.

CHAPTER 11

Gambling and sport

INTRODUCTION

Gambling is nearly as old as civilization itself. Mesopotamians used knucklebones as four-sided dice as long ago as 6000 BC, and archaeologists have found Mesopotamian six-sided dice with pips dating from 3000 BC. The Chinese invented playing cards some 1,500 years before the advent of the modern printing press, and public lotteries to raise money for civic improvements date from the 15th century.

Efforts to ban, tax, and control gambling are also centuries old and equally creative. Both organized religions and governments have long histories of edicts and laws designed to prohibit or regulate gambling on ethical grounds; ironically, some governments even profit from gambling. The Eastern Orthodox Church issued both civil and religious bans on gambling in the 6th century. Secular governments' attempts to control gambling have taken many forms over the last thousand years, including royal edicts prohibiting gambling by commoners, allowing gambling only during the Christmas season, and deeming gambling debts legally unenforceable.

Many of these prophylactic efforts were predicated on the presumed immorality of gambling, but many were also driven by economic and other governmental interests. Henry VIII enjoined certain types of gambling, such as wagering on dice and card games, bowling, and tennis in order to promote the sport of archery which benefited the kingdom's defense efforts. Laws forbidding gambling by the masses on workdays were designed to keep people working rather than wagering.

The significance of gambling, and particularly sports gambling, in modern society is apparent to even the most casual observer. Perhaps less apparent, but equally significant, is the potential of gambling to corrupt sports.

HISTORY AND DANGERS OF SPORTS GAMBLING

Just as gambling and gambling regulation went hand-in-hand, so did gambling and sports. Romans wagered on chariot races before the birth of Christ. Chinese emperor Yao is reputed to have invented a board game on which spectators wagered 4,000 years ago. The rise in popularity of baseball in the United States in the late 19th and early 20th centuries sparked a rise in gambling on the national pastime. Gambling's footprint on society in general, and the sports arena in particular, has evolved and expanded to the point where regular poker games among friends, March Madness brackets, and National Football League pools are so commonplace that most people might consider them more forms of recreation or entertainment than gambling.

Although sports gambling does not always lead to corruption and scandal, there are many instances where it has. Perhaps one of the most famous examples is the 1919 Black Sox scandal where several members of the heavily favored Chicago White Sox were accused of accepting payments from gamblers to throw the World Series against the Cincinnati Reds. This scandal brought the pervasive and insidious role which gambling had played in professional baseball for many years to the public's attention, and it marked the inception of professional sports' organized efforts to combat gambling.

In the early 1900s, it was not at all unusual for professional baseball players not to just consort with known gamblers and racketeers, but to actually bet on the outcome of baseball games. Players were not well compensated, were not unionized, had no job security or benefits, and had no free agency rights, making them susceptible to the lure of extra money that professional gamblers offered.

Most teams and clubhouses were aware that, from time to time, a player with a wager on a game might make an error or otherwise act to affect the outcome of that game to ensure he collected on his bet. Notwithstanding the prevalence of gambling and game fixing, management and players did little to remove the influence of gambling from the sport. The 1919 World Series would change that.

The motivations of the players involved (sometimes attributed merely to greed, other times to a desire for vengeance against a miserly team owner), which players were involved and to what extent, are still debated. What is not subject to argument is that several of the White Sox players conspired to throw the 1919 World Series to the underdog Cincinnati Reds.

This scandal, which brought to the public eye the pervasiveness of gambling inside the national pastime, threatened to ruin professional baseball. Baseball's response was to appoint a commissioner with actual authority to police and punish offending players, thereby setting the precedent for powerful commissioners in MLB and other sports.

Although no subsequent sports gambling scandals have been as prominent as the Black Sox scandal, there have been many. In the early 1950s, the City College of New York was at the epicenter of a college basketball point-shaving scandal that involved seven colleges in several states. Pete Rose, baseball's all-time hits leader, was banned from MLB for life because he had bet on baseball games while managing the Cincinnati Reds, even though it was never established that he had ever bet against the Reds. In the 1960s, the English "national pastime," soccer, was scandalized when it was learned that a number of professional players, led by Jimmy Gauld, had conspired to fix matches on which they had placed bets.

More recently, Asian gambling interests are thought to have fixed no less than 680 soccer games around the world, including 380 in Europe. The scheme allegedly involved players, club representatives, and over 400 referees.

Even the gentlemanly sport of cricket has not been immune. The cricket world was jolted by allegations that players on the Pakistani national team colluded with gamblers by "spot-fixing," i.e. manipulating play not to affect the outcome, but to enable bettors to win wagers placed on specific acts occurring in a game or match.

In the United States, veteran NBA referee Tim Donaghy bet on games he officiated and then made calls which affected the point spread in those games. He also was paid thousands of dollars by a gambler for providing inside information on NBA games. Donaghy's conviction on charges of conspiracy to engage in wire fraud and transmitting betting information through interstate commerce was a reminder that gambling has the potential to severely damage a sports industry that is dependent on the perception that its contests are fairly and impartially conducted.

Traditional gambling

Despite being virtually omnipresent in society—who hasn't made a nominal wager on a friend's golf putt, bought charity raffle tickets, or bet a few dollars with a fellow employee on the outcome of a football game between college rivals?—what conduct actually constitutes gambling is not always easy to determine. Since most states have laws prohibiting or limiting gambling, traditionally the courts have had to explore the issue of the nature of gambling in order to determine the applicability of those laws to particular activities.

So what is gambling? Gambling is defined by federal law (31 U.S.C. §5362(1) (A)) as:

> the staking or risking by any person of something of value upon the outcome of a contest of others, a sporting event, or a game subject to chance, upon an agreement or understanding that the person or another person will receive something of value in the event of a certain outcome.

Despite this seemingly simple definition, the courts have struggled over the application of this definition to particular activities, and even over the meaning of the terms "risk" and "game of chance."

What is a "game of chance," as opposed to a game of skill, has long been contested, and the results vary by jurisdiction. On one end of the spectrum, some states hold that any element of chance whatsoever is sufficient to constitute gambling. Other states require that the element of chance must be "material" while still others insist that the "chance" component must "predominate."

To illustrate the difficulty in determining if an activity is gambling, take the following example. A store owner has a vending machine in his shop which entitles every person who deposits a nickel into the machine to a pack of gum worth a nickel. Occasionally, the machine rewards a customer with ten packs of gum. Is this gambling? One might be inclined to say it is not since the customer does not risk anything: he or she puts in a nickel and is guaranteed no less than the value of a nickel in return. Similarly, since the customer could not "lose" and the store owner could not "win," it is not a game of chance.

The courts, however, have concluded differently. They have held that the broadest definition of gambling does not require that both parties might lose or win by chance; it is enough that one party stands to lose, or to win by chance. In other words, the courts have adopted the idea of "something for nothing" in determining what is gambling. In this example, the store owner risked losing nine packs of gum, and the customer stood to win those nine packs. That, the courts have held, is gambling.

Some ambiguity is inherent in all definitions of gambling, including statutory definitions. Chess is often used as the paradigm case of a game that is not gambling because of the level of skill involved. However, does the statistical advantage that white has in moving first, constitute an element of chance? Is the level of skill required to play poker proficiently sufficient to dwarf the element of chance?

Even trading in the stock market has been used as an example of a form of legal gambling. Although that comparison is not necessarily apt, it is worth noting that a major federal gambling statute expressly excludes the purchase and sale of securities and commodities from its scope (31 U.S.C. 5362(1)(E)).

Regulation of gambling

As discussed above, governmental efforts to regulate gambling, whether predicated on protecting virtue ethics or on other bases, are thousands of years old. In the United States, there is no shortage of federal and state legislation designed to prohibit or control gambling, including sports gambling. Federal statutes include the Wire Communications Act of 1961, the Illegal Gambling Business Act of 1970, the Racketeer-Influenced and Corrupt Organizations Act of 1970, the Professional and Amateur Sports Protection Act of 1992, the Unlawful Gambling Enforcement Act of 2006, various anti-lottery statutes, and many others.

Every state has laws banning or regulating gambling, and all but one have laws which criminalize sports gambling. In addition, non-governmental bodies such as the NCAA and professional sports leagues have rules, regulations, and contract provisions designed to protect the integrity of their sports from the deleterious effects of gambling (see, for example, Article 35A(g) of the National Basketball League Constitution, Section 15 of the Standard National Football League Player Contract, and Paragraph 3 of Exhibit 14 to the National Hockey League Collective Bargaining Agreement). Some professional teams have even banned gambling (such as card games) by players during team flights. Ethical theories supporting these rules are virtue ethics and utilitarianism.

These laws and regulations were designed to preserve the integrity of the games and contests of the various leagues and associations in the sports industry. The advent of fantasy sports gambling has created new regulatory problems and a schism in professional sports leagues between their historically anti-gambling stance and the financial benefits associated with fantasy sports gambling.

The professional sports industry's love–hate relationship with gambling

All the professional sports have traditionally and publicly denounced even the appearance of a relationship with gambling. The major professional sports leagues have until recently opposed expanding to Las Vegas, fearing the impact of such proximity to the epicenter of gambling. Prior to the NHL establishing a franchise in Las Vegas in 2016, no major league professional sports team has been located there. The Oakland Raiders announced a move there in 2017.

Baseball has been quick to invoke the "best interests of the game" doctrine to expel people for having "ties" to gamblers. All the major team sports historically publicly condemned any association with gambling, although they have been inconsistent in their responses to such association: willing to turn a blind eye in many cases involving owners while exacting severe punishment on others such as athletes.

Even superstars like Mickey Mantle, Willie Mays, and Joe Namath were not immune to the threat of punishment by their respective leagues in this regard. In 1983, MLB imposed lifetime bans on Mickey Mantle and fellow superstar Willie Mays, both long-retired from baseball, for merely working as greeters and autograph signers for legal gambling casinos. Both bans were later rescinded.

Joe Namath, the New York Jets' Super Bowl winning quarterback invested in a New York City bar at the height of his fame. The National Football League ordered him to sell his interest in the bar because it allegedly had "ties" to gamblers and others in organized crime.

These punishments were handed out, ostensibly, to protect the integrity of the sports, both real and perceived. However, the NFL, for example, conveniently overlooked ownership of the Cleveland Browns in the 1960s by a bookie and organized crime figure, and the more recent ownership of the San Francisco 49ers by a family with casino and horse racing interests. Regardless of these inconsistencies and hypocrisies, the leagues were "officially" adamantly opposed to all things gambling.

Sports leagues went well beyond self-policing in their efforts to insulate their sports from the effects of gambling. In 1992, Congress passed the Professional and Amateur Sports Protection Act (PASPA) which rendered illegal gambling on any game "in which professional and amateur athletes participate." The enactment of PASPA itself is less noteworthy than the fact that all three of the major professional team sports, MLB, the NFL and the NBA, vigorously lobbied for its passage.

Even as the leagues tried to distance themselves from any association with gambling by, for example, urging the passage of PASPA, they were increasingly recognizing the financial rewards resulting from an association with gambling, and increasingly willing to embrace that association. The NFL is not unaware that its rise to prominence coincided with and resulted from the expansion of football betting, in the form of office pools and similar contests. Similarly, the NCAA is cognizant of the importance of betting on March Madness brackets, which enhances the popularity of its annual basketball playoffs.

The popularity of fantasy baseball leagues led MLB to try to monetize the information and statistics on which those leagues are based. The emergence of daily fantasy sports resulted in the further erosion, to the point of collapse, of the separation of organized sports and gambling. With the rise of internet and fantasy sports gambling, the notion that professional leagues, their teams, and games are neither subject to the coercive effects of gambling interests nor associated in any way, has given way to actual economic partnerships between the leagues and daily fantasy sports league providers.

THE RISE OF FANTASY SPORTS

In the last 35 years, traditional sports gambling has been supplanted by fantasy and online gambling, challenging legislators and sports organizations to adapt to these new forms of sports gambling. It is unlikely that Daniel Okrent and the other creators of rotisserie baseball anticipated either the popularity of their game or its broader connection with sports gambling when they drafted their first fantasy baseball teams in 1980. Their intimate, friendly competition soon burgeoned into a national phenomenon with millions of participants in thousands of leagues.

Leagues and sports media soon sought to profit from the popularity of fantasy baseball by selling statistical information and expert advice (a modern-day internet-fueled version of the old racetrack tout) to fantasy baseball participants. This, in turn, led those same sports industry enterprises to go a step further and create actual leagues on a large scale for participants who had previously been content to compete in small leagues comprised of friends and acquaintances.

Soon, sports media giants like ESPN and CBS Sports were dominating the fantasy baseball industry by, among other things, providing host websites for fantasy leagues. The growing role of the internet and the financial benefits of fantasy baseball resulted in expansion into football, basketball, and even hockey in the late 20th century.

Coinciding with this softening of professional sports' anti-gambling position, driven by the benefits of monetizing fantasy sports, was the recognition by various states that their coffers could be fattened by gambling in the form of lotteries, in particular, sports-related lotteries. State sports lotteries run the gamut from lotteries which award tickets to an NFL game to the winner (Wisconsin) to more elaborate contests which are tied to the results of actual games, such as the Delaware lottery. In one of the sports lottery games offered by Delaware, the player selects the winners of a certain number of actual NFL games for a given week, and wins if he or she correctly selects all of the winners.

Rather than being welcomed by professional sports, Delaware's introduction of an NFL sports lottery in 1976 was met with immediate opposition. The NFL filed a suit in federal court against the state to permanently enjoin it from conducting the lottery, a suit which it lost. Although the NFL claimed that the lottery diminished its brand, reputation and other property, the "core of the [NFL's] objections to [the lottery] is what they term a 'forced association with gambling'" (*National Football League*, 1977).

In a complete turnabout from the NFL's 1976 suit to bar Delaware's lottery, the NFL and a growing number of teams and leagues have since joined forces with government sports lotteries. Massachusetts was an early entrant in this field with a state lottery which licensed the logos of the Red Sox, Patriots, Celtics, and Bruins. Other joint ventures include the Green Bay Packers and the Wisconsin lottery and the Atlanta Falcons and the Georgia lottery.

The recognition of the beneficial impact of gambling on the rise in popularity of various sports leagues, as well as the financial benefits reaped by the leagues from gambling-related activities such as lotteries and season-long fantasy sports, brought sports and gambling closer together than at any time in history. These developments also marked the transition from traditional sports gambling—that is, simple wagering on the outcome of a given game—to new forms of gambling: government-sanctioned, internet-driven, and season-long fantasy-based sports gambling. No sooner had legislators and the sports industry begun to embrace these new forms of gambling than the sports gambling playing field would be transformed again.

Daily fantasy sports

Season-long fantasy sports gambling did more than jump-start the growth of sports gambling in the 1980s and 1990s. It began the transition from traditional sports gambling, where gamblers placed bets with sports books, legal and illegal, primarily on the outcome of a given sporting event, to a much different type of wagering. Season-long fantasy sports created an industry based on gambling on a single player's performance compared to the performances of other players over the course of a season. This, in turn, paved the way for the new gambling kid on the block: Daily Fantasy Sports (DFS).

DFS sites and leagues soon filled the online vacuum left by internet poker sites after they were outlawed. Two sites, DraftKings and FanDuel, which proposed a merger in late 2016, control 90 percent of the DFS market. Estimates of DFS industry entry fees alone for the year 2015 exceed $2.6 billion. Some reports indicate that in 2015 FanDuel enrolled over 20,000 new players every day.

DFS take fantasy sports gambling well beyond the relatively languorous season-long fantasy sports to fast-paced daily or weekly competitions. Players do not select their rosters at the beginning of the season and manage that roster throughout the course of the season. DFS participants pay an entry fee to the site and then select certain players who the participant believes will perform well that day. Each athlete is assigned a "salary" value and each contest has a salary cap. The actual statistics of the players selected by each participant are compared after the sporting events conclude. The participant with the best overall statistics on that day will then be awarded a cash prize.

For example, a DFS participant wishing to enter a football contest might select an NFL quarterback, a running back and two wide receivers to comprise his or her "team" for that week. The statistical performance of his or her "team" is then compared to that of other "teams" in the same contest and a winner determined. Although professional team sports predominate, DFS include NCAA football and basketball, auto racing, mixed martial arts and other sports.

With the ascendance of DFS, the question of whether or not it is gambling—and, if so, is it illegal gambling—also arose. As with many previous iterations of sports gambling, the question is not easily answered. Laws often lag behind social, cultural, and technological changes. Sports gambling legislation is no exception, evolving far more slowly than the industry it seeks to control. The federal Unlawful Internet Gambling Enforcement Act of 2006 (UIGEA) was designed to regulate internet casinos and gambling, internet poker sites in particular. Although UIGEA expressly targeted internet casinos and related on-line gambling activities, it expressly excludes most fantasy sports gambling from its purview.

An internet fantasy sports game is exempt from the UIGEA if 1) the prizes are not determined by the number of participants or the amount of fees paid by them, 2) winning outcomes "reflect the relative knowledge and skill of the participants" and are determined by actual statistical performance of the athletes in multiple real-world events, and 3) no winning outcome is predicated on actual scores or games or the single-event performance of an athlete. This exemption spurred the rise of DFS.

The fact that DFS is seemingly outside the scope of UIGEA, however, does not answer the question of whether or not it is gambling. This exemption also does not insulate DFS from challenges by the various states, which have contended that the answer to that question is "yes."

Since DFS first gained traction, it has faced significant resistance on the state level. For every state that considers DFS legal, another opposes it. The laws are not always clear, but as of mid-2016, five states (Washington, Montana, Arizona, Louisiana, and New York) deem DFS to be illegal and DFS games cannot be conducted there. Six other states consider some forms of DFS to be illegal (Nevada, for example, requires that operators have a casino license), and as of February, 2016, over 16 states had filed suits challenging the legality of DFS, or were crafting legislation to permit, ban, or regulate DFS—Virginia being a state which recently passed a statute legalizing, while regulating, fantasy sports gambling. One participant even sued to recover his losses on the theory that the DFS games were illegal gambling operations.

Although no state court has rendered a definitive decision, three significant legal challenges were made in New York, Texas, and Illinois states which account for a large percentage of DFS revenues. In 2015, New York alone represented $267 million in DFS entry fees, $24.8 million in revenue, and ranked behind only California in DFS revenue. Illinois had 200,000 DFS participants, the fourth most participants. State laws vary, but the legal arguments on each side are similar in each case. The states contend that DFS is a game of chance, that is, gambling. Some states, such as New York, utilize the "material degree" standard, meaning that an activity is gambling if winning or losing turns on elements of chance to a material degree. Other states require only that there is some element of chance. The proponents of DFS, on the other hand, argue that it is a game of skill, not of chance like a lottery, and that the more one plays, the better one gets.

The Illinois case is illustrative of the competing claims and the path that most of the state cases have taken. On December 23, 2015, the Illinois Attorney General issued an opinion that DFS constituted gambling under Illinois law and advised DraftKings and FanDuel to prohibit Illinois residents from participating. DraftKings and FanDuel responded by commencing lawsuits against the Attorney General. Amid a number of technical, procedural, and constitutional arguments was the core contention that DFS games were complex contests of skill and therefore fell outside the scope of the Illinois gambling statute, which permits awards and compensation to the participants "in any bona fide contest for the determination of skill, speed, strength or endurance" (720 ILCS 5/28).

Similar arguments that great skill is necessary to succeed in DFS contests were made in the New York case, which has settled, with the DFS companies agreeing to be regulated. In the New York case, DraftKings contended that it had a primarily administrative role as the entity which set the rules, collected the fees, determined the winners and awarded the prizes. DraftKings asserted that choosing the athletes, navigating salary cap rules and limitations on roster moves are skill factors needed by the participant which outweigh the element of chance, likening them to the season-long fantasy games which are legal. In countering the state's contention that DFS games are similar to poker, which is illegal, DraftKings averred that DFS games were not unlike horse racing where "the horse owner competes based on the performance of his horse and jockey." DFS participants "compete based on the performance of" the players selected by the participant (DraftKings' Brief in *People of New York v. DraftKings*, 2016). The rise of DFS resurrects in a most modern context the traditional battle over what is gambling—that is, a game of chance, and what is a game of skill.

The sports industry has embraced DFS because of both the direct financial benefits and the indirect benefits: fans are more inclined to watch, and continue watching, games in which they have a betting interest. As recently as 2013, MLB's stated position was that DFS was akin to a flip of the coin, which is the definition of gambling.

How quickly things change. Virtually every NFL team now has a sponsorship or advertising deal with a DFS site—16 with FanDuel. DraftKings has sponsorship and other relationships with MLB, the NHL, and Major League Soccer, including such things as a restaurant located in the Staples Center, home of the Los Angeles Kings, Clippers and Lakers, and a lounge at Wrigley Field. FanDuel has relationships with nearly half of the teams in the professional leagues.

Sports industry companies such as Fox Sports and Madison Square Garden have invested in DFS sites—the former paying $150 million for an 11 percent interest in DraftKings and agreeing to buy a quarter million dollars in advertising. CBS holds an investment in FanDuel. Where the leagues would once have shunned a media partner such as CBS or Fox Sports for having any affiliation with gambling activity, the leagues (e.g. NBA and MLB) and team owners (e.g. Jerry Jones and Robert Kraft) now have actual ownership interests in DFS sites. Even the National Football League Players Association has agreements with these two DFS operators which allow them to use NFL players' likenesses in their advertisements. The same professional sports leagues who once decried even state-sponsored sports-based lotteries, and sought legislation designed to curb sports-related gambling, are now lobbying for laws to protect fantasy sports and DFS in particular.

In response to the judicial and legislative opposition to DFS, the major professional sports leagues are not standing on the sidelines. They have expressly endorsed DFS and have lobbied in support of them and against legislation seeking to ban them. When the NBA announced it had become an investor in FanDuel, Commissioner Adam Silver told the *New York Times* that sports betting should be regulated but legalized. NFL Commissioner Roger Goodell continues to maintain the NFL's position that gambling on sports should not be permitted, but contends that DFS is not gambling, even though most of the courts that have ruled on the subject have held that DFS is gambling. Inherent in MLB's endorsement of DraftKings as the "Official Mini Fantasy Game of MLB.com" is an endorsement of DFS. The NHL has publicly expressed concern about legalized sports betting, even as the NHL entered into a relationship with DraftKings.

However, in a classic case of wanting to have one's cake and eat it too, one week after NBA Commissioner Silver publicly endorsed the legalization of sports gambling, the NBA, the NFL, the NHL, and MLB, joined the NCAA in filing a lawsuit against the state of New Jersey to prevent it from legalizing sports betting. The ethical distinctions, if any, between sports betting and DFS are difficult to discern.

The NHL's statements regarding sports gambling reflect the sports leagues' schizophrenia in this area. Even as the league acknowledged that sports betting is a "complex issue" which "does not lend itself easily to simple 'agree' or 'disagree,'" it reiterated that sports should not become a "vehicle for betting" where the only reason a fan watches a game "is so they can cash in on a bet afterwards" (Purdum, 2014). It is clear that the anti-sports gambling tide is turning. More and more fans are placing bets, entering pools, and engaging in fantasy sports, aided by the tacit or express approval of the sports industries' leaders.

The future of sports gambling

DFS is still in its infancy, and legal and ethical questions related to it are unsettled and developing. Even as several states continue to challenge the legality of DFS, another, Massachusetts, introduced legislation to permit the state lottery, which is regulated, to offer DFS games and even allow for vendors, such as DraftKings and FanDuel, to provide online platforms for such lottery games. Curiously, PASPA has never been invoked against any DFS provider or contest. The major sports leagues, having gone from opposing all forms of sports gambling, to embracing state lotteries and DFS, now appear to be lobbying for some federal regulatory framework to govern DFS.

Although the myriad legal issues surrounding the relatively new phenomenon of DFS are being contested, there is already a new entrant in the sports gambling field. E-Sports gambling, betting on computer game competitions, is poised to become a growth industry.

The e-Sports industry generated over $300 million in revenue in 2015 (Graham, 2016). As interest in e-Sports has grown, so has interest in betting on e-Sports tournaments and other competitions. The volume of e-Sports wagering has surpassed that of golf, tennis, and rugby; and many legitimate bookmakers now take bets on e-Sports contests.

ETHICS AND LEADERSHIP IN THE MODERN SPORTS GAMBLING CONTEXT

Sports gambling, fantasy sports, and DFS in particular, seem to be here to stay—at least in most states. In 2008, 118 million Americans wagered on sports. Nearly 70 percent of all college students bet on sports. Sports gambling is the most popular form of gambling among people aged 14–22. In 2015, Americans bet more than $2 billion on March Madness games and brackets (Montana Council on Problem Gambling, 2016).

The growth and evolution of the sports betting industry present ethical and leadership issues more important than their classification as gambling or not gambling. Whether or not sports leagues should oppose DFS or embrace DFS by having investment, sponsorship, and other arrangements with DFS providers, how involved should teams and leagues be in shaping legislation, and what dangers modern sports gambling presents are three of those issues.

The financial attraction of DFS is obvious: teams and leagues stand to receive tremendous direct revenues from their investments in DFS businesses as well as substantial advertising and sponsorship revenues. DFS is also a way to expand a sport's audiences. More fans are likely to watch more games—even those in which they would otherwise have no interest—if they have a betting interest in players on those teams. Similarly, fans are more prone to stay tuned to a game that is a blowout if they have wagered on the players involved. DFS also lures new and younger, more technologically minded fans to the sports, and offers them the faster paced viewing experience they prefer.

Perhaps in part because the leagues do not want to be viewed as brazenly chasing the money that sports gambling offers, and perhaps in part to have the benefit of a more structured and supervised DFS playing field, the leaders of the major professional team sports endorse DFS legislation with varying levels of enthusiasm. A uniform regulatory structure would provide for more oversight of providers, ensuring greater consumer protection, the monetary repatriation of significant illegal sports bets ($93 billion in 2015 in illegal NFL bets alone), and a mechanism to preserve the actual and stated integrity of the game.

Sports leaders have warmly greeted the arrival of DFS in large part because it is seen as less conducive to game fixing and manipulation of sports events than traditional sports betting. In the traditional sports betting context, a single person could influence the results of a game by bribing a single player or official. Fixing a DFS contest by manipulating the underlying games would be virtually impossible, according to proponents. The number of athletes, officials and games that would have to be involved in order to influence the results of even a few of the hundreds of DFS contests that are offered daily is astronomical.

The integrity of the athletic contests, however, is only one component of the overall DFS "integrity" landscape. The inherent fairness of DFS games has come under scrutiny. Claiming that DFS is a game of skill is a double-edged sword. It separates DFS from gambling, but it also acknowledges that the games may not be fair to all players.

One study concluded that in the first half of the 2015 season, 1.3 percent of the participants in DFS MLB contests won 91 percent of the participant profits (Miller & Singer, 2015). That same study found that 80 percent of the players lost money.

The study highlights the disparity between seasoned players and novices, those who play constantly and the casual player, and those who pay substantial entry fees to play numerous higher-stakes games, and the player who pays to enter relatively few and smaller contests. The authors pointed out the concern that "the risk that skill element of daily fantasy is so high that DFS pros will wipe out recreational players."

They contended that to sustain its popularity, DFS "needs the right balance of skill versus luck" noting that while chess is popular, it is rarely played for money because "it is too skill-based; the better player wins almost every time." In contrast, poker achieved and maintains its level of popularity because, with luck, even an unseasoned amateur can beat the best professional.

Aside from the disparities created by the very nature of DFS, the integrity and fairness of DFS are susceptible to human conduct, although not the sort of manipulation of the underlying athletic event associated with traditional sports gambling. In late 2015, an employee of DraftKings came under scrutiny when he won $350,000 in rival FanDuel's NFL contest. Because he accidentally published a proprietary "percentage owned" chart of DraftKings, which would have conferred an advantage on a player who had access to it before entering a DFS contest, the same weekend in which he received his winnings, initial speculation was that the employee used the DraftKings chart to increase his chances of winning the FanDuel contest. Although it was determined, after investigation, that he did not have access to the chart until after entering the FanDuel contest, the incident raised doubts about the integrity of DFS games, and the ability of insiders to influence outcomes.

Investigations by the Attorney General of New York and the United States Attorney's office in Florida into allegations of more systemic abuse of inside information by DFS site employees, and the filing of a private class action suit in New York making similar claims, have also tarnished the image of DFS operators. Application of existing federal and state consumer protection and fair competition laws to DFS activities may be the first step in policing the DFS industry, with new legislation either banning DFS in some states, or regulating it in others, likely to follow.

CONCLUSION

The words of NBA Commissioner Adam Silver illustrate how much sports gambling is changing:

> The [DFS] industry exists, and it's my view that you have to engage in it. What's happened with daily fantasy is what happened with virtually every other industry that's out there: The Internet has disrupted it. Now that that's happened, what should our reaction be? My reaction is to engage directly. To the extent that federal or state regulators are stepping in, my reaction is, that's very positive and we'd like to be part of those conversations. Because it's ultimately our game, our intellectual property and most importantly, what's at stake is the integrity of our game.
>
> (Fainaru & Fainaru-Wada, 2015)

The traditional ethical debates over the propriety of the sports industry's association with gambling and gambling-related activities will certainly continue in the context of newer endeavors such as DFS and e-Sports betting, and future endeavors not yet conceived. Although it appears that the concept that professional sports should not in any way be associated with gambling has been relegated to the scrapheap, along with moral judgments regarding gambling, sports industry leaders will continue to wrestle with issues regarding the nature and extent of that association, the financial lure offered by that association, and the preservation of the integrity of the games they lead.

It does not appear that virtue ethics or utilitarianism is having a significant effect on these developments at this time. Whether those important ethical theories will begin to assert themselves more as time goes by remains to be seen.

ETHICAL LEADERSHIP CASE STUDY

Case study #1

You have been asked to review your state's gambling law, make recommendations about revising it, and determine if it is ethical. Currently, your state's law defines gambling as wagering on any competition where chance is involved in the determination of the results. What ethical theories support this activity, and which oppose it? What sort of ethical leadership should be exerted to get the public to consider the ethical aspects of allowing gambling?

Case study #2

You have been asked to evaluate a proposal to change your state's definition of gambling to any competition where the element of chance predominates in the determination of results.

1. Under this revised version of your state's law, is poker gambling?
2. Under your state's law, is trading in the stock market gambling?

3. How would the counter-arguments of poker and stock market proponents change as a result of the revised law?

Case study #3

You have been asked to evaluate a proposal that would legalize DFS in your state. Discuss the ethics of the following arguments:

1. Legalizing DFS would encourage more people to gamble and, in particular, would encourage people to start gambling at a younger age.
2. Legalizing DFS would reduce the incidents of game fixing.
3. Legalizing DFS would minimize the influence of organized crime and unscrupulous service providers on DFS gambling.

STUDENT LEARNING EXERCISE

Does e-Sports gambling present any unique problems or dangers that are not present in other forms of sports gambling? Formulate an ethical leadership campaign to convince the e-Sports industry to protect:

a. the integrity of the underlying e-Sport competition.
b. the integrity of the e-Sports gambling activity.

PROBLEMS/QUESTIONS

1. Define "gambling." What are the ethical arguments against it?
2. What is the difference between a game of chance and a game of skill? Why is one generally considered ethical while the other is not?
3. Are there ethical reasons why the major sports leagues have gone from denouncing sports gambling to embracing it?
4. Is it ethical for states to become involved in sports gambling?
5. What ethical dangers and risks are associated with partnerships between DFS providers and sports leagues?
6. What unique ethical issues does e-Sports gambling present that traditional, season-long fantasy and DFS gambling do not?
7. Should gambling for a good cause (such as church bingo or a poker tournament which benefits disaster victims) be treated differently ethically than "for profit" gambling?
8. Is it ethical for a player or manager to bet on his own team to win? Why or why not?
9. How would statistical data showing that "unskilled" DFS participants beat "skilled" DFS participants 50 percent of the time affect the ethical arguments about DFS?

BIBLIOGRAPHY

Ali-Shamaa, Omar, Daily Fantasy Sports: Are They Legal?, *Florida International University Law Review, Student News*, November 2, 2015.

Asinof, Eliot, *Eight Men Out* (1963).

Associated Press, New Jersey Lawmaker Seeks to Regulate Daily Fantasy Sports, cbsnews.com, November 2, 2015.

Barmasse, Jason, Fascinating Legal History of Fantasy Sports, *The Fields of Green*, September 9, 2014.

Bauder, Don, The NFL's Dirty Secret, *San Diego Reader*, July 4, 2012.

Berr, Jonathan, Is DraftKings' Ethan Haskell Just a Shrewd "Investor"?, cbsnews.com, October 14, 2015.

Boghani, Priyanka, Sports Leagues and Daily Fantasy: What's At Stake?, *PBS SOCAL*, February 9, 2016.

Breslow, Jason, How Fantasy Sports Got Around Online Gambling Laws, *PBS SOCAL*, October 15, 2015.

Breslow, Jason, Is It Gambling? How States View Daily Fantasy Sports, *PBS SOCAL*, February 8, 2016.

Breslow, Jason, Matt King: Daily Fantasy Sports Are 'Entertainment," Not Gambling, *PBS SOCAL*, February 9, 2016.

Chenard v. Marcel Motors, 387 A.2d 596 (1978).

DFS Operators Like DraftKings, FanDuel Under Federal Investigation, *Headlines and Global News*, October 9, 2015.

Edelman, Marc, A Short Treatise on Fantasy Sports and the Law: How America Regulates its New National Pastime, 3 *Harvard Law School Journal of Sports & Entertainment Law* 1 (2012).

Edelman, Marc, Is It Legal to Play Fantasy Football for Money?, forbes.com, September 3, 2012.

ESPN Pulls Fantasy Football-Sponsored Content After DFS Insider Trading Report, *Headlines and Global News*, October 6, 2015.

Fainaru, Steve & Fainaru-Wada, Mark, Adam Silver: "Should Be a Regulatory Framework" for Daily Fantasy Operators, espn.go.com, October 22, 2015.

Fischer, Howard, Bill to Exclude Fantasy Sports From Gambling Law Draws Derision, azcapitoltimes.com, February 18, 2016.

Gouker, Dustin, Illinois Attorney General Says DFS Is Gambling, Expects DraftKings, FanDuel to Leave State, legalsportsreport.com, December 23, 2015.

Graham, Luke, E-sports Betting to Become a Boon for Gambling Industry, cnbc.com, April 8, 2016.

Humphrey v. Viacom, 2007 US Dist. Lexis 44679 (D.N.J. 2007).

Illinois Compiled Statutes, 720 ILCS 5, Chapter 28.

Irwin, Neil, Daily Fantasy Sports and the Hidden Cost of America's Weird Gambling Laws, *New York Times*, September 24, 2015.

Kaplan, Michael, The Reality of Fantasy, *Cigar Aficionado*, January/February, 2016.

Lang v. Merwin, 99 Me. 486 (1905).

Linder, Douglas, The Black Sox Trial: An Account, http://law2.umkc.edu/faculty/projects/ftrials/black sox/blacksoxaccount.html, 2010.

McGugan, Ian, The Case for Legalized Gambling on Sports, nytimes.com, January 23, 2015.

Miller, Ed & Singer, Daniel, For Daily Fantasy Sports Operators, the Curse of Too Much Skill, *Sports Business Daily Journal*, July 27, 2015.

Moore, David Leon, Las Vegas Makes Plays to Lure Pro Sports Teams, usatoday.com, November 5, 2014.

Morran, Chris, Fantasy Sports Lobby Spending Millions to Push New Laws to Protect DraftKings, FanDuel, consumerist.com, 16, 2016.

Montana Council on Problem Gambling, Sports Gambling Facts, www.mtproblemgambling.org/sports-gambling-facts.aspx, 2016.

NCAA v. Christie, 730 F. 3d 208 (3rd Cir., 2013).

National Football League v. Governor of the State of Delaware, 435 F. Supp 1372 (D. Del. 1977).

People of New York v. DraftKings, Inc., New York Supreme Court Index No. 453054/15, Brief for Defendant-Appellant DraftKings, filed February 22, 2016.

Pierceall, Kimberly, DraftKings, FanDuel Face Scrutiny Under Federal Gambling Law, www.inc.com, September 14, 2015.

Prah, Pamela M., States Expand Lotteries, Online Gambling, www.govtech.com/budget-finance/States-Expand-Lotteries-Online-Gambling.html, April 26, 2013.

Purdum, David, Explaining National Basketball Association Commissioner Adam Silver's Stance on Sports Betting, espn.go.com, November 18, 2014.

Purdum, David, DraftKings, FanDuel Will Stop in NY, But Appeal, Legislation Pending, espn.go.com, March 22, 2016.

Robbins, Liz, Sports Betting in New Jersey is Challenged, nytimes.com, October 20, 2014.

Rose, I. Nelson & Owens, Jr., Martin D., *Internet Gaming Law* (2009).

Rummel, Nick, Fantasy Sports Are Skill-Based, Claims DraftKings, osga.com, February 24, 2016.

Schrotenboer, Brent, Fantasy Sports Debate: Gambling or Not Gambling?, usatoday.com, January 12, 2015.

Schwartz, David G., *Roll The Bones: The History of Gambling, Casino Edition* (2013).

Szadolci v. Hollywood Park Operating Co., 17 Cal. Rptr. 2d 356 (1993).

Unlawful Internet Gambling Enforcement Act of 2006, 31 U.S.C. §§5361 – 5367.

Wahl, Grant, MLS Invests In Its Brand By Striking Deal With Fantasy Site DraftKings, si.com, July 25, 2015.

Woodward, Curt, Fantasy Sports Bill Passes in Virginia, A Needed Win for Industry, *Boston Globe*, February 24, 2016.

CHAPTER 12

Ethical aspects of intellectual property rights in sport

INTRODUCTION

In conceptualizing the ethics of intellectual property rights in sports, it is important to keep in mind that intellectual property shares many attributes with personal property. Just as it is not ethical to steal someone's personal property, like a purse, it is unethical to steal or misappropriate someone's intellectual property, like a broadcast that is copyrighted, an identifier that is trademarked, or a product that is patented.

What makes intellectual property different from personal property is that intellectual property is usually intangible. Also, in a high-technology world, it can be very easy to misappropriate intellectual property, sometimes with just a few keystrokes.

In sports, intellectual property can be very important and valuable. Broadcast rights, team logos, scores, and images of plays and players have all been the subject of extensive litigation. As with other subjects explored in this book, the ethics of the use of intellectual property in sports has been reflected by and determined in courts and legislatures. Generally, the courts and legislatures in our democratic system are determining, in accord with utilitarianism, the greatest good for the greatest number.

These ethical problems go to the very roots of the U.S. Constitution, which provides for both freedom of speech and intellectual property rights. These rights can conflict, however, which is where the complexity enters. For example, putting the image of a famous athlete on a T-shirt and selling it is speech, but such an act conflicts with the intellectual property rights of the famous athlete. Courts must balance these competing interests, which is a difficult endeavor.

This chapter will explore these issues in the areas of player publicity rights, owner trademark rights, broadcast rights, and patent rights. These issues come up regularly in sports.

FREE SPEECH IS NOT AN ABSOLUTE RIGHT

The First Amendment of the U.S. Constitution is a well-known guarantee of free speech: "Congress shall make no law . . . abridging the freedom of speech, or of the press." However, it has long been established that this right is not absolute. One cannot, for example, shout "fire" in a crowded theater, or make jokes in an airport security line.

Nonetheless, the right to free expression is fundamental to democracy, and the suppression of it is, in the United States, generally considered immoral and wrongful.

Our Founding Fathers obviously thought that free speech in the free marketplace of ideas constituted the greatest good for the greatest number, because that was the surest path to truth. They also obviously thought that unfettered free speech would be harmful and would therefore not produce the greatest good for the greatest number.

Certainly, one of the major counters to free speech is the law relating to intellectual property, like copyright or trademark laws. These laws also originate from the U.S. Constitution, Article 1, Section 8: "Congress shall have power to promote the progress of science and useful arts, by securing for limited times to authors and inventors the exclusive right to their respective writings and discoveries." This power is important because, without such protection, there would be less intellectual property benefiting the country. Authors and inventors would be reluctant to write or invent if their work could be unethically misappropriated. Therefore, our Founding Fathers also believed that the protection of intellectual property generated the greatest good for the greatest number.

In balancing the two important rights of free speech and the protection of intellectual property, the courts have taken into account the ethical purposes of the intellectual property laws. Copyright, for example, has as its purpose the protection of the author, who alone can and should financially benefit from his or her work for a limited period of time. The time limit exists because at some point, the public, which created this right, should not have to pay for it in perpetuity.

On the other hand, trademark has as its purpose the protection of consumers from confusion. When a customer sees a trademark—for example, the logo of a professional sports team—the customer has the right to know that the item trademarked truly comes from that team, and not from another entity trying to exploit that trademark. Virtue ethics would teach that intentionally confusing another person would not be ethical.

The right of trademark may be limited, however. For example, offensive trademarks, such as certain references to Native Americans, may be prohibited. This issue is before the courts as of spring, 2017. Again, offensive trademarks would appear to be contrary to both virtue ethics and care ethics.

PLAYER PUBLICITY RIGHTS

No area in sports intellectual property rights is more complex than players' publicity rights. The value of a player's image, which he has worked years to develop and which may be his most valuable asset after he retires from sports, often conflicts with the free speech rights of those like manufacturers of videogames or operators of fantasy sports leagues.

Nothing illustrates this conflict between two basic rights better than the sole U.S. Supreme Court case on the subject (*Zacchini*, 1977). Unfortunately, nothing also illustrates better the lack of clarity in this area, because the case is dated (1977), and it involves an idiosyncratic set of facts relating to a human cannonball act. Nonetheless, it is a Supreme Court case and cannot be ignored. Both sides of the issue—those favoring free speech and those favoring publicity rights—cite the case for support.

Like athletes, the human cannonball involved in this case took years to develop his skills. Also like athletes, his skills had a limited life, and, after that limited life, all that remains is whatever publicity can be generated by what happened while the performer/ athlete possessed the skills. The entire act of the human cannonball was very brief, lasting only 15 seconds. The nightly news—an institution that is at the heart of the free speech that the First Amendment of the U.S. Constitution protects—broadcast the entire act over the human cannonball's protest.

The human cannonball sued and won. The Supreme Court held that:

> [w]herever the line in particular situations is to be drawn between media reports that are protected and those that are not, we are quite sure that the First and Fourteenth Amendments do not immunize the media when they broadcast a performer's entire act without his consent.
>
> (id.)

The court then specifically analogized the right of publicity with the well-recognized copyright:

> The Constitution no more prevents a state from requiring respondent to compensate [the human cannonball] for broadcasting his act on television than it would privilege [the television station] to film and broadcast a copyrighted dramatic work without liability to the copyright owner.
>
> (id.)

Ethically speaking, the court is advocating a theory of universalizability. One should not misappropriate the act of another because one would not want one's own act to be mis-appropriated.

Advocates of the First Amendment say that this case supports their use of athletes' images in all cases where the "entire act" is not used, as in a videogame. Advocates of the right of publicity say that this case supports their claim that the First Amendment is not absolute, and must be balanced against other rights like copyright.

Clearly, the latter argument is correct. Free speech in the U.S. legal system is balanced against intellectual property rights like copyright and trademark. Copying a copyrighted book is speech, but it is clearly illegal, because it is unethical to free-ride on the work of another. The same is true for copying a registered trademark that has been devised by another's creativity and effort. These legal theories are founded on concepts of utilitarianism, deontology, and virtue ethics.

Striking this balance has, however, been very difficult for the courts, which have only the human cannonball precedent to go by in an era of videogames and fantasy sports that did not even exist in 1977. As a result, the lower courts have devised over a half dozen different legal standards for striking this balance, some of which contradict each other. The remainder of this section will explore the ethical ramifications of these different standards, and the law that tries to reflect these ethical ramifications.

History of the right of publicity

The history of the right of publicity, which is much younger than the First Amendment, demonstrates that the courts have created many conflicting interpretations of this right.

The right of publicity did not exist before 1890. At that time two distinguished lawyers, one of whom later became a U.S. Supreme Court justice, wrote an article describing the right as part of the right of privacy (Warren & Brandeis, 1898; Katz, 2012). The right is deceptively simple: one cannot use a person's image without permission. That simplicity disappears, however, when free speech rights have to be balanced against the right of publicity.

Of course, in 1890 images were not nearly as valuable as they are today in our celebrity-driven society; in 1980 products promoting images like fantasy sports and videogames did not exist. As the authors of this far-seeing article mentioned, however, the common law system used in the United States had the capability of adjusting to new developments, because it, "in its eternal youth, grows to meet the demands of society" (Warren & Brandeis, 1898).

The early disputes about publicity rights did not go well for the athletes, who were becoming important celebrities as the 20th century progressed. For example, Davey O'Brien was an All-American football quarterback for Texas Christian University in the 1930s and also played professionally for the Philadelphia Eagles. Pabst Blue Ribbon beer put out a calendar with an image of O'Brien in his college uniform next to an image of Pabst Blue Ribbon beer. Not only was O'Brien unpaid for this, but, although it is unknown, he might well have objected to being portrayed with an alcoholic drink.

He sued, but lost (*O'Brien*, 1941). The court reasoned that he had no complaint about his privacy because he had sent many images of himself to fans and to the press—i.e. in ethical terms, his conduct was not universalizable. The court also ruled that there was no endorsement by him of Pabst Blue Ribbon beer contained in the calendar and that he did not possess any right in his likeness.

The ethical objectionableness of Pabst Blue Ribbon exploiting O'Brien's image did not impress the court. However, courts started recognizing the ethical issues in the early 1950s with a case involving baseball trading cards (*Haelen*, 1953).

Two baseball card companies were fighting over the use of the images of major league baseball players. One of them claimed that, as in the O'Brien case, the players had no independent right of publicity. The court disagreed:

> The right might be called a 'right of publicity.' For it is common knowledge that many prominent persons (especially actors and ballplayers), far from having their feelings bruised through public exposure of their likenesses, would feel sorely deprived if they no longer received money for authorizing advertisements, popularizing their countenances, displayed in newspapers, magazines, busses, trains and subways. This right of publicity would usually yield them no money unless it could be made the subject of an exclusive grant which barred any other advertiser from using their pictures.
>
> (id.)

In ethical terms, the court was supporting the proposition that misappropriating the image of another for profit without permission or compensation was neither universalizable nor utilitarian.

As ethics and mores changed, Davey O'Brien's alcohol association issue was reversed in a later case. Renowned Brooklyn Dodger pitcher, Don Newcombe, who was a recovering alcoholic, was pictured, without his permission, in a full-page advertisement for Killian's Red Beer. The court decided that Newcombe had a triable claim, even though the ad ran 34 years after Newcombe's retirement as a baseball player (*Newcombe*, 1998).

Despite Newcombe's victory, the First Amendment and free speech still had to be factored into these legal issues. A good example of that is the lawsuit by famed San Francisco 49ers quarterback, Joe Montana, against the *San Jose Mercury* newspaper. The newspaper made into posters, which it sold for five dollars apiece, some of its pages describing Montana's Super Bowl victories. Montana claimed that this violated his right of publicity; the newspaper defended on the grounds of the First Amendment.

The court ruled in favor of the newspaper, holding that the First Amendment protects the poster for two reasons, "first, because the posters themselves report newsworthy items of public interest, and second, because a newspaper has a constitutional right to promote itself by reproducing its originally protected articles or photographs" (*Montana*, 1995). In other words, free press in this case is utilitarian.

The Montana case presaged the case of another famous athlete, golfer Tiger Woods. After he won the Masters Tournament in 1997, he was centrally depicted in a poster entitled *The Masters of Augusta*. Less centrally depicted were the well-known golfers Jack Nicklaus and Arnold Palmer. A total 700 serigraphs of the poster sold for $700 each, and numerous lithographs of it sold for $5 each. As in the Montana case, Woods sued for infringement of his right of publicity, and the artist used a First Amendment defense (*ETW Corp.*, 2003).

The artist won for several reasons. First, the court found that the Masters Tournament was a newsworthy, historic event. The court ruled that the depiction of such an event— even featuring a famous athlete—does not suspend the First Amendment. In ethical terms, the free reporting of historical events is utilitarian.

Second, the court found that the First Amendment/Right of Publicity balance tilted toward free speech because Tiger Woods did not need the right of publicity in order to reap substantial financial rewards from golf. Indeed, Woods's appearance in these posters could increase his ability to earn money because of the publicity generated by the posters. On the other hand, the artist would be deprived of his ability to profit from his talent and enterprise. Therefore, the court decision was also supported by principles of universalizability.

The transformative use test

Finally, the court applied what has come to be called the "transformative effects" or the "transformative use" test, which has become very important in this legal and ethical area. That test came from a case where the comedians called The Three Stooges were depicted on a T-shirt in a charcoal drawing. A lawsuit was brought, and the artist defended with the First Amendment (Comedy III, 2001).

The court held that First Amendment protection would apply if the image of the Stooges was sufficiently transformed. Because the court held that there was not sufficient transformation in this case, The Three Stooges won.

The transformative use test is emerging as the dominant legal test for balancing the right of publicity against the First Amendment. The reason is essentially ethical: the creator of the new work is creating something new, not copying something in existence, and therefore protecting that is utilitarian. The full statement of this important rule is deceptively simple:

> [w]hether the celebrity likeness is one the 'raw materials' from which an original work is synthesized, or whether the depiction or imitation of the celebrity is the very sum and substance of the work in question . . . whether the product containing a celebrity's likeness is so transformed that it has become primarily the defendant's own expression rather than the celebrity's likeness.
>
> (id.)

It is important to note that sometimes transformativeness itself is a subjective judgment. This will become clear below when we explore the ethics of using players' images in videogames like Madden NFL.

It is also clear from the subjective analysis of transformativeness in the Tiger Woods case. The court notes that the Woods depiction is unlike that of The Three Stooges because the Woods depiction is surrounded by other images, consisting "of a collage of images in addition to Woods's image which are combined to describe, in artistic form, a historic event in sports history and to convey a message about the significance of Woods's achievement in that event" (*ETW Corp.*, 2003).

Videogames

The right of publicity has been an important issue in sports videogames. The reason is that, unlike The Three Stooges T-shirts, and like the Tiger Woods poster, videogames contain many elements other than the images of the players themselves. There are the stadium, the cheerleaders, the announcer and the software program, among many other things (Katz, 2012, 2013 ("Rights"), 2013 ("Third")). Therefore, when the manufacturer of the college football videogame was sued for infringing the players' rights of publicity by using their images without permission or compensation, the manufacturer used the First Amendment defense, augmented by the transformative effects defense.

Two courts have rejected this defense on the essentially ethical grounds that the videogame manufacturer was profiting from the images without transforming them at all. As one of the courts said of former Rutgers quarterback, Ryan Hart:

> The digital Ryan Hart does what the actual Ryan Hart did while at Rutgers: he plays college football, in digital recreations of college football stadiums, filled with all the trappings of a college football game. This is not transformative; the various digitized sights and sounds in the video game do not alter or transform the appellant's identity in a significant way.
>
> (*Hart*, 2013)

The court, however, insisted that it was not doing away with the First Amendment, but simply balancing it against the right of publicity:

> In finding that NCAA Football failed to satisfy the Transformative Use Test, we do not hold that the game loses First Amendment protection. We merely hold

that the interest protected by the right of publicity in this case outweighs the Constitutional shield.

(id.)

Fantasy sports

Free speech outweighs the right of publicity in fantasy sports. The balance between the First Amendment and the right of publicity came out precisely the opposite from the result in videogames. The reason is also ethical: the raw materials of fantasy games are statistics that are in the public domain. No baseball player, for example, owns his batting average. That would not be utilitarian.

The way that fantasy sports work in general is that one creates a sports team that can consist of players from different teams. After games are played, the statistics for the player chosen are applied to the fictitious team in order to see which team does the best (see also Chapter 11).

The court held that this public information could not, consistent with the First Amendment, be restricted: "It would be a strange law that a person would not have a *First Amendment* right to use information that is available to everyone" (C.B.C., 2007). It should be noted, however, that images of the players in a fantasy game might be treated differently, but that issue has not yet been decided by the courts.

Commercial v. expressive use

As public awareness of the ethics of the right of publicity developed, it became important whether the use of the image was commercial or expressive. There is much less protection for an advertisement—so-called "commercial speech"—than for expressive speech, such as that in newspapers or in other media. Again, this legal rule is ethically based, because the point of a commercial advertisement is ultimately not to express oneself but rather to make money. Therefore, on utilitarian grounds, it does not deserve as much First Amendment protection as expressive or political speech. However, not all advertisements are blatantly offering to sell something. So-called "image advertising," for example, is intended to enhance the image of a company so that it will be more commercially successful.

The case that best illustrates this issue was brought by the famous basketball player, Michael Jordan, against a supermarket, Jewel-Osco, which ran a congratulatory ad after Jordan was inducted into the basketball Hall of Fame (*Michael Jordan*, 2014; Brenner and Becker, 2016). The ad barely mentioned Jordan by name, but it contained an image of basketball shoes with Jordan's well-known number, 23, on them.

The ad did not overtly try to sell anything. It merely said, referring to the shoes, "A Shoe In!" It followed that up by saying:

> After six NBA Championships, scores of rewritten record books and numerous buzzer beaters, Michael Jordan's elevation in the Basketball Hall of Fame was never in doubt! Jewel-Osco salutes #23 on his many accomplishments as we honor a fellow Chicagoan who was 'just around the corner' for so many years.
>
> (*Michael Jordan*, 2014)

The court ruled that such an advertisement was commercial speech, even if it touched on public issues. Therefore, it was not entitled to First Amendment protection: "The ad is a form of image advertising aimed at promoting goodwill for the Jewel-Osco brand by exploiting public affection for Jordan at an auspicious moment in his career" (id.).

The difficulty of determining whether something is commercial or expressive speech was well illustrated in a case involving NFL Films, a company that makes films about notable NFL moments and games (Katz, 2014). The court in that case noted that the test for distinguishing expressive from commercial speech "had more holes . . . than in a wheel of good Swiss cheese" (id.). The test he used had three prongs: 1) whether the communication is an advertisement, 2) whether it refers to a specific product or service, and 3) whether the speaker has an economic motivation.

Illustrating the difficulty of applying this test, in this case the court first decided that these films were commercial speech but later in the case reversed itself and decided that the films were expressive speech. In his earlier decision, the judge held that the films were advertisements because they present a wholly positive picture of the NFL; that the product was the NFL itself; and that the NFL clearly had an economic motivation.

In the later decision—directly contradicting the earlier decision—the judge decided that the films were "a history lesson of NFL football," not an advertisement (id.). On the product issue, he also changed his mind, saying that "the productions do not promote a product separate from the productions themselves. The productions exist in their own right—they are stories of the NFL" (id.). The court maintained its position on the issue of economic motivation, but decided that that alone could not make the films commercial speech: "This is not commercial speech; it is capitalism" (id.). Ethically speaking, this court's result can be justified on utilitarian grounds. The number of people who will benefit from seeing these documentaries is much greater than the number who are only a part of the documentaries and who make their living from playing football, not appearing in documentaries.

Group licensing

So-called group licensing adds complexity to the right of publicity because group licensing acknowledges the publicity rights of journeyman players as well as of the stars. On one hand, there is no doubt that star players can garner more income from their image than journeymen. However, there is also no doubt that in team sports all must participate to even produce the game. A football star, for example, would not do very well without 10 teammates on the field with him.

Dividing revenues—for example, from team pictures in professional sports—presents ethical problems addressed by care ethics and virtue ethics. Providing resolutions to these problems are the unions to which most professional sports players in the U.S. belong.

The unions recognize both the star power of individuals and the necessity of having a group in team sports like football, basketball, baseball, and hockey. The unions permit individuals to capture the worth of their own images when less than five players are portrayed. If, however, more than five players are pictured—for example, in a videogame—then the professional player unions require an equal sharing of revenue.

TRADEMARK RIGHTS IN SPORT

Sports logos are often highly recognizable and very valuable. They present a tempting target for infringers, because of those attributes. Furthermore, the use of trademarks raises a number of ethical issues. The primary issues relate to deontology, utilitarianism, virtue ethics, and care ethics. None of those theories permit the intentional confusion of others. All of those ethical theories are reflected in U.S. trademark laws—principally one called the Lanham Act, which has as its main purpose the prevention of consumer confusion.

The Lanham Act defines a trademark as "any word, name, symbol, symbol or device ... used by a person ... to identify and distinguish his or her good ... from those manufactured and sold by others and to indicate the source of the good." The idea is that the efforts of a manufacturer of goods to endow his or her products with attributes attractive to consumers and then to enable consumers to identify that product by its trademark should not be exploited by another to attract customers to another product. Because the market for products like apparel with sports trademarks is literally billions of dollars, this law and the ethical theories underlying it are extremely important and valuable.

It is certainly not universalizable to permit exploitation of another's trademark. Nor does it generate the greatest good for the greatest number. And it is definitely neither a component of virtue nor the way to relate to another human being.

Three examples will illustrate the problems associated with trademark infringement. One deals with the National Football League team formerly known as the Baltimore Colts and now known as the Indianapolis Colts; the second deals with the Major League Baseball team formerly known as the Brooklyn Dodgers and now known as the Los Angeles Dodgers; and the third deals with the famous 12th Man trademark originated by the Texas A&M football team. The cases are similar in many ways except for the key ethical concept: the likelihood of consumer confusion.

In the Colts case, nine years after they left Baltimore, a Canadian Football League team started playing there under the not coincidental name of the Baltimore CFL Colts. The question whether this name would be confusing, particularly with respect to team apparel sales, was brought before the court when the Indianapolis Colts sued the Baltimore CFL Colts for trademark infringement. The Canadian team's main defense was that the "CFL" in its name made all the difference. A survey was taken by the NFL team, though, that the court thought proved otherwise.

The survey asked one group of consumers questions regarding the Baltimore CFL Colts and another group about a team called, for purposes of the survey, the Baltimore Horses. The survey demonstrated what the court characterized as "astonishing levels of confusion": "Among self-identified football fans, 64 percent thought that the 'Baltimore CFL Colts' was either the old (NFL) Baltimore Colts or the Indianapolis Colts" (*Indianapolis Colts*, 1994). On the other hand, the name Baltimore Horses generated much less confusion. According to the court, this focused the source of the confusion on the part of the name "Colts" rather than the part of the name "Baltimore."

The court therefore enjoined the use of "Colts." The importance of that decision was illustrated shortly thereafter, when the team formerly known as the Baltimore CFL Colts ceased to do business in Baltimore. In choosing a confusing name, the owners of that team were clearly unethically free-riding on the efforts and creativity of the original Baltimore Colts.

The second case, which had the opposite result, involved a restaurant in Brooklyn called the Brooklyn Dodger (*Major League Baseball Properties*, 1993). The case was brought over 30 years after the Dodgers baseball team had moved from Brooklyn to Los Angeles.

The Dodgers claimed that the name of the restaurant was confusing. The restaurant claimed—and the court agreed—that "the 'Brooklyn Dodgers' was a non-transportable cultural institution separate from the 'Los Angeles Dodgers.'" On the issue of confusion, the court held that, because the Brooklyn Dodger was not a baseball team, there was no risk of confusion: "No one would think the Brooklyn Dodgers baseball team reincarnated in a restaurant" (id.).

Therefore, in ethical terms, it would not constitute a violation of character ethics to use the Dodger name on a restaurant in Brooklyn after the Dodgers departed, and using such a name also results in the greatest good for the greatest number, because no one is hurt. The rule allowing the use of the name is universalizable: it is allowable to use a name that is similar or identical to another name if the new name is not confusing.

The fact that a trademark is being used in two different locations for two different kinds of businesses, however, is no guarantee that there will not be a trademark infringement. A recent case, for example, involved the 12th Man trademark used by the Texas A&M football team for many years.

The mark originated in 1922, when a Texas A&M student literally came out of the stands during a game in order to be available as a substitute because the team had sustained several injuries. A professional football team more than a thousand miles from Texas, the Seattle Seahawks, started using 12th Man in 2006.

After Texas A&M brought suit, the case was settled. The Seahawks agreed, among other things, not to use 12th Man in its social media and also agreed to pay Texas A&M a royalty based on other permitted uses by the Seahawks. Texas A&M's president was quoted as saying about the settlement, "The 12th Man is a cherished tradition" (Rajan, 2016).

Ethical theories supporting this result are virtue ethics and care ethics. It is a mark of good character not to misappropriate a long-used, successful, and widely recognized mark. Also, empathy and compassion would lead to the same result. Although professional and college football have their differences, they are definitely more similar to each other than a restaurant is to a baseball team, as in the Brooklyn Dodger case. Therefore, it would be hard to universalize a rule that would allow the Seahawks to infringe on Texas A&M's well-known mark.

Offensive trademarks

It is an open question whether offensive trademarks are allowable (see also Chapter 8). Such offensive trademarks include references to American Indians, like the University of North Dakota's former nickname (the Fighting Sioux) or the nickname of the Washington DC professional football team (the Redskins).

The NCAA made a rule proposing penalties for member schools that had offensive nicknames. This led to an extensive fight in the courts and the legislature about the Fight ing Sioux nickname. One issue was that a $100 million contribution to the university stipulated as a condition that the nickname be used indefinitely.

A second issue had to do with whether the nickname was in fact offensive. The NCAA gave the university time to pursue this issue with several tribes as part of a settlement of litigation between the school and the NCAA. Sufficient tribal support for the university was not forthcoming, and the university changed its nickname to the Fighting Hawks in 2015 (Borzi, 2016).

The free speech guaranteed by the First Amendment was not an issue in this matter, because the NCAA is a private, not a governmental, organization. The NCAA was taking an ethical stand, based on the universalizable proposition that it is not ethical to malign a racial group, on the virtue ethics proposition that such conduct does not comport with good character and on the care ethics proposition that such conduct devalues interpersonal relations, empathy, and compassion.

The Washington Redskins situation is more complicated because it involved governmental action—the issuing of trademarks. The governmental involvement implicates the First Amendment, bringing up the balancing of free speech on the one hand and the governmental interest in preventing discrimination based on race (Katz, 2015).

The Lanham Act contains a section 2(a) that prohibits "scandalous, immoral, or disparaging marks," including trademarks that disparage a religion, nation, or ethnic group. This prohibition can collide with the ethical position that free speech creates the greatest good for the greatest number and is the best way to generate truth. The trademark office of the government disallowed the trademark, which was an economic blow to the football team because it meant that, although the Washington Redskins could still use the trademark, they could not prevent others from using it. A trial court affirmed that result, which the Washington Redskins appealed to a higher court.

The grounds for the appeal appear compelling for several reasons. First, the appeal points out that the trademark office has allowed many offensive trademarks, which makes this disallowance discriminatory. Some of the allowed trademarks include "dumb blondes" and "MURDER 4 HIRE."

Second, the trademark office has been inconsistent in judging what is offensive and what is not. For example, the trademark office allowed "THE DEVIL IS A DEMOCRAT" but disallowed "HAVE YOU HEARD SATAN IS A REPUBLICAN?"

Third, a federal appellate court recently decided a similar case, striking down the entirety of section 2(a) on free speech grounds. That case involved an Asian-American band called "The Slants." The court's holding was an emphatic defense of free speech: "Section 2(a) is a viewpoint-discriminatory regulation of speech, created and applied in order to stifle the use of certain disfavored messages" (Mullin, 2015; Volokh, 2015).

The point is that one of the main purposes of the First Amendment is to protect unpopular speech. Indeed, popular speech needs no protection, because no one attacks it. Ethically speaking, the protection of unpopular speech generates the greatest good for the greatest number because it allows people to decide for themselves what to believe or respect.

The Washington Redskins case has not been finally decided as of spring, 2017. Many commentators believe that the appellate court deciding that case will rule in the same as the appellate court in The Slants case.

THE ETHICS OF SPORTS BROADCASTING

History

Perhaps nothing has contributed to the rise in popularity of organized sports more than the evolution of sports broadcasting from radio to television to digital and internet. Alongside the rise of sports broadcasting is the rise of ethical questions concerning who owns the broadcast rights and when that ownership ends. Today, the health of professional teams and leagues is dictated more by the size of broadcast contracts than by actual game attendance.

In 2014, the National Football League earned more than $6 billion in revenue from national television broadcast rights, Major League Baseball received $1.6 billion in such revenue, and the National Basketball Association pulled in nearly $1 billion (Gaines, 2014). These revenues represent the majority of the revenue received from all sources.

In the National Football League for example, 60 percent of annual revenues are from national television contracts (Bloom, 2014). In 2014, $705 million of the National Collegiate Athletic Association's total revenue of $871.6, or 81 percent, came from media rights agreement with CBS Sports and Turner Broadcasting (ncaa.org).

The values of professional teams are now predicated to a great extent on the value of local broadcasting rights. In recent history, the New York Knicks have been considered the most valuable NBA franchise in large part because of their lucrative local media rights agreements. The Los Angeles Lakers, even during two of the team's three worst years on the court, are the NBA's most profitable team by virtue of their $3.6 billion broadcast deal with Time Warner Cable (Badenhausen, 2016).

In fact, "there would be no broadcast revenues if the law had not recognized certain property rights in the accounts and descriptions of sports events" (Garrett & Hochberg, 1984). The law recognized these rights because of ethical precepts relating to the taking of another's property, in this case, intellectual property.

However, at the core of any broadcast is the expression of ideas, and the legal protections given sports broadcasts have to be balanced with freedom of speech. Issues include: 1) what spectators can report from a live contest, 2) division of rights between the players and the owners, and 3) the tension between ownership of a broadcast and news media rights. These issues are all basically ethical issues regarding the balance of free speech and property rights.

Today, it is accepted that viewing a game does not necessarily give a spectator the right to report on it to the outside world, even if it is held in a public space. However, this rule, which is clearly utilitarian and deontological, did not spring to life fully grown.

As early as 1936, baseball team owners sought judicial protection of their ownership interests in their product, including the "broadcasting" of the events on the field (*National Exhibition Co.*, 1936). In that case, the team sued broadcasters for their "dissemination over telephone wires to groups of listeners, gathered at various distances from the scene of the game, of descriptions, play by play, of the plays as they occur during the progress of baseball games" without the owner's consent.

At the heart of the suit was money. The owner feared that its income from Western Union would suffer because the telegraph company would no longer pay for the "privilege of announcing the results of innings" (id.). He was also concerned that ticket sales would decline "because telephone listeners, who would otherwise attend, prefer to get the news in places of comfort away from the [baseball] grounds" (id.). The ethical issue was how to protect the game created by the owners from exploitation by others without pay, which is sometimes called "free-riding."

The *National Exhibition Co.* court did not have the benefit of federal broadcasting laws or other express legislative guidance; therefore, it looked to common law concepts regarding property and contractual rights. The court was not persuaded by the owner's contention that it had "an exclusive property right to news of the game while it is going on." The court did not find any contractual relationship between the owner and the broadcaster and, consequently, no contractual restriction or prohibition on what might be broadcast. Nor did the court find that any property right had been misappropriated:

> What the plaintiff owned was the game; or rather it owned or employed the instrumentalities through which the game was produced. On the other hand, what the defendants conveyed to their listeners, through the voices of themselves or their representatives, was the creation of their own faculties; they told what they had seen.
>
> (id.)

It was not long before team owners were back in court, seeking a different result because of what they thought was a clearly unethical misappropriation of what they had created at substantial expense. In 1938, the Pittsburgh Pirates sought to prevent the unauthorized play-by-play broadcasts of its games (*Pittsburgh Athletic Co*, 1938). That case reached a very different conclusion on facts very similar to those in *National Exhibition Co.*, holding that the Pirates' right to control the information about its games while they are being played is a property right of the Pirates.

The court found that the unauthorized broadcasts interfered with the Pirates' property right, and that the defendant radio station, which broadcast the games in order to increase its listening audience, was appropriating profits belonging to the Pirates. The court noted that the team, "at great expense, acquired and maintains a baseball park, pays the players who play the game, and has . . . a legitimate right to capitalize on the news value of their games by selling exclusive broadcasting rights" (id.). The defendant radio station unfairly competed by acquiring its information by posting observers at vantage points outside of the field—paying the Pirates nothing, but greatly damaging the team's ability to capitalize on its property rights.

The modern ethical doctrine, which is reflected in the law, that team and league owners have exclusive ownership of their teams' broadcast rights, can trace its roots to the decision in *Pittsburgh Athletic Co.* Professional sports teams and leagues have seen legislative and judicial expansion of these rights since 1938. The Sports Broadcasting Act of 1961 enabled teams in the major professional sports leagues to pool their broadcasting rights and revenues without fear of violating antitrust laws. Live sports broadcasts, which were recorded simultaneously with their transmissions, were given federal copyright protection by the Copyright Act of 1976.

Despite these advances, for the teams and leagues the same sorts of issues addressed by these legislative and decisional pronouncements continue to arise. New media outlets, platforms, and technology have caused the courts to revisit and refine the laws governing the extent to which teams' ownership of their broadcast rights must, at times, give way to free speech, news media, and other considerations.

Technological developments

Unauthorized broadcasting through high-tech devices has created major issues. Late 1930s judicial decisions did not anticipate the growth of importance of sports broadcast rights or related technological advances. The legality of broadcasting live scores and related information in the modern era of cell phones and pagers was addressed in a 1997 case (*National Basketball Association*, 1997).

The NBA sought to prevent the manufacturer of a sports-related paging device and the company which provided the information transmitted by the SportsTrax pager from transmitting real-time scores of NBA games. The NBA claimed in its lawsuit that the defendants violated unfair competition laws and state and federal copyright acts. These laws, of course, reflect the ethical considerations surrounding the "ownership" of the games, at least for a limited period.

In reaching its decision, the court traced the evolution of sports broadcast law as well as technology. Just as *National Exhibition Co.* and *Pittsburgh Athletic Co.* applied then-existing precedent to contemporary technology (radio), so the *Motorola* court attempted to apply the extant body of law to emerging computer and pager technologies. Despite the difficulty in separating live sports events (which are not copyrightable) from the copyrightable aspects of the broadcasts, particularly in the computer age, the court found that the pager did not infringe on the NBA's copyright protections.

The court seized on the facts that game scores are not information that the NBA gathers at a cost, and Motorola was neither directly competing with the NBA, nor was it seeking to free-ride on the efforts of the NBA. Motorola was merely transmitting facts from the games, not the expression or description of the game that constitutes the broadcast.

Moreover, "any patron of an NBA game could acquire [such factual information] without any involvement from the director, cameraman, or others who contribute to the originality of a broadcast" (id.). In this case, the ethics of free speech outweigh the ethics relating to property ownership.

Even as the courts address the impact of one form of technology on sports broadcast rights, another technological innovation emerges. The popularity in the late 1980s and early 1990s of sports bars showing games which the proprietor obtained through satellite dish systems required the courts to determine whether and to what extent those broadcasts were protected by copyright laws. Again, the ethical issue was free-riding.

The leagues advanced their traditional contention that any such infringement on their broadcast rights reduces advertising revenues as well as ticket sales. The establishments showing such satellite events argued that the leagues' copyright is not unlimited, citing the Copyright Act's "home use" exemption which limits the copyright protection when the transmission is received by "apparatus of a kind commonly used in private homes" (17 U.S.C. §110(5)). Because they utilized satellite dish equipment commonly used in private homes, they asserted, the home use exemption applied to them.

The courts have rejected the sports bar use of the home use exemption on various grounds, including the legislative intent of the Copyright Act of 1976. Also, because in 1986, satellite dish antennae were outnumbered by non-satellite dish "television sets by more than 100-to-one," dish antennae were not considered commonly used equipment under the statute (*National Football League*, 1986). In ethical terms, the appropriation of these broadcasts for profit by sports bars was not universalizable.

Ever newer technologies have made the pager, which was the center of the dispute in the *Motorola* case, and the television sets discussed in *McBee & Bruno's, Inc.* quaint and obsolete (1986). More recently, the Copyright Act has been applied to deep linking of live webcast feeds by a third party (*Live Nation Motor Sports*, 2007). In that case, the court extended the Copyright Act's protections to include the defendant's provision on his website of a link to the plaintiff's live audiocasts of plaintiff's motorcycle race events, by finding that the defendant was improperly "copying" those audiocasts.

The copyright protections afforded to teams and leagues continue to be challenged by the emergence of the internet (including sites such as YouTube), internet piracy, and the capturing and then streaming of broadcast signals. Ethical problems will continue as technological advancements continue.

Player/owner revenue split

Division of broadcast rights between players and owners has been a very fractious issue. The difficulties of interpreting the copyright protections afforded team owners and leagues when challenges are made by competitors or "free-riders" are substantial. When the copyright adversaries are the teams and the players themselves, the ethical difficulties are even greater.

Players and owners have been at odds as long as there have been professional teams and professional players. Players have traditionally fought management over ethical issues such as working conditions, free agency, salary caps, and revenue sharing. The players' entitlement to share in the benefits of the owners' copyright protections is another such issue.

Less than a decade after an arbitrator invalidated the reserve clause and declared major league baseball players Dave McNally and Andy Messersmith free agents, the Major League Baseball Players Association asserted the right of its players to share in broadcast revenues. In response to the MLBPA's letter to television networks and other broadcasters of Major League Baseball games that the players had a property right in the broadcasts and that any broadcasting of games was in violation of that right, Major League Baseball pursued a lawsuit against the MLBPA (*Baltimore Orioles*, 1986). The team owners asserted the exclusivity of their copyright against the players' claim of a common law right to publicity.

The owners' right to copyright protection was predicated primarily on the facts that the broadcasts of their games 1) were fixed in a tangible form, and 2) were original works of authorship. The court found that the videotaping of the broadcasts satisfied the fixation requirement. The court also found that the broadcasts were original works of authorship, citing the creativity and originality required in making decisions regarding camera angles, types of shots, use of things such as split screens and replays. The court concluded, as had many before it, that MLB had a copyright in its broadcasts. The MLBPA contended, however, that the works in which they claim rights are their performances, rather than the telecasts of the games in which they play, and that performances per se are not fixed in tangible form. Therefore, their rights of publicity in their performances are not subject to preemption by the copyright laws.

The court acknowledged that the players' rights of publicity in their performances could be violated by, for example, the unauthorized use of the player's image to advertise a product. However, because copyright law preempted the laws under which the players claimed their rights of publicity, and because the owners held the copyright to those broadcasts, the players' rights were preempted.

The players' rights to exploit their images and performances are now a matter negotiated as part of the collective bargaining agreements between the players and the leagues. For example, television revenues are part of the "Basketball Related Income" which the National Basketball Players Association collective bargaining agreement requires the league to share with the players through the salary cap and minimum team salaries, and Article XXIV of the Major League Baseball collective bargaining agreement sets forth how broadcast and other revenue is to be shared with players. Negotiation of such rights— rather than conflict over them—is an example of care ethics.

THE ETHICS OF PATENTS AND SPORTS COMPETITION

Patents also have their basis in the U.S. Constitution. There are three types of patents: utility, design, and plant. Patents must be useful, novel, and non-obvious. If they are, the patentee may stop others from making, using, or selling something that infringes the patent for a period of 20 years.

The ethical calculus for patents is the same as it is for the other forms of intellectual property discussed above—i.e. that protecting the fruits of the labor of the patentee ensures that more patents will be generated thereby, in accord with Article I, Section 8 of the U.S. Constitution, promoting "the progress of science and the useful arts." Unlike the other forms of intellectual property discussed above, however, the ethics underlying sports completely limits the application of patent law in that arena.

The reason is simple. The purpose of sports is to find out who is the best on a level playing field. If one side has an advantage that the other side cannot use or attempt because the advantage is patented, then the whole purpose of the exercise is defeated. Such a situation would not generate the greatest good for the greatest number because it would defeat the purpose of sports (Bambauer, 2005; Rapin, 2010).

This situation would not benefit either the side with the patent or the opponent. The opponent would be at an obvious disadvantage, but the side with the patent would also suffer because the competition would become uninteresting. No one would want to watch a sporting event where a patent gave one side an advantage that would ensure victory. Indeed, such an event would be an exhibition rather than a competition.

That is why sporting organizations have to control, for example, what kind of equipment is used. A fiberglass pole will, if everything else is equal, always outperform a wooden pole in a pole vaulting event. Similarly, a fiberglass tennis racket is superior to a wooden one. That is why sporting organizations have explicit rules and regulations about what equipment can be used.

Although it has been suggested that sports moves like the slam dunk might be patentable (Kunstadt, 1996; Das, 2000), that too would defeat the purpose of sports. If one team could use a play that the other team could not also attempt, the result would not be sport but rather an exhibition. There is simply no universalizable rule that would allow one party in a sporting competition to have a patented advantage over another. For that reason, patents are generally not relevant to competitive sports.

Of course, patents are relevant to sporting equipment. If, for example, an inventor patents a superior golf club, that inventor should receive patent protection. Whether, however, that club can be used in competition is a decision of the authorities that regulate sports. A level playing field precludes patented advantages of any kind.

CONCLUSION

Intellectual property rights translate into billions of dollars in sports. That fact in turn translates into legal issues, which, in turn, reflect the underlying ethical issues. Although these issues have been prevalent for decades, the substantial amounts of money at stake have made these issues much more contentious. Participants in the sports industry will continually have to deal with these issues for the foreseeable future, and therefore must carefully monitor developments in this area.

ETHICAL LEADERSHIP CASE STUDIES

Case study #1

An organization that opposes the use of alcohol creates a poster with a drawing of a well-known athlete who is often seen drinking in public places. The athlete's lawyer complains to the organization that the poster is objectionable to the athlete because it is ruining his image. The organization replies that it is asserting its rights of free speech.

1. What are the ethical arguments supporting the position of the athlete?
2. What are the ethical arguments supporting the position of the organization?
3. Do your answers to the above questions change if the athlete is a recovering alcoholic.
4. If the athlete is a recovering alcoholic, what can he do to provide leadership on that issue on a local and national basis?
5. Do your answers change if the athlete asks for payment for the use of his image?

Case study #2

For many years a professional sports team in a city with many Irish people has been known as the Micks. The team's logo is a leprechaun with exaggerated facial features. The local Irish-American organization asks the team to change its name and logo because it is offensive. The team refuses because it has been using this name and logo for a long time, and it does not believe that either is offensive.

1. What are the ethical arguments supporting the team?
2. What are the ethical arguments supporting the Irish-American organization?
3. What role, if any, should the federal government play in this dispute?
4. What courses of action are open to the Irish-American organization outside of the legal process? How, for example, would the organization provide leadership on the issues of stereotyping and racial and ethnic slurs?

Case study #3

A well-known sneaker company invents and patents an air cushion for its shoes that enables basketball players to jump 10 percent higher. It gives an exclusive license to use that shoe to a professional team in the NBA. That team goes on to win the championship. The league then bans the shoe. The team registers a protest with the management council of the league.

1. What are the ethical arguments supporting the league?
2. What are the ethical arguments supporting the team?
3. What is the ethical significance, if any, that the shoe is patented?
4. What is the ethical support for the league if it permits the use of the shoe on the condition that all other teams be allowed to use it?
5. How can the league provide ethical leadership on this issue?

STUDENT LEARNING EXERCISE

Videogame manufacturers are criticizing NFL players for charging for their images, which increase the price of videogames. The NFL Players Association asks you to draft a memo. Prepare one about how the Players Association would ethically lead public opinion on the importance and value of protecting athletes' rights of publicity.

PROBLEMS/QUESTIONS

1. What is the relationship of free speech with rights of publicity? Copyrights? Trademarks?
2. What ethically justifies limiting free speech in the name of intellectual property?
3. Why, ethically, does a player get to protect his or her right of publicity in a videogame but not in a fantasy sports game?
4. Would your answer to question 3 above change if the players' image was used in the fantasy sports game?

5. What ethical considerations make patents of plays incompatible with sports?
6. Why, ethically, does commercial speech receive less protection than expressive speech?
7. How does utilitarianism apply to copyrighted material? Deontology? Virtue ethics? Care ethics?

BIBLIOGRAPHY

Badenhausen, Kurt, New York Knicks Head the NBA's Most Valuable Teams at $3 Billion, forbes.com, January 20, 2016.

Baltimore Orioles, Inc. v. M.L.B. Players Association, 805 F. 2d 663 (7th Cir. 1986).

Bambauer, Derek, Legal Responses to the Challenges of Sports Patents, 18 *Harvard Journal of Law & Technology* 401 (2005).

Bloom, Howard, NFL Revenue-Sharing Model Good for Business, *Sporting News*, September 5, 2014.

Borzi, Pat, The Sioux Nickname Is Gone, but North Dakota Hockey Fans Haven't Moved On, *New York Times*, March 1, 2016.

Brenner, Lee & Becker, Andreas, Do not Mess with Michael Jordan and His Right of Publicity, *DryeWit*, August 26, 2016.

C.B.C. Distribution v. Major League Baseball Advanced Media, 505 F. 3d 818 (8th Cir. 2007).

Comedy III Prods. v. Gary Saderup, 25 Cal. 4th 387 (2001).

Das, Proloy, Offensive Protection: The Potential Application of Intellectual Property Law to Scripted Sports Plays, 75 *Indiana Law Journal* 1072 (2000).

ETW Corp. v. Jireh Publishing, Inc., 332 7.3d 915 (6th Cir. 2003).

Gaines, Cork, The NFL Makes $6 Billion Annually Just From National Television Contracts, *Business Insider*, September 11, 2014.

Garrett, Robert & Hochberg, Philip, Sports Broadcasting and the Law, 59 *Indiana Law Journal* 155 (1984).

Haelen Laboratories v. Topps Chewing Gum, 202 F. 2d 866 (2d Cir. 1953).

Hart v. Electronic Arts, 717 F. 3d 141 (3d Cir. 2013).

Indianapolis Colts v. Metropolitan Baltimore Football Club, 34 F. 3d 410 (7th Cir. 1994).

Katz, Ronald, Courts, Sports and Videogames: What's In a Game?, *Law 360*, January 4, 2012.

Katz, Ron, Major NFL Match-up: Disparaging Speech versus the First Amendment, forbes.com, November 20, 2015.

Katz, Ronald, NFL Films Ruling Reverses Course, Blurs Right of Publicity, *Law 360*, October 31, 2014.

Katz, Ronald, Rights of Publicity: Contradictions in the Courts, *Law 360*, January 10, 2013.

Katz, Ronald, Third Circuit Weighs First Amendment v. Rights of Publicity, *Law 360*, July 17, 2013.

Kieff, Scott, Kramer, Robert & Kunstadt, Robert, It's Your Turn, But It's My Move: Intellectual Property Protection for Sports Moves, 25 *Santa Clara High Technology Law Journal* 764 (2009).

Kunstadt, Robert, *Are Sports Moves Next in IP Law?*, National Law Journal, May 20, 1996.

Live Nation Motor Sports, Inc. v. Davis, 81 U.S.P.Q.2d (BNA) 1826 (2007).

Major League Baseball Properties v. Sed Non Olet Denarius, Ltd., 817 F. Supp. 1103 (S.D.N.Y. 1993).

Michael Jordan v. Jewel Food Stores, No. 12–1992 (7th Cir., February 21, 2014).

Montana v. San Jose Mercury News, 34 Cal. App. 4th 790 (6th Dist. Ct. App. 1995).

Mullin, Joe, Asian-American Band "The Slants" Overturns USPTO Rule on Disparaging Trademarks, *Ars Technica*, December 23, 2015.

National Basketball Association v. Motorola, Inc., 105 F. 3d 841 (2d Cir. 1997).

National Exhibition Co. v. Teleflash, Inc., 24 F. Supp.488 (S.D.N.Y. 1936).

National Football League v. McBee & Bruno's, Inc., 792 F.2d 726 (1986).

ncaa.org, www.ncaa.org/about/resources/finances/revenue.

Newcombe v. Adolf Coors Co., 157 F. 3d 686 (9th Cir. 1998).

O'Brien v. Pabst Sales, 124 F. 2d 167 (5th Cir. 1941).

Pittsburgh Athletic Co. v. KQV Broadcasting Co., 24 F.Supp. 490 (W.D. Pa 1938).

Rajan, Greg, *Texas A&M, Seahawks Agree to New 12th Man License Agreement*, Chron, August 11, 2016.

Rapin, Jane, *A Critical Analysis of the Arguments For and Against the Granting of Patent Rights Over Sporting Apparatus and Sports Moves* (2010).

Volokh, Eugene, Federal Appeals Court Decides "The Slants" Case: Excluding Disparaging Marks from Trademark Registration Violates the First Amendment, *The Washington Post*, December 22, 2015.

Warren, Samuel & Brandeis, Louis, The Right of Privacy, 4 *Harvard Law Review* 193 (1898).

Zacchini v. Scripps-Howard, 433 U.S. 562 (1977).

CHAPTER 13

The ethics of technology in sport

INTRODUCTION

Many sports develop from a relatively simple formula: state the objective of the game, define the rules, pick teams, schedule an event, and play ball. For example, nothing more is needed in baseball than players, a playing field, a bat, a ball, and a glove. In a foot race, what adds value other than a starting point and a finish line?

Despite this simplicity, the idea of continuous improvement pervades the sporting landscape. How can one hit a ball farther? How much faster can one run? With increased focus on gaining competitive advantages, modern-day athletes look to cutting-edge training methods to become faster and stronger. Athletes test the limits of physical potential as it relates to success in sport and continually set new records throughout the sporting world. Such testing can raise ethical questions about fair play.

Although many athletes can achieve these accomplishments through their own skills, developing technology also has played a notable role in improving the quality of athletic performance and in perfecting the sport fans love. For example, improvement in the development and the function of training equipment and athletic apparel contributes to competitive success. Increased precision of in-game technology more fairly governs the games that athletes play. Medical advancements help athletes and coaches understand more about the capabilities of the human body, and creative technology enhances fan enjoyment of sporting events.

This chapter explores the history of technology in sport and presents a foundation for understanding the effects of advanced technology on athletic games. Moreover, this chapter intends to provoke thoughtful dialogue about the ethical considerations of advanced technology in sport.

In the 21st century, sport continues its vast popularity, but at what price? The market for sport in North America alone is valued at more than $60 billion (Heitner, 2015). Is the objective to win founded on the desire to be the best or based upon greed for more money? Are traditional athletic skills being compromised or diluted by advanced technology? What is responsible for improved athletic performance? Do raw athletic talent and devotion to training make an athlete successful, or do improved technology and the athlete's modern equipment? Could the advancement in technology enable athletes to gain an unfair competitive advantage? From which ethical frameworks can these questions be answered?

HISTORY OF TECHNOLOGY IN SPORT

In the ancient Olympic Games, the concept of technology or innovation had very little impact on sport. Athletes competed in the nude, using equipment such as discs, which were haphazardly made and which often were shared among the competitors. In ancient Greece, sport played out in raw form; only with time did sport evolve to the sophisticated spectacle it is today.

Perhaps the breakthrough technological advancement in sport, first patented in 1830 by inventor Edwin Beard Budding, had nothing to do with sport itself. With creative ingenuity, Budding invented the lawnmower, which provided a catalyst for the rise in popular athletics in 19th-century England.

Prior to Budding's invention, the arduous task of grass-cutting required the skilled work of specialized laborers wielding sharp blades by hand. Budding's idea derived from machines used to cut the irregular nap of woven, woolen materials. The cutting devices had rotary cylinders, and Budding envisioned that a similar device could serve the purpose of trimming grass lawns. He may have been influenced by the variable use of the word *lawn*, which can refer to both cloth and landscape (Haake, 2013).

Budding's lawnmower made cutting grass easier and a more common practice. It also allowed games to be played on flat patches of grass and provided increased opportunities for outdoor sports among the British upper classes. In fact, the rise in popularity of croquet led to the creation of The All-England Croquet Club in Wimbledon in 1868. Freshly manicured lawns became so prevalent that the more exciting game of lawn tennis surpassed croquet in popularity, resulting in the club's name-change within a decade to The All-England Lawn Tennis and Croquet Club (id.).

Almost simultaneous with the invention of Budding's lawnmower was the development of the rubber ball, which also transformed the sporting landscape. Creating an inexpensive ball that bounced to the desired height ensured the success of lawn tennis and other ball-related sports. England's Thomas Hancock and America's Charles Goodyear revolutionized the use of rubber; the rubber ball enabled the game of lawn tennis to thrive globally along with the outdoor games of American football, soccer, and rugby. Indoor sports like basketball, racquet ball, and volleyball followed as the sporting scene grew in the 1900s (id.).

This heightened sophistication of sport led to the emergence of competitive leagues. Focused training of teams began, and the entertainment value for competitors and fans grew rapidly. In the 20th century, the business model to monetize sport placed significant burden on athletes and organizations to find competitive advantages to win. Technological breakthroughs contributed to constant improvements in sporting equipment and athletic apparel.

ADVANCEMENTS IN EQUIPMENT AND APPAREL

Technology serves as "human-made means to reach human interests and goals," and technology in sport accomplishes these purposes (Loland, 2003). Sporting equipment and apparel enable athletes to train across a broad spectrum of sport from elite sport participation in the Olympics and in professional athletics to those amateur athletes engaging in leisure time sport and physical activity.

"Records are made to be broken," according to nine-time Olympic Champion Mark Spitz (Spitz, 2004). Equipment manufacturers and apparel companies certainly agree by promoting the latest gear as the key to athletes' ability to perform at a higher level. During the past two decades, sports equipment has significantly influenced athletes' perceptions that the clubs they swing or the shoes they wear give them a certain competitive advantage. From the sleek polyurethane full-body suits of Speedo that led to numerous swimming records falling in the first few summer Olympic games of the 21st century to the enhanced heads of golf clubs, the athletic-gear industry now produces lighter, stronger, and harder synthetic materials (Vanderbilt, 2014).

For example, the heavy steel-framed bicycles, which were commonplace in the 1950s and still dominated the Tour de France through the 1980s, have been replaced by lighter bicycles using carbon fiber. This material, barely researched and developed in the early 1990s, now serves as a key component of almost all sporting equipment including skis, sails, racquets, and bicycles (id.).

Similarly, in tennis, the racket has undergone a radical transformation. For much of the sport's history, racket innovations focused on increasing power and enlarging the racket's head. Tennis rackets evolved from wooden frames with small heads used in the mid-20th century to today's ultralight carbon fiber composite models with larger hitting surfaces. The racquet strings changed from a polyester blend to new synthetic material that helps players place significant topspin on the ball allowing for a much more powerful and accurate shot (Strauss, 2012).

Even the standard baseball glove has been reinvented. Initially, the baseball glove of the 1870s prevented hand injuries. In 1919, the glove-maker Rawlings came out with the first mitt that included webbing between the thumb and index finger, thus featuring a performance-related element. With the addition of a web, the area inside the glove increased, thereby making it easier to catch a baseball.

Gloves have continued to advance during the last 100 years in size, shape, material, and even the number of fingers. Specialized gloves are produced for each position. For example, a catcher's mitt does not have separated fingers but rather has extra padding. An outfielder's glove has long fingers to extend the reach of the outfielder; a first baseman's mitt is essentially a large glove of webbing to assist in making plays; and an infielder's glove is smaller and shallower to allow for quicker transfer of the ball (Depta, 2013). A new glove experiment resembles a standard black baseball glove; but it is composed primarily of synthetic microfibers, may be custom-fitted to a player's hand, and weighs up to ten ounces less than a leather glove (Kutz, 2014).

Keeping pace with the advances in equipment are those in sports apparel. Today's apparel is outfitted with specialized material advertised to help an athlete move faster, jump higher, and have an overall performance-edge on the competition. Moisture-wicking fabrics and thermal technology produce athletic clothing that reacts to body temperature and perspiration. Clothing with thermal technology keeps the athlete's body warm while the athlete performs in colder conditions and climates.

Instead of absorbing perspiration like normal fabrics, which can weigh down an athlete, this advanced clothing draws the perspiration to the surface of the fabric, allowing the moisture to evaporate. In training and in competition, such clothing helps keep an athlete drier and lighter (Lauer, 2014).

Footwear in sports emerged from protecting feet, to increasing the level of comfort, to returning energy from impact. Apparel giant Nike introduced the concept of air-in-shoe cushioning during the 1970s, a development which coincided with the era's enthusiasm for running. The air forced in during production provided a new level of comfort. Other companies, such as Reebok, customized the use of air-in cushioning and developed a system for the wearer to adjust the movable airflow to fit specific needs of comfort.

The Reebok Pump, popularized in 1989, allowed wearers to press a button at the top of the shoe tongue, pushing air through the shoe from heel to toe. Other companies offered gel-based cushioning to reduce shock placed on the foot as it recoils to spring forward for another step.

More recently, Adidas unveiled a new cushioning platform built on a more advanced type of foam. Noted as the best design to provide runners the greatest energy return, the new Energy Boost shoe incorporates thermoplastic polyurethane foam that outperforms traditional EVA foam used in varying degrees across the running-shoe line. This advanced form of foam purportedly more firmly protects a runner's feet against impact, increases comfort, and offers more durability, allowing runners to run longer without tiring too quickly (Newcomb, 2013).

Wearable technology has become a growth market in sport. A wearable product such as the FitBit or AppleWatch appeals as an accessory yet may also function as a watch and pedometer to track a person's movement and sleep activities. Sport teams outfit athletes in one or many wearables to collect as much data as possible to assess the overall performance and health of the athlete and to correlate health with athletic performance.

For example, many elite NBA players wear devices called Blast Motion Basketball and Shot Tracker. Blast Motion serves as a visualizer for a player's movement. The players clip a small sensor onto the back of their shorts or wristband for the coach to record each movement with a smartphone through the Blast Motion app. The app analyzes the physics behind the player's movement and measures activity such as jump acceleration, vertical height, ball rotation, and hang time (Brown, 2016).

Sophisticated data analysis, such as that possible with the data described previously, plays a critical role in the advancements in athletic training. Operating under the premise that more precise preparation leads to increased success, coaches look to tracking technology and the resulting data for improved training of an athlete. Such equipment as strength training machines and treadmills produce value only to the extent to which that value can be measured and understood. For example, Catapult Sports promotes a monitoring system for athletes that enables coaches and athletes to understand more about the athletes in terms of risk of injury, physical readiness, and returning to play.

Contained in a small device worn by athletes, the system tracks the athletes' movements and collects information about physical exertion and about how much work athletes can complete while still recovering properly. Athletes are predisposed to injury when they become tired, and fatigue reduces an athlete's ability to compete effectively (Catapult official website).

A similar technology measures efficiency of movement in an athlete's speed and strength, while also predicting an athlete's risk for potential injury. Sparta Science utilizes a trademarked movement signature of an athlete's nervous system after the athlete performs a series of jumps off a force plate, producing instantaneous results about the effectiveness of the athlete's movement. These results dictate how an athlete trains within the Sparta system, and the prescribed workouts change as the measurement of the athlete's movement develops. The data can also pinpoint areas of concern in the athlete's scan, which can be predictive of injury if there is no corrective action (Sparta Science official website). Innovation and change to sport-related equipment can cause significant controversy. The rise of new and more efficient equipment creates skepticism about the "de-skilling" of sport participants.

From a standpoint of cultural subjectivism, the emphasis on winning and success in sport may prevail on a cultural level, thus promoting the use of enhanced technology by athletes. Moreover, the debate over fairness continually arises. From the framework of moral relativism, if an athlete believes that the benefits of technological advancement lead to winning and are not in violation of a governing rule, then use of technology to improve play must be fair. However, if technological advancements are available to only a few athletes because of limited access or significant expense, an argument for competitive inequality can be made. That situation may contravene deontology, virtue ethics, and utilitarianism.

TECHNOLOGY IN SPORTS MEDICINE AND TRAINING

The expanding fields of sports medicine and sports training focus on helping athletes improve athletic performance, recover from injury, and prevent the occurrence of future injuries. As increased media attention generates vast exposure for sport, the injuries athletes sustain receive greater scrutiny as well. As a result, the heightened focus on sports medicine helps medical professionals develop a comprehensive understanding of how an injury occurs and how to ascertain the options available to treat the injury. A treating physician strives to keep the athlete participating in the sport safely, and the continuous advancement of technology in injury prevention and treatment enables athletes to avoid missing competitions because of injury, and, if there is injury, a more rapid return to play. Moreover, even when healthy, athletes look to advances in sports medicine and sports training methods to gain a competitive edge.

Despite such improvements and a broader understanding of the function of the human body, athletic injuries persist. Enter the surgeons, who embrace the high-pressure responsibility of putting an athlete back together, especially at the elite level. The marvel of sports medicine arguably began its modern era in 1974, when famed Los Angeles Dodger pitcher, Tommy John, suffered a serious injury to his left elbow. Team doctor, Frank Jobe, opted to perform surgery on the elbow and replaced the torn elbow ligament with a tendon from John's right wrist. The surgery and subsequent rehabilitation allowed John to continue a brilliant career, which spanned 26 seasons. The procedure, now commonly known as Tommy John surgery, repairs the damaged ulnar collateral ligament (UCL), also known as the medial collateral ligament (MCL) (Lamb, 2009).

The evolution of medical equipment enables surgeons to perform operations more quickly in a less invasive manner and with increased precision. Such developments allow athletes to rehabilitate from injuries faster with a more focused effort on returning to play. For example, athletes who suffer a tear to the anterior cruciate ligament (ACL) are often sidelined for six months to one year before a return to competitive action. ACL injuries most commonly occur in sports such as soccer, basketball, and football, each of which requires a pivoting of the leg that can lead to enough stress on the knee to tear the ligament. The traditional ACL surgery, called ACL reconstruction, involves the removal of the torn ligament and replacement with a graft of tendon most commonly taken from somewhere else in the athlete's knee or thigh.

A new version of ACL surgery, called bridge-enhanced ACL repair, involves mending the torn ends of the ACL with stitches. During the repair a sponge is placed between the two torn ends, and the patient's blood is placed onto the sponge. The sponge absorbs the blood and holds the tendons together to promote healing. The blood acts as a stimulus for healing of the ligament in the same manner in which blood helps a bone or cut heal. The sponge prevents the blood from being washed away too quickly by the fluid in the knee joint and keeps the blood in place long enough for the ACL to heal (The Micheli Center official website). This revolutionary procedure may limit the recovery time for athletes with ACL tears because the surgery would be performed only on the interior of the knee as opposed to another area being used to obtain a graft of tendon. Moreover, the natural healing process may promote better long-term benefits for athletes' quality of life after a career in sport.

After surgery, the recovery process requires sharp focus during rehabilitation therapy on the player's effort to regain strength and to prepare for return to play. In the case of a serious knee injury or surgery, researchers are developing a specialized knee band that records sounds made by the knee joint and in turn tracks the knee's rate of recovery during the rehabilitation process. The device includes a vibration sensor that contains a small microphone and is worn close to the skin on the knee joint. The sound data that the band collects is compared to a knee joint's normal range of motion to determine where in the motion problems exist. If an active athlete returns to play too quickly after surgery and therapy, the athlete may reinjure the knee.

Research shows that reinjuries are ten times more likely to occur than an initial injury. Researchers further demonstrate that sound patterns from an injured knee resonate more erratically than from those of a healthy knee. With researchers understanding more about the healthy sounds of the knee, return-to-play protocols for athletes may be more complete and may limit the chances of reinjury (Brumfeld, 2016).

As the game of football continues to dominate the American sports landscape, the concern about player safety remains at the forefront of the discussion about the future of the sport. The purpose of the helmet in football, as is the case with shoulder pads, is to protect the safety of the player. Specific to the helmet, the head gear is designed to reduce and prevent head trauma. With more studies to understand how athletes perform in the midst of competition, researchers focus additional attention on helmet design to prevent head trauma. Interestingly, the purpose of the protective gear is in question. Does the helmet, in fact, help protect the brain, or does the helmet act more as a weapon and encourage football players to hit harder?

The next edition of the football helmet will be expected to protect the head even more as a result of greater knowledge about brain trauma. For now, doctors and scientists can study the impact of a football tackle by taping a small sensor behind the ear to measure the force and direction of a hit. The medical team registers vital data to establish a picture of medium- and long-term damage that may be occurring (id.).

Physicians and trainers working in competitive sports face unique ethical challenges. A framework of care ethics burdens medical professionals with a conflict of interest. Team-employed physicians have obligations to act in the organization's best interest while also caring for the individual athlete. As such, they must balance issues like protecting the privacy of the athlete versus sharing the athlete's health information, as well as issues regarding informed consent versus paternalistic decision-making on the part of coaches in determining whether an athlete may safely compete.

Especially at the professional level, with significant financial considerations involved, the physicians have to weigh an injured athlete's own personal assessment about the level of health necessary to return to play with consideration of the athlete's long-term best interest. Evoking moral subjectivism, the coach and team may benefit from the athlete's playing in the short term, while the athlete may have long-term detrimental health consequences (Testoni, 2013). As technology develops to return an injured athlete more quickly to the playing field, should a healthy player be permitted to use this same technology to enhance his performance? Should some standard protocol regulate the use of such technology by healthy players?

TECHNOLOGY IN OFFICIATING

In the heat of competition, every inch and every second counts in determining the winner. Advancements in timing devices and the rise of video and instant replay provide officials a nearly 360-degree view of the game. With much at stake in today's sporting industry, the demand for getting the call right is critical across fields and courts.

All major sports leagues have rules committees to address the use of technology to improve the pace and flow of the game and to foster more efficient officiating. For example, the advent of the shot clock has added a layer of excitement to the game of basketball. First implemented in the NBA at the onset of the 1954–1955 season, the shot clock governs the time of possession for a team's offense. Offenses have 24 seconds to attempt to score or risk incurring a violation resulting in turning over possession of the ball to the other team. Said Maurice Podoloff, the NBA's first president: "The adoption of the (shot) clock was the most important event in the NBA" (NBA official website).

Football employs the use of a similar feature called a play clock, which allows an offensive team 40 seconds to run a play, while college baseball and triple A and double A professional baseball utilize a pitch clock, which allows a pitcher 20 seconds to deliver a pitch or risk crediting the batter with an automatic ball. These advancements enable players to develop rhythm of play and allow officials to remain focused on the nuances of the game. Although human officials still judge most games, technology serves as a safeguard to ensure fairness; in some cases, automated officiating keeps the score.

An early example of automated scoring appeared in the 1930s with the electrical scoring system in the sport of fencing. The system detected the fast touches of the blades more accurately by causing an electric current to trigger a series of lights and buzzers to identify a score. The development of the swimming touch pads in the late 1950s made race times more accurate and reduced the number of judges on the pool deck.

Beginning in the late 1960s, fully automated timing recorded track meet results electronically with precision to the hundredth of a second; and starting in the 1990s, chip timing with transponders tracked and timed individual runners in long-distance events (Springer, 2012). The potential for increased automated officiating exists in sports such as baseball where an overlay of a strike zone can be viewed live and the television viewer can clearly see whether a pitch is accurately called a strike or a ball by an umpire. Eventually, the technology could govern balls and strikes in real time and replace that particular umpiring duty.

In the absence of automated scoring, human referees must make split-second decisions, and sometimes the officials make the wrong call. To aid the officials in these tense moments, video review provides a closer look at the action. The development of the photo finish preceded today's instant replay. The first photo finish reportedly occurred at a horse race in Plainfield, New Jersey, in 1888, and forever changed the way a close race is judged. As the horse tripped a set of wires, cameras captured a series of images, which provided clarity in a close race (Karmelek, 2013).

The modern-day version of instant replay initiated by George Retzlaff, a producer for the Canadian Broadcasting Corporation's wildly popular Hockey Night in Canada, showed a replay of a goal during a game in the 1955–1956 season. Replicating the process proved cumbersome and expensive. Following in George Retzlaff's footsteps, Tony Verna experimented with videotape while working the 1960 Olympics in Rome. Verna's experience in directing football games for television motivated him to find a way to fill lulls in the action between plays, while showing viewers the game taking place away from the ball on any given play.

Verna debuted his instant replay system on December 7, 1963, during the annual Army-Navy football game. Late in the game, a replay of an Army touchdown was shown as the first display of instant replay in American sport (Allen, 2010). Soon thereafter, instant replay became more prevalent; and today some version of an instant replay system exists in every major sport, including soccer, which implemented goal-line technology in the 2014 World Cup in Brazil.

In fact, the concept of instant replay resonates so strongly that Major League Baseball, the National Football League, and the National Basketball Association each has centralized replay systems to which league officials are assigned to review in real time all games being played on a particular day. Any time there is an official review, in-game officials consult with the control room officiating crew at the centralized location to review a given play. In college, a similar system has been instituted by the Southeastern Conference in the sport of football. The collaborative process allows for game officials to rely on better support for correct outcomes (SEC, 2016).

Technology has advanced to the point where every angle of each play can be captured, resulting in numerous replays, second-guessing, and some long delays in the contests. Gone are the days of an umpire's irrefutable call. Now with replay, an official's call may stand or may be overturned. Because the technology exists to review the judgment calls of game officials, does the opportunity impose an ethical obligation to use that technology? A utilitarian approach would suggest that using technology to get a call right favorably impacts the integrity of the game and provides reassurance to fans that the fairness is being upheld. To that end, is sport approaching a time when autonomy for game officials is non-existent? What is the value of the human element in officiating?

TECHNOLOGY AND THE FAN EXPERIENCE

Missing the big game once meant having to wait until the next morning to read about the results in the newspaper or to hear about the game at the local market. Now, however, sports coverage is available everywhere, all of the time, both live and on-demand, in full replay. People may record, save, and play back any footage or find the results on mobile devices.

The media channels that broadcast sporting events use technology to share information at a faster pace than ever before. News and updates appear instantaneously on smartphones the moment the news breaks. Fans crave the access to information, and the sport business continues to grow as a result of the vast consumption of media. In fact, sport media rights account for more than $15 billion of the sport market in North America (Heitner, 2015). In addition, social media creates multiple opportunities to interact with sport. Twitter, Facebook, and other social media provide access for fans and athletes to connect, resulting in increased fan enthusiasm and enjoyment. Live tweeting captures instantaneous play-by-play from viewers whether they are watching the game from their living room lounge chair or are out with the crowd at the big game. Giving rise to a different way to watch a game, this interaction enables the sharing of different perspectives about a contest in real time with remote interlocutors.

The rise of ticket technology expands the secondary ticket market as well. Gone are the days of the costly, time-consuming, and inefficient process of scalping hard tickets outside a stadium. Today, sports fans may buy unused tickets online. Online platforms like Eventbrite allow easy and convenient access to check in and coordinate the entire ticketing process, enticing more people to attend sporting events.

Other companies like Barry's Tickets focus on selling cheaper tickets at the last minute, completely changing the "scalper" method of selling/buying tickets outside stadiums (Agrawal, 2015). This option has grown across the internet, with websites like Facebook and Craigslist offering fans the chance to purchase and sell tickets without having to navigate through ticketing websites.

Mobile apps now offer ticket purchases, with TicketsNow and StubHub bringing ticket orders to the palm of people's hands. For sports fans, making a last-minute decision to go to the game is now a reasonable and easy possibility.

Despite the ease of ticket purchasing, many fans elect to stay at home to watch the game. The luxury of lounging at home in front of a large TV screen complete with high-definition capability becomes a compelling alternative to spending hundreds of dollars and fighting traffic and crowds to attend a game in person. Being able to record, pause, and rewind makes replays of games easier and allows for a fan to attend to other business and watch a recorded game at a later time as a matter of convenience. Plus, the viewing quality of mainstream television sets simulates actually being at the game. High-definition television produces images with stunning clarity and specialized cameras capture game action from all angles, contributing to a better viewing experience at home. For example, in Major League Baseball the base camera highlights action on the base paths, while in the National Football League cameras are mounted in the end zone pylons ready to capture a pivotal moment in the game. Also, the Spidercam system enables cameras to move across a field and film the action from above to provide an entirely different viewing experience for fans.

The shifting demographics of sports fans to a younger generation leave sports teams racing to digitize their stadiums. Younger fans in particular want to use social media-related content in order to enhance the game-day experience and make the trip to the stadium more worthwhile. A Cisco report reveals that the ability to connect to the internet is as important as air, water, food, and shelter to one in three people, particularly those in the millennial generation, including college students and young professionals (Maddox, 2014). Fans now have the opportunity to interact with the sporting venue as they park their cars. Using beacon technology, sensors capture movement patterns and can turn real time crowd flow into data that is then pushed to a fan with the smartphone app.

These apps enable fans to know parking availability, the quickest point of entry, and the nearest, most efficient concession stand. Moreover, an app can signal the opportunity to upgrade to a premium seat for which a fan can pay using a smartphone, therefore creating a near seamless transaction that puts a fan closer to game action. Such technology gives the fan a reason to forgo the comforts of his recliner and high-definition television at home.

The capabilities of connectivity at the game enhance the experience, which fans can then share through social media. This simple ability registers as a highly important activity for some fans because the opportunity to boast about the experience becomes just as important as actually attending the game. For example, according to Extreme Networks, the official Wi-Fi analytics partner for the NFL, fans during the 2011 Super Bowl used approximately 177 gigabytes (GB) of network data or the equivalent of 500,000 social media posts with photos. In 2014, this data usage jumped to 624 GB, which equates to 1.8 million social media posts with photos (id.).

According to a Game Change report (Wolford, 2012), 83 percent of sports fans will browse sports-specific social media websites while watching a game at home and 63 percent of fans will check sports social media sites while attending an actual game. In addition, the connectivity inside the venue generates a litany of in-game opportunities such as the ability to watch instant replay with varying camera angles and to order food, drink, or merchandise.

The enhanced game-day experience for fans directly results in better revenue generation by providing easier opportunities to purchase concessions, merchandise, and up-sales on tickets. Management uses the customer data to devise products or in-game experiences that resonate with fans and that command a premium price. For example, a mobile app called Super Fan U provides organizations with data to help them market more efficiently to their fan base. Fan use of the technology gives management the ability to predict a fan's next move based on historical purchase patterns and movement within the facility.

From the ethical standpoint of utilitarianism, the greatest amount of good or happiness for the greatest number would be the desired outcome of using fan engagement technology. However, at what risk does this gathering of information pose to fans? What is the obligation of management to protect information of fans? Are all fan transactions secure?

VIRTUAL REALITY

Virtual reality, also referred to as immersive multimedia or computer-simulated life, replicates an environment that simulates physical presence in places in the real or imagined worlds. Gaining traction in technology circles, virtual reality offers compelling and attractive content, particularly with sports, because the technology allows athletes the capability to practice without submitting to high-intensity training and allows fans to experience action from all angles and perspectives of a game. However, the advent of the technology presents difficult ethical concerns from the vantage points of moral subjectivism and cultural relativism.

Comparing reality with virtual reality is the expectation as a result of advances in multimedia technology. Virtual reality provides a unique training opportunity for athletes (Zorowitz, undated). For example, in the sport of football, virtual reality allows interested teams to simulate game-like situations without the athletes having to walk through plays. Using a virtual reality headset, a quarterback can survey the defense as he approaches the line of scrimmage. He can look to his left and see a defender reposition, signaling a possible blitz. The quarterback can glance to his right and gesture for a receiver to go into motion, and that receiver then passes through the peripheral vision of the quarterback. The quarterback can scan the defense one more time and call through a snap count before he signals for the ball (id.).

Furthermore, virtual reality enhances the ability of recruiters who can demonstrate to prospective athletes what playing a sport in college looks like by simply putting on a virtual reality headset. Instantaneously, a college campus seems closer to recruits. Complete with tours of locker rooms, stadiums, and weight rooms, prospective student-athletes can see and hear a pre-game speech or "experience" a weight-room training session without leaving their living rooms. Moreover, tours of campus buildings such as dorms, classrooms, and the cafeteria give a prospective student a simulated view of college life.

The use of virtual reality also extends to live events when fans wear a headset and watch a sporting event live from different perspectives. Some fans desire the ability to be completely immersed in the sporting scene. Fans may want to experience the sights and sounds from the vantage point of an athlete. Virtual reality places a fan inside the team room and in the center of the team huddle. Moreover, fans can experience the view from the owner's box or from the bullpen.

Concerns have been raised about the side effects of a possible relationship between virtual reality and the concept of desensitization. Desensitization means that the person becomes unaffected by certain behavior such as violence and fails to show proper emotion like empathy as a result. This phenomenon may arise in virtual reality games in which a high level of violence exists such as in training games for the military in which soldiers engage in simulated combat scenarios (Virtual Reality, undated).

Sports training exercises can impact an athlete in a similar way. In the situation of an athlete in training, the athlete may develop desensitization to his own skills by getting too accustomed to the virtual elements of the game and becoming careless about the potential harm or physicality involved in live competition. Such desensitization suggests the need for care ethics and virtue ethics.

Another concern related to use of virtual reality is cyber-addiction. People affected by cyber-addiction become overwhelmed by virtual reality games and, as a consequence, start to blur the boundaries between real and virtual life. People spend increasing amounts of time in the virtual world, which has a detrimental impact on their daily lives (id.).

For athletes, too much virtual training could result in difficulty performing in real competition. Do the benefits of virtual reality to improve athletic training and performance outweigh any possible resulting injuries that an athlete may face in the actual competition? Should some uniform standards regulate the use of virtual reality for sports training?

ETHICAL CONSIDERATIONS SURROUNDING TECHNOLOGY AND SPORT

In basic terms, the functions of technology are mostly uncontroversial. An exploration of care ethics would highlight developers working with considerable interest on minimizing the risk of injury and offering continuous technological advancement, leading to safer outcomes in competitive athletic environments. However, tension emerges through the lens of virtue ethics when technological development leads to performance enhancement and when access to technology is limited. To what extent can enhanced performance exist without contradicting the spirit of competition?

The implementation of technology plays a significant impact in Olympic sports, in which athletes frequently set records. For example, in speed skating, experts suggest that half of the progress made in setting world records is attributable to changes in technology while the other half results from actual athletic improvement (de Konig, 2010).

One guiding case on the controversial nature of performance-enhancing technology highlights Olympian sprinter Oscar Pistorius. In the 2012 Olympics, Pistorius became the first double amputee to compete in the Olympic games against able-bodied athletes by using two leg prostheses. The prostheses comprised of curved carbon-fiber blades, which could be melded into various shapes and designs.

Known in concept as energy storage and return (ESR), the technology allows the prostheses to bend and spring forward, therefore assisting to propel a runner forward. When Pistorius sought approval to participate in both the 2008 Paralympic and Olympic games, critics claimed that the ESR prostheses created an unfair advantage by increasing the runner's speed.

As a result, the International Association of Athletics Federations (IAAF) commissioned a report which outlined that the technology provided Pistorius with a mechanical advantage over able-bodied athletes by more than 30 percent while requiring a 25 percent reduced-energy output for maintaining the same speed. After reviewing the report, the IAAF banned Pistorius from running in able-bodied events.

In response, Pistorius then commissioned a counter-report, and the ban was challenged in the Court of Arbitration for Sport. Pistorius argued that while the use of prostheses contributed to his difference from other runners, he was of the same physiological frame, powered exclusively by movement of his body. With a successful appeal, the ban was overturned; Pistorius competed in both the 2012 Paralympic and Olympic games using the ESR prostheses (Dyer, 2015).

Another case involves former professional golfer Casey Martin. Martin is a registered disabled person who suffers from a blood circulatory disorder in his leg. In 2000, Martin qualified for the Professional Golfers' Association (PGA) Tour. However, he was not allowed to use a golf cart while participating and subsequently filed suit against the PGA Tour, citing the Americans with Disabilities Act (ADA).

The U.S. Supreme Court elected to review the case and considered whether the ADA protects access to professional golf tournaments by players and whether a competitor with

a disability may be denied the use of a golf cart because of the potential to change the fundamental nature of the competition. The Supreme Court decided that the use of a golf cart by Martin did not rise to the level of altering the game of golf and therefore would not disadvantage other golfers who walk from shot to shot (id.).

Although these two cases had a legal resolution, the debate regarding the use of new technology continues. How does the development of technology that benefits both healthy individuals and physically impaired individuals affect the integrity of the game? How may the developments in technology affect changes in the rules of specific sports? What ethical considerations arise when all players do not have access to the same technological advancements?

CONCLUSION

With more people participating in athletic activity, the enhancements of sporting equipment and training devices help athletes improve both physically and technically. Injury prevention and rehabilitation enable an athlete to return to play at an ever-increasing pace. Fans utilize technology for more engagement opportunities with athletes and with each other; and at the cutting edge of developing technology, virtual reality opens an entirely new world of possibility of training and experience in sport.

Yet the virtue of constant improvement remains questionable. Does technology which helps an athlete run faster result in that athlete's ability to run better? Does protective gear shield an athlete from harm or bolster false confidence to perform more aggressively? Does one athlete who uses equipment influenced by new technology have an unfair advantage over another athlete who uses aging equipment? The answers to these ethical questions are not yet certain, and may never be.

Technological advances will continue to increase, and new technology will affect all facets of life, including the arena of sport. The development and enforcement of regulations regarding the use of technology must ensure that the competitive nature of sport and the enjoyment of the game for both athletes and fans survive technological experimentation.

ETHICAL LEADERSHIP CASE STUDIES

Case study #1

Steve Slicktrout represents his country as a member of the International Swimming Federation. The sport of swimming is experiencing a new era of competitive success. Whole-body polyurethane suits have revolutionized the sport and world records are continually broken. Of course, swimmers have always taken steps to reduce the drag on their bodies while swimming. Sometimes swimmers shave off body hair before major competitions and wear tight-fitting swimming caps to reduce any drag from head hair. However, these new swimsuits made from a thin layer of foam-like material enclose tiny pockets of gas that make a swimmer more buoyant. As a result, a swimmer floats higher in the water and is subject to less drag. Concerned about the integrity of the sport, Steve proposes to ban these new suits and set certain criteria for the use of future swimwear to be used in international competition.

1. What ethical considerations or arguments can Steve present to support his position?
2. What arguments can be made by opponents of the motion in an effort to demonstrate the value of technologically advanced swimwear to the sport of swimming?
3. What ethical leadership techniques would be most effective for Steve?

Case study #2

Thomas Johnson is a budding professional baseball player and a top MLB draft prospect as a pitcher. Lately, he has noticed some discomfort in his pitching elbow. Thomas tends to practice his pitching on a frequent basis, especially during the season. After a few days of rest, his elbow feels better, and he performs well in his next throwing session. Nevertheless, he has read about the success of Tommy John surgery, which repairs the ulnar collateral ligament (UCL) in the elbow. Some athletes have reported that after recovery they are able to throw with more velocity and with better accuracy than they were prior to the injury. Since his elbow hurts from time to time, Thomas thinks that having elective Tommy John surgery will improve his pitching prowess and ultimately will position him for a higher draft selection.

1. From the ethical perspective of both Thomas and the surgeon, why should Thomas have the surgery or why not?
2. How can the surgeon create effective, ethical leadership on the issue of not allowing sports-related surgery that is not medically indicated?

Case study #3

Since suffering numerous muscular injuries in the last few seasons with a subsequent loss of funding from her endorsement deals, professional tennis star Robin Ace has changed her practice methods to train under legendary coach Steve Winsalot. Prior to this new training regimen, Robin had to train without sport-specific support and services she once had as a funded athlete. Now, thanks to her newfound training relationship, she is able to train with access to the latest tennis specific training tool. She has spent the last few months using the tool to ensure optimal training and to utilize the varying training options, including injury prevention techniques, while also studying the data review of her movement during training to reduce the likelihood of further muscular injuries. Having thoroughly prepared for a tournament, Robin qualifies for participation. Part of her training requires her to use a monitor on her tennis outfit to gauge her fatigue level. With no restrictions prohibiting the use of the monitor, Robin intends to wear it to help her better understand how she performs. However, she will be the only competitor to use such a tool.

1. Is Robin's use of this tool ethical?
2. How can Robin use ethical leadership to make sure she can continue to use this monitor?

STUDENT LEARNING EXERCISE

Divide into small groups and debate whether continued advancement in technology is good for sport. Articulate ethical reasons why technological advancements may affect sport positively and also submit reasons why technological development may affect sport negatively. Discuss applicable ethical leadership frameworks to make the case.

PROBLEMS/QUESTIONS

1. As high-technology apparel develops with ever more efficiency for improved athletic performance, should teams or even individual members of a team ethically be allowed to wear enhanced sporting apparel that is different from the apparel the other team is wearing? Why or why not?
2. As advanced equipment and apparel lead athletes to increasing competitive success, purists of sport frequently question whether new technology exists as another form of doping. If the use of performance-enhancing drugs constitutes cheating, then does a performance-enhancing swimsuit or bicycle similarly equate to cheating? Explain your answer using an ethical framework.
3. How does access to technology affect the pool of athletes available to participate in elite college or professional athletics? How does it affect the participation in recreational leagues? Are these effects ethical?

BIBLIOGRAPHY

Agrawal, A.J., 3 Ways Technology Has Changed the Sports Industry, Inc.com, December 21, 2015.

Allen, Scott, Upon Further Review: A Brief History of Instant Replay, mentalfloss.com, October 13, 2010.

Brown, Ayliffe, What NBA Teams Are Using Wearable Tech?, wearable-technologies.com, April 20, 2016.

Brumfield, Ben, Hearing Snap, Crackle, Pop May Help Heal Your Knee, sciencedaily.com, May 23, 2016.

Catapult official website, catapultsports.com.

de Konig, J.J., How Much Technology?, *International Journal of Sports Physiology and Performance*, June 2010.

Depta, Laura, The Top Five Technological Advancements in MLB History, sportechie.com, October 21, 2013.

Dyer, Bryce, The Controversy of Sports Technology: A Systematic Review, www.ncbi.nlm.nih.gov, September 18, 2015.

Haake, Steve, Technologies in Sport: Number 1, engineeringsport.co.uk, October 2, 2013.

Haake, Steve, Technologies in Sport: Number 2, engineeringsport.co.uk, October 18, 2013.

Heitner, Darren, Sports Industry to Reach $73.5 Billion by 2019, forbes.com, October 19, 2015.

Karmelek, Mary, Winning in a Snap: A History of Photo Finishes and Horse Racing, blogs.scientific american.com, May 7, 2013.

Kutz, Steven, Is This the Baseball Glove of the Future?, marketwatch.com, October 21, 2014.

Lamb, Robert, Is Surgery Changing Baseball? health.howstuffworks.com, February 11, 2009.

Lauer, Caleb, Three Innovations in Sports Clothing Technology: Fashion vs. Function, proplayerinsiders. com, May 19, 2014.

Loland, Sigmund, Technology in Sport (Three Ideal-Typical Views and Their Implications, www.idrottsforum. org, September 10, 2003.

Maddox, Teena, Stadiums Race to Digitize: How Sports Teams are Scrambling to Keep Millennials Coming to Games, www.techrepublic.com, April 14, 2014.

The Micheli Center official website, themichelicenter.com.

National Basketball Association official website, History of the Shot Clock, nba.com.

Newcomb, Tim, From Nike Air to Adidas Boost: The Evolution of Athletic Shoe Tech, popularmechanics. com, February 26, 2013.

Recapping the Sports Tech News from the Stanford GSB Sports Innovation Conference, sporttechie.com, April 20, 2015.

SEC Approves Collaborative Process for Instant Replay, secsports.com, November 6, 2016.

Sparta Science official website, spartascience.com.

Spitz Happy to Have His Record Broken, upi.com, August 4, 2004.

Springer, Shira, Timeline: How Technology Has Affected Sports Officiating, bostonglobe.com, November 2, 2012.

Strauss, Ben, Into the Laboratory for the Secrets of Spin, nytimes.com, August 27, 2012.

Testoni, Daniela, Sports Medicine and Ethics, 13 *The American Journal of Bioethics* 4 (2013).

Vanderbilt, Tom, Lighter, Faster, Stronger: Sports Gear Over the Last 20 Years, mensjournal.com, July 16, 2014.

Virtual Reality and Ethical Issues, undated, https://www.vrs.org.uk/virtual-reality/ethical-issues.html.

Whitten, Phil, The Amazing Rise and Fall of Performance-Enhancing High-Tech Swimsuits, blogs.britannica. com, February 10, 2010.

Wolford, Josh, 83% Of Sports Fans Use Social Media While Watching the Game [Infographic] http:// www.webpronews.com/83-of-sports-fans-use-social-media-while-watching-the-game-infographic-2012- 04/ (2012).

Zorowitz, Jane, It Just Got Real – Coaches Like Bret Bielema and Bill Belichick Are Getting on the Virtual-Reality Wave, sportsworld.nbcsports.com, undated.

CHAPTER 14

Value, virtue, and meaning in sport

INTRODUCTION

Much of what has been discussed and explored in this book required us to examine the aspects of sports that are negative, requiring strong leadership in order to curb otherwise unethical behavior. Understanding the legal and ethical issues involved in sports is clearly an important part of becoming a leader or participant of any kind in this field.

Yet, an investigation and exploration of virtue and ethics in sports should not merely resemble the policing of behavior and the meting out of moral (and legal) judgments. There is an entirely different side of sport—and of being human—often overlooked if we allow this to serve as our only lens. It is the celebration of virtue itself: actions that embody what we value most, such as acting with respect and integrity, and celebrating humans acting virtuously, often in the face of external motivators to do otherwise.

This chapter will allow us to reflect on issues in sport from a positive, uplifting perspective. In doing so, we can acquire a better grasp on the moral concept of sportsmanship. In addition, we will consider actions that may not be morally required but are themselves morally praiseworthy. Some of our reactions to certain praiseworthy actions in sport may provide an alternate frame for ethical issues presented in previous chapters.

At the least, it can remind us of some of the unique riches sport provides as well as how virtues from sport can inform our own daily lives. If competitors are truly *striving together*—as the roots of the word "competition" suggest—then morally praiseworthy actions should be the norm, not the outlier.

REFLECTIONS ON VIRTUE AND MEANING IN SPORT

Albert Camus

Existential philosopher and Nobel Prize winning author Albert Camus was also a soccer goalkeeper and, at one point infamously said, "All that I know most surely about morality and the obligations of men I owe to football" (Noury, 1965). In making such a comment, Camus hoped to capture the relative simplicity of the moral nature of sport as compared to the more convoluted, seemingly unnecessarily complicated and self-serving moral frameworks espoused by politicians and religion. Instead, Camus reflected on the moral nature of friendship and fairness, all of which could be captured by sport.

Some have suggested that Camus intended his quote more as irony and even sarcasm, instead meaning that sport reflects the tribulations of the human condition and the meaningless of life more so than teaching virtue. They note that in the same essay he reflected, "I learned . . . that a ball never arrives from the direction you expected it. That helped me in later life, especially in mainland France, where nobody plays straight" (id.). Here, we get the sense that sport frames the *un*ethical nature of others as well as the unpredictability and inherent frustrations of being human. Regardless, Camus invites readers to allow sport to inform life, both in moral and metaphysical terms.

Nelson Mandela

Nelson Mandela won the Nobel Peace Prize in 1993 and went on to become the first black president of South Africa. He is best known for his ethical leadership in the anti-apartheid movement and also for how he utilized sport as a vehicle to help overcome the deep-rooted racism in South Africa.

In a seminal moment of Mandela's anti-apartheid work, he was able to bring the 1995 Rugby World Cup to Johannesburg, South Africa. Despite rugby being a white-dominated sport, Mandela saw an opportunity to unite the races. The team representing South Africa, the Springboks, had only one nonwhite player, and blacks viewed this as emblematic of the unjust racial ethos at the time. Despite this—or, actually, because of it—Mandela donned the green Springboks jersey for the championship match against New Zealand, much to the surprise of the home crowd of 65,000, which began chanting "Mandela! Mandela!" South Africa went on to win the match, resulting in blacks and whites celebrating together.

Following the match, Mandela presented the Championship Cup to the Springboks' captain, Francois Pienaar. Pienaar, like most other white members of the team and the country, had overcome a deeply engrained negative view of Mandela and, following the trophy presentation, referred to him as the "symbol of everything that is good about humanity" (Bond, 2013).

Mandela reflected on this in what has now become a famous quote for those who celebrate so much of what is good in sports:

> Sport has the power to change the world. . . . It has the power to inspire. It has the power to unite people in a way that little else does. It speaks to youth in a language they understand. Sport can create hope where once there was only despair. It is more powerful than governments in breaking down racial barriers. It laughs in the face of all types of discrimination.
>
> (Mandela, 2000)

EMBODIMENT AND SPORT: A CELEBRATION OF OUR HUMANITY

Throughout the history of philosophy dating back over 2,000 years, one of the most highly discussed and scrutinized issues has been the nature of human beings. Often referred to as the "mind–body problem," philosophers have posited the human being as either *dual* in nature—i.e. having some metaphysical component such as the mind, soul, or spirit along with the physical body—or *material*, void of anything metaphysical. This particular issue maintains great relevance in how we view athletes and the sporting experience because it forces us to consider such questions as, "Am I a mind *using* this body, or am I truly this body performing such acts?" and, "If there is a mind separate from the body, does one maintain greater relevance and importance (in education, for example) than the other, or should we value them equally?"

Such a discussion not only informs how we ought to view athletes and the entire concept of sport and play, but it provides an opportunity to explore—or, put more strongly, to *celebrate*—what it means to be human, all through the lens of sport. As sport philosopher Klaus Meier (1979) writes in *Embodiment, Sport, and Meaning*:

> Through free, creative, and meaning-bestowing movement experiences, man becomes cognizant of the limits and potentials of [human] existence. . . . In short, sport may be characterized and extolled as the celebration of man as an open and expressive embodied being.

Both theories have their virtues (and shortcomings) as they relate to sport. For the dualist, something exists above and beyond the "mere" human body: that a human *spirit* exists and, through the sporting experience, one may connect with such an essence in a way unique to no other enterprise, allowing us to extol this core of our humanity. The materialist recognizes the body as an exceptionally complex machine of sorts, coming to understand the ways in which we can best maximize our own bodies—not as vessels which hold us but as bodies which *are* us.

The materialist sees the athlete not as someone utilizing their body but, instead, as fully being a body: what modern phenomenology refers to as the "lived-body." As Meier writes:

> Play is an intrinsically rewarding, purposeless activity which requires no external justification. . . . Ultimately, play is an essential, revelatory, liberating, most human enterprise. It is 'an affair of flutes' wherein man is provided a grove in which he may listen to the fluid rhythms of inner music, cheerfully express all aspects of his being, including the affirmation of his sensual nature, and luxuriate in the intense, fully-lived release, if not explosion, of his subjectivity. And this is most worthy of praise and celebration, indeed.
>
> (Meier, 1980)

SPORTSMANSHIP

Before we look at numerous examples of sportsmanlike acts throughout sport, it is important to frame and revisit a few concepts and definitions. As you recall from Chapter 2, we defined cheating as, "Acting with the intent to gain an advantage by acting outside the stated rules and context of the sport, with the hope of going undetected." In addition to cheating, we also introduced the term, "sportsmanlike." This distinction is important because, in sports, it is possible to behave in an unethical manner yet not technically cheat—one need not break the rules or even involve the rules of the game to behave in an unsportsmanlike manner. For example, when players shake hands following a game, no rule informs their behavior stating, "You must grasp the competitor's hand firmly, look them in the eye, and honor their effort." Yet, to ignore the extended hand of one's competitor would be unsportsmanlike.

Another important distinction exists in sport involving the so-called "unwritten rules" of the particular sport. While these guidelines may not be explicitly enumerated in the rules of the game nor enforced by the referee, everyone who plays the sport is expected to adhere to them. Baseball is known for having an extensive list of such guidelines such as, "Don't step on the pitcher's mound if you're not the pitcher," and, "Immediately after you hit a home run, don't act excited about it."

An outsider—someone not familiar with the culture of baseball—would likely be confused by conversations and analyses involving actions under the umbrella of unwritten rules. For example, even if an opposing player's shortest path is over the pitcher's mound, he should consider making an effort to go around it. New York Yankees' Alex Rodriguez failed to do this as he returned to first base from third base following a foul ball and drew the ire of Oakland A's pitcher, Dallas Braden.

In another instance, Toronto Blue Jays' Jose Bautista hit a three-run home run to complete a remarkable comeback for his team in game five of the 2015 American League Division Series and, after watching it sail over the fence, flipped his bat high in the air in celebration. This caused great controversy among those entrenched in the game, such as Hall of Fame third baseman Mike Schmidt who called it, "a flagrant disrespect of the opponent" (Schmidt, 2016). Others found it perfectly acceptable for Bautista to briefly celebrate this major accomplishment and went so far as to argue that baseball would attract more young fans if more emotion were shown on the field.

Soccer has an unwritten rule which, when implemented, would also appear odd to an outsider: when a player is injured and the opposing team has the ball, they will kick it out of bounds so the injured player may be attended to. Then, when that team is awarded possession of the ball by way of a throw-in, they will return the ball to the opposing team.

These are just a few examples of unwritten rules. To break them would not result in any form of punishment by the referee of the sport, but would be considered unsportsmanlike and unethical by all those entrenched in the culture of the respective sport.

As we move forward with this discussion, it is important to keep in mind why we value sportsmanship and how we consider it a moral category of action. It is a way of showing respect to one's opponent and making sure the competition is fair. Sometimes acting in a sportsmanlike manner involves a cost to oneself: one will forgo otherwise desirable and advantageous outcomes for the sake of acting in a sportsmanlike manner. It may also, on occasion, involve an athlete actually breaking the rules in order to provide for a more fair contest.

CONCLUSION

Although the pursuit of sport ethics primarily involves a policing of sorts, meting out moral judgments and condemnations, it also involves a celebration of morally praiseworthy actions.

In this sense, the sport enthusiast is on the lookout for not just transgressions, but for achievements. Because sport does maintain some semblance of a "winning is everything" ethos, with so much on the line—be it pride, salaries, scholarships, trophies—the stakes are high. It is these high stakes which allow for an even greater opportunity for excellence.

If the results did not matter, then the opportunity for ethical courage would diminish. Once we recognize the potential for such virtue and moral praise in sports, those in a leadership position can frame the experience in such a manner, allowing for even greater opportunity for those who participate to achieve these riches and to truly *strive together* with their competitors and all those involved in the institution of sport.

ETHICAL LEADERSHIP CASE STUDIES

One of the best ways to engage in an exploration of sportsmanship and the relationship of sport and virtue is to examine case studies based on actual events that occurred throughout various sports, at all levels. As you reflect on these consider the following questions:

1. Is the athlete in question *morally required* to act in the manner he or she did?
2. If the athlete in question acted otherwise, would you consider his or her action unethical?
3. Do you consider his or her action morally *praiseworthy*?
4. Is there any moral concern with the action?
5. Does your evaluation of the action change given the age and level of the competition (i.e. youth sport, high school, college, Olympic, professional)?
6. What sort of feelings arise as you reflect on the actions of the particular athlete in question?
7. What is the leadership component of the situation in question?

Case study #1

Fallen competitor

At the 2012 Ohio State Track Meet runner Meghan Vogel rounded the final turn of the 3,200-meter race and saw a competitor up ahead who had fallen and was clearly struggling due to debilitating cramps. Instead of running past her, Vogel picked her up and carried her the remaining 30 meters to the finish line, even placing her competitor ahead of her. When asked about the event afterward Vogel commented, "She deserved to finish ahead of me" (Evans, 2014).

Case study #2

Late arrival

In a rival high school basketball game, between Milwaukee Madison and DeKalb High Schools, the starting guard from Milwaukee, senior Johntel Franklin, arrived at half-time. His mother had passed away that day following a five-year bout with cancer and, by the evening, he decided he wanted to play in the game. As the crowd cheered him on and his teammates embraced him, the referee awarded the opposing DeKalb Barbs two free throws, as per the rules regarding a player entering the game not on the game-time roster. Down just two points, the opposing coach sent a player to the free throw line to intentionally miss the shots, with the ball not even coming close to the rim. Milwaukee won 62–47, with Franklin contributing 10 second-half points. Opposing coach Dave Rohlman said after the game, "Our kids are great kids with high moral character." When interviewed about this event on ESPN, Franklin reflected, "It's love. That's all it was that day was love" (Evans, 2014).

Case study #3

Eighth batter

At an 11-and-Under Little League Baseball game, Team A arrives with just eight players (instead of the nine who typically play in a regulation baseball game). The rules allow for a team of eight to play but they also require an "out" to be recorded in this situation when the ninth place batter cannot bat. With Team B on defense in the final inning, winning by one run, Team A has runners on second and third with two outs and the number-eight batter up to bat. Instead of walking the batter, which would result in a final out of the game (due to the ninth batter being an automatic out), Team A instead pitches to the eighth hitter.

Case study #4

Medal's rightful owner

New Jersey high school swimmer Michael Sparks was declared the winner of the section Championship 100-meter backstroke race despite finishing two seconds behind another swimmer, Rich Fortels. After the race, Fortels was disqualified by race officials for wearing a non-high school affiliated cap, a cap which provided no competitive advantage. Fortels had broken a 14-year-old meet record and his school petitioned the disqualification but was denied. In the days following the race, Sparks met with Fortels and handed the medal over, declaring him the winner (Tularo, 2016).

Case study #5

Bejeweled vaulter

A high school league championship meet came down to the final event, the pole vault, to determine the winner. As South Pasadena High School senior Robin Laird completed her meet-winning vault, the opposing coach, 54-year-old Mike Knowles, approached her and the officials to report an observation he had clearly seen before the vault: Laird was wearing a cloth friendship bracelet. This broke a rule ("Jewelry shall not be worn by contestants") which resulted in Laird being disqualified, South Pasadena's victory rescinded, and Laird in tears (Where's the Sportsmanship, 2010).

Case study #6

Imperfect game

Pitching for the final out of what would be a perfect game—a feat accomplished by only 20 pitchers in the history of Major League Baseball—pitcher Armando Galarraga arrived at first base with the ball clearly ahead of the batter for what would have been the final out. But umpire Jim Joyce called him safe. Having seen the replay following the game, Joyce publicly apologized. Galarraga also went on record, saying of the situation, "Nobody's perfect," and then, at the lineup card exchange the following day, went to shake the hand of Joyce causing Joyce to become "misty-eyed" in appreciation of Galarraga's forgiveness (Amato, 2010).

Case study #7

Home away-game

Gainesville State School near Grapevine, Texas, is a correctional facility for adolescent male felons. They have a football team, yet all games are played on the road, with the players arriving in handcuffs and never a single person cheering for them aside from a handful of faculty members. But one evening, the head coach of their opponents, Kris Hogan, split his school's massive fan base in half. The Gainesville team ran through a "spirit line" to start the game for the first time in their school's history and had people cheering their successes and calling out their names in support. Although Gainesville ended up losing the game 33–14, finishing their season with a record of 0–9, they celebrated like they'd won, dousing their coach in the celebratory shower of water. One Gainesville player reflected on the game: "After the game I cried. I realized other people love you." Another commented, "I see the world in a different way now. I'm not a victim any more. There's so much love. I came from a broken home family so having all that love rolls my spirits up" (Evans, 2014).

Case study #8

Home run help

In a Great Northwest Athletic Conference softball game, Western Oregon University senior Sara Tucholsky hit a three-run home run (the first of her career). While rounding first base she suffered a severe knee injury which caused her such pain she could not continue. The umpires interpreted the rules such that if her teammates aided her in any way she would be considered out, and if a replacement runner was substituted, then her home run would only count as a single. At that point, two players from the opposing Central Washington University team, Mallory Holtman and Liz Wallace, carried Tucholsky around the base path, gently touching her foot on the remaining bases, allowing the home run to count. Western Oregon won the game 4–2 (Hays, 2008).

Case study #9

Tripping admission

In a professional German League soccer match, FC Nurnberg player Aaron Hunt was awarded a penalty shot as the referee determined he was tripped inside the penalty box. Hunt immediately let the referee know he was not tripped and, as viewers could see on video replay, he instead caught his toe on the grass while dribbling past defenders toward the goal. The referee then changed his call, awarding the other team the ball.

Earlier in that same game, a player from the opposing team, Werder Bremen, was awarded a corner kick as the referee perceived the ball going off the opposing defender and out of bounds, but the Werder Bremen player informed the referee the ball had, in fact, glanced off of him and the corner kick was rescinded (Mandel and Schwartz, 2014).

Case study #10

Righting the wrong

At a 2016 professional tennis tournament, in a close match and with Andrew Sock up 5–4 in the first set, Lleyton Hewitt hit a serve which the umpire called out. Sock voiced to Hewitt that the serve was actually in and suggested Hewitt utilize one of his official challenges to overturn the call. To the surprise of everyone, Hewitt accepted Sock's suggestion, thus overturning the call in Hewitt's favor. Hewitt went on to win the match, 7–5, 6–4 (Scott, 2016).

Case study #11

Self-penalized

In the 1925 U.S. Open golf tournament, Bobby Jones lined up a shot from the rough. As he did, he saw his ball move slightly and alerted officials to assign him a one-stroke penalty as per the rules. Officials did not see the infraction and even interviewed numerous members of the gallery there at the time with none of them witnessing any ball movement. Jones persisted, asserting that the penalty should be assigned, regardless of its not being witnessed. At the end of the four-round regulation, Jones was tied for first and, following 35 playoff holes, lost by a single stroke. When praised for self-assigning the penalty which essentially cost him the U.S. Open title, Jones responded, "You might as well praise a man for not robbing a bank" (BrainyQuote, undated).

Case study #12

Tap out while you're ahead

In a 2014 mixed martial arts cage fight, fighter Mike Pantangco had connected on repeated powerful blows to the head and face of his opponent, Jeremy Rasner. With

Rasner still standing but barely conscious, the referee allowed the fight to continue, at which point Pantangco bowed down and tapped out—referred to as "submitting"—making Rasner the victor. After the fight Pantangco shared that he could think of no option other than continuing the fight and sending Rasner to the hospital with severe injuries (Scott, 2014).

STUDENT LEARNING EXERCISES

1. Discuss any morally praiseworthy actions from either your own sports career or from your experience as a fan/spectator.
2. How do you distinguish between cheating, behaving in an unsportsmanlike manner, and breaking unwritten rules?
3. Given the roots of competition mentioned in this chapter—*striving together*—in what ways does sport deviate from this? In what ways does it adhere to it? Do your views on the various ethical issues explored throughout the institute of sport align with this definition of competition?
4. How do you evaluate Bautista's "bat flip" following his home run, in light of the unwritten rule to avoid celebrations after home runs and Schmidt's condemning it as "a flagrant disrespect of the opponent"?
5. How do you evaluate the following statement: because we consider it morally praiseworthy not to accept a call by a referee in your favor which one doesn't deserve, then to intend to get calls one doesn't deserve (such as soccer's flopping) is therefore unethical?
6. How do you evaluate Camus's quote, "All that I know most surely about morality and the obligations of men I owe to football"?
7. Evaluate Mandela's quote at the end of the section discussing his work with sport and his work combating apartheid.
8. Does your stance on any previously examined ethical issues change after learning of the numerous examples of moral courage exhibited by athletes and coaches in this chapter?

BIBLIOGRAPHY

Amato, John, Armando Galarraga is All Class After Blown Call Loses His Perfect Game, http://crooks andliars.com/john-amato/armando-galarraga-all-class-after-blown Crooks and Liars, June, 2010.

Bond, David, How Nelson Mandela Used Sport to Transform South Africa's Image, BBC, December 6, 2013.

BrainyQuote, https://brainyquote.com/quotes/authors/b/bobby-jones.html, undated.

Evans, Sean, Great Moments in Sportsmanship That Hit You in the Feels, Bleacher Report, February 9, 2014.

Hays, Graham, Central Washington Offers the Ultimate Act of Sportsmanship, espnw.com, April 28, 2008.

Jones, Matthew, Golf Wisdom From The Legends (2011).

Mandel, Nina & Nick Schwartz, Soccer Player Admits He Wasn't Fouled, Rejects Penalty Kick, *USA Today*, March 10, 2014.

Mandela, Nelson, Speech at the Inaugural Laureus Lifetime Achievement Award (2000).

Meier, Klaus V., An Affair of Flutes: An Appreciation of Play, 7 *The Journal of the Philosophy of Sport* 24 (1980).

Meier, Klaus V., Embodiment, Sport, and Meaning, Sport and the Body: A Philosophical Symposium, edited by Ellen W. Gerber and William J. Morgan (1979).

Noury, Jean, Archives du Sénat français, Comptes rendus des débats, Vol. 4, November 10, 1965.

Scott, Nate, Winning MMA Fighter Taps Out to Protect his Opponent, *USA Today*, May 20, 2014.

Scott, Nate, Jack Sock Gives Point to Lleyton Hewitt in Incredible Moment of Sportsmanship, *USA Today*, January 6, 2016.

Schmidt, Mike, Bautista Bat Flip Was 'Flagrant Disrespect,' www.sportsnet.ca/baseball/mlb/mike-schmidt-bautista-bat-flip-flagrant-disrespect/Sportsnet, March 24, 2016.

Tularo, Greg, Teen Swimmer Finishes First, Then Gives Medal to "Real" Winner, *USA Today*, February 15, 2016.

Where's the Sportsmanship? Girl disqualified for wearing bracelet, *Sports Illustrated*, May 11, 2010.

Index

ability enhancement see performance enhancement drugs
academic abilities: racial discrimination 139–40; and university sport 64–5
Act Utilitarianism 11
adaptive leadership 41
Adidas 223
adolescents see youth sport
advertisements: amateur sports 67; fantasy sports 193; players' publicity rights 201–7
advisers: for amateurs 64–5
affiliative style (leadership) 45
African-Americans: history in U.S. 133–7; see also racial discrimination
agents: for amateurs 64–5
aggression see violence
alcohol advertisements 203–4
amateurism 57–8, 71; advisors 64–5; agents 64–5; commercialism 66–7; ethical leadership case studies 71–2; exploitation dilemma 67–9; impact on academic study 65–6; improving model of 69–70; pay for play 68, 141; racial discrimination 137–41; recruitment 62–4; retention 63–4; rise of National Collegiate Athletic Association 58–62; youth injuries 100–6
America: racial discrimination 133–5
Americans with Disabilities Act 231–2
Anabolic Steroid Control Act 118
andro 114–15
anterior cruciate ligament (ACL) 225
apparel: technological developments 221–4
AppleWatch 223
arguments: ethics 1; moral 2–5
Aristotle 11–12, 24
Armstrong, Lance 117, 127–8
Association of Intercollegiate Athletics for Women (AIAW) 152
'assumption of the risk' 91–2
athletes see amateurism; professional athletes
authoritative style (leadership) 44–5
automated scoring 226–7

badminton: strategic losing 30
Baltimore CFL Colts case 208
bargaining agreements 176–7
Bartman, Steve 82
baseball: broadcasting 214–15; fan safety 77–9, 80; framing 27–8; gambling 186, 189; injuries 91–2; performance enhancement 119, 125, 126; racial integration 142–3; sportsmanship example 26
baseball gloves 222
Bash Brothers 126
basketball: gambling 187; good fouling 23, 24; video replay 226
behavioural theory (leadership) 40
Bennis, Warren 47
bicycles: technological developments 222
biomechanical performance enhancement 122–3
black Africans: history in U.S. 133–7; see also racial discrimination
Black Power 145
Blast Motion 223
Blatter, Sepp 49
blowouts 28–9
Bonds, Barry 126
'Bountygate' scandal 177
boxing: concussions 94; consent 16; violence 169
brain injury 92–3, 96–7, 225–6
Branch, Taylor 68
Brashear, Donald 175
broadcasting: intellectual property rights 211–15
Brooklyn Dodgers 209
Brown v. Board of Education 137
Budding, Edwin Beard 221
burnout 90, 105–7
Burns, James MacGregor 42

cage fighting 169
cameras: fan behaviour 76, 80–1, 84–5
Camus, Albert 236–7
Canseco, Jose 126
Cantu, Robert 95–6

care ethics 12–14; amateurism 64, 67, 70; concussions 93–4, 98; gender discrimination 152, 159; intellectual property rights 201; performance enhancement 123; racial discrimination 138–9, 144; youth sport 106–7, 108
Carlos, John 145
Categorical Imperative 8–9
Caucasians: history in U.S. 133–5; see also racial discrimination
CEOs 48–9, 51
Chambers, John 57–8
character development 58, 60; see also virtue ethics
character ethics 11–12
Chastain Effect 157
cheating: performance enhancement as 117, 124–5; recruitment 63; sports ethics 25
Chelladurai, Packianathan 50
children see youth sport
chronic traumatic encephalopathy (CTE) 99
Ciccarelli, Dino 174–5
civil courts: violence 171–3, 179–80
civil rights: gender 149, 151, 153–4; Nelson Mandela 237; race 135, 136–7
Clark, Charles 173
Clemens, Roger 117
cloning 18
clothing: technological developments 221–4
coaches: gender discrimination 156, 160; leadership 49–51; salary 62
coaching style (leadership) 46
codes of conduct: fan behaviour 83–4, 86; violence 170–1
coercive style (leadership) 44
cogent arguments 2–5
Cohen v. Brown University 154
college see university/college sports
Colts, Baltimore case 208
commercialism: amateur sports 66–7; players' publicity rights 201–7
community: leadership 36–7; performance enhancement 123
compensation see salaries; scholarships
concussions 90, 92–4; professional sport 94–100; youth sport 100–4
consent: concept of 16; formalism 22–3; hazing 179; violence 169–70
consequentialist ethics 10–11
contingency theory (leadership) 40
Controlled Substances Act 118
Copyright Act 213–15
costs: youth sport 106
creatine 115, 116
cricket: gambling 186
criminal courts: violence 174–5, 180–1

cultural relativism 7–8, 133–5
culture: ethos-based perspective 23–4; fan behaviour 81, 84–5; hazing 181; leadership 48–9, 53; performance enhancement 114, 116, 125; technological developments 224
cyber-addiction 230
cycling: performance enhancement 127–8; technology 222

Daily Fantasy Sports 191–5
death penalty example 1, 4–5
deductive validity 3–5
democratic style (leadership) 45
demographics: fan use of technology 229; racial integration 137–9
deontology 8–9; concussions 93–4, 98; fan behaviour 81, 82; gender discrimination 159; racial discrimination 144; technological developments 224
Descartes, Rene 2
desensitisation: virtual reality 230
designer steroids 116
disabled sports 231–2
discrimination see gender discrimination; racial discrimination
Disjunctive Syllogism 2–3
diuretics 115, 116
Divine Command Theory 9–10
Donaghy, Tim 187
doping 117–18, 121, 128–9; see also performance enhancement drugs
drugs see performance enhancement drugs
duty: deontology 8–9; virtue ethics 11–12

education: leadership 36; racial discrimination 137; see also university/college sports
embodiment 237–8
emotional intelligence 43–4
employment: amateurs 68–9; gender discrimination 152, 157–8
energy storage and return (ESR) 231
epoetin 115
equipment: technological developments 221–4
erythropoietin (EPO) 115, 116
ethical leadership 43, 51–3
ethics 1; see also moral frameworks; sports ethics
ethos-based perspective 23–31
executives: leadership 48–9, 51
exploitation: amateurs 67–9, 140–1

fabrics 222–3
facilities: gender discrimination 160; transgender issues 163–4
fan behaviour 74–5, 86–7; ethical leadership case study 87; history 75–6; leadership

79–80, 84–6; responsibilities 80–4; safety
    76–80
fan experience: technological developments
    228–9
fantasy sports: gambling 189–94; publicity rights
    206
Federation Internationale De Football Associations
    100
feminist ethics 12–14
fighting: hockey 99
financial issues see costs: youth sport; revenue;
    salaries
FINA: strategic losing 31
FitBit 223
fixing (gambling) 186
flopping 27–8
football: brain injury 225–6; concussions 95–7;
    injuries from sport 37–8; university/college
    sports 37; video replay 226; youth injuries
    100–2
footwear 223
formalism 22–3, 24–31
fouling: case study 32–3; fan safety 78, 80;
    formalism 23
framing 27–8
free speech 200–1, 202, 204, 206, 207, 210

gambling 185, 196; case studies 196–7; ethics
    194–5; fantasy sports 189–94; history of
    185–9; leadership 194–5
gaming: fantasy sports 189–94, 206; videogames
    205–6
Gandhi 39
Gee, Gordon 49
gender discrimination 149, 165; case studies
    165–6; history 150–1; legal issues 151–61;
    Rooney Rule 144; salaries 156, 161; sexual
    orientation 163; sportscasters 164–5; Title IX
    151–61; transgender issues 163–4; unisex
    teams 161–3
gender: leadership style 51
Gilligan, Carol 14
gloves 222
God: Divine Command Theory 9–10
Goleman, Daniel 43–6
golf: technology use 231–2
gonadotropin 115
Goodell, Roger 49
good fouling 23, 24
great man theory 39, 46
Green, Ted 174
group licensing 207
growth hormones 115, 116

Hackbart, Dale 173
hazing 168, 177–81

heading the ball 102–3
health: medical improvements 224–6;
    performance enhancement drugs 115–16;
    see also injuries from sport
Heinz Dilemma 13–14
hockey: concussions 97–9; fan safety 78, 80, 87;
    violence 169, 170, 174–5
hormones 114–15, 116; see also performance
    enhancement drugs
horse racing: performance enhancement 118
human cannonball 201–2
Hume, David 18
Hunter, Dale 175

indigenous Americans 145
inductive arguments 5
injuries from sport 90, 107–8; burnout 90, 105–7;
    case studies 108–9; concussions 90,
    92–100; fans 75, 76–7, 79; history of 91–2;
    history of sport injuries 91–2; National
    Football League 37–8; overuse 90, 104–5;
    technological developments 224–6; violence
    169; youth sport 100–4
instant replay 226–7
institutional failures: performance enhancement
    125–9
intellectual property rights 200, 216; broadcasting
    211–15; case studies 216–17; free speech
    200–1, 202, 204; patents 215–16; players'
    publicity rights 201–7; trademark rights
    208–10
intent 14–15
intentional losing 29–31
intercollegiate athletics see university/college
    sports
internet gambling 189–94
internet: social media 229
intuitionism 17–19

Jim Crow laws 136
Johnson, Lyndon, President of USA 137
John, Tommy 224
Jones v. Kappa Alpha Order 179–80
Jordan, Michael 206–7

Kant, Immanuel 8–9
Kass, Leon 18
Kohlberg, Lawrence 13
Kouzes, Jim 47

Lanham Act 208
law see legal issues
lawnmowers: history of technology 221
lawyers for amateurs 64–5
leadership 35, 51; 'Are leaders born or can
    leadership be taught?' 46; 'Are leadership

and management the same?' 46–7; attributes 47–9; coaching role 49–51; ethical leadership case studies 51–3; fan behaviour 79–80, 84–6; fouling case study 32–3; gambling 194–5; gender 51; meaning of 38–40; medical cover-up case study 19–20; performance enhancement 125–9; in society 36–7; in sport 37–8; styles 43–6, 50–1; types 41–3
leadership development 36, 46, 51
league presidents 49
legal issues: amateurism 64–5, 69; broadcasting 211–15; concussions 90, 97, 98–9; disclaimers 76–7; and ethics 1; fan safety 74, 77–9; free speech 200–1, 202, 204, 206, 207, 210; gambling 185, 187–8, 196–7; gender discrimination 151–61; hazing 179–81; injuries from sport 91–2; negligence 74, 79; performance enhancement 118, 119–21, 127–8; players' publicity rights 201–7; racial discrimination 135–7, 143–4; technological developments 231–2; violence 170–6; youth injuries 101
Lesbian Rule 24
LGBTQ athletes 163
Locke, John 16, 22–3
locker rooms: gender discrimination 160; transgender issues 163–4
logic 2–5
logical incompatibility thesis 23
logo rights 208–10
Lombardi, Vince 46
London's Amateur Athletic Club 57–8
losing intentionally 29–31
luck, moral 15

McGwire, Mark 126
McSorley, Marty 175
Maier, Jeffrey 82
Major League Baseball (MLB) 79–80
Maki, Wayne 174
management: 'Are leadership and management the same?' 46–7; fan safety 76–9
Mandela, Nelson 237
Maris, Roger 125, 126
Martin, Casey 231–2
mascots: racial discrimination 144–5
meaning in sport 236–44
media: broadcasting 211–15; fan behaviour 84–5; fan experience 228–9
medical cover-up case study 19–20
medical facilities: gender discrimination 160
medical issues see health; injuries from sport
medicine: technological developments 224–6
Meier, Klaus 237–8
'mind-body problem' 237–8
Mink, Patsy 151, 152

missing premises (moral reasoning) 4–5
mixed martial arts (MMA) 169
modus ponens 3–4
modus tollens 4
moral arguments 2–5, 16–19
moral frameworks 6–14; care ethics 12–14; cultural relativism 7–8; deontology 8–9; Divine Command Theory 9–10; moral subjectivism 6–7; nihilism 8; utilitarianism 10–11; virtue ethics 11–12
morality: and ethics 1
moral luck 15
moral subjectivism 6–7
Mothers Against School Hazing (MASH) 179, 182
Motorola case 213–14
multi-dimensional model of leadership 50

National Basketball Association: broadcasting 213–15; performance enhancement 119; violence 177
National Collegiate Athletic Association (NCAA): amateurism 58–62; concussions 93–4; gambling 188; gender 152, 158–9; recruitment 62–4
National Exhibition Co. court case 211–12
National Football League 37–8; broadcasting 211; concussions 95–7; players' publicity rights 207; violence 176–7
National Hockey League: concussions 97–9
Native Americans 145
NCAA see National Collegiate Athletic Association
negligence law 74, 79, 173
neuroscience: social intuitionism 17–19
Newcombe, Don 203–4
NFL Super Bowl 37
Nietzsche, Friedrich 8
nihilism 8
Nike 223
nutritional supplements 115, 116

obligation: deontology 8–9; virtue ethics 11–12
O'Brien, Davey 203
offensive language 85
offensive trademarks 209–10
officiating: technological developments 226–7
Olympic Games: amateurism 57, 58; gender discrimination 149, 150; performance enhancement 120–1, 125, 128–9; racial symbolic speech 145–6; strategic losing 30, 31; technology 221, 222, 231
online gambling 189–94
overuse 90, 104–5

Pabst Blue Ribbon advertising 203
pacesetting style (leadership) 45

participative leadership 43
patents 215–16
pay *see* salaries
pay for play 68, 141
Penguins disclaimer 76–7
performance enhancement drugs 113–14,
    129–30; case studies 130; as cheating 117,
    124–5; ethics 123; harm to sport 117–18;
    health risks 115–16; institutional failures
    125–9; non-drug 122–3; reasons for use
    114, 121–2; regulation 119–21; Therapeutic
    Use Exemption 125; types and forms 114–15
personal judgment: morals 6–7
Pishchainikova, Darya 128–9
Pistorius, Oscar 231
pitch framing 27–8
Pittsburgh Athletic Co. 212
players' publicity rights 201–7
political leaders 36, 42
Posner, Barry 47
power and influence theory (leadership) 40
Professional and Amateur Sports Protection Act
    (PASPA) 189
professional athletes: amateur prospects 64, 106;
    broadcasting revenues 214–15; concussions
    94–8; gambling 188–9; gender
    discrimination 157, 161; racial discrimination
    142–4; salaries 156, 161; technological
    developments 221–2; *see also* performance
    enhancement drugs
publicity: gender discrimination 160–1
publicity rights 201–7

racial discrimination 133, 146; case study
    146–7; history in US 133–5; legal history
    135–7; mascots 144–5; professional athletes
    142–4; symbolic speech 145–6;
    university/college sports 137–41
recruitment: amateurs 62–4
reductio ad absurdum 5
Reebok Pump 223
referee-as-adjudicator 26–7
referee's use of technology 226–7
regulation *see* legal issues
relativism, cultural 7–8, 133–5
religion: Divine Command Theory 9–10; gambling
    185
responsibilities: fan behaviour 74, 80–4
retention: amateurs 63–4
revenue: amateur sports 66–7; broadcasting
    211–12, 214–15; fantasy sports 192, 194–5
Rhode, Deborah 36
Richardson, Luke 174–5
Rickey, Branch 142–3
Robinson, Jackie 142–3
role models, athletes as 48

Rooney Rule 143–4
Roosevelt, Theodore 58–9
rules: cheating 25, 63, 117, 124–5; consent 16;
    ethics 22; ethos-based perspective 23–31;
    fan behaviour 83–4, 86; formalism 22–3,
    24–31; moral 8–14; performance
    enhancement 123–4; self-regulation 170–1,
    176–7; sportsmanship 239; violence 170–1,
    174–5
Rule Utilitarianism 11
Russia: performance enhancement 120–1, 125,
    128–9

safety of fans 74, 76–80
safety of players *see* injuries from sport
salaries: coaches 62; fantasy sports 191; gender
    discrimination 156, 161; scholarships
    59–60, 62–4, 68–9, 70; unpaid amateurs
    67–8, 141, 161
scholarships, university sports: employment 68–9;
    gender discrimination 158–9; National
    Collegiate Athletic Association 59–60, 70;
    racial discrimination 139–40; recruitment
    62–4
Scurry, Briana 24
self-awareness 44
self-management 44
self-regulation 170–1, 176–7
servant leadership 42–3
sexual orientation 163
Shot Tracker 223
Singer, Peter 19
situational leadership 42
skills, leadership 43–4, 47–9
Smith, Ronald E. 50
Smith, Tommie 145
Smoll, Frank 50
soccer: cheating example 25; concussions 100;
    ethos-based perspective 24–5; flopping 27,
    28; formalism 22; strategic losing 30; youth
    injuries 102–3
social awareness 44
social contract 16, 22–3
social intuitionism 17–19
social media 229
social skills 44
society: leadership 36–7; role models 48
Sosa, Sammy 126
Sparta Science 223–4
specialisation: youth sports 106–7, 108
sponsorship: amateur sports 67; *see also*
    advertisements
sportscasters: gender discrimination 164–5
sports ethics 22, 31–2; blowouts 28–9; cheating
    25; ethical leadership 43, 51–3; ethos-based
    perspective 23–31; fan behaviour 75–6,

81–3; fan safety 79–80; flopping 27–8; formalism 22–3, 24–31; framing 27–8; gambling 194–5; intentional losing 29–31; performance enhancement 123; sportsmanship 26–7; technological developments 231–2
sports injuries *see* injuries from sport
sportsmanship 26–7, 238–44
Sports Violence Act 176, 182
steroids 114, 116, 118, 121–2; *see also* performance enhancement drugs
stimulants 115, 116
strategic losing 29–31
students *see* amateurism; university/college sports
subjectivism 6–7
substance abuse *see* performance enhancement drugs
suicides 97
surgery: technological developments 225
surveillance: fan behaviour 76, 80–1, 84–5

tacit consent 16, 22–23
technological developments 220, 232; apparel 221–4; broadcasting 213–15; case studies 232–3; equipment 221–4; ethics 231–2; fan experience 228–9; history 221; medicine 224–6; officiating 226–7; online gambling 189–94; patents 215–16; training 224–6; virtual reality 229–31
television broadcasting: intellectual property rights 211–15
tennis: formalism 23; technological developments 222
Texas A&M 209
Therapeutic Use Exemption: performance enhancement 125
Thorpe, Jim 58
ticket technology 228
Title IX: history 151–6; impact 156–8; recommendations 158–61; sexual orientation 163; transgender issues 163–4; unisex teams 161–3
Tomjanovich court case 172–3
Tour de France 127
trademark rights 208–10
training: technological developments 224–6; virtual reality 230–1; wearable technology 223–4
trait theory (leadership) 40
transactional leadership 42
transformational leadership 41–2
transformative use test 204–5
transgender issues 163–4
traumatic brain injury 92–3, 96–7
travel policies: gender discrimination 159–60
Tressel, Jim 49

Trolley Car Situation 17–18
Tucholsky, Sara 28
Turgeon, Pierre 175

umpire as adjudicator 26–7
umpire's use of technology 226–7
unions: amateurism 68–9; performance enhancement 119; players' publicity rights 207
unisex teams 161–3
university/college sports: amateurs 58–62; gender discrimination 153–4, 156–7, 158–61; hazing 178–9; impact on academic study 65–6; racial discrimination 137–41; sense of community 37; unisex teams 162–3; unpaid amateurs 67–8, 141, 161
U.S.: history of racial discrimination 133–5
utilitarianism 10–11, 17–18; amateurism 59, 66, 69; fan behaviour 80, 81, 82; free speech 210; gender discrimination 152; intellectual property rights 204; performance enhancement 123; racial discrimination 144; technological developments 224
U.S. Anti-Doping Agency 127–8

validity: logic 2–5
value of sport 236–44
videogames 205–6
video replay 226–7
violence 168, 181; attempts to control 170–6; case studies 182; concussions 99; fan behaviour 74–6; hazing 168, 177–81; philosophical considerations 168–70; self- vs outside regulation 176–7
virtual reality 229–31
virtue ethics 11–12; amateurism 57, 58, 68–9; intellectual property rights 201; performance enhancement 123; racial discrimination 138–9; technological developments 224; youth sport 107
virtue in sport 236–44

Washington Redskins 145, 210
water polo: strategic losing 31
wearable technology 223–4
Williams, Gregg 169
women *see* gender discrimination
Wooden, John 38
Woods, Tiger 204, 205
World Anti-Doping Agency (WADA) 120–1, 125, 128–9

You Can Play 163
youth sport: burnout 105–6; medical issues 100–4; overuse 104–5; steroids 116; *see also* amateurism